OCEANSIDE PUBLIC LIBRARY
330 N COAST HWY

D0399180

Civic Center

The Gods of Prophetstown

The Gods of Prophetstown

The Battle of Tippecanoe
and the Holy War
for the American Frontier

———◄●►———

ADAM JORTNER

OXFORD
UNIVERSITY PRESS

OXFORD
UNIVERSITY PRESS

Oxford University Press, Inc., publishes works that further
Oxford University's objective of excellence
in research, scholarship, and education.

Oxford   New York

Auckland   Cape Town   Dar es Salaam   Hong Kong   Karachi
Kuala Lumpur   Madrid   Melbourne   Mexico City   Nairobi
New Delhi   Shanghai   Taipei   Toronto

With offices in

Argentina   Austria   Brazil   Chile   Czech Republic   France   Greece
Guatemala   Hungary   Italy   Japan   Poland   Portugal   Singapore
South Korea   Switzerland   Thailand   Turkey   Ukraine   Vietnam

Copyright © 2012 by Adam Jortner

Published by Oxford University Press, Inc.
198 Madison Avenue, New York, NY 10016

www.oup.com

Oxford is a registered trademark of Oxford University Press

All rights reserved. No part of this publication may be reproduced,
stored in a retrieval system, or transmitted, in any form or by any means,
electronic, mechanical, photocopying, recording, or otherwise,
without the prior permission of Oxford University Press.

Library of Congress Cataloging-in-Publication Data
Jortner, Adam Joseph.
The gods of Prophetstown : the Battle of Tippecanoe and
the holy war for the American frontier / Adam Jortner.
p.   cm.
Includes bibliographical references and index.
ISBN 978-0-19-976529-4
1. Tippecanoe, Battle of, Ind., 1811. 2. Tenskwatawa, Shawnee Prophet.
3. Harrison, William Henry, 1773–1841. 4. Shawnee Indians—Biography.
5. Governors—Indiana—Biography. 6. Indians of North America—Wars—1750–1815.
7. War—Religious aspects—History—19th century.
8. Indiana—History—19th century. 9. United States—Territorial expansion.
10. Frontier and pioneer life—United States. I. Title.
E83.81.J67   2011
973.5—dc23   2011016857

1 3 5 7 9 8 6 4 2

Printed in the United States of America
on acid-free paper

31232009161599

To Mom and Dad

Contents

Acknowledgments

ONLY GRADUATE STUDENTS read this part. Normal people have already skipped ahead to the introduction.

Those of you still reading probably know that no one writes a book alone. This book began as part of a dissertation at the University of Virginia, where I had the good fortune to work under Peter S. Onuf. Many of his students refer to Peter simply as "Mentor"; rarely is a title so well earned. Peter's ability to visualize an argument before the author even knows it is exceeded only by his care and concern for his students. I cannot hope to repay him for his patience, his clarity, and his advice through the entire process.

I have accrued other academic debts. H. C. Erik Midelfort and Patrick Griffin both contributed mightily to my doctoral work; their zealous attention to detail and pugnacious practicality made my thinking and my prose better than it deserved to be. Jon Lendon offered constant advice to a beleaguered graduate student, and from his perspective in the ancient Mediterranean offered timely correctives on writing and argument. Daniel Richter read an early draft of my work on Tenskwatawa and quickly set my thinking on a more promising track. Richter also oversaw the intellectual atmosphere of the McNeil Center for Early American Studies at the University of Pennsylvania, where I spent a wonderful year as the E. Rhodes and Leona B. Carpenter Fellow in American Religious History. My thanks to the fellows and staff at the center for challenging me to do my best work and for being wonderful friends when I wasn't quite up to that challenge.

In the course of this project, I received support from the Charlotte Newcombe Fellowship of the Woodrow Wilson Foundation, the Massachusetts Historical Society, the Maine Historical Society, the Kentucky Historical Society, the Everett Helm Visiting Fellowship at the Lilly Library at Indiana University, the International Center for Jefferson Studies, and the University of Virginia. I owe thanks to the librarians and staff at the Indiana Historical Society, the Abraham Lincoln Presidential Library and Museum, the American Philosophical Society, the Library Company of Philadelphia, the Ralph Brown Draughon Library at Auburn University, and the Great Lakes

Ethnohistory Archive at the Glenn A. Black Laboratory of Archaeology at Indiana University. For the last two years, Auburn University has provided a wonderful home for scholarship and creativity. I could not ask for better colleagues.

Many people read drafts and versions of this book. My agent, Rob McQuilkin, saw a potential finished product from some very rough first drafts. My editor, Timothy Bent, did a fabulous job clearing the debris from my writing. Zara Anishanslin, Simon Finger, Matthew Garrett, William Huntting Howell, Laura Keenan-Spero, Christina Snyder, Taylor Stoermer, and Anthony Stanonis all read drafts or parts of the manuscript at one time or another. Patrick Spero and Kathryn Braund read the final version, correcting errors and adding valuable insights. Special thanks are also due to Mally Anderson and the anonymous readers at Oxford University Press, and to Rick Britton, who made the fabulous maps. Any mistakes that remain are, of course, mine alone.

I had the good fortune to grow up in a family and in a place—Blacksburg, Virginia—that valued intellectual curiosity and left me with a constant sense of wonder. I am grateful for Susan and David (perpetual allies and wonderful siblings), Abby, Nathan, John, and Felicity (constant sources of hope for the future), and Emily (who knows what she means to me). My greatest debt is to my parents, whose good sense, wisdom, and love are the greatest wonders of my life. This book is dedicated to them.

Adam Jortner
Auburn, Alabama

The Gods of Prophetstown

Prologue: The Eclipse

He cured disease, saw the future, sundered curses, instilled visions, and passed into other realms. He felt the presence of witches and other agents of evil spirits hiding among the people. His powers were earthly signs of his profound connection to the divine. His followers stretched from the Appalachian foothills to the source of the Mississippi, and they thought he could change the world.

Three years earlier, he had been an undistinguished drunk, the fallen scion of a prominent family of warriors, a man who had learned the arts of war only so far as to blind himself in one eye. But on June 16, 1806, he solidified his place as a divine agent among the patchwork of Native American tribes of the Ohio Valley. That was the day he put out the sun. His supernatural power made him a man to be reckoned with, and the devotion of his followers to his cause made him the greatest political threat to American power in the calamitous and lawless world of the early American frontier. But his followers and his enemies would not have discussed him in such antiseptic terms. To them, the Prophet was the man who made the sun go dark at midday.[1]

He had previously warned those who did not accept his divine mission that he would demonstrate his power. Disbelievers, he vowed, "would see darkness come over the sun," a sign from the Master of Life presaging destruction, calamity, and "war, bloody war." He told his followers—and skeptics— at the town of Greenville, Ohio, that "he was every night in his dreams with the Spirit above" and had foreseen a coming darkness.[2]

As the sun vanished on that June Monday, he remained in his tent while panic bubbled through the community. The eclipse was "a matter of great surprise to the Indians," wrote one white commentator. Some ran in fear, some fell to their knees in prayer, and some wrapped themselves in blankets and waited to die.[3] A few wondered if the darkness might last all day, many days, "a dark year." At last he emerged and addressed followers and doubters alike: "Behold! Did I not prophesy correctly—see darkness is coming."[4] His prophecy fulfilled, his divine mission confirmed, he restored the sun.

Instantly he became a force to be reckoned with, and the devotion of his followers—an agglomeration of individuals and factions drawn from the Native American tribes of the Ohio Valley—transformed him into the greatest threat to the American authorities creeping across the western frontier.

From that day forward, recalled one witness, those who saw him darken the sun "submitted to his dictation, with a confidence that was never shaken."[5]

Like many Indians of eastern North America, he had several names. In 1806, he still bore the nickname "Lalawauthika"—a derisive sobriquet that translates as "the Rattle," or more colloquially as "Loudmouth." In the years to come he took the name Tenskwatawa—"the Open Door." The Shawnee language from which his name comes, however, employs soft consonants, and sometimes the name was written down as "Elkswatawa." Whites—who in their correspondence rarely attempted to master the subtle Indian names— usually simply referred to him as "the Prophet." At the time of the eclipse, he was not much to look at—"of a common size, rather slender, & of no great appearance"—but he preached a potent religious message of penance and sanctification to the assembled tribes of the Ohio, revealing that the Master of Life who created the world wanted his people to return to their old ways of life and reclaim their lands.[6]

Tenskwatawa had not risen to prominence on his own. He had the assistance and loyalty of his elder brother, a Shawnee war chief then of only minor note—Tecumseh. More important, he had made the right enemies. By 1806, virtually every other leader among the Indians of the Old Northwest had made common cause with the government in Washington. Black Hoof had agreed to its aggressive settlement plans. Little Turtle had been bought off. Handsome Lake, a prophet of the Senecas, had built a little fiefdom on the Finger Lakes in central New York State with the acquiescence of President Thomas Jefferson. Tenskwatawa also had enemies among the dealers in goods and annuities who routinely cheated both the American government and the Indian tribes. He was hated by the cadre of designing governors who had been appointed by the federal government and possessed a considerable interest in turning Indian land into American settlements. Foremost among these men was another scion of a distinguished clan, William Henry Harrison, territorial governor of Indiana and minister plenipotentiary to the Indians.

In some ways, the eclipse had been Harrison's idea. In the spring of 1806, Harrison had a number of crises to deal with. All of thirty-three years old, he was in principle the most powerful white in the West. All Indian treaties and land negotiations west of the Appalachians went through him. Appointed by the federal government, he had no need to bother with the niceties of local democracy; he had engineered elections of Indiana's territorial legislature to ensure that his men got the jobs. Harrison had personally reinstituted slavery in Indiana, and he lived in a stately plantation-style manor in his provincial capital. He was cunning, ruthless, and extraordinarily able.

This kind of power, however, meant little to Harrison. Governing the frontier was not the career he craved, and he felt certain his political acumen would vault him on to greater heights. He was a Virginian patrician, not a backcountry populist. Aaron Burr (who knew a thing or two about ambition) remarked, "This H. is fit for other things."[7] Yet despite his talent and his pedigree—his father had signed the Declaration of Independence—Harrison moldered in Indiana for nearly six years. Worse, his once enviable hold had begun to slip. Something like a democratic opposition had emerged to oppose his autocratic rule; abolitionists had attacked his slave codes. His opponents schemed to escape Harrison by persuading the federal government to divide Indiana in two, giving Illinois its own government. Without the Illinois country, Harrison later complained, "Indiana cannot for many years become a member of the Union, and I am heartily tired of living in a territory."[8] Into this deteriorating situation came rumors of a new prophet among the Indians.

There had been prophets among the eastern tribes since before Harrison was born, mixing a strain of monotheism into older animist beliefs. Among the Munsees, Papoonan preached a return to the customs the Creator had established. The Lenni Lenape prophet Neolin had galvanized resistance to the British in the 1760s. A decade later, Wangomend had drawn charts showing the path to hell for Indians who emulated white culture. Yet Harrison had had almost no contact with this kind of Indian visionary and no interest in it. Miracles and claims of supernatural powers were so much folklore to him. The Harrisons were Anglican gentry from Virginia, committed to the kind of mild deist philosophy that accepted a divine creator but not an involved deity. Harrison fit the family mold. In his college days, when an evangelical revival broke out on campus, Harrison left school.

The deist god did not interfere in such banal matters as individual souls. He had grand purposes that history would reveal through what George Washington called "the ways of Providence." Exact details of the plan were inscrutable, "not to be scan[ne]d by the shallow eye of humanity."[9] There was, however, a direction to human affairs, one that a discerning mind could discover. Naturally, it pointed to formation of the United States. It was providence, Washington declared, that had won the revolution, secured the peace, and finally established a government with himself at its head. Providence "induced the People of America to substitute in the place of an inadequate confederacy, a general Government, eminently calculated to secure the safety and welfare of their Country."[10]

Harrison could believe in this kind of a god: one whose creation ran inexorably toward a bright American future. He thought he also understood the lessons providence intended for the "miserable Indians" and "warlike savages." The United States was to "divert from these children of nature the ruin which hangs over them" by purchasing their lands, ridding them of superstition, and making them live like white folks, a goal he declared "consistent with the spirit of christianity, and with the principles of republicanism."[11] God was a clockmaker; there were no more miracles. Indeed, all miracles did was foment dissent among the Native Americans, and Harrison certainly could not allow an opponent of the land deals to gain stature. It ran counter to the designs of providence, and it would be poisonous for his political career.

Thus when rumors reached Harrison, in the months before June 1806, that this new prophet had not only discovered witches among the Delaware tribes of Ohio but also participated in their execution, he saw his chance. He wrote a searing letter to the Indians at Greenville. "Who is this pretended prophet," Harrison demanded to know, "who dares to speak in the name of the Great Creator? Examine him. Is he more wise or virtuous than you are yourselves, that he should be selected to convey to you the orders of your God?" It was a rhetorical question; no one could speak for God, and the religious claims of a man who claimed wondrous powers merely counterfeited a greasepaint piety to cover baser motives. It was all a sham—"Wretched delusion!"—that had been "imposed upon by the arts of an imposter." Harrison was following the deist general line. No prophecies or miracles any longer existed. God spoke through enlightened republicans, not wonder-working rabble.[12]

Harrison went a step further and designed a test that he knew the Prophet could not pass. "Demand of him some proofs at least of his being the messenger of the Deity. If God has really employed him he has doubtless authorized him to perform some miracles, that he may be known and received as a prophet." Harrison thought he had constructed an airtight argument. If a prophet claimed miracles, ask for one. According to deist dictates, miracles could not exist; therefore this prophet would fail, and that would put an end to the business. In his confidence, Harrison even offered suggestions for possible miracles to request: "Ask of him to cause the sun to stand still—the moon to alter its course—the rivers to cease to flow—or the dead to rise from their graves. If he does these things, you may then believe that he has been sent from God."[13]

Had Harrison chosen his words more carefully, the history of the Prophet might have been different. But he asked for a miracle—and the Prophet provided one. A few days later, the sun turned black at midday.

The eclipse has bothered historians since at least 1841. References to it drift in and out of correspondence and newspaper reports. The only

eyewitness accounts, however, were recorded well after the event.[14] It belongs
to oral history and should be taken with all the circumspection such evidence
entails. Rather than focus on the nature of the evidence, however, historians
have seemed more interested in verifying the accusation that Tenskwatawa
faked the eclipse, that is, that he possessed foreknowledge of it and deliberately duped his followers. This thesis is nearly as old as the biographical accounts of Tenskwatawa. Benjamin Drake, for whom Tenskwatawa was a
"crafty impostor" who played on the "superstitious credulity" of the Native
Americans, assured his readers in 1841 that the "great eclipse of the sun which
occurred in the summer of this year [1806], a knowledge of which he had by
some means attained, enabled him to carry conviction to the minds of many
of his ignorant followers, that he was really the earthly agent of the Great
Spirit."[15] A newspaper account of the eclipse—published years after the
event—insisted that Tenskwatawa knew the "superstition of his people" and
therefore deliberately lied to them about the divine nature of the eclipse.[16]
Though R. David Edmunds' 1983 biography was far less accusatory, it too
asserted that Tenskwatawa had learned of the eclipse before predicting it. Virtually all subsequent studies of the Prophet and his religion repeat this claim.[17]

What could provoke such an insistence that the Prophet not only failed to
perform a true miracle (however defined) but also deliberately misled his followers? For early commentators such as Drake, the answer was obvious: the
Prophet was a two-bit charlatan. Nearly every early account makes Tenskwatawa a villain. And nearly every early account describes Tenskwatawa as a
theocrat, deliberately keeping his people in pagan darkness, inventing a religion out of whole cloth so as to dress himself in authority and riches. Drake's
cultural narcissism and blatant racism are, thankfully, quite rare among modern historians. Yet scholars of Tenskwatawa's religion continue to "disprove"
the miracles of Tenskwatawa—or at least to suggest that he knew about the
eclipse in advance. The impulse here cannot be an effort to discredit the
Prophet; recent biographers have in fact rescued him from his older brother's
shadow. "It was Tenskwatawa, not Tecumseh," writes Edmunds, "who provided the basis for Indian resistance," while historian Andrew R. L. Cayton
credits Tenskwatawa with creating "a coherent prescription for social and
spiritual rebirth."[18] Indeed, over the last forty years, as published biographies
in popular and academic presses have slowly shed generations of stereotypes,
the concept of Native American spirituality as religion and not mere "superstition" has at last taken hold. Why, then, the difficulty in admitting a Native
American miracle or at the very least that Tenskwatawa believed he had performed a miracle?

The evidence for Tenskwatawa's foreknowledge of the eclipse is muddled at best. Edmunds writes that both Tenskwatawa and Harrison were aware of "several teams of astronomers and other scientists" studying the eclipse in Indiana, Kentucky, and Illinois. Edmunds' citation is to Glenn Tucker's 1973 *Tecumseh: Vision of Glory*; Tucker's citation, in turn, comes from R. M. Devens' *Our First Century*, from 1879. Devens indeed makes note of the 1806 eclipse, as well as an 1869 eclipse that had a similar effect. The "hordes of scientists" Devens cites, however, set up their observation stations for the eclipse in 1869, not the one in 1806. Indeed, two of the research stations mentioned in Devens were located in Springfield, Illinois, and Des Moines, Iowa—towns that did not even exist in 1806.[19] Nowhere does Devens mention the Prophet. Numerous almanacs note the eclipse on June 16 (Oram's almanac put an astonished man-in-the-moon graphic alongside the entry for "nearly totally eclipsed!").[20] More commonly, the almanacs abbreviated the coming event: "ecl[ipse]. vis[isble]." That in turn raises the question of whether, if the Prophet saw the almanacs, he could have correctly interpreted "ecl. vis.," especially given that Tenskwatawa did not speak English.[21] It also raises the question of why, if Tenskwatawa could put all this together, none of his many Native American rivals challenged him about it. If others knew about the eclipse beforehand (and some may have), why did the miracle inspire such loyalty among his followers, as almost every account of the event attests?[22] And then there is the most basic problem of all: if the Prophet believed himself to be in contact with the Master of Life and had astronomical knowledge of the eclipse beforehand, why deliberately deceive his followers? The foreknowledge hypothesis creates more problems than it solves.

There is a solution to the "problem" of the eclipse, but it lies in historical, not scientific or sociological, reasoning: to the Shawnees and other peoples of the Old Northwest, an eclipse was supernatural rather than scientific. Nature was not a clock; it was alive, and it had meaning that transcended cause and effect. Nature was imbued with powerful manitou that could heal or harm or be indifferent, part of a universe saturated with metaphysical wonder. Nature was malleable; humans could interact with and change it. Dreams, thunder, lightning, fire, the eddying of river water—all could serve as supernatural conduits, acknowledging favor, giving benefits, sharing secrets, or transmitting warnings to humanity or to individual humans.[23] It was a complex and nuanced conception of the cosmos that brought meaning and understanding to the peoples of the Eastern Woodlands.[24] In such a universe, the vanishing of the sun could not be predicted. This was something only the most powerful manitou—or even the Master of Life himself—could bring about.

Moreover, the did-he-or-didn't-he question may be the wrong one, akin to the question of whether Jesus Christ rose from the dead or Joseph Smith Jr. dug up the golden plates of the Book of Mormon. These are theological questions, the answers to which, some believe, affect the very soul. Historically, however, they are almost irrelevant. As Stuart Clark writes, the objective reality of beliefs in the supernatural is not nearly as important as "their capacity to inspire actions."[25] In explaining human society, the salient fact is not whether what the apostles or Smith claimed was true but whether people believed them. Whatever the epistemological reality behind their beliefs, Christians and Mormons are historical groups, and understanding how their beliefs affected their actions, and how those actions in turn altered events, should be the focus. So too with Tenskwatawa, the eclipse, and the Master of Life. For Tenskwatawa and his followers, the eclipse was a supernatural event. It was a sign. To suggest otherwise implies that Native American belief systems were merely the trickery and superstition that men such as Harrison assumed them to be.

That is clearly not the conclusion of modern historians, and in a sense the myth of the Prophet spying on "hordes of scientists" is actually the result of some faulty source work from 1972. Nevertheless, the story recurs in virtually every history of the Prophet or Tecumseh written since 1972. This persistence undergirds another recurring theme: the desperation of the Woodlands peoples and the inevitability of their decline. Most historians writing about the Prophet, Tecumseh, and the War of 1812 take for granted that the Shawnees and their allies were at the end of their rope. Defeated and despondent, they turned to the prophets in a last-ditch effort to preserve their way of life: "Enough desperation had accumulated among nativists—to lead some to believe it might actually happen."[26] Another historian calls Tenskwatawa's movement "a desperate attempt" by Indians "under pressure from loss of land, disease, and alcoholism . . . to combine traditional elements of Indian culture with those aspects of American technology which Indians realized they needed."[27]

Such conclusions, however, reveal more about assumptions regarding Indian history than about nineteenth-century sources. One theory in particular has colored historical writing on Tenskwatawa—that of Anthony F. C. Wallace's "revitalization." In the 1940s Wallace argued that a culture in crisis would develop new religious leaders who would introduce innovations to that culture through what he called charismatic revival. The leaders of such a movement, who were "hallucinatory" and spoke to supernatural creatures, would claim to be restoring an old way of life but would sneak in innovations to save the society under the cover of piety and new revelation. A culture under threat, in other words, would invent a new religion to save itself. Wallace applied the idea most prominently to the career of the Seneca prophet Handsome Lake. Nonetheless, he intended the idea to have greater purchase; revitalization, he wrote, also explained the emergence of Methodism, Sikhism, Islam, Christianity, and the Egyptian religion of Akhenaton, among others.[28]

Wallace's ideas tend to devalue religion as religion; faiths exist only to preserve culture rather than as sources of life-changing beliefs about ultimate reality. Indeed, Wallace later wrote (in 1966) that religion would soon vanish, anyway: "The evolutionary future of religion is extinction. . . . belief in supernatural powers is doomed to die out, all over the world, as a result of the increasing adequacy and diffusion of scientific knowledge."[29] Yet religion has not vanished in the modern world, of course, suggesting that religious beliefs play a role beyond the mere functionality that Wallace saw for them. Perhaps, then, it is also time to lay aside assumptions about revitalization, as well as its connotations of a culture weakened and helpless. Religious ideas and movements are the agents and not the outcomes of historical change.

The other modern assumption is more subtle. A "faked" eclipse is a set piece in a story of nineteenth-century Indians helpless in the face of an inevitable white conquest. In this view, Tenskwatawa's movement and the subsequent War of 1812 represented a last gasp for the tribes of the Old Northwest, who in truth had been defeated years before. This kind of story fits well with a revitalization thesis; the Indians of the Old Northwest were so desperate and politically naive that they would believe anyone who promised them succor. Tenskwatawa just showed up at the right time.

But although Tenskwatawa and Tecumseh ultimately lost, it does not follow that they were always destined to lose. Most histories of eastern Native Americans retell a familiar story, one of demographic disaster following European contact, followed by efforts to hold off white encroachment for the next three hundred years. Such stories recapitulate at least one part of the thinking among white expansionists of the nineteenth century: that the Indians were doomed.

Close analysis of the struggle between Tenskwatawa and Harrison suggests otherwise. Moments of contingency abound in their story, moments wherein events could have turned out otherwise and the history of the United States and even its borders could have been radically different. "The fate of indigenous cultures," argues historian Pekka Hämäläinen, "was not necessarily an irreversible slide toward dispossession, depopulation, and cultural declension." Decisions made on the frontier by leaders in specific circumstances between 1800 and 1815 resulted in American success and Indian defeat. As Hämäläinen warns, historians must avoid "reading Indian dispossession back in time to structure the narrative of early America" and instead examine "the multiple possibilities and contingency of historical change."[30]

Nor were those who followed Tenskwatawa blind or duped. Religious, supernatural, and moral dimensions converged to create a powerful argument for the Prophet's party. One of Tenskwatawa's followers at Greenville explained, "We all believe—He can dream to God," but the Prophet could also "tell us how to be good."[31] Professions such as these helped Tenskwatawa earn the respect and, eventually, the allegiance of the Indians in many of the tribes across the Ohio country and beyond. And as he did, he began to enact the divine plans for his people.

The Prophet formed his own settlements on the western frontier—first at Greenville in Ohio, and then at Prophetstown in Indiana. Those towns represented a threat to Harrison, as did Tenskwatawa. Harrison had his own career to consider, and a providential destiny of America to preserve. He worked assiduously to silence those who believed providence intended peace rather than glory, or coexistence on the frontier rather than bloodshed. In 1811, Harrison convinced a group of ministers to petition President Madison with their own sacred demands for the lands of the Old Northwest: "The impunity with which these savages have been so long suffered to commit crimes," they wrote, "has raised their insolence to a pitch that is no longer supportable." Madison must therefore allow Harrison to go to war—a justifiable and sacred war: "The character which some of us retain as ministers of the gospel of Christ, will shield us from the supposition that we wish to plunge our county in an unnecessary war."

The petition worked. Having goaded President Madison and his cabinet into supporting a preemptive strike against Prophetstown, Harrison marched an inexperienced regiment of federal and militia forces against Tenskwatawa in November 1811. The result was the Battle of Tippecanoe. The battle made Harrison famous—a hero—but in fact consisted of equal parts bravado and error. Indeed, Harrison's actions probably pushed more Indians into the ranks of Tecumseh and Tenskwatawa, who joined with the British the next year in an attempt to destroy the infant nation. On the frontier, then, the War of 1812 was very much a religious war—the Great Spirit against providence—with the vast expanse of the western frontier, a holy land, as the prize.

The parallel lives of Harrison and Tenskwatawa offer guideposts to the American frontier of two centuries ago. Histories of that frontier were

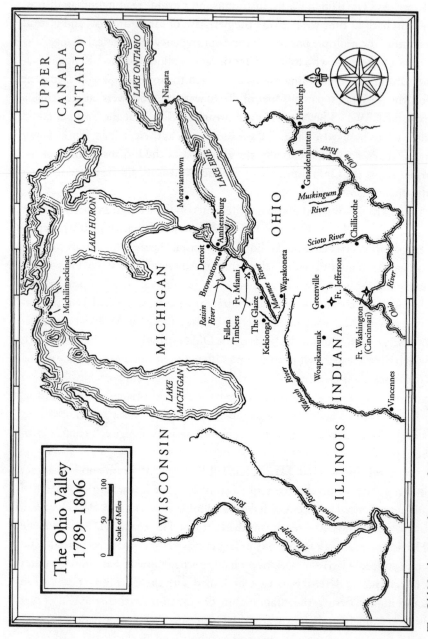

The Ohio Valley
1789–1806

Scale of Miles
0   50   100

UPPER CANADA (ONTARIO)

LAKE ONTARIO

Niagara

LAKE HURON

Michilimackinac

LAKE MICHIGAN

WISCONSIN

MICHIGAN

Moraviantown

LAKE ERIE

Amherstburg

Detroit

Brownstown

Raisin River

Ft. Miami

Fallen Timbers

The Glaze

Kekionga

Maumee River

Wapakoneta

OHIO

Pittsburgh

Gnaddenhutten

Ohio River

Muskingum River

Chillicothe

Scioto River

Greenville

Ft. Jefferson

Ft. Washington (Cincinnati)

Ohio River

Woapikamunk

Wabash River

INDIANA

Vincennes

ILLINOIS

Illinois River

Mississippi River

The Old Northwest in the Age of Harrison and Tenskwatawa

dominated for decades by tales of white people—hagiographies of white Americans heading west and conquering a supposedly virgin land. Only in the last few decades have historians tried to re-create the Native American experience and encounter with Europeans and, later, with Americans. These histories "faced east" instead of west, in the academic shorthand. More recently still, other historians have chosen to "face west" once again, to explore the cultural world of frontier Americans.[32] Whichever way they faced, these works have transformed traditional representations of the frontier—and yet the shape of the American frontier depended less on cultural factors than it did on specific religious and political actions, including the message of the Shawnee Prophet and the ambitions of Harrison. Explaining the fate of the frontier by 1815 has less to do with direction than with power—political and religious.

Most Americans know relatively little about the War of 1812 and would in any case be reluctant to consider any American war as "holy." God-fearing citizens have fought and died for their country, yet Americans are accustomed to seeing their wars dressed in the language of irrepressible political and cultural conflict. Surely a secular nation could not fight a religious war—particularly not one as obscure as the War of 1812. Yet that is precisely what happened. Two centuries ago Americans believed they had a divine destiny to claim and occupy all the lands that surrounded them, a gospel of republican independence gifted from on high in 1776 and extending through time and, most of all, space.

Harrison had worked hard to subjugate and defeat the theology and institutions of the Great Spirit, to destroy the religion of Tenskwatawa, replacing it with his own self-described "mild religion," in the process emptying the western frontier of its Native inhabitants. Native Americans, for their part, believed their god had at last given them the sacred instructions necessary to halt the white advance. Tenskwatawa and his disciples spread across the frontier from Florida to Canada to preach the word that the Great Spirit had returned, ushering in a new era of *their* independence. And so when Harrison and Tenskwatawa clashed, their gods clashed as well. Had Tenskwatawa won that struggle, any providential notion of a Manifest Destiny would have been crushed before it could be created, and the story of American nations and gods would have looked radically different. For it was the gods, as well as the people, of Prophetstown who created the American frontier, in all its terror and glory.

Thrown Away

WHEN HE HAD grown old and his great days were behind him, Tenskwatawa the Prophet allowed a white man to record the stories and legends of the Shawnee people before the coming of the Europeans. The writer was C. C. Trowbridge, a young clerk in his twenties, come to interview the infamous Indian who had led his people in the name of Kichi Manitou, Master of Life, whom the whites called the Great Spirit.

One of the stories Trowbridge heard was of Rising Sun, a legendary chief of ancient days. Rising Sun "had become much dissatisfied with his youngest son," explained Tenskwatawa. "So unhappy was he with the boy that he decided to get rid of him."[1] Rising Sun instructed his people to put out their fires and move on, leaving his son behind. The boy was dubbed Abandoned-One, or Thrown Away. As Tenskwatawa told the story, Abandoned-One survived the first winter alone with the help of his *hopawaaka*, a spirit animal that provided protection and advice. With the help of his brother *hopawaaka,* Thrown Away grew to be an accomplished warrior, and one day he returned to his tribe and rescued them from catastrophe. Trowbridge dutifully wrote it all down, perhaps thinking he was hearing some ancient lore or some forbidden piece of Indian cabalism.

It is tempting to view the story of Thrown Away as Trowbridge did in the 1820s, as an artifact of some primeval Indian past, a remnant of a simpler life. In some popular notions—both now and in Trowbridge's time—the Indians play a similar role: a people from the early morning of humanity, leading a natural way of life that the modern world has somehow lost. But these are visions created by the Romantic poets and early ethnographers, a white man's dream of what Native America should be.[2] Tenskwatawa as much as Trowbridge was a product of his age. Thrown Away was a story for a modern people.[3]

The story as Tenskwatawa told it could be understood as the story of the Shawnees themselves. They understood the pains—and the benefits—of moving from place to place; they were known even in the seventeenth century as "the greatest Travelers in America."[4] No written records exist of the first centuries of the people known as Saanwanwa. Curiously, the designation roughly translates as "southerners" in some Algonquin languages—though not in Shawnee.[5] Part of the tribe lived as far south as Alabama. There is some speculation that the ancestors of Tenskwatawa once lived yet farther south. Or perhaps the name derived from their more recent dispossession—the Iroquois invasion of the 1630s that pushed them south.[6]

In the maps in history textbooks, Native American tribes seem stable. Their names sit placidly atop geographic regions, the letters sometimes widely spaced to cover hundreds of miles, sometimes crammed together for small areas. English colonies, on the other hand, get clear borders, usually with colors. The colonists, the map says, were there to stay. The Indians were just "tribes," without cities or capitals. There are of course a number of distortions in such maps. First, for the most part, the maps show what the European colonial powers *claimed* as their territory rather than territory they actually controlled. Second, the Indians had undergone long periods of migration and movement; they had fought wars, traded territory and tribal ground, and opened new lands for settlement, not unlike certain areas of the European map in those same centuries.[7]

The first Americans, of course, had never heard of America. They traveled across the Bering land bridge far earlier than the written word, perhaps even beyond the reach of memory. One of the great waves of immigrants spoke an ancient form of the language family now known as Algonquin. (Generations upon generations later, a form of Algonquin—Shawnee—would serve the American frontier as a diplomat's language.) The Algonquians settled along the southern Mississippi and on the Gulf Coast, raising great mound structures and creating tributary kingdoms along the coast. The eleventh-century city of Cahokia formed the core of a vast inland empire. Situated near the modern city of St. Louis, at the confluence of the Mississippi and the Ohio, Cahokia numbered between 15,000 and 25,000 souls, and the city served as the spiritual center of an extensive tributary empire. Hundreds of years later, a people known as the "Fort Ancient culture" built similarly vast mound structures along the Ohio. By 1600, these American cities—their residents the first "midwesterners"—had long been abandoned.

If the Native Americans of the sixteenth and seventeenth centuries had no "cities," neither did their European counterparts. Most European colonial cities numbered in the hundreds of inhabitants, a few into the thousands. At the end of the seventeenth century, New York City had fewer than five thousand residents, Philadelphia just over two thousand.[8] Puritan settlements in New England were more numerous but no more populous. Native Americans, on the other hand, lived in portable cities. The tribes that anthropologists later designated as "Eastern Woodlands"—a designation the Indians themselves never used—gathered together in regular locations in spring and summer for collective agriculture, hunting, and worship. As the days grew shorter, members of the tribe might separate into smaller clan designations and remove to different winter quarters.

Yet these towns of the Iroquois, Delawares, Hurons, and others remained invisible to many English and French settlers, who understood "civilization" as permanent structures surrounded by roads, garrisons, and palaces. Similarly, the settlers and explorers of Europe could not see Indian agriculture, which cultivated maize, squash, and beans in plots within the forest, spread across miles, rather than on cleared lands fastidiously cultivated in rows. For generations, European settlers and white Americans would reassure themselves that Indians were merely hunter-gatherers, even though plants had been domesticated in eastern North America since 2000 BCE.[9]

There were also permanent Indian "cities," even from a European perspective, that grew up following contact between North American natives and Europeans, contact that introduced innovations to the ways of life on both continents. For their part, European settlers borrowed Indian modes of transport—canoes, moccasins, snowshoes—and later the deadlier forms of Indian guerilla warfare.[10] Native Americans quickly adopted European trade goods, iron, and firearms. They also adopted European methods of social organization, though more slowly. Indians who converted to Christianity—both its Catholic and Protestant variants—formed "praying towns" on the St. Lawrence and in New England in the seventeenth century.[11] The permanent Indian settlement called Logtown (Chiningué) in the Appalachian Mountains functioned as a watchtower to keep allies posted on the movements of their rivals; the site was so valuable that the English and French fought over whose fort should go there. The Indian town of Sonionto sat not far from Logtown. Further north, Iroquoia had the towns of Canajoharie, Tiononderoge, and Chenussio.[12]

Europeans and colonials struggled to categorize places such as Chiningué. Pierre-Joseph Céloron visited it in 1749 and thought it was a Mingo town; a British traveler seemed to think it belonged to the Shawnees.[13] Chiningué possessed sizable Delaware and Shawnee populations, as well as Iroquois, Abenakis, Ottawas, and others.[14] The Indians seem not to have worried overmuch about the tribal jurisdiction of their towns, which Europeans seemed frantic to assign to *someone*, whether Shawnee, Delaware, or Mingo.

Yet the real problem was not deciding which town belonged to which tribe. The problem was that, in a sense, there were no tribes at all, at least not in the static sense in which the Europeans conceived of them. The primary focus of Eastern Woodlands life was the village. Villages themselves often claimed allegiance to different matrilineal clans. (The Shawnees, for example, had five primary divisions, occupying numerous villages, with each division comprising various clan subgroups.)[15] Moreover, membership in village, nation, or clan was flexible; young men and women normally switched clan affiliation upon marriage. Beyond that, several Eastern Woodlands peoples practiced the tradition of "mourning war." When a village or clan lost members in combat, they might compensate for those losses by kidnapping members of an opposing tribe and "adopting" them into their own. When disease tore into the Iroquois homeland, the Five Nations adapted the mourning war tradition to replace those who died of illness. Thousands of Indians from the St. Lawrence to the Hudson to the Ohio Valley were adopted into the Iroquois nation.[16]

The Iroquois were the most practiced at the mourning war tradition, so much so that by the mid-eighteenth century Iroquois families contained members who had been born Huron, Montaignai, Mahican, or French—to say nothing of the mixed-blood children who resulted from such adoptions. Indeed, the "Iroquois" themselves were a polyglot people, formed of five smaller tribes that had banded together and each of which retained its independence. Moreover, if circumstances permitted, some Native Americans would jettison the entire social structure and initiate new traditions and new peoples, such as when disaffected members of the Iroquois simply broke away and formed the Mingo tribe.

Such complexity was standard in eastern North America by the sixteenth century, and for centuries after the arrival of the Europeans. It was only in the eighteenth century that Europeans, demonstrating an Enlightenment zeal for classification, began recording and referring to Indian nations as "tribes." Eventually Native Americans, too, began using this designation—but without discarding any of their previous forms of social organization.

This kind of ethnogenesis was not limited to North America. The British Isles of the sixteenth and seventeenth centuries had their own violent "tribal" conflicts. As late as the reign of Henry VIII, at the beginning of the sixteenth century, England was a collection of disparate peoples, languages, and lords. Indeed, before Henry's father had established control of his realm, the royal house of England spoke French. Henry VIII was only the second of the Tudor line, and he further split the "English" by breaking with the Catholic Church in 1534. That divided England into Catholic and Protestant bands—and the Protestants further subdivided into Calvinists, Anglicans, Presbyterians, and a host of other religious groups. In the middle of the seventeenth century, these religious tribes would fight a civil war that would multiply loyalties again, creating Quakers, Ranters, Diggers, and others, including the Fifth Monarchy men, whose goal was to set the end of the world in motion. To further complicate matters, the English crown sought to defray some of the fighting in England by importing Scottish Protestants to the Ulster counties in the Irish north. Escapees from all this conflict migrated to English colonies in the seventeenth century, although the occupants thereof could hardly be called English: Separating Congregationalists, Non-Separating Congregationalists, Quakers, Welsh Baptists, Ulster Scots, Ulster Irish, and so forth could not truly be classified as simply "English."[17] Meanwhile, New York was still New Amsterdam; its residents spoke Dutch well into the era of American independence. Over the next hundred years Acadians, German Pietists, Moravians, Huguenots, and others would be invited into British North America to join the Dutch and Swedes already incorporated into a British overseas experiment.

Then there were the hundreds of thousands of African slaves forcibly brought across the ocean to live out their lives on the American coasts. They and their creole descendants formed a third panoply of different traditions and languages. While the systematic and systemic violence of the American colonial slave system worked hard to destroy indigenous African culture and religion, and to separate slaves with common backgrounds from one another, traditions survived, changed, and introduced yet another group of new tribes into the New World. The true extent of the cultural diversity in the slave communities of British North America may never be known, but it certainly included peoples from the societies and empires of the Ashanti, Yoruba, Dahomey, Fon, Kongo, Mandinke, and countless others.[18]

Thus the arrival of the "Harryson" clan in Virginia from England, possibly by way of Bermuda in 1632, was one piece of a vast movement of people and cultures. The Harrisons made their new home in the swampy peninsulas of Virginia, where they displaced the Powhatan Indians living there. We know more about the origins of Harrison's family than about those of Tenskwatawa's family. Mostly the difference derives from the fact that the English and other European tribes were obsessive writers by the sixteenth century, for they believed that God was in words. (Indeed, "the word was God.") This predilection only intensified with the Renaissance and Reformation, which ushered in an era of treatises, histories, erotica, and double-entry bookkeeping, aided in the fifteenth century by Gutenberg's small improvement on a Chinese technology—the printing press.

Words also mattered to the Indians, but print did not. The ability to speak deeply, accurately, and extemporaneously was a paramount virtue among Native Americans of the Eastern Woodlands. "Their eloquence is more persuasive, lofty, and commanding, and their orators far more numerous . . . than is common among any class of people on the globe," wrote one American adopted by the Osages. By contrast, the ability to scribble with a pen mattered little; Indians often fulminated that interpreters would reduce entire speeches to mere sentences. "The Indian needs no writing," remarked Four Guns, an Oglala Sioux of a later generation. "Words that are true sink deep into his heart where they remain. He never forgets them. On the other hand, if the white man loses his paper, he is helpless."[19]

Tenskwatawa excelled in this art of oratory, and his 1824 stories, transcribed by Trowbridge, suggest that his talents had not diminished with age. He told the tale of a bitter and solitary husband transformed into a blue jay; the strange boy named Ball who slew a cannibal monster; the greedy Toadstool Man's humiliation at the hands of the Star Women. For generations, historians treated Indian oratory as simply "myth"—worth collecting as museum pieces, quaint and sad reminders of a "primitive" past. Historians now look to Native American tales as important sources, some going so far as to engage in "upstreaming"—hypothesizing about possible historical roots of cosmic mythologies. Others have attempted to interpret these stories as cultural artifacts, revealing the times, places, and people from whom they were written or recorded.[20]

There is also a third possibility: to see the story of Thrown Away not only as a story of Shawnee tradition but also as Tenskwatawa's self-portrait. Like Thrown Away, Tenskwatawa was the runt of the litter, weak, despised, useless, and rejected by his father. Born in a time of starvation for his people, the boy had been forgotten until he communed with a spirit who trained him and set him on the road to leadership. Thrown Away eventually became both civil chief and war chief—positions normally kept separate in Shawnee politics— and a rare achievement that Tenskwatawa also achieved in 1813.[21] The parallels are not perfect; Thrown Away saved his people and gained immortality, while the Prophet fell short.

And if Tenskwatawa had been abandoned by his father, it was not his father's choice. Puckenshinwa had been a war chief who died fighting the Virginians in 1774. He was killed before he could meet his son; Tenskwatawa was born early in 1775. Puckenshinwa's death and the conflict that brought it about set the pattern for Tenskwatawa's life. Stories of his father's heroism must have haunted his childhood, setting an almost impossibly high standard.

The war that killed Puckenshinwa had its origins in that long attempt in the sixteenth and seventeenth centuries to classify tribes. Along the eastern Atlantic seaboard, contact with Europeans had been sporadic until the 1600s; this inconsistent contact allowed the introduction into eastern North America of European trade goods without the arrival of European pathogens. It was only when the English finally got the hang of permanent colonies in Virginia and Massachusetts and France initiated a more active trading empire in the north that smallpox, rubella, measles, and influenza struck the clans and villages of the eastern coast. Yet the most profound result of the arrival of Europeans, from an Indian perspective, was the genesis of a new and powerful native empire—the aforementioned Five Nations of the Iroquois.[22]

Prior to 1400, the Iroquois had been at war among themselves, as the Mohawks and Senecas struggled to dominate the Oneidas, Onondagas, and Cayugas. Nevertheless, the five nations (later six) that constituted the Iroquois League all spoke similar languages, and they began experimenting with forming a confederated organization in the fifteenth century—according to legend, under the leadership of Hiawatha. In the sixteenth century, they found themselves the power to be reckoned with in an American interior crucial to the trading and geopolitical hopes of the Dutch colony of New Netherland and the French outposts along the St. Lawrence. Moreover, their cultural and religious attachment to the tradition of mourning war gave them a social solution to the problem of depopulation. In the 1620s, they dispossessed the Mahican Indians from the Hudson River Valley in order to monopolize trade with the Dutch. They invaded Shawnee territory in the 1630s.[23] Along the Great Lakes, the Hurons, Foxes, Miamis, and others were splintered and pushed west by Iroquois violence. Some Algonquin groups, such as the Eries and the Neutrals, disappeared altogether, killed by or adopted into the expanding Iroquois clans.[24] The Iroquois Empire did not exercise total control over the areas it conquered, nor were those exiled from their lands completely removed. After victory, the Iroquois usually ruled with a light hand, and exacted tribute instead—much the same way that Britain would later rule her colonies.[25]

Europeans are sometimes accused of fomenting conflict between Native American groups; there is truth to this claim. Nevertheless, it is also true that Native Americans harbored resentments, ambitions, and dreams of grandeur as surely as the Europeans did. The Iroquois used their alliances with European powers against their rivals. If colors on a map symbolize control of territory and the extent to which power can be extended over space, much of the American Northeast and Ohio Valley should have been colored in sixteenth-century maps and known as "Iroquoia."

Something similar was happening at the same time thousands of miles away among the Comanches in what is today the American Southwest. The "Lords of the Plains" had begun to emerge from their Ute patrons to lash out at neighboring tribes and the Spanish to the south. The Comanches soon created a hierarchical empire in the Southwest with a sophisticated market economy and a complex political order. Like Iroquoia, Comanchería would have been hard to detail on a map; its imperial outlines were marked by tribute, commerce, and military control rather than by a European-style border. Nevertheless, the Comanches remained the dominant power in the Southwest through 1850 and beyond.[26]

The experience of the Comanches and the Iroquois demonstrates that Indian efforts at empire building—displacing other tribes and taking the lead in diplomacy—were more than mere survival or containment techniques. The Comanches and the Iroquois played the imperial game well, and they played to win.[27] Further west, other Algonquin Indians still occupying their own lands quickly formed a defensive alliance as an alternative axis to the Five Nations in an area around the Great Lakes known as the *pays d'en haut*, or "upper lands."[28] Seventeenth-century French and Dutch settlements found themselves stymied by these Indian groups, so they entered into alliances with them. The French allied with the Indians of the *pays d'en haut*; the Dutch opted for the Iroquois.

The Iroquois formalized their power and prestige by what was later called the "covenant chain," a metaphor (as all alliances are). The Dutch had tethered their "ship" by a "rope" to a tree in Onondaga; the Iroquois sat upon the rope so that they would know if the Dutch ship was in trouble. After a time, the Iroquois replaced the rope with a chain, and invited the Dutch to "enter into League and Covenant with us."[29] When the British replaced the Dutch, they too adopted the metaphor of the covenant chain. Pennsylvania's Thomas Penn wrote to the Iroquois in 1732 that "my Father made a Chain and Covenants" and promised to "make that Chain yet stronger and brighter in our Parts that it may continue so to all generations."[30]

The covenant chain was an alliance of empires, and for a while it worked well. There were some squabbles. English agents argued that the chain meant an exclusive relationship, banning Iroquois from trade with the French, while the Iroquois continued to cultivate contacts and friendships on their western borders. Meanwhile, the agreements kept the English bottled up in the marginal lands close to the ocean (marginal, of course, to a non-seafaring people). Peace between the Iroquois and the newcomers also allowed for the Iroquois domination of other Indian tribes, expanding the geography and influence of the Five Nations. The British, on the other hand, exchanged goods and services for the semblance of peaceful relations that allowed growth while using the Iroquois as proxies to displace their more immediate coastal neighbors.

This is not to accuse the Iroquois of "collaboration" with the colonials, nor to equate their behavior with that of eighteenth-century British colonists, who demonstrated a rapacious demand for land and unconcern over Indian dispossession. It is important to underscore, however, that the story of dispossession in the eighteenth century was not simply a case of whites cheating Indians. Individual white governments dealt with particular tribes, which themselves were agglomerations of villages and clans in a fluid, polyglot social order. Europeans may have seen "Indians" as singular, but they treated with them as tribes. Similarly, seventeenth- and eighteenth-century Native Americans thought in terms of clans, villages, and tribes and acted accordingly, sometimes attempting to benefit themselves and their own people at the expense of other groups. "We conquer'd You, we made Women of you, you know you are women, and can no more sell Land than Women," boasted the Onondaga leader Canasatego to the Delawares in 1742.[31] The Iroquois willingness to dominate other tribes and benefit themselves assumed a new level of duplicity when they began to sell lands to which they had no claim.

The Treaty of Lancaster seemed plain enough. Commissioners from Virginia, Pennsylvania, and Maryland wanted to settle a squabble over land in the Shenandoah Valley. Colonial commissioners contacted the Iroquois to make the appropriate payment.[32] Canasatego led negotiations for the Iroquois. At around sixty years of age, with "a manly countenance, mixed with a good-natured smile," the Onondaga elder emphasized his position to the assembled colonial delegates.[33] The land in question, Canasatego declared, was ancient Iroquoia: "Long before One Hundred Years our Ancestors came out of this very Ground, and their Children have remained here ever since." The Iroquois drove a hard bargain, eventually obtaining more than a thousand pounds of goods for the land.

It seemed a coup for the Iroquois: they received a king's ransom for lands far from the center of their empire.[34] The only problem was that the lands in question never belonged to the Iroquois. They were Shawnee and Delaware territory, and had been for generations. The Iroquois had sent raiding parties that far south decades before the treaty, but they did not exercise any real authority over the valley. Nor was it the "very ground" from which the Iroquois claimed descent. Canasatego's speech was the first time the Iroquois ever claimed ancestors in Maryland. In short, the Iroquois had sold out the Shawnees and Delawares for a thousand pounds of commodities.[35]

Some historians suggest that the Iroquois had been misled, or never intended to sell the land.[36] It is certainly true that by 1744 the empire was weakening; efforts to expand westward in the 1720s had ended disastrously, and Pennsylvania's aggressive expansion had alienated the Mohawks from the other tribes.[37] Yet claims of ignorance do not explain Canasatego's insistence on Iroquois ownership of the land, nor his humiliation of the Delawares. They do not explain the very similar colonial agreements the Iroquois had consented to in 1701 and 1726, nor the continued land sales the Iroquois made in 1768.[38] While it would be an egregious error to suggest that Native Americans brought dispossession and land theft upon themselves, it is nevertheless crucial to recognize the culture and context in which land sales took place—a world defined by village, clan, tribe, and empire, and not a world merely divided into white and Indian halves. The Iroquois feint at Lancaster profited their empire at the expense of other tribes and the English colonists.[39]

Perhaps predictably, Canasatego's performance drove a wedge through the Iroquois Empire. Even as the Onondaga chief claimed to speak for the Iroquois nations, Mohawk chiefs seem to have been treating in Boston, also claiming to represent the whole confederacy. In the days to come, the Mohawks—the tribe geographically closest to the English colonies—would distance themselves from the rest of the Confederation.[40] The question is whether such conflict was mere posturing or whether the Mohawks had a real sense that injury had been done by one tribe against another, one that might threaten all Native peoples.

Things began to move rapidly after that. Attempts by colonial and British surveyors to measure the Shenandoah and Ohio Valleys met with stone-faced delegations of Shawnee and Delaware warriors. Those dispossessed tribes allied in 1747, and the Mingo tribe soon joined them.[41] This new faction began courting France, despite a flurry of French depredations in the *pays d'en haut*. Eventually the French agreed to join the Shawnees and Delawares and began constructing forts across the Ohio in 1752; the linchpin, Fort Duquesne, rose at the confluence of the Ohio, Allegheny, and Monongahela rivers in 1754. Virginia's governor sent a green army officer from Virginia's Northern Neck to evaluate the situation. That commander managed to fall into an accidental firefight at the fort followed by a crushing counterattack by the French and Indian forces. The result destabilized the entire region to the point that Britain and France were soon at war over North America. The bungling commander was George Washington.[42]

In Europe, the conflict is remembered as the Seven Years' War. In North America, where the fighting lasted two years longer, it is the French and

Indian War. The Indians in question were old French allies from the rival alliance around the *pays d'en haut*—Ottawas, Ojibwes, Hurons—as well as Shawnees, Delawares, and Wyandots, fighting to reverse by arms what the English colonists had "bought" through trickery.

At first the French and Indian forces scored lopsided victories against English armies. Yet Britain soon devoted new resources (and new strategies) to the war in America. By 1760, the British had taken Niagara, Quebec, and Montreal, and had even seized Fort Duquesne, near Chiningué, and renamed it after their prime minister—Fort Pitt (modern-day Pittsburgh). Canada also fell to the British. The Indian clans, tribes, and villages that had fought against the British now found they lived in a world where the British were the only colonial power.

Commissioners at the 1763 Treaty of Paris paid little attention to Native American power in North America. They should have. The nations doing the negotiating were France and Britain, and as historian Colin Calloway has written, "They argued for months over the fate of a few small islands" but "casually disposed of continents that they had never seen."[43] Britain had conquered Canada, but not the Ohio country, nor any lands west of the Appalachians. Yet now Britain (with French complicity) became the nominal rulers of the vast North American interior, and her officials immediately began governing the new possession with all the swagger of an occupying army.

For Britain was also flat broke: the war with France had carried over from North America to the Caribbean, India, and Europe. After 1763, North America's nominal masters instituted a series of policy changes intended to refill its coffers. The government in London jacked up colonial taxes, prompting the protests famous in American history. The British army occupied the line of forts once built by the French, and under the leadership of Jeffrey Amherst they drastically reduced the money spent on gifts meant to maintain diplomacy and alliances with Native American powers.[44]

These things in themselves did not bring war. But with the French threat neutralized and the British army occupying French forts, several American colonials felt comfortable pushing deeper into Indian territory. Shawnee and Delaware orators began to speak to other tribes about the need to continue the war against Britain begun in 1754. Would the Europeans ever have enough land to be satisfied? Or would they, as the Shawnee Missiweakiwa said, "deprive us entirely out of our country"? British army efforts to eject the settlers failed. The Senecas began circulating war wampum as early as 1762.[45]

Scholars have pointed to this rebellion as a crucial moment of change in American history, for it was the first widespread effort to unite Native

American tribes across North America against a common white foe. Some have even pointed to this moment as the creation of a true "Indian" identity, when commonalities between Ojibwe, Ottawa, Iroquois, and Shawnee became more important than clan or tribal differences. The alliances even extended into the southern colonies, where traditional British allies such as the Cherokees switched sides and fought against the new empire.[46]

As for Thrown Away, after leading his people for many years as both civil and war chief, he "grew weary of this type of life" and asked his spirit guardian to change him into an animal. He became a wolf, and his people became deer, beavers, bears, and turkeys; "and so all were transformed."[47] In some ways, too, the changes wrought by the events of 1763 were likewise mysterious in nature. The efforts at unity were uneven and failed in some respects, but the rebellions brought about a profound transformation in Native American religion, and became a touchstone and inspiration for the religion and rebellion of the Shawnee Prophet.

2

Master of Life

NATIVE AMERICANS OFTEN found Christianity confusing, "more probably fables than fact," according to the Wyandot Kandiaronk. After all, none of the Christians could agree what Christianity was: "The English are positive that their religion is the best, while the Jesuits cry the contrary," Kandiaronk complained. "What am I supposed to make of this, if there is only one true religion on earth? What people *don't* think their own religion is the most perfect?"[1] Indian converts to Christianity encountered theological resistance from family members: "We have all the delights that the flesh and blood of man can devise and delight in, and we taste and feel the delights of them," complained the relatives of one convert. "Would you make us believe that you have found out new joys and delights, in comparison of which all our delights do stink like dung?"[2] Their religion focused upon the joys and tragedies of living in this world; gods and spirits were more powerful than humans, yet lived much like humans, and to the extent that an afterlife existed at all, it was a place very much like the lands of Iroquoia or the Ohio Valley.

European Christians found Native American religion equally confusing. Some simply dismissed it entirely. A white missionary among the Cherokees found "nothing among them which could be called a system of religious beliefs."[3] Other whites grappled with its concepts, and scribbled down notes on what they observed—sometimes to their bafflement. John Filson, surveyor and cartographer of Kentucky, wrote of Native American religion that "although it cannot be absolutely affirmed that they have none, yet it must be confessed very difficult to define what it is." Filson could identify some sort of distant high god, who was not worshipped, and an idea of a future state.[4] He could identify some kind of afterlife, and a creator god, but little else. The eighteenth-century missionary John Heckewelder, who could not understand why Indians seemed to possess no Augustinian sense of original sin, nevertheless gleaned a tolerable understanding of how eastern Native Americans conceived of God: "All Indians believe in a supreme Being unto whom, on account of his marvelous deeds, in creating the world and all that is herein, both animate and inanimate, they have given the name 'Kitschi Manitou' which in the true sense of the words, signifies 'Supreme wonders doer.'"[5]

In fact, there was no such thing as "Indian religion." While Native American tribes possessed some similarities in worship and belief, augmented by a continuing tradition of adoption and exchange, what the white colonists saw as "Indian religion" in fact represented several different traditions.[6] Much as whites at war failed to distinguish between Indian allies and Indian enemies, white missionaries and philosophers tended to see the panoply of Indian religious beliefs as an undifferentiated mass tinged with superstition and barbarism.

The tribes now designated as the Eastern Woodlands Indians, however, shared a core of beliefs and practices that British settlers took as the Indian religion. The groups that stretched (at the time of the British invasion) from the southern Appalachians to the Great Lakes and into what is now maritime Canada lived in a universe populated by a hierarchy of spiritual beings. Most Eastern Woodlands religions featured a high god, but often one who was either distant or easily duped. The power worth seeking in the Native American cosmos came from lesser supernatural creatures. These beings went by many names, but a generic term—and one used in the eighteenth and nineteenth centuries—was "manitou." The manitou were spirits, but they were not transparent, powerless shades. They were embodiments of primal forces and natural phenomena, active players in a cosmic economy tied to human beings in reciprocal relationships of favors and exchanges. The Sac Indian leader Black Hawk recalled a manitou of his childhood who lived on "the best island on the Mississippi." "A good spirit had care of it," Black Hawk said, "with large wings like a *swan's*, but ten times larger. We were particular not to make much noise in that part of the island which he inhabited." In return for respect and quiet, the spirit allowed the Sac to forage, feast, and play. It brought forth berries, plums, apples, and nuts across the island, and made sure the "waters supplied us with fine fish."[7]

Thomas Ridout, a British surveyor who had been held captive by the Shawnees for a number of years, gained some sense of the concept of a manitou in 1788, when he demonstrated his compass' ability to point north: "Not being able to comprehend its action, they [his Shawnee captors] called it a 'Manitou,' by which they mean 'spirit,' or something incomprehensible and powerful." Ridout probably meant his comment as gentle condescension, but identifying the compass as a manitou indicates the Woodlands concept of manitou: not simply powerful spirits, but anthropomorphic invisible forces that could be supplicated or manipulated for aid, which is a plausible description, in nineteenth-century terms, for what a compass did with magnetism.[8]

The manitou, spirits of animate and inanimate objects, closer to the human world and more likely to understand and care about its affairs, usually received human succor.[9] This system of spiritual economy meant that Christianity (in comparison) was not wrong; it was simply the white people's manitou. Christian missionaries often heard shamans refer to Christianity as fine for whites but wrong for Indians.[10]

What was right for Indians changed over time. Christian missionaries generally failed to understand that "Indian religion" was not static; events in the human world could trigger or signal changes in the cosmic order. Amid the vortex of the late 1750s and 1760s, a new class of religious leader began to appear among the tribes of the Ohio. While scholars disagree over how great a disjuncture with traditional Eastern Woodlands religion this new class represented, all agree that this generation of leaders represented a shift in the religious tradition, in that the high god, normally an absentee deity, had returned to the world of humans and spirits, and had begun dictating his will through chosen followers. White observers called them "prophets."[11]

The prophet of 1763 was a Delaware named Neolin. Historians know almost nothing about his origins or his fate. His followers told the story that Neolin was "anxious to know the Master of Life" and therefore "resolved . . . to undertake a journey to Paradise." Not knowing which direction to take to reach the "celestial regions," Neolin "commenced juggling"—a word that in the eighteenth century referred to sorcery and dream interpretation rather than to flipping balls or ninepins. Having found the way in dreams, Neolin traveled across two roads that ended in "fire coming from under the ground," and then ascended a steep mountain that was smooth like glass. Naked, Neolin climbed to a strange village, "a place of unequaled beauty," where a man in white conducted him to the Master of Life.

"I am He," declared the Master of Life, "who made heaven and earth, the trees, lakes, rivers, all men, and all thou seest, and all that thou hast seen on earth," and "because I love you, you must do what I say." The Master of Life instructed Neolin about the sins of the Delawares and other tribes, whose drinking and use of European trade goods had polluted their spiritual power and allowed the whites to dominate their homeland: "Were you not wicked as you are, you would not need them." The time had now come, however, for the Indians to reclaim their birthright, for "the land on which you are, I have made for you, not for others." The High God had returned to his chosen people, the Indians, and had chastened but not forgotten them.

Through Neolin, the Master of Life outlined a program of religious reform. He had, he said, recalled animals from the forests because of Indians' evil ways. It was now time to cease all conflict among Indians, to return to the bow and arrow for hunting (indeed, to abandon white habits generally), to repeat a set prayer at morning and evening, and to cease their obeisance to the British, "those dogs in red clothing." The Master of Life, Neolin explained, had placed Indians in America and Europeans across the ocean; he had tolerated Europeans to come west and trouble the Indians in the sixteenth and seventeenth centuries, but that arrangement was now over: "Send them back to the country which I made for them."[12]

Neolin was not the first to bring such a message from the Master of Life; mentions of similar reformist rhetoric appear in colonial records going back to 1737. Twelve years before Neolin, an unnamed Delaware woman explained that the Master of Life had created Indians, blacks, and whites separately—and whites last of all, so "white people ought not to think themselves better than the Indians."[13] Wangomend, a contemporary of Neolin's, taught that there were three heavens, one each for blacks, whites, and Indians. Indians had the best of the afterlives, while whites had the worst, punished for their ill-treatment of Indians and slaves.[14] These prophets did not replace traditional Indian religions; new rituals and prayers to the Master of Life often coexisted with traditional ceremonies to the manitou and the Master of Animals.[15]

Among these prophets, Neolin had the greatest success. He and his followers traversed the Ohio country in the early 1760s, calling for moral reform and political resistance. For emphasis, Neolin drew his depiction of the cosmos on an enormous animal hide, detailing the road to a comfortable afterlife and the far more numerous paths to a fiery hell. Previous efforts at resistance against the despised British overlord Amherst had failed, and indeed had fractured the clan alliances of the *pays d'en haut*. Yet when an Ottawa named Pontiac, borrowing from Neolin's teachings, inspired a series of uprisings in 1763, the entire frontier exploded in revolt.[16] The conflict is usually known as Pontiac's War, but in fact a whole host of leaders, inspired by Neolin's message, conducted raids and campaigns against the British that year. Virtually every one of the French forts now occupied by the British fell before combined intertribal forces beginning in May 1763. In the course of a year, the Ohio Valley had gone from French territory to British empire to Indian country.

Britain still held the important forts of Detroit, Niagara, and Fort Pitt, but Pontiac's insurgents had done their job. Amherst was removed from his post for failing to prevent or contain the violence.[17] As a compromise, the government in London created the Proclamation Line of 1763, designating the lands west of the Appalachians and south of the Great Lakes as Indian territory, legally binding British colonists to the seaboard, and seemingly achieving the long-standing goal of numerous Indian peoples "to secure the limits between them" and the Europeans.[18]

Yet the line did not solve the problem. The British, for example, continued to maintain that the Ohio country still belonged to the Iroquois, under the oft-repeated rights of conquest. That meant that the Iroquois Confederacy could still sell Shawnee lands for white settlement, Proclamation Line or no—which the Iroquois did at Fort Stanwix in 1768.[19]

The other problem was the Paxton Boys. Pontiac's War had fallen hard on white and Indian settlements in western Pennsylvania, with hundreds of casualties and particularly vicious fighting on both sides. One group of white volunteers from the town of Paxton had seen the results of an Indian massacre in the Wyoming Valley of Pennsylvania. In December 1763, some veterans of the conflict heard that a group of Indians at Conestoga was planning a similar uprising (they weren't). The "Paxton Boys" went on a rampage, killing all the Indians they found at Conestoga Manor. Some of the Conestoga Indians managed to find refuge in nearby Lancaster; the Paxton Boys stormed the town and slaughtered them too. Having wiped the Conestoga Indians from the earth, they headed off to the colonial capital, Philadelphia, intent on murdering a group of Moravian Indians holed up under the protection of the state legislature, believing (correctly, as it turned out) that they were next.[20] Timely diplomacy by Benjamin Franklin—backed with threats of British imperial force—kept the Paxton delegation from overthrowing Philadelphia in a coup.

Historians have paid close attention to the Paxton Boys. Many have followed Franklin's own line of reasoning. The Paxton mob, Franklin wrote, was comprised of "Frontier People" and "barbarous men ... in defiance of government." The Paxton Boys, in this formulation, were the down-and-out rabble from the backcountry who attempted (and for the most part, succeeded in) ethnic cleansing. Yet resentment played a role as well—resentment that the king's soldiers would protect Indians over whites, a rule now dictated by the Proclamation Line. The British crown had for years ruled the colonies with a light hand while negotiating with Indian tribes and empires; now the crown ruled both. The Paxton Boys were only the first to react violently to this new arrangement.[21]

The Indian prophets and the Paxton Boys had at least one thing in common: observers at the time accused both of them of altering Christian teaching to suit their needs. Franklin accused the Paxton Boys of holding up the Bible and citing the commands of Joshua to justify their murderous actions.[22] While the language used by the Paxton Boys was predominantly secular, they took up the view that the settlers were the Israelites, and "the Indians were the Canaanites, who by God's command were to be destroyed; and that this not having been done . . . the present war might be considered as a just punishment from God for their disobedience."[23] The Paxton riot soon faded away, but the notion of a divine right to land did not.

Neolin (like Tenskwatawa) is sometimes tagged as having borrowed elements of Christianity and infused traditional beliefs with them.[24] In particular, the notion of a monotheistic god and a place of eternal damnation seem to be derived from Christian teachings that had arrived in North America with European missionaries. One colonial observer claimed that Neolin believed a "Son or Little God" would carry the prayers of the faithful to the High God, "too high & Mighty to be spoke to by them."[25] That kind of language makes Neolin's religion potentially syncretic, but not necessarily so. Indeed, given the similarities of some aspects of Eastern Woodlands religious systems and Christian teaching (such as the importance of visions, the idea of a created universe, an afterlife, and multiple levels of supernatural beings) and the absence of written records prior to European contact, it is difficult if not impossible to ascertain how Eastern religious traditions had changed prior to and during the first century of European contact. (One recent scholar writes that "Indians and Christians agreed on the general contours of religion" and merely "disagreed on the details.")[26] Making precise judgments about what was "traditional" and what was "Christian" in the visions of the Native American prophets amounts essentially to guesswork—especially since neither religion could claim an unchanging tradition from which the other might borrow. This kind of classification belongs to a similar vein as the effort to prove that Tenskwatawa faked his eclipse—it implies that Native American religious genius needed to borrow from Western sources to save itself, and that religion itself is merely functional.

In fact, much of what Neolin preached found ready listeners, eager for the chance at spiritual and political renewal. One of those listeners seems to have been Puckenshinwa, father of Tenskwatawa and Tecumseh. More is known about Puckenshinwa's warrior's death than his life, but he came from the Meshoke clan of the Shawnees, a clan that traditionally provided the war chiefs for the Shawnee nation and, indeed, for the wider Shawnee confederacy of tribes in the 1760s. He likely saw action in the Seven Years' War, Pontiac's Rebellion, and the border skirmishes with whites that followed the establishment of the Proclamation Line of 1763. Puckenshinwa's final battle, however—the one that brought his career to a bloody end and set the pattern for Tenskwatawa's life—came about in a final piece of diplomatic perfidy in 1768 that led to yet another conflict in 1774.

Tenskwatawa's father died for a cause. It had not been a simple question of Indians refusing to leave their land in the face of white advances—though many white settlers insisted on seeing things that way. In 1768, with the uneasy peace still holding in the Ohio country and the British reoccupying their forts, the declining Iroquois empire and the European colonials repeated their diplomatic dance from previous decades, with whites acknowledging weak Iroquois claims to ownership and buying land from people who did not live on it. This time it was the colony of Virginia that sought western lands for settlement. The prize was Kentucky. Once again claiming ancient rights of conquest, Iroquois negotiators "sold" Kentucky lands to Virginia in the 1768 Treaty of Fort Stanwix. The fact that the land was now occupied by Delaware, Wyandot, and Shawnee tribes mattered little to the Iroquois, safe in their Finger Lakes stronghold, and it mattered little to the Virginia government. White Virginians poured into Shawnee Kentucky—in part to prevent *their* tribal brethren, the British, from appropriating the land for other whites. The Shawnees, who had never sold their land, responded by confiscating the settlers' goods, and sometimes with violence.

It was that conflict—the battle over the right of each tribe to own its own territory—that prompted the battle that cost Puckenshinwa his life. The conflict, known as Dunmore's War (named after Virginian governor Lord Dunmore), was bloody. The Americans even earned a tribal name—the Long Knives, after the distinctive Bowie knives popular among white adventurers.[27] It was not a long war. The Shawnees and their allies were pushed back across the Ohio River, the Long Knives occupied Kentucky, and Puckenshinwa died at the Battle of Point Pleasant.

Tenskwatawa was born and grew up in Ohio, a land not truly his own; as a child he must have heard stories about the lost homeland, the murdering Long Knives who had slain his father, and the treachery of the Iroquois. And so, even as the American Revolution engulfed North America in Tenskwatawa's earliest years, he perhaps had some inkling as to why most Indian tribes failed to ally decisively with either the Americans, the British, or indeed one another.

Many historians contend that by the end of Dunmore's War the mutual transformation of European and Indian cultures had come to a critical point. Three centuries of contact had affected different Indian peoples in different ways, but by 1774 things looked grim for the Native population. Both Indians and colonists were bound by a web of social relationships and economic trade; this network improved life in European colonies while it merely permitted life in Indian towns and villages. Native cultures had created extensive commercial networks. Yet they had experienced less success as producers of goods, especially iron and gunpowder. Then there was the increasing demographic imbalance: the ravages of disease had badly reduced their populations, while the population of the English colonies of the eastern seaboard had passed the million mark. English laws and politics had rarely respected Native American land claims, and with Dunmore's War the colonists had achieved a massive and bloody intrusion into the southern edge of the *pays d'en haut.* Taking these transformations together, many have determined that with the end of Pontiac's Rebellion, and certainly with defeat in Dunmore's War, the era of Indian independence had effectively ended. What remained was predetermined to failure, a doomed effort.[28]

Yet if all that is true, why did Indian resistance continue? Why were so many different Indian leaders continuing to seek unity among the tribes, and so many others seeking to advance their own tribal interests? There is another way of understanding the situation, one that better explains the politics of the Ohio Valley for the forty years following Dunmore's War. The apparent universal decline of Indian culture and power was in fact a regional decline of the two largest northeastern empires; the Iroquois and the Grand Alliance of the *pays d'en haut* began to fail simultaneously, though in different ways. These declensions created an opening for the new arrangements and alliances born after the end of the Revolution, as new Indian leaders (and religions) sought to establish themselves. The Six Nations had managed to back the winning side in the Seven Years' War, yet lost status and influence. Victory made the Iroquois exclusively dependent on the British while removing the barrier to British extension into the *pays d'en haut.* Internal squabbles fractured the Six Nations, with different tribes and clans pursuing different strategies.[29] And after years of selling other people's lands to the British, the Iroquois had forfeited prestige and power.

Further west, the much looser alliances of the *pays d'en haut* suffered similar internal decay. Canny British diplomacy had separated the Shawnees and the Delawares from the alliance, but the true division was becoming clear: the one between civil chiefs and military leaders.[30] This political division of leadership would set the stage for the coming struggle. The battle was not only between Native Americans and American citizens; it also took place within Native communities themselves, in the political balance between civil and war chiefs. The increasing numbers of white settlers and government authorities would seek to control this balance. They were not, however, the only applicants for the job: leaders of the smaller component tribes of the Grand Alliance, now free of Iroquois perfidy and interference, made their own bids for power and dominance. Some of these leaders sought accommodation with the United States, but others preferred a policy of armed resistance. A regional struggle for dominance better explains the diverse ways in which these leaders—with or without their people's support—interacted with the politics of the Revolution and post-Revolutionary period. The wars of 1774–1815 were not the last gasp of a dying people; they were the birth pangs of a new Indian empire. This was the reason Puckenshinwa had gone to his death.

Of course, beating the Americans to imperial power would be a hefty task. A new generation of white American leaders had their own "Great Spirit" with visions of the supernatural order and his favored people within that order. One of those leaders was William Henry Harrison, and as it happened, Dunmore had managed to destroy his childhood as well.

3

Primogeniture

VIRGINIA'S PLANTER CLASS dominated the political and economic life of the colony, and the Harrisons had long been part of this Virginian aristocracy. The stately mansion known as Berkeley, just up the road from the forts of Jamestown, had seen a long line of Benjamins Harrison since the first of the name arrived in Virginia in 1632. Each of the Benjamins had served in Virginia government. Traditional deference to gentility in colonial Virginia gave the Harrison clan cultural capital for leadership; control over the trade in human chattel and a popular addictive drug (tobacco) provided their economic and social power.[1]

The records on William Henry's early life are sparse; his early years were spent in the midst of a revolution, and family attention undoubtedly focused on matters greater than the education and upbringing of a three-year-old child. Moreover, like Tenskwatawa, Harrison was a younger son and thus not perceived as destined for greatness. William Henry's father and brother served together in the American Revolution—Benjamin V in Congress and as a signer of the Declaration of Independence, and Benjamin VI as paymaster general for the southern army.[2] And, like Tenskwatawa, Harrison had an older brother being groomed to fill their father's shoes.

Benjamin Harrison V was either an important prelate or "an indolent, luxurious, heavy gentleman," depending on whom you asked (in the latter case, John Adams).[3] As a member of one of the first families of Virginia, he held a seat in the House of Burgesses by dint of status as much as by elective qualifications. By ancestry or by marriage, Benjamin V could claim kinship with the other great families of Virginia—the Carters, the Randolphs, and the Washingtons. The Harrisons embodied the social order of deference and prestige in eighteenth-century Virginia. By then, most Virginians (slave and free) had been born in the New World, permitting the consolidation of a local governing elite to run the colony; only the governor came from royal appointment. Wealth and status were passed among the long-established Tidewater families, who in turn expected deference from their social inferiors. "Assumptions about social difference were fundamental to the legitimation of political authority between local elites and their social inferiors," historian Michael

J. Braddick writes. In the words of an eighteenth-century Virginian, "We were accustomed to look upon what were called *gentle folks*, as being of a superior order."[4]

William Henry's rather pompous and "uncommonly large" father was therefore an unlikely choice to back the Revolution; the Harrisons benefited from a world in which political authority derived from social position, rather than from any concept of natural rights, let alone an appeal to "the people."[5] Yet Harrison ultimately supported the Revolution—in part because of Lord Dunmore.

The governor's trumped-up war for settler land and property claims had already taken the life of Puckenshinwa in 1774 and pushed the Shawnees into Ohio. When his white subjects rebelled against the crown in 1775, Dunmore made another fateful stand on Virginian property, emancipating "all Indentured Servants, Negroes, and Others" so long as they were "able and willing to bear arms" against the rebel forces. In November 1775, he began freeing and arming slaves—which slaveholders would have regarded not just as a violation of property rights but as a terrifying reversal of power. The timing of Dunmore's proclamation arming the slaves coincided with Benjamin Harrison's decision to support revolution. In 1774, Harrison had been a conservative delegate to the Continental Congress, opposing arming colonists against Great Britain. In November 1775, he took the lead in securing assistance from France and Spain.

Dunmore's "Ethiopian Regiment" had another important role to play, both in the Revolution and among the Harrison family. As the freedman soldiers moved up the Atlantic coast in December 1775, they landed near the Harrison homestead and battled patriots near Norfolk. Unfortunately, while camped out near Portsmouth, Virginia, they contracted smallpox. Reports claimed that as many as eight slaves a day were joining the regiment. They succumbed to the variola virus just as quickly. Disease scuttled a potentially devastating loyalist force.[6]

Benjamin Harrison V understood both slavery and smallpox. A year before William was born, the disease had broken out at Berkeley; "not being able to stop the progress of the small pox in my family, I have determined to inoculate immediately," William's father wrote. The inoculation apparently did its job and ended the outbreak. In choosing to inoculate, Harrison made a risky decision in the days before professional medicine; it was not a decision every planter would have made (thus the susceptibility of Dunmore's Ethiopian Regiment). As for slaves, Harrison had many—and a perpetual problem with runaways. In the pages of the *Virginia Gazette*, where he had politely warned his neighbors to avoid the outbreak at Berkeley in 1772, Harrison also advertised for those who had left Berkeley for other reasons: Aaron in 1767, Nick in 1770, and Dublin in 1773. (Like most of the enslaved of Virginia, Harrison's bondsmen usually had only one name.) Nick escaped a second time in 1775, and the second notice included a detail perhaps derived from the first escape: "Some little time since he was whipped and had many fresh marks on his Back."[7] Whether Harrison himself delivered those blows or paid an overseer to do it is not known.

By 1776, the thirteen colonies were in full revolt. News of "victory" over the Ethiopian Regiment (the freedmen were found on Gwyn's Island, among dozens of bodies "in a state of putrefaction" strewn over two miles "without a shovelful of earth on them," while those still alive crawled to the water's edge) appeared in the *Gazette* in the very same July issue that carried the news that Congress had declared the colonies independent of Great Britain.[8] The Harrisons had joined the cause, but in some ways they fought to preserve their own status and influence, in effect their rights over other Virginians—legal rights to own slaves and social mastery over whites. Lord Dunmore had forged another leader, this time one who brought up his children with a mixture of revolutionary rhetoric and convictions about the inviolability of slavery.

Resistance did not come without cost. Revolutionary Virginia was a world at war, and though his father might have been, in John Adams' words, "of no Use in Congress or Committee," nevertheless William Henry would have grown up knowing his father could hang for treason. Of course, wartime at Berkeley had comforts as well: the dozens of enslaved servants made their life easier, and the blessings of rational Christianity offered reassurances.[9]

The Episcopalian Harrisons embraced such a religion. Benjamin Harrison and other revolutionary leaders followed a set of doctrines nearly unrecognizable to many Christian groups in the United States today. George Washington attended church but never took communion. Benjamin Franklin doubted the divinity of Christ, as did Jefferson, who considered himself "a Christian, in the only sense in which he [Christ] wished anyone to be; sincerely attached to his doctrines, in preference to all others." Jesus possessed "every human excellence," Jefferson wrote to Benjamin Rush, but "never claimed any other."[10] Rush himself was probably the most devout of all the signers of the Declaration of Independence. Religious groups in the twenty-first century have made Rush something of a hero for his piety and cite his desire to have the Bible distributed in public schools as a sign that all the Founders were religious men.[11] But Rush himself was a Universalist: he did not believe in hell or eternal damnation. Moreover, he had wanted the Bible handed out to all so as to counteract the pernicious tendency of sectarians to teach only those parts of scripture that defended their own interpretation.[12]

The heterodox Christianity of Rush, Jefferson, Washington, and other Founders owed much to the influence of deism. Deism—an eighteenth-century religious and intellectual movement—was manifold in character, and often seemed all things to all men. (Indeed, deism is easy to attribute in part because it is so difficult to define.) Some deists thought Christ was a god, others that he was an inspired human prophet; still others thought he was just a man. Some deists thought miracles had ended with the resurrection; others said that they had ended with creation, and still others believed that there had never been a creation at all—matter had always existed and always would exist.[13] Some argued for revelation, but most argued from nature. Nonetheless, deists usually agreed on a rejection of the stern God of Calvinism, who retained the ultimate ability to save or damn based on his own unfathomable workings ("The wishes expressed in your last favor," Jefferson wrote to John Adams in 1823, "that I may continue in life and health until I become a Calvinist . . . would make me immortal").[14] To make matters still more difficult, deists were scattered throughout the American denominations—there was no deist "church" to make classification easier.

The term "deist" emerged in the seventeenth century and first appears in English as a counterweight to "atheist."[15] If atheists denied the existence of God, deists acknowledged a god but denied divine revelation. Jonathan Edwards wrote that deists admitted "the being of a God" but "deny any revealed religion, or any word of God at all; and say that God has given mankind no other light to walk by but their own reason."[16]

Edwards lacked the willingness or the patience to make fine distinctions regarding the deists, but he fully understood the radical basis of their platform: reason above all. "The sources of hope and consolation to the human race are to be sought for in the energy of intellectual powers," wrote the great deistic popularizer Elihu Palmer.[17] That is not to say that previous Christians had never worshipped God through their intellect. Augustine, Anselm, and Calvin (among others) were all intellectuals; Luther was a college professor. The deist difference was one of emphasis and formulation. Reason was not simply *a* method of understanding religion, it was *the* method; indeed, reason was a divine gift that could unravel all the mysteries of religion. Jefferson's advice to his nephew on the method of religious study was simple: "Fix reason firmly in her seat, and call to her tribunal every fact, every opinion. Question with boldness even the existence of a god; because, if there be one, he must more approve the homage of reason, than that of blindfolded fear."[18] "The strength of the human understanding is incalculable," wrote Palmer, "its keenness of discernment would ultimately penetrate into every part of nature, were it permitted to operate with uncontrolled and unqualified freedom."[19]

This exaltation of the human mind joined American life and letters via the European Enlightenment. From Newton and the scientific revolution came the notion of immutable laws of nature, which human thought and observation might unravel, given time and effort. Newton's elegant solution to the problem of astrophysics—that the same laws that governed small objects (like apples) also governed large objects (like planets)—suggested a universe of subtle but comprehensible laws, beautiful in their simplicity. The deist universe was a clockwork mechanism, and the deist god a watchmaker.

This formulation, applied to Christianity, immediately ran into the problem of miracles. If God ran the universe according to immutable laws, and miracles were by definition violations of natural laws, how could miracles ever take place? The Protestants of Reformation Europe insisted that the age of miracles had closed, and that more recent wonders were merely the fabrications of a corrupt Catholic Church. Deists took the argument one step further: there were no miracles at all, and all claims to the contrary were efforts by organized religion to enslave the minds of the credulous. Miracles were nothing more than "mental lying" that made God out to have "the character of a showman," according to Thomas Paine, and the doctrine of miracles had led to "the most detestable wickedness, the most horrid cruelties, and the greatest miseries."[20]

Some deists were insistent on this point. "Zealots persuade themselves and one another that they have supernatural communion with the Holy Ghost . . . and in their frenzy are proof against reason and argument," wrote Ethan Allen. "Miracles are opposed to and counteract the laws of nature."[21] In practice, however, the American deists tended toward a more moderate stance. In reviewing deist America, historian David Holmes distinguished between Christian deism and non-Christian deism. It was perfectly appropriate for a deist to believe in God; few deists, however, took communion, "the most supernatural level of church activity." Moreover, deists might attend church to hear moral and religious precepts rather than to celebrate the ascension of the risen Christ. Thus, non-Christian deists would rarely attend church, and Christian deists would attend but avoid ceremonies such as the Eucharist or confirmation. Washington fit the Christian deist bill perfectly; he attended church, believed in God, but dismissed supernaturalism and repeatedly referred to god as "Providence" or "the Great Architect."[22]

Historians have often connected the American Revolution of 1776 with the religious revivalism of the 1730s and 1740s, but this argument is rarely persuasive.[23] Even ignoring the generation gap between the so-called Great Awakening and the War for Independence, religious rhetoric was never the Revolution's strong suit. Historian Jon Butler called the Revolution a "profoundly secular event," not because there were no orthodox Christians in the war but because "the causes that brought it into being and the ideologies that shaped it placed religious concerns more at its margins than at its center." The Declaration of Independence invoked "Nature's God"—a mild deistic formulation—yet mentioned no religious concerns in its list of grievances against Britain.[24] True, the beneficiaries of the Awakening (such as the Baptist churches) strongly supported the Revolution, but they did so for political and not religious reasons. Baptist churches demanded legal recognition as the price of their loyalty, and they got it—with the help of the deists.

When Dunmore's government fell, Baptist churches saw their chance to end the long institutional hegemony of the Anglican Church—colonial Virginia's only state religion. Advocates of the separation of church and state, such as James Madison and George Mason, pushed through the Declaration of Rights in the Virginia Assembly, a bill that included Article 16: "All men are equally entitled to the free exercise of religion." An organized and vigorous campaign by Virginia Baptists promised the deistic revolutionaries strong political and military support if the state did away with the taxes levied on non-Anglican churches. The taxes soon vanished. A political decision gave the revolution religious support.[25] (In Massachusetts, where the crown defended Baptist rights against a Congregationalist establishment, the Baptists turned loyalist.)[26]

The religion of the American Founding and the American Revolution was therefore a deistic one. The Bible existed only for the less observant, a kind of divine cheat sheet. "Nature's God and Providence," not Christ crucified, were the gods of the revolution. Benjamin Harrison V fit right in with such sentiments; a fellow member of the Continental Congress referred to him as "another John Falstaff . . . profane, impious, perpetually ridiculing the bible."[27]

Yet deism should not be thought of as mere secularism. Its advocates may have disdained direct appearances of divine miracles—which Ethan Allen classified as an "ignorance of the nature of things"—but they often approved of more subtle indications of the divine will.[28] God was a watchmaker. He was, however, a watchmaker with a purpose, and American deists spent a great deal of time attempting to discern that purpose. Conveniently, God's purposes in nature often matched their political objectives.

For deists, the key term was "providence." A sermon of 1755 explained that year's severe earthquakes—and particularly the devastating one in Lisbon—by defining providence as the "Operations of these natural *Agents*" that were God's "Workmanship . . . making and moving them in perfect Wisdom, and as having in View every Effect they were to produce when first He formed them." Nature ran on its own, but so precise was God's calibration at the beginning of time that all nature worked out the divine will as the clock ran down.[29] Deists often based their case for God's existence on the argument from design, in that the very orderliness of the universe required the existence of a divine watchmaker. Even Jefferson agreed: "When we take a view of the Universe, in its parts general or particular, it is impossible for the human mind not to perceive and feel a conviction of design, consummate skill, and indefinite power in every atom of its composition."[30]

Thus American deism—both Christian and non-Christian—became obsessed with uncovering the "design of Divine Providence" in history and nature. American Christianity sought to discover through observation what it was God wanted from humanity, for "'tis by his providence that all intercourse between GOD and his rational creatures is maintained," as one minister explained in 1778.[31] The notion that history had a plan, and that human beings could discern and follow that plan, was a religious dictum of the highest order in the eighteenth century.

The problem, of course, is that while Americans might agree that history and nature reflected the commands of the godhead, they disagreed on what those commands were. Revolutionaries were adamant that history showed the progression of humanity to republican principles, and that, for example, the patriot General Gates' "most distinguish'd conquest" in 1777 was an "Amazing work of providence!"[32] Yet loyalists were equally sure that God's design favored them; one loyalist, whose family had been attacked by a patriot mob, wrote that "a great number of Stones each so large as to have killd any person they had hit, were thrown about the table where the family were at Supper, but Providence directd 'em so that they did not fall on any person."[33] Given that partisans could select any event from history or specimen from nature as an element of God's plan, the sheer quantity of evidence virtually ensured multiple explanations of providential destiny.

For the most part, the stories selected justified the theology attributed to the design. Victory against the odds at the Battle of Concord ("a few of our brave militia . . . by God's assistance, turned the enemy's boasted victory, into shameful flight") was a providence for patriots; the death of Casimir Pulaski

at the Battle of Savannah in 1779 was one for loyalists ("a parricide with parri-
cides to die / and vindicate the pow'r that reigns on high").[34]

The same event might produce opposite interpretations. Consider the
infamous Dark Day, "the most Remarkable Day Ever known in this Land,"
according to diarist John Gates, when at midmorning "it grew very Dark,
much darker than usual and continued above three hours . . . to that Degree
that many people lit up candles" and "every appearance seemed like night."[35]
On May 19, 1780, dark clouds without rain covered New England at noonday,
ash dropped from the sky, and the air stank of brimstone.[36] In the years that
followed, multiple explanations were offered—forest fires, the interposition
of another planet, or even a Canadian volcano.[37] In the immediate aftermath,
however, providentialists drafted the darkness into divine instructions. The
pamphleteer known as "The Farmer, of Massachusetts Bay" acknowledged
that though the Dark Day came about by natural causes, it was nevertheless
divine: "NATURE'S GOD hath given the power of motion *to natural causes*, and
always co-operates with them, *otherwise they would effect nothing*."[38] Congregationalist Samuel Gatchel agreed that there was "no greater *evidence*" of the
voice of God than the confinement of the uncommon darkness to New England, and connected the Dark Day to the providential patriot victory at Lexington and Concord.[39] Gatchel and the Farmer reached opposite conclusions
about just what God intended humanity to learn from the Dark Day. The
Farmer took it as a call for repentance and reconciliation with Britain: "*Oh!*
Backsliding New-England, attend now to the *things which belong to your*
peace. . . . *Let us strive to live in peace, so that the* GOD *of peace may be with us*
always."[40] Gatchel used the same logic to reach precisely the opposite conclusion: "The sinners in *Zion* dishonor GOD who dwelleth there" by refusing
independence. American men must take up arms: "You sons of *Zion* that are
of a martial spirit . . . do boldly march forth to the valley of decision." This
holy war even entailed submission to the standing order ("God in his providence hath provided a Congress to lead and guide us, and shall we murmur
against GOD, and such as he hath appointed to lead us?") and the expulsion of
loyalists and traitors.[41]

Providentialism was therefore a popular argument, but one that might say
just as much about the speaker as it did about history or God's intentions. Yet
it was also extraordinarily useful. First, it provided a way to incorporate
extraordinary natural events—"wonders," as they were called in the eighteenth and nineteenth centuries—into a Protestant system that denied miracles. A popular play about the American siege of Quebec had one character
warn the others, "Look not for miracles, or hand of heaven . . . supernatural

display to man is left to general laws." Another character, however, upbraids his fellows and audience alike that though there were no more miracles, "heavenly Providence, in this late age, accompanies our steps, and guides our every action."[42]

Perhaps as important, the language of providence bridged deism and orthodox Christianity by allowing both to fit the independence of the United States, as unlikely as it had seemed, into the story of God's divine plan. The 1780 Massachusetts constitution, drafted a few weeks after the Dark Day, made Congregationalism the official state church. It also included a clause "acknowledging with grateful hearts, the goodness of the great Legislator of the universe, in affording us, in the course of His providence, an opportunity . . . of forming a new constitution of civil government for ourselves and posterity; and devoutly imploring His direction in so interesting a design." Similarly, Jefferson's Act for Establishing Religious Freedom invoked "the plan of the Holy Author of our religion." The argument from design could be drafted into Jefferson's argument against establishment, and into a Massachusetts constitution that *did* establish a state religion.

Yet envisioning the independence of the United States as the culmination of history could have bleak consequences, for if white civilization was the height of human development, what was the nadir? For many deists and Christians alike, the answer was not hard to find. The same Enlightenment philosophies that made God a watchmaker and gave divine purpose to the success of the revolution could also account for the state of Indians and African American slaves. Their misery, too, was God's will and plan.

The intellectual conception of human cultures as a ladder, with savagery at the bottom and civilization at the top, derived from Scottish Enlightenment thinkers. It was not solely the province of the deists and such deist-tainted thinkers as Adam Smith and David Hume, but also that of their intellectual adversaries, such as Scottish historian and divine (and historiographer royal to George III) William Robertson.[43] Hume often used Native America (or what he thought he knew about Native America) as a case in point. There, in contrast to civilized Europe, "barbarous Indians" ruled by superstition.[44] Robertson's history of colonization went a bit further; "the character of the savage [Indian]," he argued, came "almost entirely from his sentiments or feelings as an individual, and is but little influenced by his imperfect subjection to government and order." Robertson's case was not based on much better evidence than Hume's was, but his version of events suggested that all people might one day rise to the perfection of eighteenth-century Britain (naturally, the most civilized people on earth). This kind of "stadial" thinking—the notion that nations and peoples all existed along a spectrum of civilization, and could move up or down as their lot improved or declined—became central to early American concepts of providence and Manifest Destiny.[45]

Such ideas had a long germination prior to the eighteenth century, of course; European philosophers had ruminated about a "state of nature" ever since Columbus landed on the Caribbean islands. A perennial set piece of modern political philosophy, the idea of a "state of nature"—a world before political organization—derived from sixteenth-century efforts to classify American societies and cultures. This debate unsurprisingly ended up declaring that Europeans were fully developed human beings, while the Indians were trapped in a primitive state. Curiously, however, these debates also suggested that Europeans themselves had once been savages, and could be again, if they were not careful. The state of nature was held in check only by the restraint of government and morality.[46] In the nineteenth century, such views became imbued with Romantic wistfulness about nationalism and antiquity, allowing European poets and dreamers to idealize themselves by idealizing Indians. Walter Scott's protagonist in *The Pirate* (1821) pined for the days of yore in the British Orkneys, where "sacrifices were made to Thor and Odin." He "longed to possess the power of the Voluspae and divining women of our ancient race."[47] Philip Freneau wrote of the simpler "children of the forest" to whom "reason's self shall bow the knee / to shadows and delusions here."[48] John Adams once inquired of Jefferson if he knew whether the Indians had a priestly class like the druids of old.[49]

Such ideas had potential benefits for colonizing nations. Conveniently ignoring the grand cities of the Maya and Aztecs, the idea of the Americas as a "state of nature" perpetuated a myth of the New World as a *vacuum domicilium*—an empty space that belonged to the first people to "discover" it. The "Doctrine of Discovery" was employed to justify land grabs in America and Africa from the fifteenth to the nineteenth centuries, and in 1823 the Supreme Court adopted the Doctrine of Discovery as the fundamental law governing treaties with Native Americans. "Nature" might give human beings the capacity for freedom, but only "civilization" provided property. For centuries, European governments relied on this idea to justify their occupation and ownership of lands they "discovered." After the Revolution, American governments hoped to follow suit.[50]

In practice, the patriots of the Revolution usually made little distinction between Indian allies and enemies. The Shawnee chief Cornstalk was murdered trying to preserve peace between his clan and the Americans. In 1782, a militia ambushed Christian Indians praying at Gnadenhutten in Pennsylvania. These Indian converts had adopted pacifism and played no role in the Revolution; they prayed to Christ for deliverance as the militia hacked them to pieces. Victory over Britain therefore seemingly entailed victory over Indian America; the 1783 Treaty of Paris famously granted the nascent United States sovereignty over North America east of the Mississippi and south of the Great Lakes. The vast lands Britain had once designated as an Indian buffer state were now American territory (at least on a map). The American government promptly invoked the rights of conquest and civilization. The Iroquois, for example, were summarily informed that "you are a subdued people."[51]

Native Americans possessed a rather different view of their position and sovereignty after the Revolution. Despite their active role in the war (Indians as individuals, clans, and tribes had fought on both sides), no Indian peoples had a place at the bargaining table in Paris, and they found themselves left out of the Treaty of Paris. What is more, most Indians were perfectly well aware that they had been left out. A coalition of ten tribes declared, "We, the Indians, were disappointed, finding ourselves not included in that peace [of 1783], according to our expectations . . . you kindled your council fires where you thought proper, without consulting us."[52] It was, as one tribe informed the British, "an act of cruelty and injustice that Christians *only* were capable of doing."[53]

The Treaty of Paris was good enough for white settlers, however, who poured into western Pennsylvania and Ohio, seeking cheap land and a new start. The Indians, in particular those of the Ohio Valley, found themselves in the same position as 1763: they had not lost anything, and yet an imperial power claimed to be their new masters. As in 1763, they prepared to fight. Wampum belts began to circulate among the western tribes. Frontier incursions by whites prompted violent resistance from Ohio Valley Indians. The settlements of Vincennes and Hamtramck in the Northwest Territory suffered constant attacks in 1788; Wheeling, Virginia, had the same in 1789. Surveyors in particular faced constant military harassment. Nor was the fledgling American army quiescent; the Shawnee town of Chillicothe was sacked and rebuilt four times between 1778 and 1790.[54]

This recurrent violence colored the early years of William Henry Harrison. War often threatened genteel Berkeley—in 1775, when Dunmore's regiment of freed slaves moved up the southern seaboard, and in 1777, when patriot propaganda over the murder of Jane McCrea by Native Americans associated with the British prompted outrage (and a surge in recruitment to the patriot cause). In 1781, the violence finally arrived. Benedict Arnold, now siding with the British, landed a force of loyalist and Hessian troops on the Virginian peninsula and, among other things, stopped to sack Berkeley. The mansion suffered—but during the course of five generations the Harrisons had acquired more than one plantation, and William and his family had other homes to flee to when the sack occurred.[55] Even after the war, threats of Indian violence continued on the frontier and in Appalachia.

Military operations ended when William was ten; his father would not hang for treason after all, and the Harrison family had every hope of continuing in their patrician tradition. In the years to come, Benjamin V became Governor Harrison of Virginia. Yet young William was having difficulties. His father and brother had attended William and Mary, but William Henry was sent west, to Hampden-Sydney. An enthusiastic religious revival broke out there in 1787, however, and William was called home. It would not do for the Harrisons to have their son risk his immortal soul by cavorting with those who considered emotion and feeling to be the essence of religion. Jefferson wrote that the school was "going to nothing, owing to the religious phrensy they have inspired into the boys young and old, which their parents have no taste for."[56] As a later critic put it, such revivalists disregarded doctrine and thereby fell into error: "Under the influence of these enthusiastic mistakes men may positively conclude this or that doctrine to be true or false, not because they find or do not find it in the holy scriptures; but because they felt so and so, when praying."[57]

Things were changing. Deistic Christianity would soon discover that it had a rival in the form of enthusiastic Protestant worship, born out of the fervor of such frontier revivals. Similarly, the genteel Harrisons would face challenges to their hegemony based on social order in a world where free whites could head west to start their own farms and seek their own fortunes. Heading west, of course, depended on extinguishing Indian titles to lands—a task at which the early American government was proving singularly incompetent. Congress, under the Articles of Confederation, signed at least eight treaties with Indian groups between 1781 and 1789, each of which claimed that the Native American signers could sell lands to and buy goods only from the United States. Congress was unable to enforce any of these claims. Similarly, the Northwest Ordinance of 1787 promised freedom of religion and public schools for all its future (white) citizens, but these utopian ideals meant nothing in a territory effectively controlled by Ohio's Indian insurgency.[58]

After the ratification of the Constitution, the Washington administration proved that it could do little better. Washington sent Arthur St. Clair and the army to the Ohio country to engage the Indians and validate American land claims—by force if necessary. St. Clair's forces were massacred in an ambush. It was precisely at this point that William Henry decided on a military career.

For 1791 also marked the end of Benjamin Harrison V—conservative revolutionary, governor, lawmaker, slave owner, and Virginian grandee. As expected, the bulk of his estate went to his namesake and eldest son, Benjamin VI. William Henry received a parcel of land, but he sold it to his brother and shipped out to the West. It was, after all, a new world, and the youngest son of a well-connected family had options should he wish to overreach a pompous older brother who had sat out the Revolution in the relatively safe job of paymaster. Meanwhile, in a coincidence almost providential, Benjamin Harrison V was succeeded in office by another Virginia planter—John Tyler of Williamsburg. Fifty years later, John Tyler Jr. would succeed William Henry in the Oval Office.

4

Defeat

ARTHUR ST. CLAIR called his battle with the Ohio Indians "a very unfortunate campaign . . . increased by bitter calumnies."[1] St. Clair knew how to turn a phrase: when he wrote of "the disappointment of fond hopes" he meant nine hundred casualties out of fourteen hundred soldiers, possibly the worst defeat in U.S. military history.[2] The Americans had been flattened, pure and simple. One report told of victorious Indians stuffing the mouths of their fallen adversaries with dirt. If Americans were so hungry for land, let them eat it.[3]

Despite the boasting of American commissioners that they had conquered the Indian tribes in the Revolution, the United States government and not the Indian alliances steadily weakened through the 1780s. State rivalries undercut federal cooperation. Debt spiraled—national, state, private. Breakaway efforts flared, under Daniel Shays in Massachusetts in 1786 and under Adonijah Matthews in Virginia a year later. In 1786, the states agreed to send representatives to Annapolis to improve the Articles of Confederation. Only five bothered to send any. In 1787, America was a failed state.

These internal squabbles often involved land, usually Indian land. New York feared Massachusetts had designs on the Iroquois territory that it planned to divide and hand out to grateful voters. The vast Northwest was coveted and claimed by Pennsylvania, Virginia, Massachusetts, and (of all places) Connecticut. The Articles insisted that "the legislative right of any state within its own limits be not infringed," which states took to mean that they, not the federal Congress, had the right to treat with Indian nations. This situation provoked an anarchic struggle to intimidate the Indians.[4]

In 1784, when New York's delegation to the Six Nations attempted to ply Iroquois chiefs with alcohol, federal agents seized the alcohol. New York sheriffs in turn arrested the federal officials. Pennsylvania's commissioners took advantage of the confusion to negotiate with the Iroquois on the side. When the Iroquois refused to negotiate for land, New York soldiers took the Iroquois hostage. The resulting Treaty of Fort Stanwix (1784) received little support from Congress and had to be renegotiated after the collapse of the Articles of Confederation.[5]

New York's martial enthusiasm belied the country's real weakness in confronting the Indians: soldiers and dollars were in short supply. Within two years, Henry Lee would write to George Washington, "We have too much reason to fear a war, which among other evils will encrease our financ[ial] embarrassment."[6] Lee and Washington knew that the British army still occupied the forts along the Great Lakes and could keep Indians stocked with arms, ammunition, and supplies. The dubious state treaties under the Articles were rarely enforced. White settlers understood the West was still Indian country, and they both feared and coveted it.

The Six Nations rejected the legality of the shotgun treaty at Fort Stanwix outright. What the Six Nations did, however, no longer made much difference. In fact, New York negotiated primarily with the Oneidas, who with their allies accounted for 460 of the 613 delegates attending, though they were neither the most populous nor the most prestigious tribe. The Oneidas had supported the Americans in the Revolution, and in the postwar chaos they sought and received preferential treatment from the new American government. The Iroquois were a confederacy in name only.[7]

The breakdown of the Iroquois Confederacy typified efforts at Native American unity at the end of the American Revolution. Most Native peoples in the northern states and Northwest Territory once again adopted the cooperative rhetoric of Neolin, Pontiac, and their allies of 1763, though words were always easier to come by than actions. In May 1785, a council made up of Shawnees, Delawares, Mingoes, and Ohio Cherokees declared, "The people of one color are united, so that we make but one man and one mind." Their ground had been "given to us by the Great Spirit" and could not be sold. The Shawnee leader Moluntha sought a reasonable accommodation, however: Americans might stay where they were and the Indians where they were. Kekewepellethe—a Shawnee known to the Americans as "Captain Johnny"— insisted that legally the Shawnees had signed away no lands and the last generation's borders were still in effect: "According to the lines settled by our forefathers, the Ohio is the boundary." Then a religious note: "You are encroaching," he warned, "on the grounds given to us by the Great Spirit." Yet despite brave words about Indian unity, several Indian tribes continued to sell the lands on which other people lived. The Iroquois had signed away land in Pennsylvania, while groups from the Wyandot, Delaware, and Ojibwe nations signed away Shawnee land at Fort McIntosh in 1785. Even the Shawnee leadership signed away lands at the Treaty of Fort Finney.[8]

Like the floundering government in Philadelphia, the political structure of the Ohio Confederacy was shaky. Native American efforts to revise and strengthen that structure, however, achieved spectacular successes from 1786 to 1794. That success proved temporary. Two Shawnee brothers who lived through it would not forget the political lessons those years taught them.

The American effort to overthrow its own government and replace it with a sleeker and more agile federal apparatus took place largely sub rosa. The fifty-five delegates to the Constitutional Convention pledged that they would neither reveal their debates nor publish their notes, a pledge they kept; the texts of the debates we have today come from James Madison's notes, published posthumously. The unveiling of the proposed Constitution foisted a terrific surprise on the voting populace—which was precisely what irritated some of its opponents. It took some electoral shenanigans to get the thing passed, and in fact it did not pass in the form the framers wanted. The Bill of Rights, the part of the Constitution most famous in the minds of many Americans, was not included in the original draft of the document.

The Constitution attempted to solve interstate conflict by placing a variety of troublesome squabbles under federal jurisdiction, including Indian affairs. It forbade state governments from engaging in foreign affairs. It also stipulated that Native Americans were foreign nationals living in U.S. territory—asserting (in theory) ultimate sovereignty over lands held at that time by Native American tribes and their armies, and proscribing such agreements as the disastrous Treaty of Fort Stanwix.

Changing the American government involved a fair amount of political sleight of hand, but the "Miracle at Philadelphia" was straightforward compared to what was happening on the frontier. Most Eastern Woodlands Indian nations in the eighteenth and nineteenth centuries possessed a dual political leadership structure. The Shawnees, Iroquois, Delawares, and other tribes had two sets of political leaders: village chiefs and war chiefs. Village chiefs dealt with civil affairs, and their appointment often involved a hereditary component; sons (and only sons) of chiefs generally took their father's place. Yet as one Shawnee said in an interview some years after the war for the Ohio, "If there be no sons left," any man of the tribe might become a village chief. All "fit persons not related to the deceased" also received consideration, and "to the decisions of the chiefs & principal men in such cases, the nation at large cheerfully submit." Tenskwatawa likely received his own civil power through such consensus—he was the aforementioned Shawnee who described the system.[9]

Even Tenskwatawa admitted that the office of war chief was "more important & more honorable than the other."[10] Unsurprisingly, war chiefs took charge of military matters, and indeed ruled their nation during times of declared conflict. Their appointment was almost always based on merit and experience. Village chiefs spoke first at council and sat at the head of their people and warriors until the moment war was declared. At that point the war chief assumed both power and primacy until the conflict ended.

Nevertheless, both war and village chiefs relied primarily on soft power and informal authority to compel obedience. To declare war required the consent of the tribe, and "the head chief and counselors may interpose," wrote Jedidiah Morse in 1822. As for decision making, "it is seldom a town is unanimous," and "the nation never is."[11] During the crisis of the 1780s, Tenskwatawa's own Shawnee tribe split over whether to continue the fight. A considerable number of Shawnees accepted the invitation of the Spanish government to settle west of the Mississippi. They simply went; neither war chief nor civil leader could compel them to do otherwise.

The Shawnees and certain other tribes also had a second level of ruling power: the female councils, "appointed, as well for war as for peace."[12] Sometimes called "the female chiefs," these women were often related to the village chief and his allies. Tenskwatawa—who would eventually eliminate this limit on his power—described their duties as "not numerous nor arduous." The female chiefs might have disagreed.[13] It fell to them "to prevent unnecessary effusion of blood"; if a war chief or faction was bent on a pointless war, the *"peace woman"* was to lecture him, "setting before him the care and anxiety & pain which women experience," and plead with him to spare "the innocent & unoffending."[14] Her powers, therefore, were limited to her rhetorical and emotional skills in persuasion. In practice the female councils also had charge of all the women's duties—which included effective control of agriculture. (Farming, in Eastern Woodlands cultures, was women's work.) The councils often wielded their power to great effect. When the Iroquois leader Joseph Brant suggested that the Six Nations relocate to Canada, it was the clan matrons who revised the plan to keep some of the Iroquois in the United States and send some to British territory, the matrons trusting neither Americans nor Canadians.[15]

Central authority in the Old Northwest and the Great Lakes was dispersed. The reasoning was cultural. Nonetheless, it also had its uses. The United States, reasoning with wildly different cultural assumptions, developed a similar system of separation of powers in the Constitution of 1787. The executive branch was put in charge of the armed forces, but the ability to establish and regulate those forces, as well as to declare war, was left to the legislature, since "powers properly belonging to one of the departments ought not to be directly and completely administered by either of the other departments," according to the *Federalist*.[16]

Unlike the Federalists, however, by 1787 the war chiefs of the Ohio were generally moving away from separation of powers. The imperial wars of the eighteenth century favored war chiefs, since they could provide the military support the French and British required. In return, the war chiefs received the largesse and gifts of their European allies—which they in turn distributed to their people. As in many societies, the distribution of cheap or free goods created goodwill among the populace, and war chiefs began to overcome supposed checks on their power.[17]

The suddenness of the American peace and the catastrophe (from the Native perspective) of the Treaty of Paris filtered slowly and unevenly through Indian country. The Indians had not lost the war; the British had asked them to stop fighting. The Americans claimed their land but had not won it in battle. Were the Indians still at war? And if so, which nations? In a political system in which leadership depended on the presence or absence of formal hostilities, an unclear and uneasy peace was a political disaster. The Ohio Valley peoples experienced frenetic changes of leadership in the 1780s. The blind headman Koguetagechton led most of the Delawares into an alliance with the Americans; the pro-British war chief Buckonghelas seceded with his own followers after the massacre at Gnadenhutten, a village in Ohio where ninety-six Christian Indians, mostly Delawares, were murdered by an American officer named David Williams and his militia.[18] Among the Shawnees, civil chiefs reassumed power, with Moluntha holding primary authority, though he quickly lost it to his rivals Blue Jacket and Captain Johnny.[19] Among the Miamis, Pacane and Little Turtle rose to prominence.[20] By 1791, the "Head Warriors of Wyondots . . . contradict the sentiments of these chiefs."[21]

The confusion did not occur only among Native Americans; the young republic had plenty of tribal units pursuing their own courses. Squatters have become the most infamous of the frontier Americans, generally characterized as a crowd of rowdies who "threatened to kill every Indian who should attempt to settle on the Muskingum."[22] Whites' land hunger drove settlers onto Indian lands, sometimes those ceded under the dubious state treaties and sometimes those unquestionably part of Indian territory. The squatters had a "pretty prevalent" reputation, according to General William Irvine, of wishing to see the Indians "driven over the Mississippi and the Lakes, entirely beyond American lines."[23]

Squatters pressured the American government for assistance, but the government had its own problems. Although James Duane reassured the Confederation Congress that the Indians had been "aggressors in the war" and therefore had forfeited their right to the Ohio country, the Congress had little power to enforce that from Princeton, New Jersey; they had fled Philadelphia after Continental soldiers put the statehouse under siege, demanding back pay.[24] U.S. commissioners talked tough in the 1780s, but in practice Indian policy vacillated. In 1785, American troops marched into Indian country—to dispossess *white* squatters and settlers. Cabins illegally constructed by whites on Indian land were torn down, and cornfields illegally planted were burned. Moreover, some Ohio officials invited Indians to settle such regions on the Indian side of the border, hoping thicker settlement by Indians would make for a firmer border and more peaceful relations.[25]

Along with these attempts at amity, treaty making with pliant chiefs continued, as did surveys of the supposedly ceded lands.[26] Such treaties, noted a British agent in Detroit, bred "great confusion amongst them [Indians], blaming each other for consenting thereto." Yet by May 1785, the agents knew that "several deputations are gone from the Delawares & Shawanese to Council with the Western Nations this Spring since the particulars of the treaty has been made known to them." These deputations were looking to form a confederation "in case of an attempt to drive them from their Country."[27] Two years before the Federalists did so in Philadelphia, the Indians of the Old Northwest created a new, stronger central government as an exercise in self-preservation.

The origins of the 1785 Confederacy are vague. It is not known, for example, who provided the leadership or suggested the ideas behind it, although the Shawnee chief Blue Jacket, among others, seems to have played a significant role. The accomplishments of the Confederacy lie in the reshaping of the geographical and social lives of Native Americans and, perhaps more important, the increased power vested in the war chiefs. Led by the Shawnees, those tribes or parts of tribes that consented to the Confederacy began relocating to militarily and geographically defensible locations, particularly after 1790. The largest and most important of these was the Glaize, the "capital of the Shawnee," as one resident called it.[28] The Glaize, in what is now northwest Ohio on the Maumee River, actually consisted of several towns in close proximity, each of which was headed by a prominent war chief. A British trading station sat within the circle of villages, ensuring access to manufactured goods and gunpowder. One of the men manning the station there was Matthew Elliott, who had a long career in front of him as one of Canada's strongest advocates of Indian independence.[29]

Tenskwatawa and Tecumseh were likely there, too. Tecumseh had organized raiding parties against the slow-moving flatboats bringing immigrants to Ohio, and his younger brother (then still Lalawauthika) would probably have joined in. The brothers were not full-time residents of the Glaize; they had traveled as far south as Tennessee in the 1780s in search of Cherokee allies for the struggle. Still, the example and precedent of the Glaize no doubt played an important role in shaping the dreams of the Prophet and his brother in the decades to come.[30]

The war chiefs at the Glaize were an impressive group. While all had outstanding military credentials, few of them matched the stereotype of "savages" that whites who had conquered Kentucky insisted on applying to them. Blue Jacket himself was an experienced diplomat as well as a warrior who lived in a European-style house with a four-poster bed and ran entrepreneurial enterprises in trade goods and cattle breeding.[31] Little Turtle, the probable strategist of the victory over St. Clair, was praised as a gentleman when he visited Philadelphia; he responded, "I always thought I was a gentleman."[32] The Glaize had a fraternal organization (not unlike the Masons) for Native Americans.[33] Tetapatchsit, the "Grand Glaize king," lived there, as did Captain Johnny, who stood seven feet tall, "as frightfully ugly as he was large," according to one account, and who had long protested the fiction that the Indians had lost the Revolution.[34] It is impossible to know, of course, how much the example of such a collection of male war chiefs, fiercely opposed to American expansion and relatively unhindered by civil leadership or female councils, influenced the young Tenskwatawa, but the Glaize probably served as the prototype for Prophetstown.

Although details are somewhat hazy, the war chiefs do seem to have achieved far greater autonomy than previously, perhaps an autonomy they intended to hold in perpetuity. Moluntha, the civil chief who favored peace with the Americans, admitted in 1786 that the Shawnee nation had simply written off the civil chiefs as those who had "sold both land and warriors."[35] When Hendrick Aupamat visited the Glaize for a council in 1791, his allies from the Iroquois objected that the Shawnees and others "have set up such custom that the Chief Warriors should be foremost in doing business" and insisted that only the civil chiefs "are the proper managers of publick affairs."[36]

The Indians of the Glaize had little patience for such systems, and indeed, even the civil chiefs there (such as the Delaware Big Cat) raised no objections and refused to respond to Iroquois pleas to take their rightful place at the council. Big Cat had a role to play—he offered the speech that presented peace terms to the United States, and he seemed content with that function.[37]

There was one final office at the Glaize that may have influenced the young Tenskwatawa: the city had a prophet. She was an Iroquois woman named

Coocoochee, who lived apart from all the towns on the Glaize. Coocoochee served as "a sort of priestess, to whom the Indians applied before going on any important war expedition" and was also "an esteemed medicine woman." She was also understood to have "influence with the good spirits, with whom she professed to hold daily intercourse."[38] Coocoochee's role appears to have been advisory; she does not seem to have participated in the decision making of the Confederacy. Nevertheless, O. M. Spencer, a white captive living at the Glaize, recalled a developing religious consensus at the Glaize; he heard sermons to the effect that the whites, or "first murderers," had succeeded only because the Great Spirit was angry at his favored race, the Indians, and that "late victories over the whites . . . were evidences of the returning favor of the Great Spirit."[39]

The Confederacy was not, however, a centralized or hierarchical system; individuals, leaders, and tribes still had a great deal of autonomy. The Shawnees, for example, stormed off in the middle of the 1791 council and left it to their allies to soothe ruffled feathers from the American and Iroquois delegations. Nevertheless, the shifts in political organization provided, according to historian Leroy V. Eid, "an administrative atmosphere which permitted military cooperation between disparate tribes," some of whom had been enemies prior to 1785.[40] As the Iroquois objections show, of course, not all tribes or factions participated. Even among the fiercely anti-American Shawnees, Moluntha led a contingent of moderates. Moderation, however, became less popular in 1786, when the Kentuckian Benjamin Logan led an attack on Moluntha's town on Mad River. Moluntha ran up a flag of peace. The Americans ignored it, seized the town, and took Moluntha hostage. An American colonel buried a tomahawk in the chief's face.[41]

Things began to move rapidly after that. Logan's raid provoked a military response by George Rogers Clark that the Confederacy stymied. As peace disintegrated, the Confederacy appears to have gained in strength and prestige. It was not, however, merely due to their apparent prescience in formulating a workable resistance. They also began to win.

The first coordinated U.S. effort to dislodge the Confederacy from the lands it held on the Ohio came with General Josiah Harmar's expedition in 1790, and it failed spectacularly. Attacks on settlers by Indians—whether from the Confederacy or not—had effectively limited white encroachment into the Ohio between 1787 and 1790. It helped that the American government underwent its own extensive reshuffle in those years, first reclassifying the western lands into the Northwest Territory and then revising its own central authority under the Constitution. The federal government finally opted for a limited attack on the "banditti" of the Ohio, and placed the Revolutionary War veteran Harmar in charge.[42]

Harmar headed north toward the Maumee, pausing to set fire to abandoned Native American villages and food stores, so as to starve the Confederacy to the bargaining table. But on October 20, 1790, the Confederacy struck back, raking his columns with gunfire across an Ohio morass. Harmar's columns broke and fled to the abandoned Miami town of Kekionga, where two days later the Confederacy completed the rout and sent the Americans fleeing "helter skelter." Ironically, the bulk of Harmar's force consisted of frontier militia—the same supposedly savage, supposedly intransigent whites whose hardened guerilla skills were supposed to make American victory inevitable. By most reports, those same militiamen were the first to flee when the shooting started.[43]

The systemic violence of the American frontier is often attributed to "Indian-hating"; the latter half of the eighteenth century, the argument goes, saw a marked rise in demonization of Native Americans and demands for the elimination of the Indian threat through violent means, up to and including genocide. The seething anger of frontier whites wiped the Indians from the West. It is probably true that most white Americans on the frontier feared, hated, or mistrusted Native Americans. Yet Indian-hating was hardly new in 1763 or in 1786. Moreover, virulent words do not always produce violent actions—and even more rarely do they produce effective violent actions. Despite the legend of the white frontiersman and his supposed extraordinary abilities and courage, in the conflicts of the frontier wars he was almost always the loser, just as during Harmar's expedition. Americans mythologized the American "irregulars" as "half horse, half alligator" wild men, who made up for what they lacked in training with tenacity, passion, and grit. They were no match for the Confederacy. From 1786 through 1794, it was the Indians—who did not take a rosy view of white people, either—who pushed the Americans east.[44]

The main case in point came in 1791, when Arthur St. Clair attempted to recoup Harmar's losses. St. Clair's defeat is often blamed on his incompetence, but this accusation is unfair to St. Clair, as well as to Blue Jacket, Little Turtle, and Buckonghelas, who vanquished him. In a sense, the mythology of St. Clair's mismanagement must be maintained to preserve the story of the inevitability of American occupation of the frontier. A loss by an incompetent American commander preserves Manifest Destiny; defeat by superior Indian forces does not. It is an interesting myopia of American history that the story of inevitable conquest also includes the worst military defeat in American history.

St. Clair learned from Harmar's mistakes. He built a bigger army. He moved slowly and cautiously, to avoid the signature Indian ambush tactics that had devastated Harmar's forces, and he skirted the boggy marshes for the same reason.[45] He placed two hundred sentries across a mile of territory to prevent surprise attacks. He lost anyway.

Once again, the unified political-military structure of the Confederacy translated into swift and effective battlefield performance. The Confederacy's forces opened with a rush against an isolated series of militia units, which broke almost instantly; the Maumee Indians apparently also had learned from Harmar's defeat. In an impressive tactical stroke, the Indians eliminated a mile's worth of sentries, and though the Americans defeated an initial rush, a secondary attack, centered on the American artillery, broke the left flank.[46] Nearly half of St. Clair's soldiers were killed; hundreds more were injured. Six hundred U.S. soldiers died in 1791 under St. Clair, more than in 1876 under George Armstrong Custer.[47] Worse, American arms—especially artillery— were now in the hands of the Confederacy. St. Clair lacked sufficient military intelligence, and the bulk of his men were militia. These factors, derived from the structures of American society and military, exerted greater influence on the outcome than the decisions of one commander. Perhaps St. Clair's famous apology to Washington is less excuse than analysis: "I am not conscious," he wrote, "that any thing within my power to have produced a more happy Issue, was neglected."[48]

For the confederated Indians—and for the teenage Tenskwatawa and Tecumseh—it was a seminal moment: their homeland defended, the haughty Americans brought low. U.S. military operations in the Ohio Valley ground almost to a standstill, and the American diplomatic corps hurried to broker some kind of peace deal before the situation deteriorated any further. At the Glaize, Spencer heard Indians declaring that "their late signal defeat of St. Clair" confirmed the Great Spirit's favor.[49]

The phenomenal success of Indian resistance in the first decade of American independence provided the historical memory for the followers of Tenskwatawa two decades later. Unlike historians, who often view Indian resistance after the Revolution as a romantic lost cause, the Natives who fought against the Untied States in 1811 knew they could win; after all, their forefathers had done it just twenty years earlier. Though histories of the Ohio sometimes rush from St. Clair's defeat to the arrival of Wayne (and Harrison) in the next few years, no one in 1791 could have foreseen the later events. When Harrison entered the army that year, he was joining the losing side.[50]

WHY DID HARRISON even sign up? His presidential campaign materials from 1840 made it out to be a case of Indian-hating, pure and simple: "The increased and barbarous hostilities of the Indian on our northwestern borders, began to excite a feeling of indignation throughout the whole country. In this general excitement our young student [Harrison] participated so warmly, that he resolved to relinquish his professional pursuits, and join the army."[51] Such a sentiment would have won applause from some American voters in the later age of Indian removal.

But like most campaign biographies, this statement extols a rhetoric rather than a man. The "barbarous hostilities" were hardly unprovoked, and the "indignation throughout the whole country" was uneven at best. Some thought it was time to quit. Senator William Maclay grumbled that "Indian war is forced forward to justify our having a standing army"; he thought the money better spent elsewhere.[52] "Is the war with the Indians a *just* one?" asked one newspaper. "Have they not the same rights to their hunting grounds (which afford them their only means of subsistence) that we have to our houses and farms?" Victory for Native Americans meant defeat for land speculators, and that was just how some Americans liked it. A war for Indian land would enrich Americans who had the money or capital to buy and resell land; peace with the Indians favored those who already owned land. The war was "calculated for land jobbers only"; therefore, "let offense operations cease."[53]

Romance rather than patriotism might have pushed William Henry west. As a young man, Harrison may have pursued a young woman named Sarah Cutler, and when he failed suddenly headed for the Ohio. The American army of the 1790s provided opportunities for more than advancement in rank: amorous liaisons and sexual encounters were part of camp life. Virtually every army in the early republic traveled with a collection of "camp followers"—women who performed provisioning work and domestic duties for the soldiers. The soldiers and camp followers might engage in affairs, sometimes scandalously. (Indeed, Harrison would eventually owe his first command to a superior officer's adultery.)[54]

While he never had Alexander Hamilton's reputation as a cad, Harrison made efforts at love affairs. In the afterglow of the Battle of Fallen Timbers in August 1794, he pursued a "Miss M," with whom he tried to speak without "encountering *vexation Mortification Chagrin* or *Discomfort*," as he wrote to his brother Carter. Apparently Harrison must have encountered one of those, for Miss M appears no more in his correspondence. Harrison also picked up a soldier's penchant for frank speech that occasionally broke through the professional demeanor, as when he privately congratulated a friend on exchanging "the solitary life of a batchelor for the soft silken bands of Hymen ... feast my dear Sir with a Keen appetite."[55]

Then again, Harrison might have left Virginia out of boredom, pride, or shame. After leaving Hampden-Sydney, he apprenticed to a doctor in Richmond and then to one in Philadelphia. Neither took. It may have been a combination of idealism, patriotism, unrequited love, and an inferiority complex that pressed Harrison into service at such an inauspicious time (although he could not have known when he received his commission in August that the American army would fail in November). There was one other reason: on April 24, 1791, his father died.

Harrison rarely mentions his father in his own letters or his public speeches. The later presidential biographies lauded the grandeur of his lineage, but they seldom mentioned Harrison's relationship to his father. William Henry seems to have been reticent at best toward Benjamin V.

There was a financial aspect to it as well. What little Harrison inherited from his parents, he sold to his brother Benjamin VI for a pittance.[56] Perhaps he was giving up; perhaps he knew that at Berkeley he would always be the younger Mr. Harrison. Perhaps he wanted to play a different game—to succeed in the martial profession that Five and Six had only played at in the Revolution. If that was the case, then he needed to see combat—and the place to do that in 1791 was the Ohio country.

Whatever his motives, Harrison did not reject his heritage outright; family connections allowed him to finagle his army appointment. The ancient patriot Richard Henry Lee was a distant cousin and sitting senator, and he personally handed Harrison's request to President Washington—to whom Harrison was also related (by marriage). Washington signed Harrison's commission on August 16, 1791. "In 24 hours from the first conception of the idea," Harrison wrote to a friend years later, "I was an Ensign in the 1st U.S. regiment."[57] An ensign was the lowest possible commissioned officer. Four months after his father's death, Harrison left Virginia for war.

THE YOUNG VIRGINIAN arrived to find a disheveled army. A fair number of the soldiers had abandoned their "arms and accoutrements" in the flight from the Indian forces. When the troops returned to Fort Jefferson, they discovered they were out of provisions.[58] Congress initiated an investigation while the Washington administration dithered, quietly keeping St. Clair on as military commander and as governor of the Northwest Territory. For a short while, St. Clair's army (or what was left of it) was placed under the command of James Wilkinson—who was at that point secretly on the Spanish government's payroll. Meanwhile, the president appointed a succession of envoys to the Indians to make a formal treaty; the envoys were murdered upon arrival.

One envoy, Rufus Putnam, did eventually make a treaty—with Indian tribes not formally at war with the United States. Putnam worked extraordinarily hard to follow Indian protocol, going so far as to abandon military dress for civilian clothes; Putnam needed to emphasize that he represented his tribe's *civil* chiefs. "I speak from my heart, not with my lips only," Putnam declared. "The United States don't mean to wrong you out of your lands. They don't want to take away your lands by force. They want to do you justice."[59]

For once, in making such a statement, the American commissioner had the full support of the executive branch behind him. Secretary of War Henry Knox informed the prospective commissioners that "if the relinquishment of any lands, in the said space, should be an ultimatum with the said Indians, and a line could be agreed upon which would be free from dispute, you may, in order to effect a peace, make such a relinquishment."[60]

The generous terms virtually guaranteed Indian claims to just about all lands north of Kentucky. The chiefs signed, Washington approved (the president, it turned out, had yet another potential war on his hands against the southern tribes), and the treaty was duly submitted to the Senate for ratification. Putnam's work was significant: the United States had surrendered to the Indians. Had the Senate agreed with Washington, the inevitable American victory would have been scuttled, and the entire history of the West would have been radically different. Instead, it rejected Putnam's treaty. Despite Putnam's words, it appeared that the United States did not want to sign a treaty that would preclude the country from getting more Indian land.

As negotiations foundered in the Senate, Harrison and the rudderless army garrisoned themselves in Fort Washington, near Cincinnati, to wait out Putnam's negotiations. Harrison applied his limited medical training to tending to the wounded. When not so engaged, St. Clair sent him out to round up the frequent deserters. Harrison's expertise at wrangling soldiers often led him to confront the heavy drinking that was a part of life in the Washingtonian armies.[61]

Alcohol played an enormous role on the early American frontier. "The progress of intemperance amongst us outstrips indeed all Calculation," Harrison once wrote of frontier life.[62] Military commanders spent much of their time regulating the alcohol intake of soldiers, and rewards and payments often came to regulars and militiamen in the form of a gill or a dram.[63] Not that officers minded: rumor suggested that both Harmar and St. Clair enjoyed

tipping back the bottle.[64] But if they did, their predilection did not signifi-
cantly differ from that of most Americans, who consumed alcohol at a prodi-
gious rate; the turnpike between Lancaster and Philadelphia, Pennsylvania,
had sixty-one taverns along its sixty-six-mile length.[65] One Dartmouth student informed the headmaster that he drank at least "two to three pints
daily."[66] As Americans fought to extend white settlement north of the Ohio,
a territorial judge of the Northwest represented the character of white settlers
by being "found almost every day to be drunk . . . so drunk he could not
ascend without assistance" as he attempted to reach the bench.[67]

For whiskey won the American Revolution as surely as did the patriots:
wartime restrictions on tea and molasses (and therefore rum) made whiskey
the drink of choice from 1774 on. Whiskey could be produced domestically;
indeed, west of the Appalachians, it *had* to be produced domestically. Crops
produced far from eastern population centers might rot on the river trip
down the Mississippi and back up the Atlantic coast, and they would surely
putrefy if sent on the even longer (in terms of time) overland journey. Thus,
easterners grew the food, and westerners "grew" the booze to go with it.
Whiskey was an American drink, both economically and culturally. To
drink—and drink to excess—embodied personal choice, a liberation from all
masters, be they kings, ministers, or fathers. When the federal government
attempted to tax firewater in the 1790s, the result was the Whiskey Rebellion.
Restrictions on alcohol were tyrannical for antebellum white men. As historian W. J. Rohrabaugh wrote, "To be drunk was to be free."[68]

Harrison's own relationship to alcohol was fickle: half a century after he
whipped drunks in the army, he ran for president on a campaign ticket that
praised his sobriety and leadership, but which also gained notoriety for the
plentiful hard cider to be had at its rallies. As governor of Indiana, he would
restrict the sale of alcohol even as he built his own still.

The man who eventually took charge of Harrison's regiment had little
patience for drunkenness. Anthony Wayne, a veteran of Valley Forge, took
the place of the departed St. Clair. "Mad Anthony" got the nod from Washington only after two other generals declined the honor of taking on the foe
that had humiliated the last two American armies sent against it. Wayne took
the job after insisting that Washington name him commander in chief of the
entire U.S. Army, and then he set off for Ohio.[69]

Wayne did not try to eliminate drinking, but he did issue orders to curtail
it. For Wayne, freedom meant order, and order meant rules. He initiated
"stated days and hours" for practice "in firing a marks, and in marching
and maneuvering."[70] He issued numerous new regulations to curb desertion,

absenteeism, and drunkenness. Such was the state of drunkenness and discipline in the army that early in his tenure, Wayne actually had to issue a general order prohibiting soldiers from becoming so drunk that they fired off muskets and pistols in camp.[71]

Given that an increase in rules was unlikely to stem desertion and drunkenness, Wayne calmly initiated reprisals. On taking charge of the army at Philadelphia in May 1792, he ordered two deserters whipped before the companies even left town.[72] Drunkards were routinely whipped, and drunk officers were busted in rank.[73] More than once, William Henry wielded the whip.

Did Harrison enjoy meting out punishment to his fellow soldiers? He certainly would have known how to from his childhood at Berkeley. If he himself had never beaten a slave, he surely had seen slaves whipped and gained some familiarity with the method of drawing off flesh and blood from a human being who could not legally retaliate. Whether he had done it before or not, Harrison showed enthusiasm for his task in 1792: in Wilkinson's brief tenure as commander of Fort Washington, an order went out that soldiers drunk outside the garrison would receive "fifty Lashes on the spot." One night while on patrol for his commander, Harrison encountered an intoxicated civilian ordnance worker. Without bothering to distinguish between soldier and civilian, Harrison applied the lash. When the offender's friend protested, Harrison, on his own authority, gave that man ten lashes. When the civilian officers came to arrest Harrison for violence against an American civilian, Harrison entered into an "altercation" with the arresting sheriff. Harrison spent twenty-four hours in jail, to say nothing of the legal troubles that followed. Timely petitions from his commanding officer to the president helped resolve the situation.[74]

Wayne began policing his soldiers' sexual peccadilloes. His concern was not merely moralistic: "The last detachment brought with them another malady besides the *small pox*," Wayne complained in 1792. "Many . . . are afflicted with a virulent *Veneri*."[75] Wayne refused to house his men at Fort Washington because the nearby village of Cincinnati had too many taverns and brothels.[76] His efforts to control this more clandestine aspect of soldiering was less successful; only when the men managed to make their affairs public could any significant crime be shown, as when one Sergeant Hopkins received demotion "for riotously beating a Woman kept by him as a Mistress."[77]

One such affair changed Harrison's life. Captain Ballard Smith was court-martialed in October 1792 "for behavior unlike a Gentleman and Officer and repugnant to the dignity of the army." Smith had apparently been "keeping a woman, claim'd and known to be, the wife of Sergeant Sprague of his own Company." This delicate situation seemed to be an open secret at the camp, and Smith's mistress apparently had taken to lording her status over the men of the company, including perhaps even her husband; unsurprisingly, this had "produced discontent to the Sergeant." Wayne took action only when the affair became public, after a shouting match during which Smith's mistress "threaten'd to take the Captains Pistols." Smith was also drunk during this incident. Wayne suspended Smith and promoted the next-highest officer—William Henry, "now the Lieutenant Harrison."[78]

Military discipline included the death penalty. Wayne seems to have shown reluctance to apply the ultimate punishment, whatever his later reputation. The first execution ordered in his forces was for striking an officer; a soldier had struck an ensign—Harrison's rank, and the lowest officer class—and received the death penalty. Wayne pardoned the soldier in the hopes that such a dire warning would stem disobedience.[79]

It didn't. Desertions and drunkenness continued apace. Less than a month after his first pardon, Wayne was issuing death sentences for desertion, and even offering "a reward of ten *dollars*, to any *Soldier*, who will discover any intention of desertion in any other Solider or Soldiers" so that such potential deserters might receive punishment "agreeably to the rules and Articles of War."[80]

Three days after this offer was issued, Wayne punished five deserters in a grim display of power and authority. Four of the men were sentenced to death. The fifth had his head and eyebrows shaved and received one hundred lashes. Then a "D"—for "deserter"—was branded onto his forehead. Finally, the branded man was forced to act as the executioner for his four fellow deserters. Wayne mustered every man under his command to observe the humiliation and the executions.[81] In the first experience of power Harrison could call his own, his tutor had been a man very different from the amiable Benjamin V. His father had played the politics of the possible. Wayne—and William Henry—preferred fiat, enforcement, and, when necessary, death.

All these preparations would mean nothing if the army could not fight. Even after the Senate rejected Putnam's treaty, Washington and Jefferson continued to press for peace negotiations. The border remained the sticking point: Americans demanded the land to the Muskingum River, while the Confederacy remained obstinate that the border was the Ohio and that neither treaty nor conquest had ever taken that land from them.[82]

This diplomatic intransigence may amount to a missed moment for the Confederacy. The Iroquois begged them to settle with the Americans in 1791 when it would be easy: "Every time the Big knifes come to fight against you, you throw them down. If they had thrown you down as you did to them, then it would be difficult to make peace with them."[83] The possibility of a negotiated peace with the Muskingum as the border is an intriguing one, and but for two votes in the Senate it would have happened in 1792—a counterfactual world worth exploring, especially by those who skip from Harmar to St. Clair to Wayne without considering the time between, and therefore see American dispossession as inevitable.

Yet like the Americans, the Confederacy could not see the future, either. They had thrown down the Americans twice and could do it again; they knew as well (and cheered) that the slaves of Haiti had just rebelled and thrown off their European shackles.[84] The Confederacy, not the Americans, negotiated from a position of strength and for what it considered to be just: the disavowal of the dubious treaties and the removal of the Americans from the Ohio country. As the Confederacy wrote its case to President Washington in 1793, "We ask for nothing but what the great spirit gave us."[85]

Despite their forthright determination, however, hairline fractures appeared in the Confederacy. Alexander McKee, one of the British traders at the Glaize, noted that "jealousies and divisions" had emerged in the leadership, perhaps due to the refusal to take the American deal, and that consequently "the opposition to the American army establishing themselves in this Country is every day growing less."[86] In particular, the Ojibwes had withdrawn further north; warriors who had provided crucial support in 1791 would not fight for the Confederacy in 1794.

One further loss—of one man—hampered Blue Jacket and helped Wayne. The warrior Apekonit (Wild Carrot), a white man adopted into the Miami tribe at the end of the Revolution, came to Kentucky on a typical trading mission in 1792, where he accidentally ran into his biological brother. The enigmatic Apekonit was convinced to switch sides, whereupon he resumed his white name—William Wells. Wells spoke several Indian languages fluently, and knew the appropriate diplomatic and social customs. He moved easily between the worlds, providing the Americans with reliable interpretation and valuable intelligence. Wells even showed the Americans where the Confederacy had stashed the artillery captured from St. Clair, and he became a "principal Guide & Spy" in Wayne's campaign.[87] The Confederacy won in 1790 and 1791, and the Americans in 1794; Wells won all three encounters. His amazing facility for victory—and his flexible loyalty— would become a hallmark of the history of the Shawnees and the early American republic.

Wayne moved his forces north from Fort Greenville in late July 1794. Once again the American army targeted the Glaize in hopes of crushing the Shawnee capital, and once again the army took the time to burn Indian houses and grain stores en route.[88] Several diaries of the campaign exist, most notably that of William Clark, later the famous partner of Meriwether Lewis. Clark's account, however, reveals considerable irritation at Wayne's seemingly contradictory orders to march quickly *and* fortify the camps. When Wells reported that the Potawatomies had not yet reached the Glaize but were expected soon, Clark despaired. The reinforcements would aid the Confederacy; Wayne's delays had doomed the mission. The Confederacy, he wrote, was like "the long talked of Hydra," and he for one would much rather have fought it without one of its heads. Such a move would have "weakened" the creature, "& perhaps saved much effusion of blood, but that is no consideration with some folks."[89]

The battle, when it came, was fairly straightforward. The two armies had circled each other for days. Wayne's spy network located the Confederacy's main force on the rainy morning of August 20. A brief skirmish followed, then Wayne launched a massive counterattack. Indian forces again attempted to turn the left flank, but Wayne persevered with the frontal assault and sent them fleeing.[90]

Both sides probably assumed that the Indian retreat offered only a lull in the battle. The Indian army had encamped very close to the British-held Fort Miami, and the Confederacy had long treated with the British and been assured of support. The Indian forces likely assumed that the British would provide them with shelter and support within the fort—as did Clark, who spent August 21 "full of expectation & anxiety, of storming the British Garrison."[91] It was not to be. When the fleeing Indian forces requested entry to Fort Miami, the commander of the fort refused. The Confederacy's fallback strategy had disintegrated.[92]

Instead of an Indian force secure in a British redoubt, the Americans discovered that the Indians had dispersed completely. Alexander McKee, watching from Fort Miami, recorded what happened next: "The American Army have left Evident marks of their boasted Humanity behind them, besides scalping & mutilating the Indians who were killed in action they have opened the peaceful graves in different parts of the Country, Exposed the Bones of the consumed & consuming Bodies, and horrid to relate they have with unparalleled barbarity driven stakes through them and left them objects calling for more than human vengeance."[93]

Numerous legends grew up around the Battle of Fallen Timbers. One American soldier with the unfortunate name of Robert MisCampbell had the greater misfortune to die of his wounds, and over the years historians and folklorists began to report that a "Miss Campbell" had been killed in the action. Andrew Coffinberry extolled the mythical female lieutenant in his 1842 poem *The Forest Rangers:* "Tears distilled from many an eye, / That saw the beardless hero die. / Wrenching apart the bloody vest, / Lo! They exposed a maiden's breast."[94]

A greater myth was that the victory itself brought the Confederacy to the negotiating table. The Battle of Fallen Timbers concluded on August 20, 1794, and peace negotiations did not begin until the following summer. Nor was this delay merely by Wayne's choice, as he sent messengers to the Confederacy seeking peace negotiations in September 1794 but received no response.[95] Moreover, Indian depredations continued throughout the year; though one Wayne biographer assured readers that the terrified Indians never again would have the courage to mount a frontal assault, Wayne himself certainly feared they would. He wrote to Knox in October begging for more men, lest an Indian counterattack wipe out his gains. He privately worried that there might be no treaty at all.[96]

The Battle of Fallen Timbers dealt a blow to the Glaize, but the ultimate defeat of the Northwest Confederacy came through Wayne's ability to split the alliance along pre-1786 tribal and social lines. Wayne did not win the peace at Fallen Timbers; rather, he used Fallen Timbers as a wedge to bring pliable chiefs and wavering tribes to the negotiating table.

The Miami were the first to fall. The Iroquois leader Joseph Brant wrote in October that "the Indians in that quarter are in much Confusion—owing to their late bad Success and in bad Temper by not receiving any assistance from the English."[97] Brant urged the Confederation "to avoid making separate or partial Treaties with the Americans, which if they do their Country will be lost forever, but to keep firm and united untill Spring," when there might be a change of fortune.[98] But the Miamis had had enough; they arrived at Greenville to negotiate in December 1794. That month Tarhe of the Wyandots also arrived to treat with Wayne.[99] Wayne resisted making individual treaties, however, and instead insisted that the Indians who wanted peace would have to return to Greenville with representatives from all the confederated tribes. Wayne waited until he had his cat's-paw, and then moved in to seize victory.

Diplomatic developments unrelated to Fallen Timbers aided Wayne's diplomacy. News of Jay's Treaty—which reopened American trade with the

British—arrived in the Northwest; the oft-maligned treaty sparked protests against the Washington administration for agreeing to British trade restrictions and allowing British traders to remain in Indian country without becoming U.S. citizens. In terms of security arrangements, however, the treaty strengthened Wayne: the British were now formally to abandon their forts along the Great Lakes, and that signaled, if the British commander's behavior at Fort Miami had not already done so, that the Confederacy did not have any significant backing from the British.[100]

The Confederacy collapsed in spectacular fashion. The Treaty of Greenville, which established the peace, gave the United States lands far beyond the Muskingum, very nearly up to the Maumee River itself. The tribes agreed to place themselves under U.S. oversight, thereby accepting that in the future, land sales could take place only with the federal government, which would also mediate all future intertribal conflicts.

The leaders of the Confederacy lost power as well. Several war chiefs had sent delegations to Greenville determined not to sign anything, but accommodationist leaders sick of the fighting showed up as well. After the setbacks and loss of life at Fallen Timbers, these leaders carried the day and, indeed, assumed control over the peoples of the Northwest during the next decade. Black Hoof became preeminent leader of the Shawnees. The war chief had once again become a situational office. More tribes, it seemed, were willing to cede power to the accommodationists, and land to the Americans.

Later in that same year, President Washington established another brilliant victory, riding at the head of an army to put down the Whiskey Rebellion in western Pennsylvania. (Of course, that victory, too, involved political as well as military maneuvers, "the Federal Party in that Quarter being stronger and more numerous than the Insurgents.")[101] The victories of Wayne and Washington buttressed federal power in the trans-Appalachian west; fears of breakaway republics and border wars shifted from Pennsylvania and Ohio to the banks of the Mississippi, where Spain and Britain still lurked. Perhaps as important, British trading had been severely reduced, allowing American traders to flood the frontier with goods—and whiskey.

Alcohol affected Harrison's army before Fallen Timbers; it probably affected Tenskwatawa after. If Tenskwatawa fought there—and he might have—his apprenticeship would not have been nearly as glorious as Harrison's. Having watched a nascent political order achieve victory in arms and diplomacy in 1791, Tenskwatawa now saw the old divisions steal that victory away. It would stand to follow that this year might have marked the beginning of his descent into alcoholism.

Current research suggests that Native Americans are not more genetically susceptible to alcoholism than any other group. Perhaps antebellum complaints about "Indian drunkenness" were merely a matter of whites blaming Indians for a condition they overlooked among themselves. One English traveler in Indiana remarked that the backwoodsmen "are very similar in their habits and manners to the aborigines, only perhaps more prodigal and more careless of life." Moreover, while whites often recorded scenes of horror and violence when facing drunk Indians, Indians had fewer chances to record the horror and violence they suffered at the hands of drunken whites—but it happened all the same. In fact, when the Choctaws—an American ally—arrived at Cincinnati after the Battle of Fallen Timbers, they found themselves surrounded by a drunken mob of white men "armed and accoutered for War" and "putting them in great Terror." The men heard that Indians had kidnapped a white girl, and they did not much care which Indians they might catch for it.[102]

It is also possible that the two cultures used alcohol in fundamentally different ways, with whites maintaining a constant "buzz," drinking at a steady pace over each day, while Indians drank to excess on particular occasions. In light of such a theory—and it is only a theory—then perhaps nineteenth-century Native American alcohol use was related to Indian religious beliefs. Several Eastern Woodlands cultures emphasized the importance of religious ecstasy as means to achieve trance states or sacred dreams. By the early nineteenth century, some Ojibwes had incorporated alcohol into their healing rituals. Perhaps that is why Tenskwatawa began to drink—to dream. Or perhaps he drank because in defeat he had little left to live for.[103]

Harrison, on the other hand, rose in stature. Generals wrote in praise of him as a capable administrator and a man who understood both settlers and Indians. They also touted his bravery under fire; one observer even pronounced him "a second Washington."[104] The Federalist Party needed a territorial representative from the Northwest, and the young man from Berkeley was available. By 1799, Harrison's decision to abandon medicine and join the army looked prescient; his gamble had paid off. He was going to Congress.

5

The Careerist

WILLIAM HENRY HARRISON began his political career the way so many eighteenth-century Virginians before him had: he married into it. He met Anna Tuthill Symmes in 1795 in Lexington, Kentucky, not long after his uninspired wooing of "Miss M." Three months later, Harrison asked Anna to marry him. She agreed. However, the potential groom did not suit her father, Judge John Cleves Symmes, the man behind Harrison's 1792 arrest for whipping a drunk civilian. That political imbroglio had gone all the way to Secretary of State Jefferson. Symmes wrote to a friend that "I know not well how to state objections" to Harrison, and then went on to enumerate several. Mostly the problem was that Harrison, son of the gentry, "was bred to no business" and unlikely to make money in the new American marketplace. The gentry status that had secured power and prestige twenty years previously could now be seen as a liability.[1]

It was a new market for marriages, too. Harrison and Anna simply eloped. Anna "made rather a run away match of it," Judge Symmes grumbled, "married at my house in my absence." Symmes nonetheless made the best of it and was agreeably referring to his daughter as "Mrs. Harrison" less than a month after the scandalous marriage. It would not be the last time Harrison presented an opponent with a fait accompli.[2]

The match brought Harrison excellent political prospects. A war hero with a famous name but little money had become the son-in-law of a well-connected land speculator, giving him valuable contacts both on the East Coast and on the frontier. Symmes had served in the Continental Congress after the Revolution, a role that undoubtedly helped him acquire title to his million acres in southern Ohio. Symmes maintained correspondence and connections with a host of politicos from his home state of New Jersey and elsewhere, among them Robert Morris, John Jay, and Alexander Hamilton. Harrison's marriage also linked him to influential connections that included William Short (Jefferson's right-hand man) and his own former commander, James Wilkinson.

Symmes seems to have liked Harrison and quickly got his son-in-law involved in the land business. Neither Harrison nor Symmes, however, possessed much of a knack for business. Symmes offered his Ohio lands for sale at half the price the government wanted for its Ohio lands, but he paid little attention to surveys, titles, or accounting and was frequently in legal trouble because of it. Harrison attempted to enter the horse-breeding business, with lackluster results.[3]

Perhaps the two men found commonalities in their religion. Symmes had a nominal Presbyterian background, but he tended toward rational religion and good-humored skepticism. "There be many modes of worshipping the Supreme God," he wrote to Anna. These included Methodists, who "worship him by grunts and groans," while "Newlights, worship Him by screaming, clapping hands, crying hell fire and damnation, as loud as they can yell . . . But the best religion after all is to fear God and to do good." In typical deist fashion, Symmes also knew how to poke fun at religion. When he failed to get his land patent in 1794, he joked that "like a true Presbyterian I will suppose the time is not yet come which was predestined from eternity that I should receive it."[4]

That time never did seem to arrive: Symmes' land holdings turned into a quagmire. Part of the problem was the intransigence of Governor Arthur St. Clair, Symmes' nemesis. St. Clair had, with good reason, prevented Symmes from selling lands with unclear ownership. In 1797, however, Symmes struck back, and his weapon was his increasingly useful son-in-law. Harrison (probably with Symmes' help) received recommendations from Federalist stalwarts Winthrop Sargeant and Robert Goodloe Harper, and successfully petitioned President Adams for an appointment as secretary of the Northwest Territory. That set the young man up for the 1798 election for territorial delegate to Congress. St. Clair's son entered as his father's candidate, and Harrison, naturally, was Symmes'. In the proxy election that followed, Harrison won a narrow victory.[5] Harrison chose a dangerous moment to arrive at the nation's capital (at the time, Philadelphia). Yellow fever had broken out, and thanks to President Adams' flaccid diplomacy and the intransigence of French officials, a quasi war with France was on. Spain held the Louisiana Territory and, more important, the port of New Orleans, and it was trying to build up St. Louis and New Madrid on the Mississippi as further bulwarks against American expansion. New Madrid presented a particular problem, because Spain had populated it with ex-Americans. Settlers and farmers eager for guaranteed access to the Mississippi simply swapped their American citizenship for Spanish suzerainty, took an oath of loyalty to the king, and moved to New Madrid. (So much for the unshakable patriotism of the Revolutionary generation.) Other western settlers were considering establishing "a Separate independent Government," a "maggot I know is in the head of some people," according to the diplomat Rufus Putnam. A friend confided to James Wilkinson that America was full of "Spanish agents, who at different times have endeavored to persuade the people of a certain section of the Union, to pursue a different mode to obtain the free navigation of the Mississippi . . . There has been found partizans of their schemes among our own Citizens, who have encouraged the idea of a secession of the Western people from the Union." The friend was right about the agents but wrong about the person in whom he confided: Wilkinson, as noted earlier, had secretly pledged his loyalty to the Spanish crown. At the time he was the supreme commander of the American armed forces.[6]

The Spanish spies—a handful of real ones and hordes of imagined ones—represented one class of internal enemies. The French Revolution sparked fears of others, an ever-expanding international terror. One rumor had it that "an American party to the number 110 had displayed the standard of the French republic" and "adopted the name of Sans Culottes"—the working-class rebels of the French Revolution, known for bare-knuckled support for the Terror and for their interesting hats—"and said they would acknowledge no other laws but the French laws."[7] The rumor might not have been true, but plenty of Americans and some elected officials had taken to wearing sansculotte hats and costume.[8] Indeed, the ambassador from revolutionary France, Citizen Genet (he took no other title in deference to the egalitarian ethos of the French Revolution), openly organized expeditions against Spanish territory, outfitted ships to fight the British, and threatened to go over the head of President Washington and appeal to the American people directly if the government dared to disagree.[9]

Of course, not all such "maggot" plots came from overseas: plenty were homegrown. The year before Harrison arrived in Congress, a sitting U.S. senator had been censured and ejected from that body for plotting an overthrow of Spanish domains in the Southwest. That senator, William Blount, was rumored to be thinking of setting himself up as a dictator on American borders. Blount had helped draft the Constitution in 1787.

The United States was in bad shape in 1798.

By the time Harrison arrived in Philadelphia, his Federalist allies and patrons increasingly identified the internal enemies and traitors with the pro-French Jeffersonian opposition. Federalists clung to a durable political mythology: the notion that all *true* citizens of a republic would arrive at a consensus on the proper course of statecraft. Having won a bruising contest to remake the standing order in 1787, the Federalists took power in 1789 under

Washington with the assumption that they had won the right to rule. In one modern historical analysis, "the Federalists' close association with the founding of the nation led them to imagine that they owned it."[10]

Yet the same forces that had opposed ratification opposed the Washington administration. The Federalists won early political victories, enabling the federal assumption of state debt and the creation of a national bank. Both notions emerged from the mind of Treasury Secretary Alexander Hamilton, who quickly became a favorite target of the opposition. Hamilton's opponents feared that the secretary planned to increase federal power until the republic fell so that Hamilton himself, like Augustus, could assume the role of emperor. The Republicans viewed the Federalists as monarchists and Anglo men.[11]

For their part, the Federalists thought their opponents rabble-rousers, interested only in reducing an honorable and wise regime to an emasculated government run by farmhands and, as Harrison Gray Otis put it, "hordes of wild Irishmen." The close ties between Genet and the opposition—increasingly identified with Jefferson—seemed damning evidence to Federalists that the opposition faction favored a mobocracy under which no liberty could function. Indeed, David Tappan of Harvard's Divinity School denounced secret French collaborators whose "unhappy influence in this country" had "assiduously and too successfully promote[d]" the Whiskey Rebellion, "the late dangerous and expensive western insurrection."[12] Mutual suspicion easily spilled over into violence. In Congress, a literal battle erupted on the floor of the House of Representatives between Matthew Lyon of Vermont and Roger Griswold of Connecticut. (Griswold won by employing a hickory cane.)[13]

The Federalist tendency to blame foreigners for internal political dissent would become a central tenet of Harrison's political life. Federalist Philadelphia gave him a political education. The central lesson came from the Federalist Party's most infamous policy—the Alien and Sedition Acts, proposed by Harrison's own advocate, Robert Goodloe Harper.

Harper embodied many of the qualities Harrison later exemplified as governor: he had sympathies with both the Jeffersonians and Hamiltonians, and he did not mind taking the low road to electoral victory. In 1796, for example, Harper worked hard to keep Charles Pinckney in the vice presidential contest by spreading the rumor that the real desire of Federalists was a Pinckney presidency. It was all part of a labyrinthine plot to split the Jefferson vote.[14]

Championed by Harper, the Alien and Sedition Acts gave the president the right to expel any foreigner without charge and without recourse to trial. For good measure, Congress also made it a crime to print anything that would bring the government "into contempt or disrepute." Federalist prosecutors brought seventeen indictments under the Sedition Act; one culprit was none other than the Irish-born Congressman Lyon.[15] These coercive acts embodied the Federalist view of the world. It was the style in which Harrison would eventually cast his persona.[16]

The Federalists won substantial electoral victories, including Harrison's, under the banner of the Alien and Sedition Acts. The anti-administration bloc in Congress began to dissolve. The 1798 Federalists and President Adams did have help from some ham-fisted French diplomacy: the pseudonymous French agents X, Y, and Z had demanded that American ministers make concessions before they would revoke French decrees against American shipping, and the resulting outrage fueled public support for Adams' quasi war against the French navy. (Jefferson dismissed it all as the "X.Y.Z. dish cooked up by [John] Marshall" purely for electoral gains.) Harrison's lesson, then, was that hostility to foreigners and a low tolerance for criticism combined with vigorous military response could lead to electoral success. In this autocratic period of American history, Harrison learned lessons that would make him fairly autocratic as governor, with a tenure marked by fear of foreigners, paranoia about spies, and the resolute belief that to criticize the government was perforce to undermine it.

Yet though Harrison saw the Alien and Sedition Acts succeed, he also saw them fail. By 1800, Jefferson and the opposition—now widely called "Republicans"—parlayed an opposition to the Alien and Sedition Acts into a clarion call to victory. The acts embodied the kind of coercive federal government Anti-Federalists feared; Jeffersonians completed a skillful ideological turn by accusing the writers of the Constitution of violating the Constitution. As Fisher Ames wrote dryly, "The implacable foes of the Constitution ... became full of tender fears lest it should be violated by the alien and sedition laws."[17] Federalists had adopted the Constitution as a basis for centralized power; now the Jeffersonians embraced it as the limits of centralized power.

The Anti-Federalist persuasion had always been ideologically diverse (as was Federalism), so in part reaction to the Alien and Sedition Acts gave a polyglot political movement a cause to rally around. Defeated at the federal level, Jeffersonians turned to the states. The legislatures of Virginia and Kentucky approved resolutions condemning the acts and implying that they might just have to nullify that federal law if such violations persisted. Emphasizing state power in pursuit of national office, Jeffersonian rhetoric became red-hot in the campaign of 1800. By then, Jefferson had clearly established himself at the head of the opposition, while the Federalists reluctantly backed the malleable President Adams. The partisans of Jefferson—a college-educated, violin-playing slave owner—chided the farmer's son Adams as an elitist.[18]

Whipping up electoral support for both factions required a war of words, and it quickly spread to religious topics. Federalists attacked Jefferson's deism, even daring to call it atheism. Alexander Hamilton urged New York's John Jay "to prevent an *Atheist* in Religion and a *Fanatic* in politics from getting possession of the helm of the State."[19] The *Gazette of the United States* asked its readers whether they would vote for "allegiance to God—and a Religious President; Or impiously declare for Jefferson—and No God!!!"[20] In response, the Jeffersonians offered a very deist argument: religious liberty was preserved by principles, not private morality, or as a Rhode Islander wrote, "A very good man may indeed make a very bad President." That was a swipe at President Adams, a solid Christian who had shown "official deformities" in office.[21] The deist position was also very popular among newer and smaller churches and particularly among Baptists. But the fact remained that in the contest between the deist politician and the Christian politician in 1800, the deist won a close contest, seventy-three electoral votes to sixty-five.

Harrison could see the shift coming, but reading the political winds in 1800 bore little resemblance to the incessant electoral predictions of twenty-first-century America. For starters, many states chose electors through legislative votes, rather than statewide elections. Nor did the presidential votes all take place on the same day, or even the same month. The election of Thomas Jefferson involved a process of weeks—and that was before a constitutional snafu forced an extension in the form of an unexpected showdown between Jefferson and his would-be vice president, Aaron Burr.

So although Jefferson later referred to his election as "the revolution of 1800," for Harrison it was a drawn-out affair. The care and discretion he took in preserving his own political career was similarly painstaking. Harrison had impeccable Federalist credentials: ancient lineage, suitable family wealth and credit, and a reputation as a no-nonsense martinet under Wayne. Despite this Federalist resume, Harrison also had some claims to a Jeffersonian identity. He represented the freewheeling Northwest Territory, where Federalist protections of Christianity and maritime trade mattered little. Moreover, his marriage to Anna had connected him with Jeffersonians as well as Federalists, specifically with the Short family of Virginia, neighbors and longtime allies of Thomas Jefferson.

In 1800, with the political geography in flux, Harrison played both sides of the ideological divide like a veteran pol. He wrote and pushed through a

Congress an eminently Jeffersonian bill, the Land Act of 1800, and justified it with rousing rhetoric taken from the Federalist camp. The Land Act was also good politics for a Western leader: it made it easier for whites to buy land from the government.

The "land bubble" of the early republic bears some similarities to the real estate bubble of 2008, with speculators going into debt to buy land in hopes of reselling it to settlers in smaller parcels. Land was sold in large, expensive lots, and thus capital was required to start the process. Jeffersonians loathed this arrangement. Fearing a consolidation by the wealthy class, they were determined to find ways to make sure their landless voters got rewarded for casting Jeffersonian ballots. Harrison, still a nominal Federalist, carefully constructed his speeches to Congress to reflect security concerns. He warned that if whites failed to populate the western lands, the territories would become de facto rival Indian states. Thus Harrison earned Jeffersonian goodwill while emphasizing the (Federalist) obsession with security during a quasi war.[22]

When President Adams named Harrison governor of the newly created Indiana Territory, Harrison hesitated, for if the president lost the 1800 election, Harrison too would be out of a job. Then again, if Harrison jumped ship too soon and Adams then won, the result would be exactly the same. In the end, Harrison's political and marital contacts resolved the dilemma nicely: Harrison received lukewarm signals from Jefferson that he would be able to keep the office should Jefferson win. It was enough. And so, although the 1800 election was one of the closest in American history, and although balloting in the House of Representatives continued through March 1801, Harrison had arranged matters so that the outcome hardly mattered. He and his family were already off to the provincial capital of Indiana.

6

Grouseland

INDIANA WAS NOT much of a territory to speak of in 1800; the only land whites could legally occupy was a thin corridor just north of the Ohio River, and while the capital city itself was, as one anonymous traveler described it, "beautifully situated . . . full of Apple & peach orchards," it was surrounded by "2nd rate land . . . hilly, badly watered, and [with] thinly scattered inhabitants afflicted with ague."[1] Kentucky flourished, and Ohio received thousands of new settlers every year, but Indiana was a backwater.

Harrison decided that would have to change. Perhaps the construction of a patrician Virginia home in the middle of frontier country might mask the reality of this less-than-suitable soil—and perhaps a great estate would encourage permanent settlers rather than land jobbers. Thus, almost as soon as he arrived in the territory, Harrison set about making plans to create a grand plantation home in Vincennes. Constructed over several years, Harrison's house was a Federal-style brick home set in a walnut arbor 150 yards from the Wabash River. Harrison called his home Grouseland, and it would not have been out of place in the Virginia Tidewater.[2]

Grouseland was a traditional Virginian home, and as such, it required slave quarters. In fact, Harrison thought slave quarters across the territory would be a good idea. His first days as governor were spent getting his administration in order, but after that his primary and continual objective was the introduction of slavery and slave labor in Indiana. It was all part of a comprehensive campaign by Harrison to turn the Indiana Territory into the most autocratic government in America.

The problem was that the Northwest Ordinance had banned slavery north of the Ohio in 1787. Jefferson intended that "neither slavery nor involuntary servitude" exist in the Northwest. Harrison had to find a way around that. The ordinance itself had been yet another attempt to solve the problem of squabbling state governments: the national government would administer the territories west of the Appalachians, which in turn would eventually organize themselves into states and enter the Union on equal footing with the original thirteen.[3] The anti-slavery Article VI was a last-minute addition, perhaps intended to encourage the emigration of the mythical independent freeholders Jefferson dreamed of as the foundation of a republic. More likely, the provisions were a sop to northerners. After all, the Northwest Ordinance prohibited slavery but did not free any slaves. It also required the return of fugitive slaves.[4]

Indiana had not been free territory prior to 1787. French and Métis—people of mixed European and indigenous heritage—inhabitants had long held slaves, usually in small numbers. Article VI left those slaveholders and slaves in legal limbo. Slave owners of the Northwest began circulating petitions and querying governors about the state of their human property. In 1793, Governor St. Clair offered a typically dithering response, assuring slave owners that Article VI was "no more than the Declaration of a Principle" and did not apply to slaves already held.[5] Nevertheless, petitions went out from concerned slaveholders to Congress in 1796, 1799, and 1800.[6]

The number of slaves in the territory was never great; by the time Harrison arrived, there were 23 slaves in Vincennes and 135 in the entire territory. Harrison brought one more.[7] But though the number of slaveholders was small, they were the faction Harrison sought as allies. His most recent biographer suggests that behind the governor's reasoning was simply the generic white understanding of race and freedom in the early republic: "the greatest and most direct demonstration" of freedom and power "was being a master to slaves . . . to be a truly independent man, he had to rule others."[8]

On the other hand, Harrison might have been following his political instincts. He had, after all, just jumped ranks to the Jeffersonians, the more pro-slavery faction of American politics. Moreover, the Constitution's three-fifths clause meant that slaves increased the territory's population without increasing its voter rolls, an ideal situation for an enterprising young politician seeking to lead his people into statehood. And then, of course, there was the matter of his sponsors and advisors: Jefferson, Harper, Symmes, and Wayne were or had been slaveholders. Harrison's first close ally in the territory, Judge Henry Vandenburgh, owned at least two slaves, and Grouseland had been built to house more than that.[9]

Whatever the reason, Harrison pursued the legalization of slavery in Indiana with vigor. Federal response to the 1800 petitions requesting a revocation of the ordinance's ban on slavery proved tepid, so Harrison simply banned the ban. In December 1802, he suspended all anti-slavery articles of the Northwest Ordinance in Indiana for ten years. He called for a state convention to debate the annulment of Article VI. On Christmas Day, 1802, the convention met and commemorated the birth of their Savior by voting to extend slavery in Indiana for ten years.[10]

Such dubious annulment of federal law produced some uncomfortable objections, so in 1803 Harrison substituted a territorial code that required that any slaves brought into Indiana must fulfill their "terms of contract." A slave was, of course, bound for life. In other words, Harrison played with the letter of the law: slavery couldn't be *created* in Indiana, but it could be imported and perpetuated. Advertisements for runaway slaves began to appear in Indiana's newspaper, echoing those published in the Virginia papers of Harrison's youth, identifying runaways by the scars likely inflicted by slave owners' discipline. Advertisements posted calls looking for "a young negroe fellow named JOE, about 20 years of age . . . the little finger of one of his hands very much bent, having been formerly broken" or "a negro man named SAM, about 28 or 29 years of age. . . . both his feet and legs have been severely scalded."[11]

Congress did not follow Harrison's lead; the congressional committee that examined the petition ruled that Article VI would remain in force.[12] Harrison continued pressing for revocation, and pushed through a law legalizing indentures for up to ninety years, creating a system that allowed slaves to be brought into Indiana, "freed," and then forced into ninety years of indentured servitude—and after "the expiration of said term" the indentured "shall be free to all interests and purposes."[13] While Harrison waited for Congress to make his de facto slave state official, he sought to make the legal system of Indiana as hospitable as possible to slavery by passing some of the most extreme race laws in the United States. As of September 1803, "negroes, mulattoes, and Indians" were denied the right to testify in court. Harrison also passed some of the first of the "blood quanta" laws in U.S. history: any person who had one grandparent of African descent, "altho' all his other progenitors, except that descending from a negro, shall have been white persons, shall be deemed a mulatto," and hence be denied the right to testify in court.[14]

Even after Harrison had gone and Indiana became a free state, the laws remained, making Indiana less than welcoming to African Americans. The freedman Aaron Siddles settled in Indiana, and "would have rather remained," but "I was not allowed my oath." When Ephraim Waterford learned that a black man could not bequeath his estate to his wife, he informed an all-white court that "if that was republican government, I would try a monarchical one." Waterford moved to Canada.[15]

During his tenure, Harrison became personally involved in these laws. A middleman named Simon Vannorsdell attempted to sell two Indiana slaves to a different set of owners in Kentucky. Harrison halted the sale because the slaves, known only as George and Peggy, were officially "indentured servants."

To prevent such "kidnapping," Harrison stopped their extradition. As the case dragged on in court, Harrison found a way to make George his own indentured servant. Peggy eventually went free and tried to sue her owner for lost wages. She lost, of course; as a person of African descent, she had no right under Harrison's law to testify in court.[16]

Harrison's enthusiasm and activism for slavery eventually got him into trouble. Anti-slavery rhetoric provided a rallying point for his critics in the Illinois country—though those towns were more heavily enslaved. Robert Morrison, one of Harrison's political enemies in Illinois, railed against Harrison's "laws in open Violation of the Ordinance of 1787" and "the indenturing of servants for an unusual length of time." Such "Collusions through the Executive" were "invariably directed to one point, the aggrandizing of Vincennes where his possessions are, at the expense of every other consideration."[17]

Whatever the ultimate political cost, Harrison succeeded in his goal. Without question, slavery expanded under his leadership. Just over 100 slaves in 1800 became 230 by 1810, with nearly 400 others likely in "indentured" status. Illinois had nearly a thousand by 1820.[18] A Vincennes visitor in 1821 found "many slaves in the town."[19]

Harrison's remarkable ability to craft and pass laws of his own choosing came in part from the extraordinary powers granted him as territorial governor. Robert Morrison's fears were not unfounded: Harrison was an autocrat-in-chief. As a territorial governor, Harrison held office by presidential appointment and therefore could exercise power unchecked by elections or public concern. He wielded enormous power, both legal and informal, with few of the checks and balances that had been forced upon the federal government. Harrison was the chief executive and head of the militia; for the first few years, he ruled without a legislature, collaborating with three federal judges to administer the entire region. One judge was his friend Henry Vanderburgh; another was John Griffin, "a man of no great force."[20] By 1806, Harrison wangled the presidential appointment of two more of his close allies as federal judges.[21] Lawmaking in early Indiana therefore consisted of Harrison meeting with this cadre, and then the decreeing of such laws as Harrison thought useful.[22] Within five years, he also became minister plenipotentiary to the Indians, a major landowner, and the president of the territory's only university.[23] He served briefly as the governor of Louisiana *and* Indiana—and his own constituents described him as "cloathed with an absolute and arbitrary power, to make such laws and to execute them in such manner as may seem to you [Harrison] just and right."[24] In the center of a supposedly democratizing United States, Harrison had collected unto himself virtually every important social and political office in the territory. The only station he did not occupy was an official religious role; but then, a deist republic had no chief priest. As president of Vincennes University, however, Harrison acknowledged the power of "rational religion" as "the source of the only solid and imperishable glory, which nations can acquire."[25] He himself openly informed the citizens of Indiana that he possessed "unlimited power . . . over your proceedings."[26]

Harrison became so fond of ruling by fiat (and with his little cluster of judges) that he decided not to relinquish that power. When the time came to create a territorial legislature—a legal requirement known as the "second grade" of government—Harrison paid lip service to "the Good people of the Territory" while he orchestrated an enormous vote fraud to maintain his grip on power.[27] The second grade would institute a legislative branch with both elected and appointed members. The elective positions presented the greatest potential rival to Harrison's power. While some citizens remained convinced of Harrison's "attachment to the principles of republicanism," others detested Harrison's high-handed rule.[28] The Indiana *Gazette* featured spirited debate (and not a few insults) between the governor's supporters and his opponents. The latter decried him as a cronyist who surrounded himself with "sattellites" who automatically supported his decrees.[29] A Vincennes lawyer named Benjamin Parke wrote vociferously in defense of the governor in subsequent issues of the *Gazette*—and by summer's end, Harrison rewarded Parke by making him Indiana's attorney general.[30]

To ensure a legislature of "sattellites" Harrison adopted a simple but effective piece of skullduggery: swift elections. On August 4, 1804, he declared that the plebiscite to advance to the second grade (and elect a legislative council) would be held on September 11. Such celerity virtually ensured that the only locations in which voters could reliably get to the polls on time (recall the slowness of land travel in the roadless frontier in 1804) would be the districts near Vincennes, full of Harrison supporters. The western principalities—especially near Kaskaskia—would be unlikely to receive the information in time.[31] When the first vote confirmed the move to second grade, Harrison pulled the same trick to get his legislature: he declared that Indiana had achieved the second grade on December 5, 1804, and on the same day set the elections for the house for January 3, 1805.[32]

The plan worked. Only some four hundred citizens voted, and those who did supported the move to second grade and elected a thoroughly pro-Harrison assembly. As for the seats in the territorial senate, known as the

Legislative Council, candidates for those positions, according to law, would be nominated by the assembly and approved by the president. Jefferson, however, simply delegated that authority to Harrison, essentially allowing the governor to pick his own senate.[33] Harrison, as a recent historian noted, was building his very own "court party" in Indiana, a rubber-stamp group of officials who supported him in return for private gain and public offices.[34]

Westerners complained, and Congress declared the January 3 election null and void. "They say," Harrison wrote, "that the writ of election did not arrive in time—but I believe the Truth is that they Are determined not to have any thing to do with us."[35] But he did not let this setback distress him for long; after all, as territorial governor, he had the authority to prorogue the legislature at will—an authority he invoked in August 1806.[36]

Part of Harrison's power came from his popularity. He could not have rigged these elections on his own. He won supporters by promising to expand the borders of white settlement. The first piece of intelligence Harrison received from Indiana advised him to start divvying up land for white settlement and to establish boundaries with Native tribes.[37] The governor pursued that goal with all the ruthlessness of his Federalist training and all the ideological legerdemain of his adopted Republicanism.

The Jefferson administration had chosen as the basis of its Indian policy a more aggressive and virulent form of acculturation originally developed by Secretary of War Henry Knox. The nominal idea was to subsidize efforts to teach Native Americans to live like whites. Once that transformation had taken place, the geopolitical and security problems of the frontier would simply vanish. The administration's intention toward the Indians, Jefferson wrote, was "to cultivate their love."

The president explained this agenda to Harrison in greater detail in an 1803 letter that revealed an important caveat: in order "to cultivate their love," officials needed to buy their land. To Jefferson, any treaty that turned Indian hunting ground into white farms would improve relations with the Indians. Indians *needed* to lose their land, Jefferson thought, so that they might abandon their traditional lives, live like whites, and, once acculturation and civilization had taken hold, ultimately join in the American republic.[38]

This logic was not all simply distorted altruism. Incorporation offered security in a hostile world. The problem of frontier loyalty loomed over the politics of the early republic. The British, French, and Spanish remained dire threats, and Putnam's "maggots" still dreamed of abandoning American suzerainty. French purchase of Louisiana made things even more complicated. The western rivers all flowed to the Mississippi; control of the

Mississippi therefore meant control of western farmers. As Jefferson wrote in a letter to his Republican colleague Robert R. Livingston, "There is on the globe one single spot, the possessor of which is our natural and habitual enemy. It is New Orleans, through which the produce of three-eighths of our territory must pass to market."[39] Spain, Jefferson complained, "might have retained it quietly for years," but the counterrevolutionary Napoleon could not be counted on to do so. And the French had always been better than the Americans at forging alliances with Native Americans. Secretary of War Henry Dearborn—a veteran of Bunker Hill whom Jefferson had tapped for his cabinet—wrote that the United States wanted "friendship and harmony with our Indian neighbors," but there were also "artful and designing men" in the West who might make the Indians "the dupes of their wicked and mischievous Acts, and a war should be the consequence."[40]

The Northwest Indians therefore represented a potential destabilizing force, inhibiting American settlement and tempting the enemies of liberty. Yet if those tribes themselves would become settlers of the land alongside white Americans, yeoman farmers of both races might possess the land, create the nation, and deal the European monocrats a crushing defeat. When the Indians "withdraw themselves to the culture of a small piece of land," Jefferson wrote to Harrison, "they will perceive how useless to them are their extensive forests, and will be willing to pare them off from time to time in exchange for necessaries for their farms & families."[41] The Jeffersonian exchange was simple: Indians provided land, "which they have to spare and we want," and whites provided necessaries, "which we have to spare and they want." In selling goods below cost, Jefferson further speculated, whites could subsidize Indian agriculture and hence civilization, while driving private traders—land gobblers who wished to form a new American aristocracy of wealth—out of business. Once the moneyed men, who had neither the Indians' nor the Americans' true interests at heart, were out of the picture, the Jeffersonian yeoman republic could flourish. Ties of love would unite Indians and Americans into one people, "consolidate our whole country into one nation only," and create an empire of liberty prepared to defend itself on the world stage.[42] The policy was for white Americans to circumscribe Indian settlement, so that "they will in time either incorporate with us as citizens of the United States, or move beyond the Mississippi." Jefferson always understood, however, that the threat remained: "Should any tribe be foolhardy enough to take up the hatchet at any time, the seizing [of] the whole country of that tribe and driving them across the Missisipi, as the only condition of peace, would be an example to others, and the furtherance of our final consolidation."

In other words, if Indians would not agree to the Jeffersonian plan, force remained a viable alternative: "Our strength and their weakness is by now so visible that they must see that we have only to shut our hand to crush them."[43]

Accommodation and incorporation made wonderful sense to expansionist Republicans; they sounded less enticing to Indians. Beyond the fact that many Native Americans did not want to abandon their way of life to live like whites, officials who actually attempted to institute agricultural reform often spent more time criticizing Indian culture than actually producing yield. The apparatchiks sent into the Ohio country to teach agriculture wanted to see geometric rows, not climbing vines in the woods. More important, they wanted to see *men* farming.

Americans seemed perpetually puzzled that women did the farming among Eastern Woodlands people. Quaker missionaries instructed the Shawnees that "white people, in order to get their land cultivated, find it necessary that their young men should be employed in it, and not their women."[44] Many whites likely agreed with John Audubon, who, when traveling by canoe with a Shawnee party, assumed the men were simply lazy, seeing "all of the labour of paddling performed by the squaws" while "the hunters laid down and positively slept during the whole passage."[45] Some assumed that this distinct cultural division of labor was due merely to a lack of forethought by the Indians. Thus, the missionary Gerald Hopkins, in a lecture to Indian listeners in 1804, explained why his cultural arrangements concerning gender and work were the *correct* way of doing things:

> Women are less than men. They are not as strong as men. They are not able to endure fatigue as men. It is the business of our women to be employed in our houses, to keep them clean, to sew, to knit, spin, and weave, to dress food for themselves and families, to keep the clothes of their families clean, and to take care of their children.[46]

Some Native American leaders could accept such a social shift, or at least promised to try. The Massanonga Clear Sky heard Hopkins' plea and promised to "be the first young man to take hold" of a plow.[47] More commonly, however, insistence on male labor for agriculture insulted Indian men and created yet another obstacle to Jefferson's pledge of "aiding their endeavors to learn the culture of the earth and to raise useful animals."[48]

Despite these handicaps, Harrison found Indian leaders interested in negotiating with Americans and pursuing an accommodationist course. Black Hoof and Little Turtle were rivals with one another, but they both saw advantages in working with the American government. What neither Black Hoof nor Little Turtle anticipated was the ruthlessness with which Harrison pursued his goals.[49]

Harrison's first effort at a land treaty ended up mostly as a diplomatic shuffle. Despite his proclamations that no whites could settle on Indian lands, the governor never designated an enforcement mechanism. A series of reciprocal murders had raised tensions in the territory, and both Secretary of War Dearborn and Harrison wanted to settle title to lands surrounding Vincennes.

Harrison offered up soaring rhetoric about the divine providence behind American intentions. "My children, our Great Father, who lives in heaven, has admirably contrived this earth for the comfort and happiness of his children, but from the beginning he has made it a law that man should earn his food by his own exertions. . . . There is nothing so pleasing to God as to see his children employed in the cultivation of the earth." This divine instruction now passed to the Indians through Jefferson, who "has directed me to take every means in my power to have you instructed in those arts, which the Great Spirit has long ago communicated to the white people, and from which they derive food and clothing in abundance."[50]

Neither the rhetoric nor the gifts he offered the civil chiefs—at least $1,500 in silver—moved the chiefs to sign. Harrison had little to offer, and the numerous collected chiefs had little to gain.[51] The gathering did produce one important alliance, however: Harrison met Little Turtle of the Miamis and the inscrutable William Wells.

It had been seven years since Wells switched sides at Fallen Timbers, and like Harrison, he had spent the intervening time advancing himself. He too had completed a marriage that offered political advantages, wedding Little Turtle's daughter Sweet Breeze. He had helped the French scientist and antiquarian Constantin Volney make a dictionary of the Miami language and had escorted the Moravian missionary John Heckwelder across the Northwest. Wells told Volney he preferred white agriculture to hunting as a provision for care in old age, but he had not in this preference lost any of the skills learned when he was the Indian scout Apekonit. Heckewelder watched him slay a bear and then taunt it; the missionary reported that Wells insulted the bear's corpse, and told it that "he ought to die like a man, like a hero, and not like an old woman."[52]

Little Turtle adopted Apekonit's enthusiasm for white civilization. After Greenville, he became one of the most prominent advocates for the federal agriculturalization programs. He began to wear white clothing, and was invited to Philadelphia to meet with Presidents Washington and Adams.

Washington gave him a ceremonial sword; Adams gave his son-in-law a job.[53] When Jefferson took office, Wells became a U.S. Indian agent at Fort Wayne. He enjoyed his new salary, which permitted him to own, at one time, six slaves—thanks to Harrison's new laws.[54]

Of all the representatives at the 1802 talks—and there were many—Wells and Little Turtle had the most to gain from a new treaty ceding lands around Vincennes. Little Turtle had lobbied President Washington to establish firm boundaries, in the hopes that such boundaries would settle vague land claims that encouraged white encroachment. He repeated his request at the 1802 negotiations; in an ultimately ironic turn of phrase, Little Turtle insisted that "reservations should be made for the white people in our country" so that "white people should not settle over the line" established by the Treaty of Greenville.[55] Even with the aid of Wells and Little Turtle, however, the best Harrison could wrangle was a provisional treaty signed by Little Turtle and three other accommodationist chiefs, with the understanding that the treaty would be reviewed for final acceptance or rejection in a year's time.[56]

Over the course of that year, Harrison allied with Wells and received that letter from Jefferson on how to cultivate Indian love. When the time came to reconsider the 1802 provisional treaty, Harrison had become a much tougher negotiator. In 1803, he summoned the relevant chiefs to Fort Wayne to discuss the treaty—and announced that only those chiefs who signed the treaty could receive their annuities. To come home without gifts would ruin a civil chief's reputation at best, and devastate a tribe's economics at worst. Moreover, it became apparent to the assembled chiefs that Little Turtle and a few others did intend to sign—opening the way for white settlement, with or without other signatures. Harrison offered those chiefs a choice between goods for land and nothing.

Like Little Turtle, Black Hoof had faith that the agriculturalist program would work, and marshaled his political clout to make it happen. Unlike Little Turtle, Black Hoof did not have William Wells, whom Black Hoof accused of deliberately misleading the Shawnees in previous negotiations. By 1802, virtually nothing had arrived from the federal Indian agents to inaugurate European-style agriculture at Black Hoof's Shawnee town, Wapakoneta. Black Hoof in fact wrote to Jefferson to "inform you that we will not have any thing to do with them & *Mr. Wells* in particular."[57]

Wells and Harrison had outflanked Black Hoof, however; at the 1803 negotiations, Little Turtle had agreed to sign for a clear boundary and the promise of future preferment. Faced with the choice of not signing and returning home with nothing—and never getting the agricultural program off the ground—or signing and returning home with some goods, several civil chiefs, including the Shawnees Black Hoof and Hockingpompsga, took the political gamble and signed. There was little organized dissent from the civil chiefs at this point—although one chief, a small-time warrior named Tecumseh, had so little faith in the American negotiators that he had not even bothered to attend.

Harrison's next treaty established the modus operandi he would use in all future negotiations. This time, the governor deliberately chose to negotiate with a relatively unimportant tribe. For this second treaty of 1803, Harrison made his deal with the Kaskaskias, a small tribe living in what is now Illinois. The land Harrison purchased, adjacent to Vincennes, was land that, Harrison wrote, the tribe had "anciently owned."[58] During the negotiations, Harrison took the time to explain to the assembled Indians that God did not want them to have all that land: "The kind of life you lead is neither productive of happiness to yourselves nor acceptable to the Great Spirit."[59] Much better to sell it to the Americans. To sweeten the deal, the American government bought Ducoigne, chief of the Kaskaskias, his own house.[60]

It was the Sac tribe who protested most vociferously; they were the ones living on the ceded land, and if anyone was to sell the land, it should be them. Several Sac and Fox warriors—acting on their own—rebelled in 1803 and murdered whites on the frontier, seeking to start an open conflict. The civil chiefs of the Sac and Fox peoples, however, went immediately to Harrison to explain the situation and restore neutrality. It was, perhaps, a wise geopolitical decision—but Harrison refused to accept their apologies unless they also sold lands to the United States. The chiefs signed further land treaties as the price of peace.[61]

Harrison may not have cultivated the love of Native Americans, but he did obtain their land from treaties, and Jefferson granted him a second term as governor. Nor was Harrison finished. In 1805, he persuaded the recalcitrant Delawares to agree to some dubious land transfers in the Treaty of Grouseland, and at the end of the same year he made a land treaty with the Piankeshaw tribe on the basis of the treaty with the Kaskaskias from 1803.[62] It was "highly advantageous to the United States," Harrison wrote to Dearborn.[63]

Harrison could hardly have known just how advantageous it would turn out to be. In 1823, years after Harrison had left Indiana and Indian diplomacy, a Supreme Court case would erupt over the lands for which he had secured title two decades before. This case—*Johnson v. McIntosh*—established the legal framework for future land seizures. All Indians, wrote Chief Justice John Marshall in the *McIntosh* decision, were in a state of nature, and hence Christian colonizers of the previous centuries—all the way back to Jamestown—had an absolute "right to take possession, notwithstanding the occupancy of the natives, who were heathen," and that right had descended to the U.S. government. Marshall invoked a favorite antebellum argument, that of the unstoppable success of white culture: "Frequent and bloody wars, in which the whites were not always the aggressors, unavoidably ensued. European policy, numbers, and skills prevailed . . . the Indians necessarily receded." In this way, the delicate and contingent diplomatic negotiations (and skullduggery) of Harrison, and decades of collaboration between factions within white and Indian communities, were rewritten by Marshall into a story of inevitable white victory (without Native allies) by virtue of inherent cultural and religious superiority. Legal scholar N. Bruce Duthu notes that this legal attitude lasted a very long time. As late as 1955, the Supreme Court followed the same logic by ruling that "every American schoolboy knows that the savage tribes of this continent were deprived of their ancestral ranges by force . . . it was not a sale but the conqueror's will that deprived them of their land." The justices either did not know or did not care that Harrison's key land acquisitions, which set U.S. policy between 1802 and 1809, had been sales and not conquests.[64]

Harrison offers modern observers plenty of evidence that he knew exactly what he was doing when he made these sales. Indeed, in 1803 he wrote a letter to the administration specifically outlining his next plan for Indian cessions. He would deal with the Delaware tribes, he explained, because they were newcomers to the area and thus more likely to sell the land. Harrison knew that more than one tribe could claim land ownership; he planned to buy from the peoples with weaker claims, thereby obviating the need "to Negotiate with the other tribes who are more tenacious of their land" and had resided longer on it.[65]

Moreover, Harrison and other officials knew the value of land. Harrison wanted to buy it for far less than it was worth. "The compensation for the tract which has been ceded," he wrote in 1805, "amounts as nearly as I can ascertain it to about *one cent per acre*. This is much higher than I could have wished it to be but it was impossible to make it less."[66] Dearborn, meanwhile, would be willing to purchase at two cents an acre, but no higher.[67] The U.S. government intended to sell such lands, under the terms of Harrison's 1800 land law, for at least *two dollars* an acre. Harrison well knew this was a swindle. In 1805, he warned Dearborn that "a knowledge of the value of land is fast gaining ground amongst the Indians" and that they would need to finalize more land purchases before such truth could alter the political economy of the Ohio Valley tribes.[68] Indeed, Hull bragged to Dearborn that lots near Detroit "of one hundred feet Square have been sold as high as six hundred dollars."[69]

The tribes of the Old Northwest also probably understood the dubious legality of the sales. Wells and Little Turtle—who had supported the 1803 Fort Wayne Treaty—objected furiously to the treaties that followed. Indeed, Harrison reported widespread Indian discontent over those treaties, chalking it up to the influence of Wells and the Turtle.[70] Nevertheless, Chiefs Little Turtle, Paccan, and Richardville all made legal objections that they owned land ceded to the United States in treaties they had not signed. Wells and Little Turtle wrote to Jefferson detailing their legal objections and suggesting that without greater deference shown them by the United States, their people might become violent. Jefferson wrote to Harrison in 1805 with the recommendation that they purchase Little Turtle's acquiescence. Harrison offered him fifty dollars and "a negro man from Kentucky"—that is, a slave. The idea that all of this was based upon a deep cultural "misunderstanding" about the nature of land cannot be sustained. The taking of Indian lands by underhanded means was a conscious choice by Harrison and, by extension, the Jefferson administration.

In addition to the purely legal objections, tribes also deplored the American government's failure to live up to its end of the treaties. Black Hoof complained that the agricultural goods he received consisted only of "old Blankets and damaged goods."[71] Blacksmiths and other experts promised by treaty never arrived.[72] The government appointed agents "to teach the Indians the arts of agriculture . . . without experience or observation."[73] Wyandots complained of the endless delays between their voicing of complaints and federal response.[74]

This last point made a great difference. The land treaties did not merely deal with territory; they also declared that the signatory tribes were under the protection of the United States—and therefore that conflicts between those tribes, or between the tribes and American citizens, would be mediated by the American government. In theory, such a situation would prevent bloodshed and provide economic and jurisdictional benefits to the chiefs who signed. Given the government's slow response time, however, chiefs who bothered to apply for redress when attacked or threatened by other Indian groups found that the clause was a trap. If they acted on their own and counterattacked, they would be condemned by the Americans. If they waited for help, they would be unable to secure justice or honor for their tribes. And in a world where the civil chiefs had to maintain a political balance between caution and the aggressive young men of the warrior class, such an ineffectual response proved a severe disadvantage.

Thus, as the treaties mounted up from 1802 to 1805 and knowledge of the American perfidy surrounding those treaties spread among the tribes, the political goodwill that kept civil chiefs in power, and diplomacy between Americans and the Ohio Valley tribes polite, began to corrode. Hull warned Dearborn in 1805 that certain Indians had begun to declare "that the People of the US are their natural Enemies, and that their object is their total extirpation." Americans in the west should "be prepared for *all events*."[75]

The stirrings of opposition among whites and Indians north of the Ohio River mirrored the spiritual revivals taking place on the frontier, although for the moment they were mainly limited to the states of the Union rather than the territories. Indiana remained a redoubt of infidelity. In 1805 one frontier town celebrated Christmas "by drinking whiskey, and after they had quaffed to the full, they, to be sure must take another glass because it was Christmas and because they were brave fellows."[76]

Such was not the case across the river in Kentucky in the years 1801–5, where a string of revivals marked the first great outpouring of enthusiastic religion in the independent United States. Centered at the Cane Ridge church near Paris, the revivals featured ecstatic worship, speaking in tongues, involuntary spasms, visions, and trances, things "so like miracles," wrote one participant, "that if they were not, they had the same effects as miracles on infidels and unbelievers."[77] The revivalist John Lyle similarly confided to his diary that the exercises "might answer instead of ancient miracles to arouse the attention of a sleeping world."[78]

The Cane Ridge revivals, oddly enough, had their origins back in Hampden-Sydney; the same enthusiasm that chased Harrison out of college in Virginia later came to haunt the frontier he ruled. One of the visitors to the Hampden-Sydney revival was James MacGready, who liked what he saw in 1790 and brought it to his own congregation in Logan County, in southwest Kentucky, in 1798.[79] In this "day of general awakening," as MacGready termed it, the revival spread from minister to minister until it reached Cane Ridge and the Reverend Barton Warren Stone.[80]

The good Reverend Stone oversaw some entirely new elements, most particularly tongues-speaking and a kind of fit that he later termed the "falling exercise." George Baxter, president of Washington Academy (later Washington and Lee University), wrote a letter describing these trances as a kind of faux death: "Their pulse grows weak, and they draw a hard breath about once a minute. And in some instances their hands and feet become cold, and their pulse, and breath, and all the symptoms of life forsake them for nearly an hour."[81] In his memoirs, Stone referred to "the jerks," an exercise wherein an invisible force pushed the afflicted person's head back and forth or side to side "so quickly that the features of the face could not be distinguished."[82] Some revivalists placed small sticks and stumps on the ground for the penitent to hang on to if the jerks began.[83]

Deists seemed to be particular targets of the exercises. If preachers' reports are to be believed, it would be difficult to attend a Kentucky revival without having to dodge falling deists. "Doctor C——, a professed Deist," fell at Indian River in July, and when "10 or 12 of his companions ran to see," the falling exercise caught them, too: "in less than half an hour, they were all lying on the ground near the Doctor."[84] MacGready noted that one Ohio Valley town he called "Satan's seat, a second Hell," had seen revival, and "some professed Deists have, we hope, got real religion."[85]

One of the revivalists was Harrison's future biographer. Across the river in Kentucky lived Robert McAfee, a nineteen-year-old diarist in the full flood of the revivals. He saw "unusual religious exercises," in which one penitent "turned round three or four times very swift then hollord out & fell down he made his feet rattle on the flo[o]r." He heard sermons, read Jonathan Edwards, involved himself in religious disputes, and experienced the "hot headedness of zealots." Those zealots quickly took advantage of American disestablishment, shattering old denominational lines and creating new church organizations; McAfee could hear "three different denominations this day preach within three miles"—and of course, he also saw "the people much animated with Dancing & the jirks." McAfee went to Cane Ridge itself to see the huge communion services that marked the events, in which figured "vast numbers of people & much exercise of dancing & falling down & Jirking." And then, barely a week later, McAfee went "to consult a water witch" to end the local drought. Not only Indians coordinated magic with religion in an effort to make the world work right.[86]

These revivals were a far cry from the religion of the Harrison clan. Even as the revivals wound around Kentucky, tragedy struck the family when Anna's sister Maria died. The family's religious response was summarized by Judge Symmes' stoic deism. It was "painful beyond utterance to realize her death," yet "I have some phylosophy and firmness on the Most distressing & alarming Occasions—I know it is the lot of Mortals to mourn for a departed friend." No radical turn toward a forgiving, personal god would comfort this family amid crisis. Harrison had nothing to add, or if he did, he refused to commit it to paper.[87]

Perhaps the most unexpected result of these revivals was the arrival of the Shakers, also known as the United Society of Believers in Christ's Second Appearing. What made the Shakers different from other Christian believers was that they thought Christ had *already* come again—in the person of Ann Lee, the illiterate wife of a blacksmith who had immigrated to New England in the 1770s. Lee had been the Second Eve to Christ's Second Adam, completing the work of salvation and instituting a system of communal living and ecstatic worship (thus "Shakers"). In 1804, two decades after Lee's death, the Shakers remained a thoroughly New England sect. But when they heard of the remarkable exercises going on in Kentucky, the Shaker leadership sent missionaries, and several utopian villages sprang up on the American frontier.

What was truly remarkable about the Shakers, in terms of Harrison's world, was that they continued to see the work of God in the Ohio Valley even after the Cane Ridge revivals died out in 1805. The power of God, they believed, had translated from the whites in Kentucky to the Indians gathered around a particular Indian preacher who worked miracles. The Spirit of God had forsaken Americans, wrote the Shaker Richard McNemar, and had come to "the trembling Shawnee, obedient to the Good Spirit in Lal-lu-e-tsee-ka."[88] McNemar was referring to Lalawauthika, better known as Tenskwatawa, who did indeed receive a vision of God just as the fires of Cane Ridge began to burn low. Quite a different revival was about to take place among the Indians.

7

Prophecy

IT WAS THE winter of 1804–5; the exact date is unknown. No one, it seemed, would ever challenge the Americans in the Ohio country again. To the west, the Sacs and Potawatomies made rumblings, occasionally joined by the Sioux, a tribe so distant from the moving line of white settlement as to seem almost mythical. The generation that had fought at Fallen Timbers had all but retired. Blue Jacket lived near Detroit, where he still had scalps taken from St. Clair's and Harmar's forces, but he now made a quiet living trading in English and American goods and acting as a go-between for American officials.[1] Little Turtle and Wells lived off their American bribes as grandees of the Miamis. Buckonghelas was dead. The tribes of the Northwest might remember the political resistance of fifteen years before and, if they were old enough, even the religious resistance of forty years ago. But such ideas had no advocate.

On the morning of the vision, Tenskwatawa sat near the fire to get warm. Another nameless disease had struck the village, though that was not why he had nothing to occupy him at that moment. The English trader Henry Timberlake once derisively wrote that "the sole occupations of an Indian life, are hunting, and warring abroad, and lazying about at home." Having failed at the first two, Tenskwatawa apparently had devoted himself to the third. What little is known about his life in the decade after 1795 is not encouraging. He drifted through several villages in eastern Indiana, and although he married and had children, he proved unable to provide for them by hunting or other means. Most observers agree that before the vision came, Tenskwatawa had allowed his life to disintegrate, and he passed his days with the resigned and bitter patience that often graces alcoholics.

And then he collapsed. His family and friends—those he had remaining— found him motionless on the ground. Some later disciples reported that he had only lost consciousness; others insisted that he had actually died, and that his body had been laid out for burial. If so, his family would have begun preparing his body with ritual paint. Mourning rites nonetheless would have been limited. Tenskwatawa was not a distinguished man.

Dead or merely dreaming, he found himself transported to a fork in the road. The left-hand path led to three houses. "He saw vast crowds going swift along the left hand road," one follower later explained, "and great multitudes in each of the houses, under different degrees of judgment and misery." Drunkards were forced to swallow molten lead, and "upon drinking it his bowels were seized with an exquisite burning. This draught he often had to repeat." Tenskwatawa "saw vast multitudes of every colour going in to this left hand road, & many would not forsake it but were running swiftly to the last house." From that house, he "heard them scream . . . like the falls of a river." This third house, Tenskwatawa was told, was called *"Eternity."*[2]

Along the right-hand path, Tenskwatawa found "everything beautiful, sweet, and pleasant" and "interspersed with flowers of a delicious smell." This land the Prophet later described as "a rich, fertile country, abounding in game, fish, pleasant hunting grounds and fine corn fields." Now an admonition descended from the Great Spirit: Tenskwatawa was to warn the world. And in this way he became the Prophet.

Whatever shock his family and tribesmen may have had at his recovery (or resurrection) was likely abbreviated, for Tenskwatawa began to preach as soon as he awoke. Once Tenskwatawa returned, "he began to speak to them in great distress," Blue Jacket explained, "and would weep and tremble while addressing them. Some believed—were greatly alarmed—began to confess their sins—forsake them, and set out to be good."

This first sermon—like so many of Tenskwatawa's teachings—was not recorded, but it was as much performance as plea. The Great Spirit had sent the vision because he "found fault with his way of living," and the reform of Tenskwatawa's life would "also instruct all the red people [in] the proper way of living." Tenskwatawa promised to mend his ways, as evidence and example of the new teaching. Surely if he could change, so could all Indians.

The example proved effective. Word of the Prophet's vision and personal reformation began to spread, first among Indians in the Ohio Valley and then slowly into Pennsylvania, New York, the Illinois country, and unorganized territory farther up the Mississippi. Over the next year, delegations from the Ottawa, Wyandot, and Seneca nations arrived at Wapakoneta to hear what the Prophet had to say—as did numerous individual Indians from a host of tribes: "Shawnees, Wyandots, Potawatomies, Tawas, Chippewas, Winnepans, Maboninese, Malockese, Secawgoes."[3] In November 1805, an enormous delegation arrived at Wapakoneta to hear the Prophet tell his story and to explain what the Great Spirit now required of them.

Listeners gathered, then converts. Tenskwatawa's teaching became more complex. Over the next eighteen to twenty months, he developed his message into a thoroughgoing program of reform. Some of these new strictures were implicit in his first vision; some, apparently, came from further revelations the Master of Life granted the Prophet. (The exact number and timing of the visions are not clear.) Nor can historians lay out exactly when each element of Tenskwatawa's new Lenten season were adopted by his followers. Yet the visions were only prelude to the religion, which sought to recall Native Americans to their rightful place in the cosmic order. And if exact details of the visions are hazy at a distance of two hundred years, the content of Tenskwatawa's teaching is not.

First, true followers of the Great Spirit would give up alcohol; "it was not made for them," wrote Tenskwatawa (through an interpreter), and "it is the cause of all the mischiefs which the Indians suffer." As might be expected from those who believed in Tenskwatawa's vision—wherein drunkards had flames licking the insides of their mouths—virtually all those who joined the movement agreed to this point. By 1807, William Wells reported that the believing Indians "are quitting the practice of Drinking whiskey very fast notwithstanding the traders Leave nothing undone that is in their power to keep the Indians supplied with this article."[4] Whatever credit Tenskwatawa managed to earn among white Christians largely derived from his restrictions on alcohol—though, as missionaries noted, other Native American leaders had made similar pledges before.

White observers were less sanguine about some of the Prophet's other prohibitions. Tenskwatawa preached a separation from white society and culture: according to some of his followers, the Master of Life acknowledged his creation of the Indians but told Tenskwatawa, "The *Americans* I did not make—They are not my *Children*. But the *Children* of the *Evil Spirit*—*They grew from the Scum of the great water, when it was troubled by the Evil Spirit*."[5] Consequently, the Prophet's followers were not to sell their goods to whites, nor even eat food cooked by a white person; dogs and cats—introduced by Europeans—must no longer cohabit with Indian families. "Many killed their dogs," reported the adopted Shawnee John Tanner. Hats, coats, and other articles of clothing in the European style could not be worn, and in fact "were to be given to the first white men they met." Firearms, another European introduction, could be used in self-defense but not for hunting; for that, followers needed to trust in the traditional bow and arrow.[6]

Whites and Indians were not even to live in close proximity; they might have cordial relations, nothing more. If Indians found a white man starving, they might give him food, but they were not to sell it. "We ought to live agreeably to our several customs," Tenskwatawa said, "the red people after their mode, and the white people after theirs." Indeed, the ban on alcohol so

admired by white missionaries was probably just one aspect of the larger prohibition against white goods and culture. To Shawnee observers, whiskey
simply seemed an omnipresent part of American culture, one that "white
people . . . alone know how to use." The Great Spirit insisted on these changes,
Tenskwatawa taught, "so that the nations might become genuine Indians."[7]

As his ministry developed, the Prophet's teachings on this point became
more insistent. Indians who lived with whites were commanded to return
home. Those who obeyed may not have done so willingly. Mixed marriages—
between Indians and whites—fell under a similar prohibition and sparked
numerous clashes. At the Moravian Christian mission on the White River in
Ohio, Christian Indians living with whites suffered repeated harassment by
the Prophet's followers and allies. Some of the Christianized Indians left
freely, as the minister Andrew Luckenbach wrote mournfully, "to listen to the
foolish teaching of the lying prophet." Yet other Indians at the mission left
"out of fear." That fear at the Moravian mission would prove well founded.[8]

Expunging white elements from Indian life was only the first step. Tenskwatawa's vision initiated more radical reforms yet. Indians were to reject
tribal affiliations entirely. There would be no more separate nations. Shawnee,
Kickapoo, Iroquois, and other designations no longer existed in any mean-
ingful sense. Rather, all Indians were to identify themselves simply as "Indians," so that all might belong to a single nation in the caring demesnes of the
Great Spirit. "The Indians were once different people," declared Tenskwatawa, "they are now but one: They are all determined to practice what I have
communicated to them, that has come immediately from the Great Spirit
through me."[9]

To facilitate the separation from white culture and the merging of all
tribes, the Prophet established a new town for his followers—just as Indian
factions of the Eastern Woodlands had done for centuries. Tenskwatawa
insisted, however, that the Master of Life had ordained *this* town, and "told
him to separate from these wicked chiefs and their people, and shewed him
particularly where to come, towards the big fort where the peace was concluded with the Americans."[10] That fort was none other than Greenville. In
late 1805 or early 1806, the Prophet established his own polyglot town there,
dedicated to the worship of the Master of Life and to the purification of
Indian life.[11]

Tenskwatawa's followers built the town from almost nothing; like many
forts of the 1790s, Greenville had been abandoned. At the center of the new
city was an enormous longhouse, reckoned at 150 feet, surrounded in 1807
by sixty or so cottages.[12] The Shakers—those despised children of the Great

Revival—heard about the preaching at Greenville: "Sometimes we heard one thing & sometimes another, but we fully believed that the Spirit of God was at work among them."[13] The Shakers determined to find out for themselves, and sent a delegation of elders, including theologian and evangelist Benjamin Youngs and the Cane Ridge luminary Richard McNemar. When Youngs reached the town, he felt "sensibly struck with the resemblance this place bore to places of encampment during the late revival, In Kentucky & Ohio &c." In addition to longhouses and dwellings, he found long rows of seats, made of hewn logs, and large tents, in all "resembling the old stands for preaching." There were even small trees similar to those the revivalists had seized when attacked by the jerks.[14]

The Shakers also encountered the Prophet's most illustrious convert to date: Blue Jacket, the aging advocate of the Glaize. Blue Jacket had likely encountered Tenskwatawa in the course of his diplomatic career; he spoke with Michigan's Governor Hull about the hubbub in the summer of 1806, and then headed down to meet with the Prophet. Perhaps he was sent to evaluate the situation, or to encourage the new preacher to cooperate with the Americans.[15] But as the saying goes, those who come to condemn often stay to pray. By 1807, Blue Jacket had joined the believers, and sat down with the Shakers to explain the doctrines of the new religion.

He told the Shakers that the Indians at Greenville required confession (as did the Shakers) and that they must admit to sins such as fornication, murder, and "beating their wives."[16] He emphasized that the Prophet's preaching differed from Christianity because it had no written text; followers believed "that a person could have the knowledge of the *good spirit* & know what was good by an inward feeling without going to school & learning letters."[17] As for alcohol, "we never taste it," and Blue Jacket promised to smash any whiskey barrels he found and pour the poisonous liquid into the soil.

Blue Jacket then brought the Shakers to a worship service in the heart of Greenville, a place the visitors found as terrible and great as the worship places of the biblical Jacob. The Prophet's followers, they wrote, had built holy sites "for the worship of the *Great spirit* that smile with his presence—& the very air filled with his fear & a solemn sense of eternal things." The service began with an hourlong invocation by a speaker standing on a log to the southeast, where worshippers might overlook the fort, two miles away. The people shouted their assent at the appropriate pauses. Finally Tenskwatawa appeared, "hailed the opening day with loud aspirations of gratitude to the *Good Spirit*; and encouraged the obedient followers of Divine light to persevere." Youngs saw in Tenskwatawa a "person of a common size, rather slender, & of no great appearance," but one who, when "he began to speak & with his eyes closed," became "very eloquent and emphatical" with "solemn voice" and "grave countenance."[18] McNemar was even more emphatic: "We felt," he wrote, "as though we were among the tribes of Israel, on their march to Canaan."[19]

Some contemporary observers—and not a few modern historians—have assumed that the reasons behind the adherence of figures such as Blue Jacket to the Prophet's cause were political rather than religious.[20] In the case of Blue Jacket, the devotion seemed genuine; a year after Blue Jacket met the Prophet, Hull referred to him as "the friend and principal adviser of the Prophet."[21] Yet it was not an either-or proposition; as with previous religious movements in the Ohio Valley, the gathering at Greenville also served a political function— and caused a political problem.

First, there was the simple question of numbers. Many Native Americans, particularly in the first years after the Prophet's vision, seemed attracted by his message. They undertook pilgrimages, sometimes en masse. Official government correspondence between 1806 and 1808 buzzes with stories of Indians "assembling from a great distance . . . to direct themselves entirely to the prophet" at Greenville.[22] Sometimes the faithful would send messages north, "inviting them to come and settle at [G]reenvill[e] telling them that this is the place appointed by the great spirit for the Indians to reside." A white settler in what is now Wisconsin found that "the Indians are crouding down upon us from the Green Bay on their way as they say to see the Shawonese at Greenville."[23]

More visitors and followers meant more prestige—and in Native American politics, prestige meant power. Power also depended on an ability to persuade and gather allies, and with Blue Jacket on his side, the Prophet had done well on that point. The Shakers found five Delaware chiefs at Tenskwatawa's town, and the Wyandot chief Roundhead had joined the cause. (Roundhead would later add his brothers Splitlog and Warrow to the coalition.)[24] The white leadership in the Northwest grew nervous. What were "the intentions of this Shawnese prophet"? The petulant Wells believed they were nothing less than "to destroy the chiefs of his nation and be come the first chief himself."[25]

Tenskwatawa's intentions are hard to grasp at a distance of two centuries, but his religious message did provide a working alternative to the accommodationist policies of the Indian leadership that had held sway since 1795. Not all Indians, nor even all those who visited Greenville, embraced the message of Indian autonomy and a holy life away from whites. Yet the idea that Indians needed a spiritual and political order other than that offered by the

American "civilization" program made Tenskwatawa not only a religious teacher but also an opposition political leader.

Tenskwatawa's emergence from 1804 to 1807 coincided with some of the great failures of the accommodationist cause. These years saw the Sac tribe cave to Harrison's threats and the Piankeshaws selling out the tribes of Indiana, again through Harrison's cunning. Hockingpompsga of the Delawares had been trying to backtrack after signing the hated Treaty of Greenville, but he was reduced to signing ineffectual protest documents sent to various white governments. In 1802, Black Hoof—still the best-known Shawnee chief—had sent a delegation to Jefferson to ask for agricultural assistance. Jefferson offered uplifting blandishments, but funding would not arrive until 1807. When it did finally arrive, the men rather than the women had to work the fields. "To raise corn and domestic animals, by the culture of the earth and to let your women spin and weave," wrote President Jefferson to the tribes, was "the wisest resolution you have ever formed." To the nineteenth-century Shawnee mind, the decision looked quite different: Black Hoof was simultaneously kowtowing to the Americans and unmanning his warriors. Little wonder that most observers wrote that it was the "young men"—the warrior class—that flocked to Greenville. Greenville's religious message, viewed in the context of such humiliating concessions, offered a clear political and policy alternative—and a resurrection of the reign of the war chiefs from the days of Blue Jacket.

Tenskwatawa had no patience for white agriculture. The Master of Life, he told his followers, had given white people "Cattle, Sheep, Swine and poultry for themselves only. You are not to keep any of these Animals, nor to eat their meat—To you I have given the Deer, the Bear, and all wild animals."[26] Indians could fish and grow food in their traditional way, with corn, beans, and squash all sown together. But husbandry or lined fields were forbidden. When offered farming implements, an emissary from the Prophet politely declined: "Father, you can give us nothing that will be acceptable to us."

Even his choice of enemies may have gained the Prophet adherents. The Prophet's entire enterprise made William Wells apoplectic, and even the accommodationists hated Wells. When Wells made his way to Greenville in 1807 and publicly ordered everyone there to leave, Tenskwatawa's quiet defiance likely earned him allies.[27] As for the whites, Tenskwatawa made it abundantly clear what he thought of them. In a discussion with an Indian trader, the Prophet apparently "spoke very disdainfully of the people of the United States saying he could turn them over as easy as a basin of water: that he cared no more for them than he did for the wind of his backside, and verified his assertion by a blast from that quarter."[28]

Yet it was whites who claimed that Tenskwatawa had political motives; when Indians were asked why they went to Greenville, they invariably responded that they wanted religious instruction. The Quaker William Kirk, from Wapakoneta, saw many small groups travel to and from Greenville, and wrote "that their only object is to hear the Prophet preach, that the[y] all appear sober & friendly."[29] Simon Kenton—who reported the story of the Prophet's fart to his superiors—also noted that "the reason given by the Indians for coming to Greenville, is to listen to the Prophet."[30] When the governor of Ohio asked why they had gathered at Greenville, a collection of Indians replied that they had come "to try to l[e]arn them good things, to worship the great god above us."[31] The Prophet addressed a crowd at Greenville and reminded them that "they did not remove to this place because it was a pretty place, or very valuable, for it was neither; but because it was revealed to him that the place was a proper one to establish his doctrines," which "were not his own, nor were they taught him by man, but by the supreme ruler of the universe."[32]

At his mission, Luckenbach saw Indians flocking through the village on their way to one of the Prophet's ceremonies, and he reported that they spoke with the "greatest wonder and respect about these lies."[33] Lies to Luckenbach, perhaps, but not to the faithful followers of the Prophet, or to curious onlookers among the Eastern Woodlands nations. Where whites saw fear and superstition as the driving forces behind conversions to the Prophet's cause, Native American listeners in those first few years saw hope, power, and religious truth. At least initially, the more Tenskwatawa spoke about his message, the more followers seemed drawn to his cause.

It was important, too, that this message was spoken. Oratory and storytelling were paramount art forms in Eastern Woodlands cultures, and by all accounts Tenskwatawa had great abilities in this regard. He was an articulate and moving speaker, "solemn and feeling." "I cannot tell you," said Blue Jacket, "the wonderful strange things which he speaks." Even Harrison, who found the Prophet bombastic and duplicitous, was also forced to admit that Tenskwatawa possessed "considerable talents" in "art and address." Tenskwatawa cultivated such skills in his followers as well (whether intentionally or not). A follower named Skelawway supposedly could be heard preaching at a distance of a mile, while an Ottawa known as the Trout preached across Michigan and Wisconsin in 1807. Tecumseh himself became one of North America's greatest orators.

Tenskwatawa's religious movement cannot be separated from the wonders he performed (or those performed in his name). The spirit world and his command of it were as much a part of his message as his teachings, his politics, and his missionary activities. Those who flocked to his town came in the same year he defied Harrison and Harrison's god by putting "the sun under my feet."[34] He had "been given the power to know all that is concealed and to uncover even the thoughts of people." Animals gathered about him, so hunting was easy. Some white observers actually referred to Tenskwatawa as a manitou in the flesh. "It is even said," went one report, "*he can fly.*"[35]

A Winnebago legend (collected in the early twentieth century) tells of what may have been the Prophet's first miracle, soon after his vision. A fellow Shawnee declared the Prophet crazy, and told him to stop repeating the story of his journey to the Master of Life. Tenskwatawa responded by gathering the tribe together; he placed a war club on the ground and declared, "If anyone can lift this, then I will not say it." No one could lift the club.[36]

Did Tenskwatawa have any spiritual bona fides prior to his transforming vision that might have lent credence to his teachings? Most white contemporaries dismissed Lalawauthika's life prior to his prophethood as seedy and unsettled; "a perfect vagabond," one critic sniffed. Certainly he had never been a prominent figure in the villages. Still, a few clues suggest that his dream-death of the afterlife was not his first foray into religious matters. Accounts from the Shakers refer to him as a "doctor," caring for the sick during epidemics in Indian country. In 1805, "doctor" could mean a variety of different things. Noah Webster's dictionary defined it first as "teacher," and also applied the term to the early fathers of the Christian church. A "doctor" was a wise man, not necessarily—or even primarily—a physician. The term may have also referred to the "medicine man," who served in Native American practice as both spiritual leader and healer. There is the suggestion that Lalawauthika had apprenticed himself to another Shawnee holy man—Penagashea, or "Change-of-Feathers." It may be that when Penagashea died (probably in 1803 or 1804), Lalawauthika assumed his position, if not his power.

It is an intriguing possibility, though there are good reasons to doubt it. The story originates with Anthony Shane, a half-blooded Shawnee and critic of the Prophet. Years after the Prophet faded from influence, Shane (and others) used the presumed connection to Penagashea to dismiss the Prophet as an opportunist who "took up the old man's business." In his unkind 1841 biography, Benjamin Drake wrote that Tenskwatawa "adroitly caught up the mantle of the dying prophet" so that he might initiate "that career of cunning and pretended sorcery, which enabled him to sway the Indian mind in a wonderful degree." Rather than describe the relationship with Penagashea as one of teacher and disciple, Drake (and later historians) described the shift from

Penagashea to Tenskwatawa as that of an honest religious man being succeeded by a charlatan.

In truth, it is impossible to describe accurately the relationship between
the two men, since records of Change-of-Feathers are thin indeed. But
should Tenskwatawa have sought religious training prior to his vision,
such an apprenticeship placed him squarely within a tradition of Shawnee
religious leadership. Spiritual power existed between the individual and
the supernatural forces of the world. If Change-of-Feathers indeed taught
Tenskwatawa and identified him as a leading student, Tenskwatawa would
have had some legitimate claim to succession. Claim and relationship, in
the Native American cosmos, were not enough; Tenskwatawa had to reveal
his own power. His countrymen and his followers therefore might have
understood Tenskwatawa's vision in this light, as a necessary demonstration of the supernatural world's approval and its designation of this man as
a prophet.

Yet Tenskwatawa offered a very different kind of religious leadership, for
the Great Spirit had given him one final instruction for the Indians. The
Shawnees carried power as they traveled. Warriors and shamans carried small
bundles that whites called medicine bags and the Shawnees called *mishaami*.
"In these we place the highest confidence," one warrior admitted in 1825. "We
take them when we go to war; that we administer of their contents to our relations when sick . . . deeming them indispens[a]ble to obtain success against
our enemies."[37] Such bundles appeared among many Native American tribes;
in the Old Northwest, the Shawnees, Sacs, Foxes, and Kickapoos were best
known for them. The reticence with which the Indians spoke of their bundles
left many white settlers mystified. One befuddled eighteenth-century observer could only conclude, "They carry their god in a bag."[38]

The Great Spirit apparently wanted no more of this. "All medicine bags,"
reported the Indian agent Thomas Forsythe, "were to be destroyed in the *pre-
sens* of the whole of the people."[39] The *mishaami* could no longer be trusted,
Tenskwatawa explained, for they did not contain spiritual power derived from
the manitou. Instead, said the Prophet, each medicine bag contained a strip of
flesh from the Great Serpent, a creature with a body "like that of a snake & he
had the head, horns & neck of a large buck." Primeval magicians had cut this
serpent "into small pieces, and everything connected with it, even to the ex-
crement, was carefully preserved." These bygone sorcerers—the world's first
witches—mixed the pieces of the Great Serpent with the carcass of another
evil reptilian beast (one Tenskwatawa's translator could not clearly identify),
and this noxious concoction "forms the medicine which the witches use."[40]

Medicine bundles contained spiritual power, but it was fetid and dangerous. Better to destroy them.

Jefferson called Tenskwatawa's program a "budget of reform," and if so, the condemnation of medicine bundles constituted one of its most radical proposals. It is likely that most Shawnees believed some medicine bundles contained pieces of the Serpent. An ancient Delaware tradition held that medicine men might occasionally obtain pieces of the Great Serpent and draw on its great spiritual power to perform remarkable deeds. Indeed, the description of the Great Serpent that Tenskwatawa provided his interpreter bears a strong resemblance to the powerful and monstrous Uktena of Cherokee legend. A beast of the underworld, the Uktena posed a mortal threat to humanity—and yet he also oversaw the realm controlling water and fertility. This double-edged spiritual power was dangerous, no question. Yet such energy could be harnessed for good, and its inherent menace gave it potency. Tenskwatawa rejected such subtleties. *All* medicine bundles possessed shards of the Great Serpent and were to be destroyed.

Once the faithful had burned their bags, they were to make "open confession to the Great Spirit in a loud voice of all the bad deeds that he or she had committed during their lifetime, and beg forgiveness as the Great Spirit was too good to refuse." With the destruction of medicine bags and the public admission of past sin, the penitent could become members of Tenskwatawa's new Indian nation. It was to be a sacred nation, as befit a polity that required a spiritual sacrifice and a confession to join. Indeed, setting aside Tenskwatawa's charisma and the political winds blowing in his favor, it was ultimately his teaching—and the supernatural power that accompanied it—that brought followers to him.

Nonetheless, his knowledge of the operations of the Great Serpent and his campaign against the perversion of the medicine bags got him into trouble. In the spring of 1806, a witch scare had fallen upon some of the Delaware tribes in Ohio. Having heard of Tenskwatawa's powers, and perhaps also of his declaration that sorcerers had infected the sacred medicine bundles of the nations, a group of Delaware warriors invited the Prophet to come and seek out the witches among them. It was in this context that Harrison first heard of the man who was to become his chief adversary. From the very outset, the collision between Harrison and the Prophet was over religious truth—over whose god should rule the Ohio country.

8

Witchcraft

AMERICANS OF THE twenty-first century often dismiss the history of witchcraft beliefs and trials as a medieval extrusion provoked by the ignorance with which modern society scarcely need concern itself. This shibboleth is comforting; it is also wrong. Belief in witchcraft remains strong throughout the world, with very real political and religious consequences. Witchcraft trials occurred in the 1990s in South Africa and Tanzania.[1] A large number of Americans ascribe to a variety of creeds and rituals they refer to as witchcraft (if also shorn of all connotations of evil or malice). Such traditions are recognized as a religion by the American government—even, as of 1996, by the U.S. military. A similarly large number of Americans continue to believe that such self-proclaimed witches are practitioners of real satanic magic. And modern America, no less than modern Africa or Asia, has seen legal and political crises erupt due to widespread fears of devil worship. In the 1980s, legends of a satanic day care cult gripped the American public, leading to investigations in California, Minnesota, New York, Tennessee, Massachusetts, and other states. The Manhattan Beach case in California became the most expensive public trial (at the time) in American history.[2]

That the Delawares would believe in witches is not unusual. What is unusual was their recourse to Tenskwatawa, given that the Delawares had their own prophetess. Beata (or Beade) was born in 1769, the daughter of two Christian Indians in Pennsylvania. German-speaking Moravians baptized her with a name meaning "blessed." Blessed or not, Beata and her family left the Moravians a few years later. Little else is known of her until more than thirty years later, when she arrived in the Indiana Territory, in Woapikamunk, just across the border from Black Hoof's Shawnee town of Wapakoneta. There, another set of Moravians would watch her career very carefully.

Beata may have preached her own message, but there are good reasons to think that when Beata arrived at Woapikamunk in 1805 she did so as an apostle of Tenskwatawa.[3] A Moravian missionary diary, kept by Abraham Luckenbach, recorded some of the details of her ministry, the Prophet's arrival, and the witch trials that followed. Luckenbach began the diary in 1799 and for several years provided a workaday account of a mostly unsuccessful mission. The Moravians managed to make few converts. Their insistence that Christian Indians live at the mission, instead of among the heathens at Woap-ikamunk, probably inhibited their efforts. Their most enthusiastic convert, an exuberant young Mohican baptized Joshua, had joined the church before the missionaries arrived in Ohio. The missionaries had great hopes to convert the Delaware chief Tetapatchsit, a periodic visitor to the mission, but Tetapatch-sit avoided definitive commitments.

Then in February 1805, the Moravians first noted Beata, "the greatest lying prophet," who "pretends to have seen God Himself and also an angel."[4] She "had had a vision," according to Luckenbach's Indian source. Two angels came to her and declared that God was not satisfied with the Indians, who were to return to the lifestyle of the days before white contact. If the Indians would not do so, an apocalyptic storm would break over the valley, leveling all the trees, destroying everyone.[5]

In the vision, these angels threw down "seven wooden spoons" and began to argue over what kind of sign the people of the Ohio Valley could expect as confirmation of the new message. The argument between the divine person-ages suggests that what Luckenbach called angels were actually manitou—contending spirit forces with their own agendas. At any rate, the Moravians never heard of any of the proposed signs coming to pass, though they did witness their converts shifting allegiance to the prophetess; after Beata arrived, "the old baptized souls have become heathen again."[6]

Her message might have been obscure to whites, but not to Indians. Beata was a convincing preacher. Converts to Christianity began to leave the mis-sion to hear Beata preach, and found themselves reconverted to the worship of the manitou and the Master of Life.[7] "The Indians flocked through our village on their way to the appointed house of sacrifice," wrote Luckenbach, "and spoke with the greatest wonder and respect about these lies."[8]

Her preaching style seems to have been as fire-and-brimstone as any Cane Ridge revivalist's. Tetapatchsit heard her say that all those who would not come to the appointed sacrificial feast would perish.[9] Worse, if the Indians failed to sacrifice diligently, within a month they would all be destroyed by a whirlwind.[10] And in a remarkable inversion of an old Christian assumption, Indians who heard Beata claimed that it was Christianity, not Indian religion, that was a front for satanism. Those who believed and accepted the teachings of the white people would go straight to hell. They were, she said, in a cove-nant with the devil and belonged to him.[11]

Beata's preaching and behavior followed those of Tenskwatawa. Her cen-tral message advocated a return to ritual sacrifices and a total prohibition on alcohol.[12] She also emphasized the authority of the "young men" and denounced the older accommodationist chiefs and all collaboration with whites. By July 1805, the Delaware warriors had increased their harassment of the Moravians, attempting to push them off their land.[13] Beata did have original elements in her preaching; she claimed, for example, to have "swallowed three times a light that appeared to her," and by this means "spoke only the Word of God."[14] Yet her monotheistic visions, warnings of hellfire, and ban on whiskey—and her appearance soon after the initial vision of the Shawnee Prophet—all suggest a connection to Tenskwatawa.

Beata's real place as Tenskwatawa's apostle, however, is indicated by the fact that she facilitated his visits. By February 17, just weeks after Beata arrived, the Moravians learned that the Delawares expected a visit from a "heathen teacher of the Shawano nation."[15] Tenskwatawa had previously visited Woapikamunk in December 1805, before the witchcraft accusations began, and preached his message, apparently without conflict with Beata. He explained another vision to the Delawares, this one of a crab—"from Boston"—with claws full of seaweed. The crab had brought with it some land from there, and if followers heeded his message, they would come into possession of it.[16]

Beata first declared to the Delawares that witches were rife among them; they flew about the skies at night, turned themselves into animals, and brought misery upon all good people. This news created panic among the Delaware chiefs, who sent messengers to "spend many days and nights in sacrificing" to the other manitou to save them from the witches.[17]

Though Beata announced the presence of witchcraft, she could not cure it. The Delawares wanted a new holy man, one who had argued compellingly that the medicine bundles of the First Peoples were an infection spreading a mystical death, and who therefore could discern "who among the people had poison or possessed the unhallowed gift of sorcery to bring about the death of Indians."[18] If witches had taken hold in the village, the evil that had befallen the Delawares could be explained. And yet, until the witches were unmasked and defeated, they certainly would ensure that all tribal efforts would continue to fail. Their power to make things go wrong would corrupt efforts at food production, social order, military affairs, and tribal leadership. In short, the problem was not merely religious; it was political, social, and economic.[19]

A campaign against witches and evil magic had always been part of Tenskwatawa's reform program. The Indians gathered at Greenville reported that Prophet preached against witches who "can go a thousand miles in less than an hour & back again & poison any body they hate."[20] Indeed, his first vision listed the crimes that led humans down the left-hand path to eternal torment, and along with wife beating, drinking, and murder, he included "*witchcraft* or the art of hurting & torturing one another with a certain kind of poison."[21] Harm and destruction made witchcraft a social problem as well as a supernatural one. It led to hell, and unraveled the Indian way of life on earth (as Tenskwatawa envisioned it). True power extended through the physical realm into the metaphysical, and in this case that power was a malign force. Agents of evil had tangible weapons, such as alcohol and land treaties, but they could strike invisibly as well. Only combined metaphysical and physical power could overcome them.

Thus, when Tenskwatawa arrived at the Delaware villages on Lake Erie in March 1806, he entered into a systemic crisis, a failure of religious orthodoxy that the existing leadership had been unable to address. He had been invited to restore order by identifying witches, and in so doing return the Delawares to a state of sacred and secular equilibrium. The witchcraft trials were Tenskwatawa's first major political test. They would alter the existing order of power among the Ohio Delawares. If Tenskwatawa was to move forward with his dream of reconverting the Native Americans and saving their independence, he would need first to restore and reconstruct the political and religious order on the Great Lakes. The crisis of witchcraft offered a perfect opportunity.

Whites often derided Native American belief in witchcraft as a sign of the barbarism of Indian beliefs; more than one observer likened Indian religion to satanism. Henry Rowe Schoolcraft, the nineteenth-century white chronicler of Indian America, spent a lifetime recording stories and traditions of Native Americans. He summed up Indian beliefs in the supernatural, prophecy, and witchcraft as "superstition" produced by the "operations of a class of men amongst them, called prophets, medicine-men, or jugglers . . . the greatest rascals in the tribe."[22] According to white discourse, Christians did not believe in such things as witches, magic, or the supernatural; only savages believed in such superstition. "As a rule," declared the white author of *The Journal of Pontiac's Conspiracy*, "all the Indians, even those who are enlightened, are subject to superstition."[23] Samuel Kirkland, who lived among the Iroquois, was "astonished" to find belief in witchcraft widespread among the peoples of the Six Nations, even those who had converted to Christianity.[24]

But white scholars and missionaries like Kirkland had a beam in their own eye: witchcraft beliefs were rife among whites in the early American republic. Among rich and poor, educated and ignorant, beliefs in supernatural powers and malignant magic percolated. In nineteenth-century New England, for example, a robust tradition of vampire hunting took hold. Unlike Stoker's later bloodsucking count, these antebellum vampires rose from their graves to sicken their living relatives. In Vermont, Connecticut, and Rhode Island, citizens exhumed suspected vampiric corpses and then reburied them, adjusting bones or breaking off plants that had grown over the skeleton, and thus set the spirit to rest.[25] When an unfortunate Dartmouth College student died of consumption, his relatives removed his heart and burned it to prevent the spread of vampirism—a decade after Tenskwatawa's trials.[26]

Vampires were not the only things being dug up by white Americans in Jeffersonian America; the search for buried treasure attracted an even wider following. Visiting New England in 1807 and 1808, traveler Edward Augustus Kendall noted that people indulged in an "unconquerable expectation" of finding money buried in the earth.[27] Legends of gold buried by pirates, Native Americans, or loyalists fleeing the Revolution sparked a postwar craze of treasure-digging. Kendall even wrote of farmers letting fields go fallow so that they could follow a cadre of "prophets," wise men who claimed the ability to locate treasure with divining rods, "grown in the mystic form."

Such mysticism permeated American treasure-digging. Scrawled maps marked with an X had nothing to do with finding pirate gold; to unearth buried treasure in the early years of the American republic, seekers needed a magician. Magical rods, spells, or dreams could locate treasure, and so could arcane rituals. The nineteenth-century politician Thurlow Weed recalled a treasure search in his youth that required the sacrifice of a cat; the direction of the blood spray showed the location of the treasure. Hen's blood mixed with pig dung also worked in a pinch. Less violent measures could include mystical circles of wood, scythes embedded in the ground, or ritual silences to placate the ghosts who invariably guarded buried treasure.[28] Eyewitness reports of treasure seekers often ended with a tragic violation of this taboo, as when an 1814 Rochester searcher hit a box of treasure and cried, "Damn me, I've found it!" whereupon—with a sound like hissing serpents—the treasure vanished.[29]

Historian Alan Taylor has identified dozens of cases of treasure-digging in America in the first sixty years of independence, almost all of which involved the services of a mystic who could locate riches by dreams, rods, seer-stones, or spells. Taylor (and some observers in the nineteenth century) assumed that such beliefs persisted only among the very poor or the very ignorant.

Actually, stories of white Americans casting spells for Captain Kidd's gold involved the wealthy and prominent. A Vermont paper claimed that it could name "at least five hundred respectable men who do in the simplicity and sincerity of their hearts believe that immense treasures lie concealed upon our

Green Mountains."[30] An 1834 newspaper discussed the spectacle of "all the fashionables" at a treasure hunt, joining the rabble and wearing "their best attire."[31] John Greenleaf Whittier observed the very top of New England society—"deacons, squires, and General Court members"—digging for gold in the swamps of Poplin, New Hampshire, after an old woman dreamed of gold buried there. They never found gold, but in the yawning pit they left behind, Whittier found a "commentary upon 'The Age of Progress.'"[32]

This era also saw the rise of Moll Pitcher, the famed witch of Marblehead, who became rich off her prognostications of ocean voyages from that Massachusetts seaport; she apparently lived in the clichéd house overlooking a cliff, with a gate made from great whalebones.[33] Magic items could be purchased from cunning folk in order to defeat witchcraft. Paul Coffin reported from Maine in 1795 that magic iron was sold to save a young boy "tormented in the air by a number of witches and then left him in the crotch of a tree."[34] Such a supernatural economy was illegal in New Hampshire, where in 1818 Luman Walter was imprisoned for "pretended knowledge of magic, palmistry, conjuration, &c." Pretense at magic was also illegal in New York, Delaware, and South Carolina. White Americans in the early republic—like Native Americans—clearly possessed a host of beliefs about witchcraft and the supernatural. And just as among the Delawares, those beliefs could translate into violence.

For the Salem trials of 1692 were not the last time in American history that people died under suspicion of witchcraft. The courts were no longer involved, but mobs could exact a brutal form of summary justice without recourse to law. Witch lynchings or suspected deaths by witchcraft occurred in Virginia in 1795, Maine in 1796, North Carolina in 1800, and Virginia again in 1822.[35] That same year, a slave identified as Gullah Jack, "a necromancer," was convicted in the failed Denmark Vesey slave uprising in South Carolina. Jack participated in the revolt by crafting magical charms that would protect the freedom fighters. The judge in the case convicted the conspirators of treason but singled Jack out for special opprobrium in sentencing: "You were not satisfied with resorting to natural and ordinary means, but endeavored to enlist on your behalf, all the powers of darkness, and employed for that purpose, the most disgusting mummery and superstition."[36] As late as 1855, a white man in Connecticut was convicted of the murder of a woman he swore was a witch.[37]

One lynching in particular suggests the extent to which post-Revolutionary America was a land haunted by witches. In the summer of 1787, as delegates gathered for the Constitutional Convention, the people of Philadelphia attacked an old woman named Korbmacher, "on a supposition she was a witch."[38] Korbmacher survived her first beating on May 5, but a week later the

Philadelphia *Independent Gazetteer* reported that she was again attacked for witchcraft and carried through the streets of Philadelphia while the mob threw stones and other objects.[39] Korbmacher sustained massive injuries, lingered for a few weeks, and finally died from complications.[40] The notion that witchcraft beliefs existed only among the unenlightened cannot be sustained. The same city that crafted the Constitution also hosted a witch lynching.

In this context, Harrison's reaction to the trial among the Delawares ("Wretched delusion!") takes on a different meaning. He did not speak as an emissary of a culture from which magic and witchcraft had vanished; he spoke as a Jeffersonian republican from a world in which enlightenment and magic coexisted. When Harrison demanded that those who "convey to you the orders of your God" be "wise or virtuous" rather than wonder-workers, he was not telling the Delawares something all white Americans agreed on. He was advocating—perhaps somewhat plaintively—for his own quiet, disenchanted, deist universe.

The story of the trials is also the story of a power shift. Over the course of Beata's ministry, the civil chiefs steadily lost power and the young men and the warrior class claimed it. Beata's doctrines seem to have led to the harassment of the Moravians in July 1805; the Moravians in turn concluded that the Lenni Lenape chiefs were powerless to stop the young men.[41] The relevant new teachings also coincided with Tetapatchsit's gradual expulsion from Delaware leadership that same month. "No one," he told the Moravians, "pays any attention to me."[42] In keeping with the general political direction of Tenskwatawa's new religious program, the resurgence of the warrior class among the Delawares seems to indicate that Beata's preaching had extended the Prophet's reach into Woapikamunk.

The shifting political order initiated its stand against witchcraft in late February 1806. All the Indians of the region were ordered to gather for "the examination to determine who had poison or practiced sorcery." Messengers arrived at the Moravian mission on February 22, bearing a string of black wampum and demanding that the Christians at the mission return for the gathering.[43] The few Christian Indians remaining at the mission appear to have disregarded the ultimatum. Perhaps in response, the new Delaware leadership accused the missionaries of a secret plan to drive away game. The Moravian leadership responded by sending a small delegation with white wampum to negotiate. In a brazen display of contempt, the "Chief"—Luckenbach did not identify him by name—roughly handed back the wampum and declared that "the old no longer has any weight because the old people no longer have anything to say. The young people now rule."[44]

And so they did. On March 13, seven Indians with painted faces arrived at the mission. Their quarry was the convert Joshua. The pacifist Moravians could not stop the witch-finders, who forcibly removed Joshua. The Delawares explained that "the young people had banded together," deposed the old chiefs, and resolved to uncover the witches among them. To that end, they had "appointed a great day on which to sit in judgment upon all who were suspected of dealing out poison."[45] The revolution at Black Hoof's country had truly gotten under way.

The March 15 arrival in Woapikamunk was already a victory for Tenskwatawa. According to John Heckewelder, Tenskwatawa's arrival drew sizable crowds, "witnesses to the actions of so extraordinary a character."[46] Heckewelder attributed the attendance to Tenskwatawa's novel doctrines. However, it seems equally likely that motivation came from a genuine fear of witches.[47] Delawares might also have sought to evaluate firsthand the emerging new political order, the powerlessness of old chiefs and accommodationism. If the new order wanted to solve the crisis, it needed to uncover the witches and thereby validate the leaders of the silent coup at Woapikamunk. For when the painted Delawares took Joshua, Luckenbach wrote, it was a sure sign they had "deposed their chiefs."[48]

Tenskwatawa's search for witches did not last long. He performed a series of ceremonies, then gathered Indians of both sexes in a circle around him. He named at least ten witches, four of whom had connections to the accommodationist power structure: Tetapatchsit, Hockingpompsga, Billy Patterson, and Ann Charity.[49] Tetapatchsit had been suspected of witchcraft for some time, and had signed the hated Treaty of Greenville. Hockingpompsga, too, was a civil chief associated with the old passivity. Patterson was Tetapatchsit's "aid[e] & nephew," and Ann Charity (also called Caltas) was a "chief among the women" and likely a member or leader of the women's council. Charity also had connections to the Moravians, suggesting that she too sided with accommodationism.[50]

As with the witch trials in Christian Europe, torture was used to extract confessions. Probably several victims—certainly Tetapatchsit, and possibly Charity as well—were "brought to confess through fire."[51] Such interrogations produced remarkable insights into the activities of witches. One suspect admitted to using his grandmother's medicine bag to fly "over Kentucky, to the banks of the Mississippi and back again, between twilight and dinner."[52] Tetapatchsit, when faced with the flames, both confessed to witchcraft and implicated Joshua in his crimes, thus prompting the seizure of the accused from the mission. When Joshua arrived at the trials, Tenskwatawa cleared him of witchcraft, but asserted that Joshua nevertheless "had an evil spirit in him by means of which he could bring about the death of the Indians"—a crime that, like witchcraft, carried a sentence of death.[53]

Ann Charity died first, by pyre. Joshua was struck by a tomahawk and then burned. As the Moravians told the story, Joshua's martyrdom itself revealed supernatural power—not of witchcraft or the Master of Life, but of Jesus Christ. Joshua's body, like that of the saints of the church, remained inviolable. Though thrown into an enormous bonfire, it did not burn until the following morning.[54]

Tetapatchsit's death was particularly spectacular. Before execution, the "old king" insisted on dressing in his finest apparel.[55] The warriors dragged him to the Moravian mission and, in full view of the Christian faithful, set him on fire. As Tetapatchsit screamed, the nearby prairie caught fire as well, and the whole encampment filled with smoke and fumes. The executioners forced their way into the mission and demanded food and tobacco.[56] The pacifist Moravians had little choice but to provide it. Then, in a particularly cruel act of psychological warfare, the executioners promised the Moravians they would not put Joshua to death. In fact, Joshua had been killed the day before, as the warriors must have known.[57]

The trials lingered into April, with the deaths of Patterson and at least one other individual.[58] Yet when the time came to execute Hockingpompsga and the widow of Tetapatchsit, a group of protesters pleaded for leniency. These pleas were accompanied by a series of fines (or bribes, depending on who told the story). The protesters gave Tenskwatawa "several hundred strings of wampum, besides gifts of silver and cows."[59] Tenskwatawa and the Delawares were apparently ready to accept fines rather than executions as fealty to the Master of Life.

The trials continued, however, although not among the Delawares. Soon after returning to Greenville, a group of "young Wyandots" invited the Prophet to identify witches in their village at Sandusky.[60] The Prophet agreed, and identified and sentenced to death "four of the best women in the nation" for witchcraft there. Having initiated a custom of accepting fines rather than blood, however, the Prophet found it difficult to carry out the executions. Though he appointed executioners, "the chiefs stopped the prophet in his murderous designs," according to the missionary Joseph Badger. The Prophet may once again have accepted gifts to appease the Master of Life—or he may have revoked his sentence after one of the appointed executioners fled rather than carry out his orders.[61]

The refusal to execute Wyandots did not end the witchcraft scare. Luckenbach reported in August 1806 that a contingent of younger Indians had maintained that witchcraft continued to be a threat, and in that they would take all necessary measures against witches, meaning "cut them to death and burn them, as you saw us doing that spring."[62] Such threats would be carried out in the era of the Prophet's reign; in 1809, a Kickapoo Indian was burned to death for refusing to give up his medicine bag. In 1810, the Sandusky Wyandots executed a witch, and "tomahawked him till his Bra[i]n Came out & his Eye Balls Started out & yet he lived several hours afterwards."[63]

Some have interpreted these witch trials as a religious cover for a political power grab. Nor did this observation originate in twentieth-century scholarship. In 1821 Shane, for one, thought that Tenskwatawa "pointed out all the chiefs or such as he wished to get clear of as witches."[64] Twentieth-century scholarship took a more subtle turn, arguing that witchcraft trials represented an effort by communities to expunge dissonance from their midst; those people who violated social norms received the designation of "witch," and once the witches were removed, the communities' boundaries were strengthened and peace reigned. Killing witches strengthened communities, or as one scholar put it regarding the 1806 trials, "Those killed for their deviancy were hardly innocent bystanders. Each committed antisocial acts that upset other Delawares," and "by purging the witches, the Delaware established their boundaries and strengthened their cultural reintegration." One wonders whether Ann Charity would have agreed.[65]

Neither interpretation truly satisfies. As numerous writers have pointed out, witchcraft trials rarely resolve problems of social stress; the divisions in Salem, Massachusetts, persisted long after 1692. Similarly, the trials at Woapikamunk did not resolve divisions among the Delawares and other Native American groups. Nor were the trials a mere power grab or an effort to gain control over the Indians at Woapikamunk and Sandusky. Had they been, the trials would have to be seen as failures, as Tenskwatawa did not gain ascendancy in those tribes, and he certainly did not advance his position among the Shawnees. One historian concluded that Tenskwatawa had "failed completely" in trying to depose Black Hoof and other accommodationist Shawnee chiefs.[66]

Tenskwatawa was playing for higher stakes; it had never been simply a matter of tribal rulership.[67] The vision of the forked road had not told Tenskwatawa to assume control only of the Shawnees; it had told him to reach out to all Indians. He intended to dismantle tribal divisions and craft a new basis for pan-Indian resistance. To this end, the trials were remarkably successful. Tetapatchsit—who signed the hated Treaty of Greenville—was dead.[68] Hockingpompsga returned to power severely

Tecumseh. The war chief of Prophetstown was probably a devotee of his brother's religion. *Indiana Historical Society.*

Tenskwatawa. The Prophet in later life, when he had returned to the practice of wearing European-style dress. *Indiana Historical Society.*

William Henry Harrison. Rembrandt Peale's 1815 oil painting of a young General Harrison, just a few years removed from his reign in Indiana. *National Portrait Gallery, Smithsonian Institution / Art Resource, NY.*

Little Turtle. One of the architects of St. Clair's defeat in 1791, this Miami leader became an accommodationist later in life but found Tenskwatawa and the nativists far more challenging to deal with than the American army. *Indiana Historical Society.*

William Hull. As governor of the Michigan Territory, the Revolutionary War veteran poisoned Jefferson's later efforts at comity with the Northwestern tribes. He ended up surrendering Detroit to a faction of those tribes allied with the British. *National Portrait Gallery, Smithsonian Institution / Art Resource, NY.*

John Johnston. A constant foe of William Wells, Johnston worked hard but—ultimately—fruitlessly to maintain cordiality between white Americans and Indian tribes. *Indiana Historical Society.*

Jonathan Jennings. Harrison's political nemesis won by a narrow margin to become the territorial delegate to the U.S. Congress, providing a stage for criticisms of Harrison's heavy-handed rule. *Indiana Historical Society.*

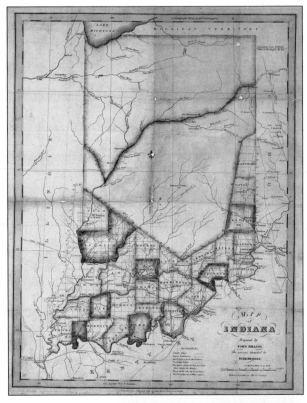

Indiana Land Cessions. White settlement of Indiana proceeded north from the border of slaveholding Kentucky; Harrison's political career—and his extension of slavery—looked southward for political support. *Indiana Historical Society.*

The Council at Vincennes. Tecumseh and Harrison nearly came to blows at a summit to discuss the Treaty of Fort Wayne. The standoff was emblematic of the political situation: Harrison had promised to sell the land to white settlers, and Tenkswatawa had vowed that the land would never even be surveyed by whites. *Indiana Historical Society.*

Tippecanoe. Harrison's jingoism (and later success in the War of 1812) transformed a bungled stalemate into this vision of a victory by a horde of white soldiers vanquishing the perfidious Indians. In fact, the battle had little military effect other than to send the Old Northwest to war. *Indiana Historical Society.*

. . . **and Tyler too!** An older Harrison as he would have appeared in campaign materials in 1836 and 1840. *Indiana Historical Society.*

Scalp. As the standoff with the Northwest Indian coalition dragged on, white tales of Indian barbarity became more common. By the 1860s, Benson J. Lossing could include this picture of a scalp in an Indian's hand as an illustration for his *Pictorial Field Book of the War of 1812* (New York: Harper and Brothers, 1868) without having to explain its meaning or, indeed, to provide any context. It is a nameless Indian hand, doing what the "Indians" of the white imagination did.

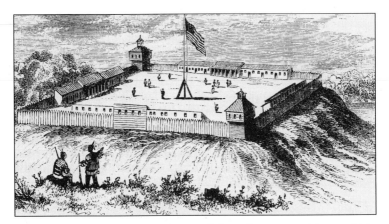

Fort Wayne in 1812. The fort was the site of the infamous 1809 Treaty, which took weeks to negotiate and was later foisted upon the tribes who refused to sign or send delegates. As with Fort Greenville, Tenskwatawa attempted to transform the symbol of white American presence in the holy land into a symbol of victory by followers of the Master of Life; he besieged the fort in 1812. *Indiana Historical Society.*

Washington Falls, 1814. British troops set fire to the American capital in retaliation for what they saw as an upstart war against Great Britain in its hour of need. Even the White House burned—a sign of how close the War of 1812 came to unmaking the United States. *Art Resource, NY.*

chastened; the experience of his own accusation and the discernment, confession, and removal of witches altered his views and political adherence, for after Tenskwatawa left, the Delawares "did not reaffirm their previous friendly relations with the Moravian missionaries and instead embraced a nativist program."[69] Indeed, when the Prophet had gone his way, the Moravians begged the "new chief" of the Delawares to honor the promise made by his predecessors and protect them against "the wild young savages." The chief replied, "They will not obey me."[70] Even as the trials receded, the refrain that the Moravians heard about the power of the young men and warriors began to be heard by American officials across the Northwest: rumors spread of "private councils of the Chiefs and Warriors" that planned on "restoring to the *Aborigines* their former independence."[71] Tenskwatawa had pushed the balance of power among the Delawares toward his followers.[72]

Witchcraft trials—at least in this instance—were not merely hunts for outsiders or political struggles garbed in religion; they were the working out of old and new conceptions of authority. Witches and witchcraft prosecution, in Europe and in Ohio, reflected essential understandings of the nature of power— legal, supernatural, and traditional—and in that sense they were political. In his comprehensive examination of the rhetorical and intellectual world of demon-ologists, Stuart Clark writes, "In describing witchcraft as a social evil authors necessarily invoked a conception of the social order, an idea of *communitas* . . . they committed themselves to views about authority and about the general de-sirability of certain forms of rulership."[73] Tenskwatawa's trials among the Dela-wares offered a very real concept of rulership: power came not through civil chiefs, who had allowed the witches to flourish, but through the Prophet and the warrior class, who had unveiled the secret stratagems of the Great Serpent.[74]

Tenskwatawa also defeated the missionaries. The persecutions suffered by the Moravians at the hands of the warriors—to say nothing of the trials— prompted the Moravian evacuation of Woapikamunk in the autumn of 1806.[75] At the same time, Beata returned, emphasizing the preeminence of the new religion and its powers; she hosted "a great heathen festival" in the Ohio country, featuring a version of the Iroquoian false-face ceremony. Hocking-pompsga, embracing his new nativist position, demanded compensation from the Moravians, and when they demurred, he threatened to ban all trade with them, and promised to set the "young people" to "keep a strict watch."[76]

And the trials produced one further victory for Tenskwatawa: the eclipse. It was one final opportunity to encourage adherence, defy accommodation-ism, and demonstrate the power he had over the enemies of the Indians— witches, missionaries, and accommodationists.

From an Indian perspective, therefore, Harrison's taunting letter to the Prophet failed spectacularly. His letter did not even arrive in Woapikamunk until the trials were over (in mid-April), and the Delawares received it "briefly and with indifference."[77] Indeed, Harrison's scoffing demand that the Shawnee Prophet demonstrate his power provided Tenskwatawa with the opportunity to rise to that supernatural challenge, changing the very course of the sun. Tenskwatawa emerged from the witchcraft trials more popular and powerful than ever—the most infamous Indian in the Northwest.

9

Conspiracies

OPPOSING HARRISON IN the Old Northwest was a risky proposition. On the evening of December 7, 1808, in the Illinois town of Kaskaskia, a rising politician named Rice Jones made his way home from visiting with friends. Across the street, a man on horseback dismounted, called out to Jones to stop, and then shot him through the chest with a pistol. The bullet passed through Jones' heart, and he died minutes later. The victim had been one of Harrison's most acerbic opponents, and his murderer, John Dunlap, was a Harrison ally. A friend of the deceased blamed the crime on Indiana's "men in power": "Nothing is too sacred to be assailed, not even life, when it stands in competition with their plans."[1]

The Jeffersonian Revolution was not above political murder, and Native Americans like Tenskwatawa were not the only leaders on the continent who employed violence to remove or influence rivals. Rice Jones had become the wit of the anti-Harrison movement in the western counties; he was the son of John Rice Jones, a Welsh immigrant who once served as Harrison's attorney general. As Harrison turned his appointees into his junto, however, the elder Jones demurred. The younger Jones joined in, campaigning against Shadrach Bond, a yes-man for Harrison, in the 1808 elections for Indiana's assembly. At a town meeting, Jones called Bond a tool of Harrison, "governed by unworthy motives." The insulted Bond challenged Jones to duel, with Dunlap as his second. Both Bond and Jones survived the duel, but Dunlap returned later to exact satisfaction.[2]

In the August 27 edition of the *Western Sun,* Dunlap published an account of the duel wherein he quoted Jones as making statements that Jones later denied.[3] Jones protested Dunlap's account in a series of essays in the *Sun* that lampooned Dunlap as a fool and an incompetent doctor. Unfortunately for Jones, Dunlap did not follow the honor protocols as closely as Bond. After shooting Jones, Dunlap lit out for Spanish America.[4] In the words of Jones' ally John Badollet, the murder might not have been directly ordered by Harrison. Nevertheless, a politician "assassinated in the streets of Kaskaskia" showed "what kind of men he [Harrison] fosters" and the "audacity they think that under his shield they can permit themselves to reach."[5]

In some ways, the early American political system functioned on violence. The eighteenth-century culture that gave rise to the first congresses did not yet have a party system; politicians thought more in terms of honor and faction. They had jettisoned royal patronage as a means of ascertaining trustworthiness and had not yet replaced it with party ideologies and loyalty. They were left with honor: elected officials defended their reputations in a series of complex social rituals designed to prove they were honorable—and hence loyal to the country.[6] Even when there was not murder, there was plenty of ferocious rhetoric. Harrison's ally Elijah Backus informed the opposition's Robert Morrison a few months before the Jones murder, "I wish you sir to consider me as designated by the finger of providence to be your executioner. If it pleases god to spare my life you shall meet me in the field of blood."[7]

Honor was tested through dueling; the insulted party could answer an insult by demanding to meet his accuser on "the field of blood." This structure provided a useful political tool. Charges of calumny, treason, or sexual impropriety could be neutralized by staring down death calmly, armed with a pistol. In practice, duels need not end in an actual shooting; simply agreeing to meet one's rival often allowed for the duelists' associates to work out a compromise. Alternatively, duelists might fire in the air, deliberately miss, or aim for the leg. A duel of that sort occurred in Jeffersonville, Indiana, in 1809, between Humphrey Marshall and a rising politician named Henry Clay (who took the shot in the thigh).[8] Clearly, the odium of Jones' murder did not outweigh the political benefits of dueling. It provided an ersatz form of combat in a political system committed to open elections but fearful of enemies and factions out to destroy the system from within.[9]

Unsurprisingly, it produced a system in which a lot of people got shot. Republican Brockholst Livingston killed Federalist James Jones in 1798.[10] In 1802, Federalist congressman John Stanly killed Republican ex-governor Richard Dobbs Spaight in North Carolina.[11] In 1806, a young Tennessee lawyer named Andrew Jackson took on the legendary duelist Charles Dickinson after an argument regarding a horse race. Old Hickory carried a bullet from Dickinson in his chest for the rest of his life, but his honor survived. Dickinson did not.[12]

The most famous affair of honor—the most famous murder—of the Age of Jefferson concerned the vice president and a former cabinet secretary. Officially, Burr and Hamilton fought the duel over a series of pompous pamphlets authored by Hamilton, but their animosity was of long standing. They met on the New Jersey Palisades, across from New York City, on July 11, 1804. Historians and enthusiasts have debated the events of that morning in numbing detail: the intentions, the weapons, the shots. What is sure is that when it was over, Hamilton lay bleeding on the ground; he lingered for a few days and then died. Burr was shouted down as a murderer.

Yet even this catastrophe did not end his career. Burr continued in his role as vice president, presiding over the Senate and delivering a farewell address that brought senators to tears. And the equally scurrilous General Wilkinson met with Burr in the winter of 1804 to discuss the possibility of "liberating" Mexican lands and bringing them into the United States. Clearly, Burr had future political plans. Wilkinson thought he knew just the man to help bring them about. In 1805, with Burr out of office, Wilkinson wrote to Harrison, suggesting that the governor make Aaron Burr the next territorial delegate from Indiana.[13]

Jeffersonian America abounded with rumors of plots, counterplots, and treason. Like most Federalists and Republicans of that day, Harrison read conspiracy into opposition and saw threats everywhere, almost always assuming that these threats and disagreements came from a well-organized opposition that sought not only political victory but an overthrow of liberty and civilization. In his early career, Harrison had been largely successful; it was only when the water became choppy and opposition to his rule emerged from Greenville and from Illinois (among other locations) that he began acting on his fears—and eventually using those fears to convince his superiors that an armed reaction was both justified and prudent. Harrison's second term was an exercise in finding patterns in shadows. He was not the only one so employed. Jefferson also saw conspiracies, and turned the American government upside down to stop the man he believed was responsible: Aaron Burr. Burr, in the meantime, made contact with Harrison.

Ostensibly, this visit by the disgraced vice president was perfectly natural, as Burr was a close friend of James Wilkinson, Harrison's old army associate and brother-in-law. Yet within a few months after the visit, both Wilkinson and Burr were under suspicion of treason. Wilkinson squealed first, accusing Burr of attempting to woo western territories away from the United States, to form a new country where Burr might be president. The charges were never proved. Burr's evening at Grouseland in 1805 is intriguing, for if he indeed had been planning a revolution in the west, Harrison would have been the ideal man to have on his side. Was Burr sounding out Harrison on such an idea? Or perhaps sizing the governor up? Would Harrison have been attracted by the idea of his own state, more than a thousand miles west of Washington, where he could wield the real power he craved? We will never know if such a proposal was offered, and if so, to what degree Harrison was tempted by it, for

Burr soon departed on his shadowy mission to the West, and events in Indiana soon demanded all of the governor's time.

Assimilation was failing. Much of the blame derived from the halfhearted implementation of the high-sounding rhetoric of the accommodationist program. Poor supplies and incompetent administrators slowed or halted the shift to European-style agriculture. Black Hoof's Shawnees finally received their farming implements in 1807, but the Chippewas, Ottawas, Wyandots, and Potawatomies, among others, still awaited the agricultural planners and equipment promised in 1795.[14] Worse, the accommodationists had committed themselves to treaties that gave United States government a large role in establishing justice in Native lands, through arbitration of all intertribal and Indian-white disputes. It was not a task many western governors pursued with great vigor or attention. When the Sandusky Wyandots requested the removal of the corrupt trader Isaac Williams, Michigan governor William Hull responded with eloquent words and a flat refusal to remove Williams.[15] Similarly, when a Kickapoo murdered a Kaskaskia Indian in 1807, the Kaskaskias demanded that the Americans retrieve the murderer for them. Harrison sent "a strong speech" to the Kickapoos, who offered remuneration but did not give up the murderer, leaving Harrison with no options short of war. Harrison took no further action, thereby leaving the Kaskaskias with a weakened headman.[16] And while the United States had a legal system to deal with Indian violations of treaties, the various tribes and villages of the Northwest had no system of their own to handle whites' violations of the treaties. Indeed, sometimes the very men tasked with enforcing treaties did not know their particulars, as when Dearborn had to explain to Hull the provisions of the Treaty of Grouseland eleven months after the fact.[17]

In 1807, a coalition of Shawnee accommodationists, including Black Hoof, attempted to circumvent the powerful Western governors by writing to Jefferson directly. "They see with concern that incroachments on their Boundaries remain unchecked," wrote Louis Lorimier, and even sought to head to Washington to talk to the president directly. They soon discovered they could not do so unless the government paid their way, which would not be the case.[18]

Persistent raids by the trans-Mississippi Osage tribe complicated matters further. Several tribes of the Old Northwest had suffered at the hands of such raids, and sought reprisal in war. Still, American commissioners insisted on negotiating a peace, since the tribes east of the Mississippi had agreed to let the United States arbitrate conflicts between Indian nations. Letting Americans restrain the warrior classes—even if such restraints were temporary—probably did not aid the prestige of civil chiefs. Nor did the rhetoric of Harrison, who had the audacity to declare during a peace treaty, "Red Men, Children, listen to us, for we are your friends[.] What do we ask of you[?] Is it land? No! We have enough of it."[19]

The United States—or at least those who had charge of Indian affairs—had little interest or experience in dealing with inter-Indian conflict. Tenskwatawa, on the other hand, had solved witchcraft problems in Wyandot and Delaware territory and with his eclipse defied the arrogant Harrison to boot. By 1807, as white American politics stumbled through the Burr trial, the Prophet rose to become one of the paramount Indian leaders, if not *the* paramount leader, in the Northwest. Frederick Bates, secretary of the Louisiana Territory, wrote that "His Divinityship [Tenskwatawa] has indeed created some little stir and bustle, as these imposters always do," and "that his Apotheosis" was "chanted from Dan to Beersheba, from the Lakes to the Missouri."[20]

William Wells, once again reconciled to Harrison and the United States and living at Fort Wayne, suggested violence as a solution. "The Indians are religiously *mad*," Wells wrote, and recommended a military response; driving the Shawnee Prophet and his band from Greenville "can not be done with words." Of course, should the U.S. forcibly exile the Prophet, Little Turtle might be restored to prominence. Once again, Wells had the interests of white America and his Miami in-laws in mind.[21]

Other American officials were less eager for a military response, but they confirmed the growing reputation of the Prophet. Hull reported a surprising recalcitrance in Native American groups as far north as Green Bay; from the Ohio to the headwaters of the Mississippi, Indians were talking about the possibility "for all the Nations to form a League, disconnect themselves with the White People and resume their ancient habits and mode of living." Hull thought it was impossible for such an idea to have come from one Shawnee at Greenville; a conspiracy was more likely, though Hull could not decide if it came from the French, Spanish, or Iroquois. Almost as an afterthought, Hull added that he supposed Tenskwatawa's influence might have come "from his own arrangements & enthusiasms."[22]

Tenskwatawa's prominence heightened tensions that kept Harrison quite busy through the summer and fall of 1806. In case the rumors of a conspiracy were true, Harrison made some effort to palliate some Indian complaints, thereby limiting potential allies for the Prophet, Britain, or Spain. He ordered the surveyor general to draw the treaty lines scrupulously, lest any "infring[e]ment of an Article of a Solemn Treaty" convince any Native Americans "to join in a war against us." He and other American diplomats also abandoned the effort to stop military reprisals against the Osages.[23]

Harrison also invoked the deity more often. With voters alarmed at Indian assertiveness, and growing discontent with Harrison's fondness for autocratic rule, the governor fell back upon the promises of deist providentialism. In the closing months of 1806, he addressed the General Assembly in broad and self-congratulatory terms. (The address was reprinted in the newspaper, so it served simultaneously as an address to political leaders and to the electorate.)

Like the rest of the world, Harrison declared, Indiana was in a great process of development, "the progress of a Country from a state of Nature to that of Civilization." The Indians had once ruled here, he said—a premise more hope than fact, since despite all the treaties much of Indiana remained under tribal rule. "Too long has this fine Country possessing all the advantages of Climate Soil and situation been the haunt of the uncultivated savage. It is about to assume the Character to which it was destined by nature. A Virtuous and industrious people will soon render it the abode of Wealth Civilization and Science."

It was one of Harrison's first full explications of the stadial theory of development, one he would tinker with all his life. Industrious whites occupied a higher stage of civilization, and thus had rights to land. And Indians agreed, according to Harrison; they were "fully Convinced" of their inability to stem the tide of destiny. The myth of inevitable American victory over the Northwestern tribes is as old as the conflict between the Americans and the Northwestern tribes.

Harrison foresaw complications, however. A war might emerge if whites committed "injustice and oppression." He therefore charged citizens and legislatures to inculcate "an abhorrence of that unchristian and detestable doctrine which would make a distinction of guilt between the murder of a white man and an Indian." Harrison also attacked intemperance among whites and Indians, and declared his intention to pass a law reducing the number of taverns and drinking establishments—even as he attempted to open his own still. Nor did the hypocrisy end there; he bemoaned threats to republican government, even as he bragged about the "unlimited power" he wielded.

The speech was less statement of fact than an attempt to create the world it described. Harrison knew the state of violence and temperance in Indiana when he declared that listeners all practiced "the necessity of Industry economy and a faithful obedience to the laws." He knew of the complaints and protestations against his political tactics even as he lauded "the Uniform Confidence which I have experienced from my fellow Citizens through the whole Course of my administration." He asked his listeners to offer their "grateful acknowledgements to the Almighty ruler of Universe," who "seems to have made the happiness of the American people his peculiar Care."[24]

As a spackle for woe, the effort might have worked, had not the European death struggle between Britain and France made its way to the American interior. On June 22, 1807, the British warship *Leopard* pulled alongside the American frigate *Chesapeake* off the coast of Virginia. The *Leopard*'s captain demanded return of all British-born sailors serving on the *Chesapeake*. The American captain refused, and the *Leopard* raked the American ship with cannon fire until he relented. The *Chesapeake* managed to fire only a single cannon shot in reprisal. (It missed.) The *Leopard*'s crew boarded, press-ganged the four British deserters, and left the Americans to bail out the waterlogged *Chesapeake*.[25]

For Britain, the incident mattered little; His Majesty's government had to focus on Napoleon. The new emperor of France—crowned three years previously—had made 1807 his most audacious year, defeating the combined European forces at Austerlitz and Jena, and forcing Russia into his European system at Tilsit. London and Paris were each trying to strangle the other. Britain had imposed a blockade on the Continent in an effort to starve Napoleonic Europe. In response, France declared it would seize all ships and cargoes that touched British ports. (Her diplomats kindly offered to rescind this decision for American ships if the United States would declare war on Britain.)[26]

The British response to France included impressment of former Royal Navy men from neutral American ships, which served as a crude form of recruitment; to maintain its strength, the British navy needed thirty thousand new sailors a year. London, however, took a liberal view of what constituted a British sailor. Anyone who had ever served under the Union Jack was considered a legitimate target. The *Chesapeake* incident was typical. One of those taken off the American ship was a British deserter (who later was hanged for his crime); two others had legally left the British navy and emigrated to America. The penchant for taking sailors under the rubric of "once an Englishman, always an Englishman" prompted John Adams to define impressment as "kidnapping on the ocean."[27]

With the Atlantic between them and Napoleon, Americans saw things differently. ("Americans," wrote Canada's John Askin, "generally make great noise & stick at triffles.")[28] The competing European blockades stymied American ships and shipping, inflicting worrisome losses, particularly in New England. Napoleon's European System and the British Orders in Council turned every American captain into Odysseus, sailing between Scylla and Charybdis, and few measured up to the task. European observers, however, might have thought America got off easy; when neutral Denmark refused to submit to Britain's blockade, the Royal Navy bombarded Copenhagen for three straight days. With their capital reduced to splinters, the Danish acqui-esced to British demands. The fight in Europe was a fight to the death.[29]

Few Americans had Copenhagen on the brain; they treated the *Chesa-peake* affair as a crisis. "The honor and independence of our nation insulted beyond the possibility of further forbearance," declared the *Pittsburgh Gazette*.[30] The *National Intelligencer* published a description of "the late atro-cious insult on our national honor," which informed readers that the affair came down to "whether we shall have a government uncontrolled by foreign power, or degraded from its rank among the nations."[31] Calls for war prolifer-ated, an understandable consequence considering that some of the initial reports accessorized their accounts with rumor. The *Scioto Gazette* (and other papers) embellished on the *Chesapeake* incident by reporting that the British had invaded Virginia.[32]

The Northwest, however, had concerns different from those of the rest of the nation. Ohio's governor, Thomas Kirker, received depositions of citizens who worried that British saber-rattling would "come to the Indians ears and incourage them to let loose their natural propensity to Blood and Rapine."[33] In Michigan, Hull reported that while his citizens were outraged by the *Chesapeake-Leopard* affair, he also had a very different assessment of the situ-ation. "You cannot be insensible to our situation here—In the neighborhood of a British Garrison, and settlements, and accessible to vast bodies of Indi-ans, on whose friendship and fidelity, it is impossible to make certain calcu-lations. . . . We have only to depend on our own exertions for safety."[34]

Harrison expressed no such worries, at least in public; God would protect the American frontiers. "A beneficent and discriminating providence will make us the objects of his peculiar care," he told his territorial legislature, "another WASHINGTON will arise to lead our armies to victory and glory, and the TYRANTS of the world will be taught the useful lesson, that a nation of FREE MEN are not to be insulted with impunity!" The *Vincennes Sun* printed the address on August 22, and later reprinted it in pamphlet form so that citizens of Indiana could hear his reassurance—and his warning. Providence preferred the United States, but enemies were still abroad. Harrison won-dered aloud whether the Indians living in the territory might not take advan-tage of the situation and perhaps even be "let loose to slaughter our women and children."[35]

As the international situation intensified, Harrison's penchant for con-spiracy theory did as well. The simultaneous increase in British aggression and rise of the Shawnee Prophet were no coincidence to Harrison. "I really fear that this said Prophet is an Engine set to work by the British for some bad purpose."[36] Worse, Harrison did not know how white Americans could defend themselves against an Indian rebellion. He described his hodgepodge militia as "Cavalry without Swords," infantry without bayonets, and battalions armed with "fowling pieces, broken muskets and sticks."[37]

President Jefferson found his solution to the crisis in his careworn ideology of the virtuous yeoman. The president knew the country could not afford a war, no matter how much the East Coast called for one, for the Republicans had assiduously cut the military budgets to reduce federal expenditure. And as whispers and rumors rippled out from the Burr trials, Jefferson could not swear to the loyalty of the endangered western territories. But Jefferson believed—and always had—that the small farmers of the United States could produce everything they needed, and indeed that their independence from the moneyed classes of the seaboard better protected republican virtue. The solution was an embargo: the United States would close its ports to all foreign shipping. America would blockade itself. Jefferson would snub the tyrants of Britain and France, and call on white Americans to work together to produce what America needed.

Jefferson's fervent belief, however, did not make his economic plans any more realistic. Shuttering imports and exports strangled the American economy. Ships from New Hampshire to Georgia sat idle. Thirty thousand sailors lost their jobs. The discontented jeered at the "dambargo." A New Englander penned a doggerel history of the event: "Our ships all in motion once whitened the ocean. / They sailed and returned with a cargo. / Now doomed to decay, they are fallen a prey / to Jefferson, worms, and EMBARGO." Worse still, the embargo did not even much curtail trade with Britain. The yeomanry might praise patriotic sentiment, but they wanted their imported goods; Yankees lived up to their enterprising reputations in finding ways to smuggle British manufactures from Canada. A clandestine trace cut through New York's forests was dubbed "Embargo Road."[38]

The embargo did succeed in resuscitating the moribund Federalist opposition. Even though American politics was not yet party politics, Federalist leaders managed the issue with the skill of twenty-first-century political professionals. Federalists initially joined Jefferson in outrage against the *Leopard* and its British masters, but they soon turned against the embargo as a measure designed to goad the nation into an unnecessary war with Britain. Then they condemned the Jeffersonian efforts to quash opposition to the embargo. Some of these approaches—such as Treasury Secretary Albert Gallatin's request to make open opposition to the embargo a federal crime— resembled the hated Alien and Sedition Acts.[39] The Federalist veteran Robert

Troup wrote that in New England, the embargo "has rekindled the fire of 1774, 5, & 6."[40] The Federalists, by 1808, had turned the tables on Republican claims of a more representative government, as Congressman Joshua Masters explained to the House: "The voice of the nation is against the proceedings of the Government, and this system is not the system of the people." When Republicans rolled out an Enforcement Act to prosecute smugglers, the Federalist *New England Palladium* issued a special supplement entitled "*The CONSTITUTION Gone!!*"[41]

Federalists vastly improved their electoral fortunes in the 1808 elections, but the party had been so anemic beforehand that even the near doubling of their numbers in the House of Representatives did not earn them a majority. Similarly, the consensus Federalist presidential candidate in 1808 was Charles Cotesworth Pinckney, whom Jefferson had throttled in 1804. This time around, Pinckney had a more respectable showing—but still lost.

Even if the Federalists were not yet overturning Jeffersonianism, at least they presented a viable alternative—and that meant trouble for Harrison's one-party state. His anti-slavery opponents and the partisans of Illinois independence began to coalesce. Robert Morrison, in Kaskaskia, moved to the forefront of the opposition, denouncing Harrison's "Collusions," his patronage of slavery, and "the aggrandizing of Vincennes where his possessions are."[42] Morrison collected a promising cast of politicians to run against Harrison's men, as part of the newly vigorous anti-Jeffersonianism. These included John Badollet, Jesse Thomas, Jonathan Jennings—and John Rice Jones.

The Indiana "Federalists"—connections to the inchoate national party were few—outperformed their national counterparts. In October 1808, they handed Harrison his first defeat: they reversed the composition of Indiana's lower house, winning a bare majority of six of ten seats. (The legislature soon passed anti-slavery laws and reversed the spurious black indenture codes, but Harrison refused to sign them into law.)[43] John Rice Jones sang the praises of the victory; they had burned Thomas in effigy at Vincennes, but that, he joked, "had the effect of increasing your popularity."[44] A month later, Jones was dead at the hands of Dunlap.

There is no evidence that Harrison was in any way involved in the murder. But it was the kind of act that might be expected in the tense politics of the Jeffersonian frontier, where political defeat could imply both treason and personal dishonor, and where the political opposition meant faction and conspiracy to destroy liberty.

The murder stunned the Harrisonian opposition—then galvanized them. Rice Jones was their martyr, territorial division their church. The "Atrocity of the Crime and the Circumstances involved in the Commission of it," wrote Robert Morrison, "furnishes us with an example of turpitude that no rational being could ever have conceived of." His grief was real, but Morrison also hoped that it would be an occasion to offer the territory's citizens an uncorrupted government."[45]

Dunlap, on the lam, never faced justice for his crime. Jones' allies, however, did successfully parlay his murder into a victory for their faction and their cause: in January 1809, the anti-Harrison men finally won their debate in Washington and secured territorial separation. Illinois went its own way. A few weeks later, Jonathan Jennings defeated Harrison's handpicked candidate for territorial delegate to Congress. Indiana now had an anti-slavery man in Washington. Harrison was left badly beaten in a whittled-down kingdom. Perhaps his defeat at the hands of the "conspiracy" in the West contributed to his resolve to defeat the "conspiracy" to his east: in the midst of the war scare and the Federalist revival, Harrison also ordered the Prophet to leave Greenville.

Greenville

THE FOLLOWERS OF Tenskwatawa stripped bare the forests for acres around their encampment. An immense house for worship stood at its center, surrounded by cottages and land for cultivating corn. This was the town of Greenville, and unlike the Greenville of the 1795 treaty (little more than a fort, a few miles from the Prophet's new settlement), it was populated by Tenskwatawa's adherents. No longer would that name serve as a byword for American power in the Ohio; now it was a city of Indians.

When the Shakers visited the city in 1807, they found it divided into religious and residential sections. The former had hewn logs for seats, and a long walk "beat as smooth as a house floor," surrounded in turn by tents and stumps for seating. As at Cane Ridge and other revival sites, preaching stands had been set up, and one large tent—from which Tenskwatawa preached, presumably—dominated the scene.[1]

The town, as the Shakers described it, was separate from the religious site. The Shaker accounts mention cottages and that enormous central house, with tents and wigwams surrounding. That layout may suggest that Greenville was only the largest of several small Indian towns (as with the Glaize, 1786–94), or more likely that the permanent town was surrounded by camps of traveling Indians who had arrived to meet with the Prophet. As dusk fell, a speaker addressed the assembled Indians in a voice so solemn that the Shaker Richard McNemar, who spoke no Indian languages, declared, "Our feelings were like Jacob's when he cried out, *'How dreadful is this place! Surely the Lord is in this place!'* And the world knew it not."[2]

By 1807, "a little revolution" was under way at Greenville. Territorial judge A. B. Woodward, writing from Michigan, identified two sources of the "unusual" changes in Native American life. One was the preaching of the Shawnee Prophet, "the bitter reproachment," he wrote, for abandoning the "manner and customs of their forefathers." The other was "the interruption of their usual commercial transactions from the exclusion of the English from the continental market for furs." Jefferson's embargo was strengthening the Prophet.[3]

The fur trade provided the major economic activity in Indian country; furs sold anywhere in North America, however, usually had the same destination: Europe. With the embargo in effect, this system fell apart. Trade with Canada became clandestine, and trade with Americans—who no longer had European markets to feed—also dropped precipitously. It "has left the Indians of the upper country destitute of those comforts to which they have been accustomed, and which are indispens[a]ble during the winter season," wrote Frederick Bates. Worse still, the loss of the Canadian trade exposed the other deficiency in the Indian economy: when goods could not be obtained by treaty or trade, Indian societies were dependent on the goodwill of Canadians or Americans. With the Canadians legally prohibited from sending trade delegations, wrote Bates, "it has been expected by the Indians, that we supply them and that if we do not their affections and confidence will be greatly alienated." The laxity with which American officials fulfilled Indian needs for goods was already infamous. American policy toward Europe was making the Indians poorer. More ominously for Harrison and his fellow officials, the embargo was providing the Indians with a geopolitical lesson on the relative importance of British trade versus American annuities.[4]

The Prophet took advantage of this period of expansion to restructure his political world. Most prominently, he dissolved the female councils that had so often acted as a brake to violence and the intentions of the warrior class. Women continued to do much of the labor around town—farming, cutting firewood, cooking—but they no longer had a say in the governing of their new tribe. In some respects, this decision ran counter to Tenskwatawa's declarations ending polygamy. On the other hand, eliminating female councils and their traditional powers of peace strengthened the position of warriors and war chiefs while continuing the political consolidation of Greenville.[5]

The Prophet's own family and sexual life remains vague, and it is difficult to separate history from rumor. *The Colonial History of Vincennes*, written a quarter century after Tenskwatawa's death, claimed that his wife demanded the appellation "Queen" among the Greenville residents, and "possessed an influence over the female portion of the tribe not less potent than her husband's," urging them particularly toward cruelty to whites. John Ruddell (brother of the translator Stephen Ruddell, who actually knew the Prophet) doubted the Prophet's wife had such influence.[6] An 1889 letter claimed the Prophet had several wives and sired a number of children; one of his sons eventually traded under the name "John Prophet."[7]

The age of the embargo marked a great period of expansion for the Prophet; his message and his teachings had achieved some purchase among the Delawares, Shawnees, and Wyandots of the Ohio Valley, but the true "revolution" took place among tribes farther west. White reports from across the Northwest and even beyond claimed that individual Indians and entire villages were siding with the Prophet or making plans to visit him. In Green Bay, the local Ojibwe and Ottawa tribes "adhere firmly to the doctrine of their prophet" and "in their looks and deportment they do not appear to be cordial or friendly."[8] In Michigan, a Saginaw chief, under instructions from the Prophet, refused all money and goods from Americans.[9] In what is now Minnesota, the trader and former Shawnee adoptee John Tanner encountered the teachings of the Prophet and saw several of his Indian friends converted. In Wisconsin, Menominee warriors under the chief Tomah rejected his previous cautions against the Prophet and joined the movement. An Ojibwe village near Chequamegon Bay embraced the Prophet's message and hurled their medicine bags into Lake Superior.[10]

The Kickapoos soon allied with the Prophet, notwithstanding the plaintive letter Harrison had written them, cautioning them not to retract their support for American leadership. "What injury has your father done you?" Harrison wrote. With no apparent sense of irony, he added, "He has always listened to you, and will listen to you still; you will certainly not raise your arm against him." In spite of this plea—or perhaps because of it—the Kickapoo joined the Prophet at Greenville, and arranged for thirteen other tribes to meet with him in 1807, the same year George Blue Jacket also joined. Even the Wyandot, despite their chief Tarhe's general intransigence, sent a delegation to visit the Prophet at his new city. And of course, there were "men among the chippeways ottaways and Poutawatamys," according to Wells, "disattisfued with the conduct of their chief, and appear anxious to follow the example of this Shawnese."[11]

The spread of the Prophet's religion resembled other new religions blossoming in the American soil. Methodists were the most famous; the sect had not formally existed in 1776 but had hundreds of congregations by 1810. Baptists also came into their own in this era as a piece of the American religious bedrock. More radical sects also spread rapidly: Universalists transformed the religious landscape of the Northeast, and the Christian Movement (forerunners of the Churches of Christ) did the same in Ohio and the Appalachians. Like these Protestant Christians with whom he competed, Tenskwatawa taught a proselytizing religion; like the other upstart sects of the early republic, his relied on an extended system of itinerating preachers to spread his message. Beata was probably one such missionary. In Ojibwe country, John Tanner encountered a series of men who brought him the doctrines of the Prophet; like the folkloric American itinerant, they spoke to Tanner one-on-one but also gave longer addresses to crowds at the council houses, explaining doctrines at length. Like the itinerating Methodists, Tenskwatawa's emissaries knew how to make a spiritual hard sell. Tanner wrote that one acolyte claimed "that the preservation of your life, for a single moment, depends on your entire obedience" to the new teaching. They had with them a string, apparently made of "the flesh of the prophet," and asked converts to pull the string through their hands.

Tenskwatawa's best-traveled and most effective apostle was Le Maigouis— the Trout. He was "brother of the princip[a]l Chief at *Arbre Croche*" (in Michigan) and served the Prophet much the way Paul had served the early Church, scurrying from one village to another.[12] In 1807, the Trout journeyed "to Lake Superior to initiate the Savages of that quarter into its mysteries." He traveled to Greenville and then to Michilimackinac, Grand River, Saginaw Bay, Sault Ste. Marie, and Whitefish Bay. Once he was nearly arrested (like Paul) but slipped away at the last moment to give his sermon in the shadow of an American fort.[13]

Le Maigouis intended his speeches for Indians only, but a copy of one came into the hands of the American agent Charles Dunham. The sermon described the vision and transformation of the Prophet, whose teaching would last for three lifetimes, after which the world would be destroyed. The speech also contained strong invectives against whites; Trout emphasized the description of the Americans as the progeny of the Great Serpent and the scum of the waters, "*froth . . . driven into the Woods by a strong east wind.*"[14]

The speech was a religious document: it discussed supernatural origins of the world and humanity's place in it, and it promised rewards for those who followed the correct religious path. Nevertheless, it had elements that would have appealed to Indians and Indian tribes stymied by the embargo and disappointed by American neglect. It told them that God did not want them to raise animals, although corn was fine; it was white agriculture and whites themselves—as well as Indian quiescence toward them—that were to blame for hunger and want. The speech began with an offer of wampum, and it concluded with the Master of Life's directive for all tribes to send two representatives to Greenville for discussions with the Shawnee Prophet. In other words, it was a diplomatic offer as well as a sermon—and it was remarkably effective. "The enclosed *Talk*," Dunham wrote, "has been industriously spread among them" and "seems to have had considerable effect on their minds." And in his discussion with western tribes, Dunham was told that he should not think of getting "*one hand's breadth* of our Lands, for we have not so much to Spare.'" Ominously, Dunham noted, they called him "brother" instead of the usual "father."[15]

The Trout was not the only apostle in the West with a reputation as a troublemaker. The Christian preacher Peter Cartwright, for example, believed in Jesus' sacrificial salvation but not in turning the other cheek; he once chased a "camp rowdy" from a revival with a homemade club.[16] "Crazy" Lorenzo Dow wrote hundreds of pages chronicling his own journeys across the frontier, the South, and both New and Old England; like Cartwright, he watched the exercises at the Cane Ridge revivals of 1800, where Tenskwatawa may also have been an observer. Like the Trout, Dow preached against an older form of his tradition, attacking Calvinist notions that only some of humanity could be saved; like the Trout, he was often chased out of towns and forced to preach on the sly. He, too, fought the Great Serpent: "Satan pursues me from place to place: oh! how can people dispute there being a devil! If they underwent as much as I do with his buffetings, they would dispute it no more."[17] Finally, like the Trout, Dow stopped only where his own "people" were: when traveling through Creek and Chickasaw territory (as Tecumseh would in 1811), he preached only to white audiences. Itinerating preachers aimed for friendly enclaves to preach their message. When they failed—as Cartwright, Dow, and the Trout sometimes did—they were often hounded out of town.

The white government's response to the Prophet's missionary activity was at best anemic and at worst insulting. Dunham responded to the Trout's arrival in his neighborhood by giving a sermon of his own to an assembly of Ojibwes and Ottawas, where he explained what it was the Great Spirit really wanted: "Brothers, the Great Spirit would never tell you, that the American were *not his Children*. He loves the Americans." The Great Spirit—or at least Dunham—had a short memory: "And when the Indians take up the *War Club* or the hatchet against them, he is always on the Americans' side." Dunham also informed the Indians that God preferred agriculture to hunting, that God had never given the Prophet a divine commission, and that Indians had a moral obligation to pay their traders in full, even if they had been cheated by them.[18] Dunham's efforts had, unsurprisingly, little effect.

Harrison decided to put an end to diplomatic niceties. He suggested a more aggressive approach in his address to the General Assembly in 1807, where his certitude about "the agency of a foreign power in producing the discontents among the Indians" came with a more specific warning about "a few individuals are believed to be decidedly hostile."[19] His promises to arrest the white murderers of Indians—promises never fulfilled—were accompanied by a stadial reminder of white superiority: "A powerful nation rendering justice to a petty tribe of savages is a sublime spectacle."

A few weeks later, Harrison wrote to Dearborn suggesting force as a solution. The British were behind it all, he told Dearborn, and the Shawnees, Ottawas, Ojibwes, and Potawatomies probably planned to attack the whites. He also wrote to the government back east that Tenskwatawa was a British "engine" and that "war belts have been passing through all the Tribes from the Gulf of Florida to the Lakes. The Shawnees are the bearers of these belts and they have never been our friends." Without waiting for confirmation from Washington, Harrison sent John Connor to Greenville with an ultimatum: leave peacefully or be forced out by the Americans.[20]

Some of what Harrison had to say in his message to the Greenville Indians employed the same religious emphases as Dunham's ham-handed efforts to speak for the Great Spirit. "The sacred spot where the great council fire was kindled" in 1795, "the very spot where the Great Spirit saw his red and white children encircle themselves with the chain of friendship—that place has been selected for dark and bloody councils." Harrison described the treaties of Wayne's time as wise and godly, but now, Harrison said, the Indians were listening to a "fool who speaks not the words of the Great Spirit, but those of the devil and of the British agents." Harrison condemned the Prophet as an impostor and advised the Indians to "let him go to the lakes; he can hear the British more distinctly."[21]

Harrison clearly thought he had issued an ultimatum, "requiring an immediate removal of the Impostor from our [American] Territory, and the dispersion of the Warriors he had collected around him." Those at least were his words in a letter to Dearborn written after Connor had left for Greenville. But the message from Harrison to the Greenville Indians did not actually contain such specific language. It only declared that "the white settlers near you" wished them to send away the Prophet. Harrison does not seem to have noticed the difference. Tenskwatawa did.[22]

Tenskwatawa received Connor, heard the talk, and offered a diplomatic masterstroke in response. Since Harrison's message (intentionally or not) failed to include the direct order that Harrison wrote to Dearborn, the Prophet saw no need to respond directly to the ultimatum. He neither denied nor acquiesced to Harrison's authority; he merely told the governor that he had been misinformed. "I never had a word with the British, and I never sent for any Indians. They came here themselves to listen, and hear the words of the Great Spirit." Then Tenskwatawa gave Harrison a gentle rebuke ("I wish you would not listen any more to the voice of bad birds") and magnanimously offered a gesture of peace: if they heard of any violence or British-inspired revolts, "we will rather try to stop any such proceedings than encourage them."[23]

The response reinforced Tenskwatawa's authority and his right to be in Greenville, while never expressly defying Harrison; the Prophet had found a diplomatic way to thwart Harrison while simultaneously forcing the governor into the position of aggressor should violence break out. Tenskwatawa was not entirely honest in his response—certainly his acolytes in the Northwest *had* invited Indians to visit Greenville—but as an assertion of strength, Harrison's ultimatum failed.

President Jefferson didn't think much of Harrison's bombast, either. Clearly, the governor had forgotten the need to "cultivate their love." Jefferson had already instructed Secretary of War Dearborn to issue the western governors their marching orders: Americans need to "confirm our friends with redoubled acts of justice and favor, and endeavour to draw over the individuals indisposed to us." The governors might call out the militia, but no more.[24] The United States had enough security concerns without opening a second front. Harrison in particular received orders to reverse course; he was to end his aggressive stance and instead "gain over the prophet, who is no doubt a scoundrel and only needs his price."[25]

Harrison acquiesced to a pacific course, although reluctantly and not solely based on Jefferson's orders. When Connor returned with Tenskwatawa's reply, he informed Harrison that hundreds more warriors than anticipated had arrived at Greenville "and that a larger body were hourly expected." In a prescient moment, Harrison realized that any military effort to remove the Prophet entailed too many political risks. The Indians, he wrote, would defend Tenskwatawa "with all their force," and an unsuccessful attempt to drive them off "would no doubt confirm his influence."[26] A strike against Greenville would cost American lives and strengthen the Prophet's following. Ironically, when an almost identical situation arose in 1811, Harrison either ignored or had forgotten his own advice.

But in 1807, Jefferson and Harrison also could not risk a conflict at Greenville because of a developing headache in Detroit. Connecticut-born William Hull had received Jefferson's appointment as governor of Michigan and had a long career of mismanagement ahead of him. In the late summer and autumn of 1807, Hull was busily trying to achieve in Michigan what Harrison had done in Indiana: gain title to large swaths of Indian territory through questionable means. Jefferson worried about Hull's proposed treaty, writing, "It is an unlucky time for Governor Hull to press the purchase of our lands." Not only was it a "point on which the Indians feel very sore," as Jefferson observed, but if war broke out, the lands could not be settled for years anyway, and if peace prevailed, the government would get land on better terms once the

British threat was neutralized. If Hull was going to antagonize the tribes in Michigan, Jefferson could not have Harrison start a war in Ohio.

Hull did antagonize the tribes in Michigan, as it happened, and he did it in spectacular fashion. He pushed through the treaty, despite Jefferson's reticence, British opposition, and, in his opinion, the "influence of the Prophet."[27] The treaty ceded thousands of acres in Michigan and northwest Ohio. A selection of Indian leaders signed it in November, and Hull sent it to the Senate for approval, complete with a series of slavish "Indian" speeches praising U.S. wisdom and the beneficence of land treaties.

Those speeches were forged. Some of the signatures were as well. If Harrison had bent the rules of protocol and ignored Indian claims that did not originate with his allies, Hull had taken the next logical step and simply lied. Alexander McKee, the Canadian trader, examined the treaty and found that several of the chiefs who had "signed" could not have been in Detroit when the treaty was drawn up. "One of the Chiefs," McKee wrote, "reported to have delivered the first speech, very fortunately came in this morning, to whom I read the said speech who positively deny'd the whole."[28] Another signatory, Little Cedar, affixed his name to the document with the understanding that if he signed, the Americans would cancel the manhunt for his son, who had escaped from prison.[29]

The Treaty of Detroit gave northwestern tribes even less reason to support American accommodation. Harrison blamed the British for the trouble, "using the treaties which have been made as a pretext," but the Indians had long been aware of irregularities in American treaty making—in part thanks to Harrison's own efforts.[30]

Tenskwatawa again proved himself to be the only Indian leader in the Northwest to defy the Americans successfully. Harrison heard that an unnamed tribe had crossed into Indiana for the specific purpose of being "adopted into the tribe of the Shawnees."[31] In February, emissaries from the Sac and Fox tribes arrived at Wapakoneta to convince Black Hoof (or at least the warriors under him) of the rightness and righteousness of the Prophet's cause.[32] The Prophet sent word that he wanted to meet with the Iowas, Winnebagoes, and Menominees.[33] One party of Indians arrived at Greenville and "declared it to be the intention of their tribe to support the prophet against all his enemies."[34]

Harrison very much wanted to be one of those enemies. While he never struck at Greenville (and never really made plans to), he continually informed his correspondents that Indians were up to no good. In September he banned arms and ammunition sales to all Indians, including friendly and neutral tribes. He warned the General Assembly of "the probability that at no very distant period we Shall be involved in Hostilities with Some of the Indian tribes." In such a case, Harrison would not follow Jeffersonian protocol: "fear not love will restrain them."[35]

Perhaps to take his mind off his frustrations with the Prophet, Harrison redoubled his efforts to root out traitors among the whites and extinguish freedom among the blacks. He persuaded the Indiana legislature—which he had helped pick—to pass a resolution declaring, "It is not a question of liberty or Slavery. Slavery now exists in the United States and in this Territory. It was the crime of England and their misfortune." Slaves could now be held in Indiana until they had reached the age of thirty-five for males or thirty-two for females.[36] At the same time, he fell back on his old Federalist training, accusing the French citizens of Vincennes of planning an uprising. Harrison's attacks were so vituperative that a group claiming to be "the French citizens of Vincennes" published a notice in the *Sun* saying that they "perceive with great surprise and indignation that there appears to exist in the mind of the Governor suspicions of our Patriotism and Fidelity to The United States."[37] Forced to explain himself, Harrison blamed the British again, this time for misleading the "French citizens" into ever thinking their governor would suspect them. Both decisions aided Harrison's political enemies, who were setting up to make 1808 the year of their first real victories against him. Tenskwatawa, meanwhile, had largely obviated his opposition by the spring of 1808. He had become the preeminent Indian political leader in the Northwest. Greenville was a success.

Yet Tenskwatawa's purpose was not merely political; he was to listen to the Master of Life in all things, and in the spring of 1808 the Prophet received instructions from the Master of Life that would radically alter American geopolitics, reverse the political alignments of Governor Harrison and the Prophet, and bring the two men face-to-face for the first time. The Great Spirit had commanded that a new city be built, a city of Native American origin, design, and rule, from which a new cultural and political dynasty might be forged. The only trouble was that this new city would be located in the nominal jurisdiction of William Henry Harrison. The governor and the Prophet were about to be neighbors.

The Nation of Prophetstown

AMONG THE FIRST to oppose Tenskwatawa's move were the accommodationist Indians. In April 1808, Little Turtle declared, on behalf of a council of Indians including the Miami and Delaware tribes, that "they had sufficient Evidence before them that the Shawnese prophet had determined to settle low down on the Wabash and Draw all the western Indians together and commence war." "Low down on the Wabash" was also land claimed by Little Turtle's Miamis. That was not a problem for Tenskwatawa, who believed all Indians were one tribe and owned land in common, but Little Turtle had no intention of recognizing Tenskwatawa's right to live there. On the journey from Ohio to the Wabash, Little Turtle and his men confronted Tenskwatawa and his followers—in their canoes—on the Mississinewa River.[1]

The Turtle informed the Prophet of his impromptu council's decision not to let him settle in Indiana. The Prophet dismissed the idea, saying "his plans had been layed by all the Indians in america and had be[en] san[c]tioned by the Great spirit. . . . He would go on and nothing could stop him." If that was a threat, it was the only one Tenskwatawa issued. Little Turtle, lacking a clear mandate or substantial military force, backed down. The Prophet's canoes continued on their western course.[2]

The move to Indiana remains something of a mystery. The Prophet had a committed following in Ohio and had managed to fend off threats to his person and his movement. Nonetheless, the new city, Prophetstown, did offer some advantages: it was closer to the Prophet's base of support (the Shawnee leadership in Ohio had not much warmed to his message, but the western Ojibwes and Potawatomies had), it put him closer to allies in Canada, and it had excellent agricultural prospects. Nonetheless, Greenville seemed to be working, so why leave?[3]

On this point, the Prophet and his followers were clear: the Master of Life had demanded it. The Prophet simply said that he "had been directed by the Great Spirit to assemble all the Indians that he could collect, & that he would continue to do so."[4] Tecumseh gave a similar explanation: "The great Spirit above has appointed this place for us to light our fires and here we shall remain."[5] Tecumseh had used much the same logic regarding Greenville,

when he told an emissary from Ohio governor Thomas Kirker that the
Prophet had settled Greenville "because it was revealed to him."[6]

Religion was the primary motivation in moving, but Prophetstown had
political advantages as well. The city was closer to the western tribes attracted
to his message of resistance, which would make pilgrimages (and military
defense, if necessary) easier.[7] Moreover, if the Prophet truly meant to have a
pan-Indian city as his capital, perhaps it would not do to be surrounded by
the Americanizing Indians under Black Hoof. Throughout history, new
cities—Constantinople, St. Petersburg, Washington—have provided rulers
and peoples with opportunities to enact their version of social and religious
truth in layout, architecture, and structure. And it was in Prophetstown—
both rhetorically and structurally—that the Prophet began building his pan-
Indian future.

Tenskwatawa placed his new city at the confluence of the Wabash and a
river known to local Indians as "Kithtapaconnoeu." Whites called it Tippecanoe. The site was both highly defensible (it could only be approached from
the south or west) and highly commercial (the only way to transport goods
across the West was by water).[8] "It is impossible," Harrison later observed,
"that a more favorable location could have been chosen." Tenskwatawa's followers cut down the trees surrounding the town, apparently to deny any
approaching forces the benefit of cover. Beyond the city lay thickets and
swamps—difficult terrain for white armies to negotiate. North of the city
they left the forest as it was, for the harvesting of game. The rivers provided
fish, and an adjoining prairie provided crops for cultivation. Two packed
roads, each three feet wide, passed out of the town along the rivers—"the
Appian Way," as a traveler later described it, "of this ancient western capital."[9]

The lands of Prophetstown already had a past life as a site of Indian defiance of whites. In 1742, at the Indian town of "Kitepikano," the Miami rulers
fitted two captured Frenchmen with slave collars and made the captives dance
for their amusement.[10] By the 1790s, the area south of the Tippecanoe had
villages of Miamis, Potawatomies, Kickapoos, and Frenchmen; during the
frontier wars of St. Clair, Americans put the villages to the torch. Once again,
Tenskwatawa would center his empire on a site associated with a previous
U.S. incursion.[11]

Unlike other Indian towns, Tenskwatawa's was laid out in rows; it featured
both European-style dwellings and wigwams, plus a large storehouse.[12] Its villages and cornfields stretched for a mile, according to one witness.[13] Like
Greenville before it, the town was dominated by a large central structure
called the House of the Stranger, a symbol of Tenskwatawa's new pan-Indian

nation, where any Indian would be welcomed and invited to stay.[14] Harrison eventually pegged the population at three thousand men, including a nearby Wea village. Assessing historical populations without a census is tricky work, but if Harrison was correct, Prophetstown and its surrounding areas could have had an overall population of perhaps six thousand. Not a large city on the East Coast—though it would have made the list of the top twenty-five American cities overall in 1810—but bigger than every white settlement on the northwest frontier.[15] Most important, it was growing. Within two years, Tenskwatawa had built a town bigger than Pittsburgh, Cincinnati, and Lexington. With the exception of New Orleans, the largest city in America west of the Appalachians was Native American.[16]

It was at Prophetstown that Tenskwatawa began to articulate his political vision in its clearest terms. What had been assumed or suggested by his teachings at Greenville became explicit when the Prophet addressed The Earth, an Eel River chief, in 1808. According to The Earth, it was in 1808 that the Prophet explicitly called out the civil chiefs for collusion with the Americans—they had "abandoned the Interests of their respective nation[s] and sold all the Indians land to the united states." Land sales, Tenskwatawa continued, meant subjugation, and he specifically pointed to Black Hoof. He even told The Earth that "the President intended [on] making women of the Indians" but that once they united, "they would be respected by the President as men."[17] The Prophet's admonitions on communal land ownership and resistance to Western-style agriculture had been ignored in Ohio; in Prophetstown, he would have an opportunity to show how they could work in practice. Perhaps as a further sign of a shift in emphasis, it was at this time that the Prophet lost his old sobriquet, "Lalawauthika," and began to refer to himself as Tenskwatawa, "the Open Door."

Historians hesitate before assigning the term "nation-state" to Indian country and Indian towns. In maps, as noted earlier, these regions often do not receive the bold borders and colors reserved for independent nations, nor the star by which a textbook denotes a capital. Earlier historians simply dismissed the idea that Indians had civilization; their modern descendants have rectified that by undermining the myth of Indians as savage or nomadic. Yet although historians recognize Native America's cultural equality with white groups, there is (legitimate) concern as to whether Native America in the eighteenth and nineteenth century constituted a modern state. The friable politics of Indian communities of Ohio and the Great Lakes lacked a recognized central authority with monopolies on legitimate use of force; what bureaucratic structures existed were at best creations of Indian-U.S.

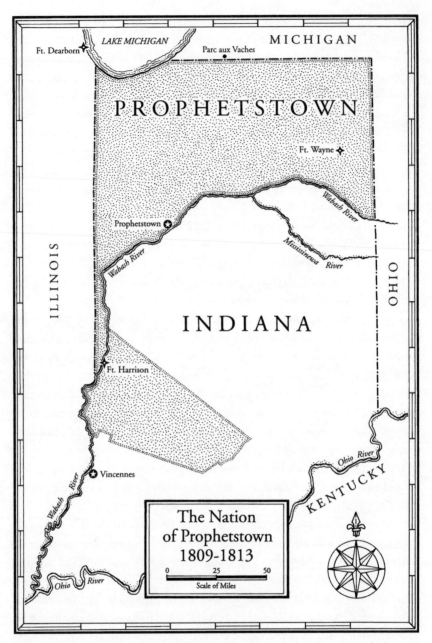

In this cartographer's rendition, Prophetstown is imagined as a city-state, with the 1809 Fort Wayne Treaty lands forming its border with the United States.

collaboration. Few regions could claim definite borders. Each of these circumstances makes it difficult to use the term "state" in discussing Indian country (although in fairness, the litany of conditions for statehood itself derives from the study of European civilizations and their descendants).

Therein lies the dream and the achievement of Prophetstown: Tenskwatawa sought to construct an Indian city-state possessing more "Western" political structures, based on religious teachings that combined the novel and the traditional. At least, that was the conclusion of Indian agent John Johnston; Tecumseh (and his "brawling, mischievous" brother) "aimed at the independence of his people by a nation of all the Indians, North and South."[18] Tenskwatawa's Prophetstown exhibited many of the characteristics of an independent state—diplomats, emissaries, borders, a national religion, a military. The language of the early American republic might lead us to expect this situation; constitutionally, Native American tribes were (and remain) independent nations. Prophetstown functioned independently of U.S. jurisdiction, with its own codes and legal system. The United States even made a strike against it in 1811. While it endured, it was a city-state.

Could it have survived longer than it did? Could a semi-autonomous or fully independent Indian state have existed side by side with the United States in the nineteenth century? While white Americans outnumbered the Indians of the Northwest Territory, this imbalance would not necessarily have guaranteed military victory; in 1812 Canada had a population not much larger than that of the Indians west of the Ohio, and the United States failed to capture Canada. Indeed, at the very moment of Prophetstown's founding, the Comanches ruled what is now the American Southwest, in defiance of a much larger Spanish force. Long-term independence of an Indian "state" would be a long shot—but history is full of long shots that made it. That possibility, of a theocratic and egalitarian Indian state on the Great Lakes, animated Tenskwatawa's followers and made their movement more—and more dangerous—than a fool's errand.[19]

A clear, defensible border was first on Tenskwatawa's list. It was also a task more easily completed in Harrison's Indiana than in Ohio. As the Prophet told Little Turtle, if the Indians were united at Prophetstown, they would "be able to watch the Boundry Line between the Indians and white people." Two years later, Tecumseh used the same terms to describe what had occurred at Prophetstown: "Warriors now manage the affairs of our Nation; and we sit at or near, the Borders where the contest will begin."[20] Moreover, even though whites constantly complained of the flexibility of Indian borders, Tenskwatawa had a specific border in mind, since he intended to defend all the lands theoretically sold under the Treaty of Fort Wayne, and he declared as much in negotiations with Harrison: "The old boundary line should continue, and that the crossing would be attended with bad consequences."[21]

Tenskwatawa sought to rework Indian economics as well. When confronted by Little Turtle, he expounded a vision of Indian life free from bitter exchanges at the hands of traders, and free as well from the constraints imposed by the embargo, a world where "a shirt would cost no more than a raccoon skin—and a Blanket a Deer skin." Such utopian ideals were indicative of the independent course Tenskwatawa intended for Prophetstown, though it does not appear that he ever implemented this kind of price control. He did, however, attempt to make the city self-sufficient, at least from Americans. Tenskwatawa seems to have increased the amount of land under cultivation while refusing American agricultural aid.[22] Several years after Tippecanoe, George Winter reported finding the ruins of a blacksmith shop at Prophetstown.[23] Ash and slag remains discovered at the Prophetstown archaeological site support Winter's observations. That suggests that Tenskwatawa and his followers were intent on self-sufficiency. Americans often boasted of their ability to produce guns and powder, and more than once Harrison pointed to that ability as an unchanging truth that guaranteed white superiority. A Prophetstown blacksmithing operation, combined with the mining operations among the Sacs and Foxes, suggests at least an attempt to develop an indigenous production facility.[24]

Recent archaeological excavations at likely sites for Prophetstown also reveal a surprising profusion of European goods: glass bottles, kettles, creamware, porcelain.[25] Tenskwatawa appears to have kept up at least some commerce despite the embargo. Yet the presence of such European goods seems odd for a town founded on the very principle of separation from whites. Some of these goods, of course, may date from previous occupations, but the Prophet did allow exceptions to his rules.[26] Firearms, for example, were required in warfare but discouraged for hunting. The presence of such goods suggests that the Prophet made domestic exceptions as well—or encouraged illicit trade with Canada—as he tried to build up his state. It may also suggest that not everyone at Prophetstown followed the Prophet's dictates.

Diplomacy had been a hallmark of almost all Native American nations since the Revolution, and it would take a great deal of it to prevent violence between Vincennes and Prophetstown. When Tenskwatawa settled his new town, he identified Harrison as one of the officials poisoning the Indian way of life. There were several men who were "always persuading the Indians to sell their Land and by these means they made them[selves] great men by cheating the Indians," namely, "the man at vincennes the one at Fort wayne and the one at Detroit" (Harrison, Wells, Hull). The president did not want Indian land sold, the Prophet declared, and was opposed by this cadre, for they well knew that when the Indians were united in their resolve, "they would no longer be able to buy the Indians lands." In this Tenskwatawa was certainly wrong: aside from the exception made in 1807–8, the president desired the purchase of land.[27]

Harrison reciprocated Tenskwatawa's chill. "The Shawnese Imposter has acquired such an ascendancy over the minds of the Indians that there can be little doubt of their pursuing any course which he may dictate to them," he wrote to Dearborn in May 1808. Worse, the Prophet's removal had confirmed his transition, in Harrison's mind, from religious to political power. Although Indians "may not be converted to his divine mission," he wrote, "they are under the greatest apprehension of his temporal power." The new city was also far distant from the Delawares and other tribes Harrison considered pliable, thus making it more difficult to keep tabs on the Prophet's activities. Harrison concluded that the Prophet's "combination of Religion and warlike exercises" continued to pose a threat to the country, and he requested that "the President would think himself authorized to have him [Tenskwatawa] seized and conveyed to the interior of the United States until the present appearance of war is removed."[28]

Jefferson, however, was in no mood to grant Harrison's request. Things had, if possible, gotten worse for the president in the year since the *Chesapeake* incident. The embargo had failed to cow Britain, though it had poisoned Jefferson's own party, and despite indicting Burr multiple times, no jury ever handed down a conviction. The administration took a wary official line: Harrison "ought not to show any improper anxiety for cultivating peace with those Indians, who may have hostile views," but neither was he to move against them. American diplomacy would, according to Secretary of War Dearborn, "depend on their own conduct." The United States would respond should any of the tribes ally with Britain in a war—but not before.[29]

The executive branch's instructions came at a good time for Tenskwatawa. The Prophet had major plans for his new city, but he had not counted on the exigencies of the weather. Food supplies had been strained at Greenville, where the arrival of thousands of followers necessitated severe rationing; Richard McNemar and the Shakers saw more than thirty Indians forced to split the meat from a single turkey. When John Connor reached Prophetstown that spring, he found them "living on nothing but meat and roots." Tenskwatawa's enemies took the famine as evidence of the Prophet's rank incompetence. Unfortunately, later biographers followed suit.[30] Such conclusions, however, assume that because Greenville possessed an enthusiastic nativist religion and a food shortage, the two were necessarily related. In fact, anecdotal evidence suggests that whites also faced shortages in those years. In 1806 a "tremendous drought" struck the Northwest, and at the White River mission, "large streams were entirely dry. Many people have to get their drinking water 2 miles away and drive their cattle still farther."[31] In May 1807 (around the same time the Shakers saw famine in Greenville), Charles Dunham at Michilimackinac reported, "*We are out of provisions . . . There is not an oz. of bread or flour on this Island.*"[32] Moreover, Indian tribes (and whites) were suffering in 1807 and 1808 from lack of supplies, thanks to the embargo.[33] In some ways, therefore, the famine may be more Jefferson's fault than Tenskwatawa's, and the decision to move to an area of lower population density (i.e., Prophetstown) was perhaps a sign of political wisdom rather than ignorance.

Whatever the cause, the food shortage was real enough. Tenskwatawa confirmed that "in consequence of our removal, we are in great distress."[34] Some members of the Ottawa and Ojibwe tribes blamed the Prophet both for shortages and for the lack of success in their war on the Osages. The Prophet, however, adapted quickly to his new situation, and in a deft display of leadership he turned a developing threat into a source of aid.

The threat came from Harrison, who continued to monitor the Prophet. Tenskwatawa was, after all, now living in the murky territory that technically belonged both to the United States and to Little Turtle's Miamis (and on land Tenskwatawa claimed for his own). Although Jefferson urged restraint, Harrison took reports of Indian horse rustling as an opportunity to rattle sabers. In June, he sent John Connor to visit the Prophet again and demand the return of stolen horses. (When caught with the horses, the supposed culprits explained that they "found them.")[35]

The last time Harrison challenged him, in 1807, the Prophet had avoided apologies but offered condolences for the rumors that "bad birds" had brought to Harrison. In Ohio, however, the Prophet had had little need for white allies. Things had changed—he was now in Harrison's nominal territory. Shortages strapped his Prophetstown project. He had the option of allying with the British; Colonel William Claus invited the Shawnee to a secret meeting at Amherstburg, Canada, in March, where Claus indicated that if a war came, the Indians could "regain the Country taken from you by the Americans."[36]

Tenskwatawa passed on Claus' offer—an important rejoinder to those who later dismissed him as a mere British puppet or a bloodthirsty, war-prone fanatic. Given the choice of a martial alliance with the British or seeking amity with the hated Harrison, Tenskwatawa chose to seek peace with the governor. The British offered a future solution, but a truce with Harrison—or at least an end to the standoff—offered an immediate possibility of solving all these problems at once.

Therefore, Tenskwatawa decided to risk it—on *his* terms. Once again he insisted to Harrison that the governor had heard only rumors ("the bad reports you have heard of me are all false"). More important, he reassured Harrison that "it was never my intention to lift up my hand against the Americans" but instead intended "to follow the advice of the Great Spirit, who has told us that our former conduct is not right" and "to live in peace upon the land he has given us." The statement was a deft piece of diplomatic language, simultaneously asserting benign intentions and a religious right to the land. Tenskwatawa had no intention of mimicking what he considered the pusillanimous language of the treaty chiefs. He was not going to beg.[37]

In that spirit, Tenskwatawa simply told Harrison that they should have a summit. "I am now very much engaged in making my new settlement," he told the governor, "but as soon as it is completed I will pay you a visit." To ensure that Harrison would not think the move a military feint, Tenskwatawa sent ahead to Vincennes a contingent of women and children as human collateral. He suggested that Harrison feed these noncombatants—thereby alleviating some of the shortages at the same time. He also offered some of his most conciliatory language yet: "It is my determination to obey the voice of the great spirit and live in peace with you and your people." And then, in contrast to earlier sermons by the Trout and others about Americans rising from the scum of the ocean, Tenskwatawa added, "This is what the Great Spirit has told us repeatedly. We are all made by him, although we differ a little in colour."[38]

Harrison found the speech "pacific and conciliatory." He offered a terse reply in which he admitted "that I have heard a very bad report of you . . . that you are endeavoring to alienate the minds of Indians, from the great Father, the President of the 17 fires, and once more bring them under the influence of the British." (The "17 fires" were, of course, the states in the American union.) Such a choice would lead, Harrison warned, "to certain misery and ruin," for the United States "wants the aid of no power on earth." Then—again without any apparent sense of irony—Harrison declared that Americans relied on their "own strength and the favor of the great spirit who always takes the side of the injured."[39]

In the end, Harrison had little choice but to accept the Prophet's unilateral declaration of a summit. He had good reason to be wary: the Prophet had sent his brother to Canada for meetings and provisions as recently as May, in one of the first times that officials took notice of Tecumseh—though they still referred to him merely as "the Prophet's Brother."[40] Yet if both Jefferson and Tenskwatawa wanted peace, Harrison could hardly instigate a war. Accepting Tenskwatawa's "solemn assurances," Harrison prepared for the arrival of the Prophet. The time was right for an unlikely summit and an even more unlikely alliance.

They met at Vincennes in August 1808. Despite his hostilities, his fears, and his objections to the Prophet's proclivity for witch hunting, Harrison ended up rather liking the Shawnee holy man. Tenskwatawa opened with a joke: "Father, I heard you intended to hang me." He proceeded to blame any bad blood or lingering rumors on William Wells, a thorn in both men's sides. Tenskwatawa stressed his reform program, mentioning specifically his desire to keep alcohol out of Prophetstown. Harrison invited the Prophet to stay on in Vincennes for a few weeks.[41]

They talked about religion. Harrison finally witnessed Tenskwatawa's preaching and came away amazed by the "art and address by which he manages the Indians." Tenskwatawa spoke to Harrison about the Great Spirit's plan for "peace and friendship" between peoples, and Harrison returned the favor, speaking of his own beliefs. He explained American Christianity in a very deist way: "The mild religion which we possess will not permit us to use any other means than argument and reason to induce others to adopt our opinions." As for religious practice, "it is an inviolable rule with the 17 fires to permit every man to worship the great spirit in the manner he may think best."[42]

This cheerful exchange continued through the summer, even when Tenskwatawa had to remind Harrison (politely) that the governor could deal only with *him*, as there were no other tribes: "Those Indians were once different people. They are now one. They are all determined to practice what I have communicated to them that has come immediately from the Great Spirit through me." Perhaps Tenskwatawa was taking Harrison at his word, for if, as the governor suggested, everyone should worship the Great Spirit as they saw fit, Tenskwatawa's rule should be recognized. Harrison at least tacitly seemed to agree; he wrote to Secretary Dearborn, "I am inclined to think that the influence which the Prophet has acquired will prove rather advantageous than otherwise to the United States." As a token of their new relationship, Harrison agreed to send funds to Prophetstown to procure much-needed provisions.[43] Tenskwatawa returned the favor; when the American forces began to build Fort Dearborn in Winnebago country that September, it was the Prophet who advised the tribe against going to war.[44] When the Winnebago and Iowa tribes came to blows in April 1809, the *Western Sun* assured its readers, "We are authorized by Governor Harrison, explicitly to state, that he has every reason to believe that the tribes of the Wabash continue firm and unshaken in their attachment to the United States."[45] Incredibly, the Americans and the Prophet were now allies.

Détente worked well for the Prophet. Having secured supplies, he began extending his political program at Prophetstown by intensifying the restrictions on women beyond the abolition of the female councils. He limited the number of wives one man could have, advocated the beating of wives for laziness or disobedience (formerly a banned practice), encouraged the timely marriage of single men, and sought the return of women married to whites to his community—by force, if necessary.

Harrison's remaking of Indiana, by contrast, seemed to be disintegrating. His handpicked representative from Clark County, Davis Floyd, had been implicated and arrested in the Burr conspiracy. Indicted in June 1807, Floyd confessed that all the purchases he had made for Burr and Wilkinson had been done under false pretenses; he had thought he was buying items for the United States. Floyd was convicted and sentenced to three hours in jail and a ten-dollar fine. When he was released, the Indiana legislature promptly elected him state clerk. He was, after all, the governor's man. The citizenry exploded. The remonstrances to Congress and editorials in the *Vincennes Sun* did little to change the situation, but the scandal added momentum to the anti-Harrison forces gathering under an abolitionist named John Badollet and the opportunistic Jonathan Jennings. Harrison's challengers prepared legal cases against the governor's rule and his slavery proclamations. In 1808, the governor needed all the allies he could find—even the defiant, witch-hunting Prophet.

By December 1808, it appeared that the chief American saber-rattler had become an advocate for Jefferson's policy of peacekeeping. Perhaps because of the rosier relationship Harrison now enjoyed with the Prophet, the American government saw no more reason to fund Black Hoof's homesteading experiments; funding was revoked and Tenskwatawa won another (inadvertent) victory over his foes. If the story had ended in 1808, it would have been the tale of a successful negotiation of peace on the frontier. It did not end up that way, of course, because to Harrison, peace meant something different than it did to Tenskwatawa. For Harrison, a break in the tension was the ideal opportunity to negotiate for more Indian land. His effort to do so in 1809 would undo all he had worked for the previous summer.

12

The Bargain

ON FEBRUARY 3, 1809, the opposition completed its humiliation of Harrison. Undoubtedly helped along by the murder of Rice Jones two months previously, the cause of pro-independence western counties convinced Congress to split the Indiana territory. The new territory of Illinois was named after one of the Native American groups in the territory. Folk wisdom sometimes claims the word means "tribe of superior men," but in fact the word is a Francophone version of a Miami appellation filtered through the Ojibwe language—an appropriate etymology for the layers of culture and power in the Old Northwest.[1]

Separation potentially scuttled Harrison's hopes of moving forward in his political career. In 1810 would come the census, and if Indiana had a population equal to half that of the least populous state, it could itself apply for statehood and make Harrison a proper governor. The separation of Illinois made that goal much more difficult.

The Illinois divorce did the most damage, but plenty of other things had gone wrong in Harrison's political world. In May 1809, the anti-slavery advocate Jonathan Jennings won a three-way race for delegate to Congress. Harrison and his allies immediately denounced the elections as fraudulent and impugned Jennings as a "pitiful Coward." The courts took a peremptory look at the accusations, but little came of it. After all, Harrison did not possess a sterling record on electioneering himself, and as his grip slackened at the end of the decade he intensified his own questionable methods. In 1810, a militia captain ordered the troops under his command into "a Solid Column" and commanded them to keep silent while "a friend to Govr. Harrison" gave a political speech to the men, "in opposition to their feelings."[2]

Indiana politics had soured on Harrison. The embargo continued to foul the economy. Harrison had to plead ignorance when his former attorney general was accused of taking bribes.[3] The war between the Osages and the tribes east of the Mississippi failed to resolve itself, despite the efforts of Harrison and Jefferson to broker a compromise. The intended territorial institution of higher learning, Vincennes University, had almost no money, and efforts by its trustees to raise funds through a lottery failed. The lottery—run by Harrison—offered its tickets on credit; purchasers could come to Vincennes and pay what they owed *after* the drawing. "These lenient terms," the trustees wrote in retrospect, "have not it is believed produced any beneficial results."[4]

Despite his troubles as a politician and his failings as a college president, Harrison retained at least one post in which he had the final say: minister plenipotentiary to the Indians. He still stood to gain by wringing lands out of the tribes. It offered Harrison a way out, personally and politically. "Without such further purchase," Harrison later admitted, "Indiana cannot for many years become a member of the Union, and I am heartily tired of living in a territory."[5]

Tenskwatawa, meanwhile, scored two major political victories. In April 1809, William Wells was at last fired from his government position.[6] That was followed by the ultimate failure of the accommodationists at Wapakoneta: the Quaker agent, William Kirk, was sent packing by the government. Despite progress at Black Hoof's village, there were "base slanders" against Kirk, according to John Johnston, including the rumor "of his having contracted a disease the of[f]spring of vice."[7] Black Hoof and other accommodationist chiefs wrote to Dearborn and Madison, mentioning in particular that "our young men are always very glad to have our friend [Kirk] working with them." Dearborn ignored Black Hoof's veiled plea for continued help in controlling his warrior class.[8] The secretary concluded that Kirk's work was unsatisfactory, and so he effectively abandoned Black Hoof.[9]

Tenskwatawa sent numerous reassurances to Vincennes about his peaceful intentions, resulting in some improvements in public relations with the white population. A May headline in the *Western Sun* of Vincennes announced, "All Prospect of an Indian War at an End."[10] Enemies defeated, and still in power: it would have been a successful year if Tenskwatawa had been a political official.

But the Prophet's office involved more than mere political powers, and therefore Tenskwatawa had a year almost as bad as Harrison's. Prophetstown had survived with the aid from Harrison, but the fierce winter of 1808–9 exacted a gruesome toll on the city nevertheless. At Fort Wayne, snow three feet deep "has ocationed the distruction of nearly all the cows and Horses among the Indians—they have not been able to Hunt and have consumed all the corn they raised last season," and the Native Americans now faced the prospect of starvation.[11] The "uncommon Weather" continued "verry Cold and wet all the Growing Part of the Season What there was But Little Raised" all that summer. "This Country never was so poor and Harrased Since it was

Settled as it is now," complained one Illinois farmer.[12] Mohawks and other Shawnee tribes appealed to the Canadian British for famine relief, but the Canadians had little to give.[13]

American officials assumed that discontent with the Prophet stemmed from this inability to control the evils of winter. Wells—before he was fired—wrote that the Prophetstown winter was so bad that "the Indians have abandoned the prophet."[14] Then again, Wells had made the exact same declaration almost a year before, when he claimed "the Indians of this country are in a perfect state of starvation at this time. This has been [occasioned] by their neglecting their farms and attending the Shawnese prophet last year."[15] William Clark, territorial governor of Louisiana, reported exactly the opposite: the Prophet had *gained* in strength over the winter and was "attempting to seduce" the Kickapoo and Sac tribes living along the Mississippi and Illinois Rivers.[16]

Harrison vacillated, altering policy based on whatever contradictory information came to hand. On April 18, 1809, he wrote to the War Department to express his fears that "those on the Wabash who adhere to the Shawnese Prophet" intended to "fall upon our settlements."[17] Then on April 26, he wrote, "I have received information which has in a great measure dissipated all my anxiety"[18] On May 3, he corrected himself again: "The information which I have received since my letter of the 26 ult. was written is entirely contradictory to that which I then detailed."[19] On May 16, he wrote instead that "there no longer exists the least probability of a rupture with any of the Indian tribes of this frontier."[20]

It is always difficult (and historically problematic) to view Prophetstown from the standpoint of Vincennes. For the summer of 1809, however, the Native American sources are nearly silent. In part, this absence of documentation may derive from a brushfire war between the Ottawas, the Ojibwes, and the Prophet's forces; Michigan's Hull reported breathlessly in June that the former two tribes "were preparing to make an expedition" against Prophetstown, seeking vengeance for those who had died on pilgrimages to the Prophet in former years. Hull tried to calm the situation by lecturing the Ojibwes and Ottawas on the virtues of accommodationism; after all, if they had "attended to their agriculture," he told them, "they would not have sustained the injuries they now complain of." That did not work, so Hull took the radical step of placing the Prophet under U.S. protection.[21]

Placing a man who thought the whites were the spawn of the Great Serpent under American protection was not as radical as it might at first seem. The Prophet had, after all, settled into a kind of truce with the Americans, and it was an established policy of territorial governors to prevent intertribal conflict (a policy that previously had favored the Prophet's movement in a very different way). Hull's interdiction perhaps derived from a desire to avoid frontier violence that might deter white emigrants, rather than from any favoritism toward the Prophet.

The Prophet was probably not in any danger, in any case; once again, Hull was a little slow on the uptake. Harrison was more suspicious. As early as April, Harrison had heard the story that the Ojibwes and Ottawas intended to attack the Prophet, but he dismissed it as a British stratagem.[22] While Hull worried about a supposed assassination of one of the Prophet's followers, Harrison discovered that the victim had actually died a natural death and then been "tomahawked and scalped by some of the Prophet's party to carry on the deception and prevent us from taking the alarm at the force he is collecting and which he pretends is to protect him against the Chippewas and Ottawas."[23]

Harrison's concerns seem hardly less conspiratorial than those of Wells, but both Harrison and John Johnston—Wells' replacement at Fort Wayne—opted to investigate the situation by talking to Tenskwatawa. Johnston spent four days in council with the Prophet at Fort Wayne. Tenskwatawa "denied in the most solemn manner, having any views inimical to our peace or welfare." He blamed Wells and Little Turtle for starting the rumors. Johnston interviewed Indians and white traders, and ultimately concluded that there was no cause for alarm. His conclusion is perhaps more reliable because he began his investigation with an assumption of guilt, but agreed in the end that the rumors had come from the Janus-faced Wells. According to Johnston, Wells, facing dismissal, had cooked up the scheme to get Harrison to militarize the situation, strike at the Prophet, and remove the Prophet from the land claimed by his father-in-law, Little Turtle.[24]

Harrison decided to meet with Tenskwatawa as well. After the Prophet finished at Fort Wayne, he returned to Vincennes for a second summit. The timing worked well for him, for he again needed American support. When Harrison pointedly asked the Prophet if he had been propositioned by the British, Tenskwatawa answered that he had. Contrary to myriad accusations of artfulness and deception, the Prophet appears to have valued his détente with Harrison and been as forthright as possible concerning British policies. Harrison nevertheless became irritated that the Prophet had not informed him earlier. As for the scuffles and transits of warriors in the territory, Tenskwatawa explained that such aggression was confined to Indians on the upper Mississippi; according to Harrison, Tenskwatawa even "claims the merit of having prevailed upon them to relinquish their intentions." Given Tenskwatawa's answers regarding the British, there is no reason to doubt this claim, but Harrison did so anyway. "I must confess," he wrote, "that my suspicions of his guilt have been rather strengthened than diminished in every interview."[25]

Tenskwatawa got what he wanted out of the meeting: Harrison agreed to provision a number of "starved wretches" the Prophet had brought with him, though he was not happy about it. "I gave them as little as possible," he explained to William Eustis, who succeeded Dearborn as secretary of war when James Madison became president in March 1809.[26] Indeed, it is not clear what Harrison hoped to achieve from the summit. Reports had already declared the scuffles with the Ottawas and Ojibwes to be over, and both Harrison and even the Vincennes newspapers reported that the Prophet had lost in the exchange. If the summit of 1808 had been a courageous and radical diplomatic move, the summit of 1809 seems dilatory, a routine checkup.

That may have been Harrison's object. For the governor was not as forthright with the Prophet as the Prophet was with him. Harrison had decided sometime beforehand to resume the process of land sales, and the summit simply may have been a ploy to see firsthand whether the Prophet represented a threat to those plans. Harrison met with the Prophet in July, but as early as May he had written to Eustis with news that the Prophet was beaten: "The Party which the Prophet had assembled have dispersed." Harrison took the Prophet's failure to attack Vincennes as weakness rather than acumen. (Harrison did note in an aside that the Prophet might not have attacked the white settlements because he never intended to do so.) The important thing, Harrison continued, was that with the Prophet weakened, "the time has arrived when the Purchase may be attempted with a considerable Prospect of Success."[27]

Secretary Eustis concurred with Harrison and authorized him to proceed, as long as the cession "will excite no disagreeable apprehensions." In July, as Harrison concluded his dealings with Tenskwatawa, President Madison instructed Harrison "to take advantage of the most favorable moment for extinguishing the Indian Title to the Lands lying to the East of the Wabash."[28]

Harrison prepared for the purchase of new Indian lands by rehiring the most notorious and unscrupulous agent in the American employ: by July 1809, Wells was back and working for Harrison as an interpreter and assistant at Fort Wayne. Wells arrived in Vincennes in time for the summit with Tenskwatawa. Henry Dearborn worried that Wells was "too much under the influence of Little Turtle," but his influence with the Miami chief may have been one of the reasons Harrison rehired him.[29] Wells, out of a job, was only too glad to offer "my aid in effecting a purch[ase] of land from the Indians."[30] One of his first suggestions to the governor at the time was to "starve all those which appertained to the prophet."

Now allied with Wells, Harrison began a courtship of Little Turtle, a mutual enemy of Tenskwatawa's pan-Indian policy, which was sapping warriors from the Miami nation. If Tenskwatawa would not sell land, perhaps Little Turtle would prove more amenable—especially if the land was closer to the Prophet.

Little Turtle *was* more amenable, as it turned out. Just as with Tenskwatawa and Harrison, the embargo years had complicated the Miami chief's reign. Jefferson, the Turtle's onetime accomplice, had lost patience with him when the chief made vast claims to territory within Indiana. "All the lands on the waters of the Wabash do not belong to the Miamis alone," Jefferson wrote in exasperation. In December 1808, Jefferson relinquished his embargo-driven caution and resumed his usual tactic of urging the Miamis to sell land, establish firm boundaries, and allow the Americans to help them "improve the lands they retain" in order that they could live by farming and not "the chase."[31]

Thus in the fall of 1809, Wells, Little Turtle, and Harrison all possessed a vested interest in obtaining a land cession. Wells needed the job and (as always) worked with his father-in-law, who wanted American funds and prestige. Harrison needed to buttress his support with his superiors in Washington and to find ways to attract new immigrants to Indiana in an attempt to stanch the bleeding of his own political fortunes.

All three men also knew that the land Harrison wanted to buy was claimed by multiple tribes. Harrison made his usual plans to treat with the most pliable tribes first—Little Turtle's Miamis, the anti-Prophet Delawares, and the disaffected Potawatomies. Only after that treaty was signed, Harrison figured, would he approach the Weas and Kickapoos, so as to "put them out of the way of bad advisers," that is, Tenskwatawa, whom Harrison did not plan to meet with at all. That perhaps had been the ultimate result of the July summit.[32] Harrison arranged for an early fall gathering in 1809 at Fort Wayne; Delawares, Potawatomies, and Miamis had been duly invited. Harrison also declared that the invited tribes would receive their U.S. annuities only after the end of the treaty negotiations. This arrangement allowed Harrison to set the goods the American government legally owed the tribes as the incentive for a successful negotiation for more land. He also invited the branch of the Potawatomi nation that he described as stricken with "poverty and wretchedness," as they presumably would add another Indian voice in favor of a large cession.[33]

Harrison's plans quickly came undone. Negotiations were delayed by the absence of numerous important chiefs—Hockingpompsga, Five Medals, the Beaver, and Richardville did not show. The delay provided enough time for rumor to infiltrate the camps. The gathered tribes heard whispers that a detachment of American troops was on its way, and Harrison's whole treaty was mere pretense for wiping out the Indian leadership. The "young men" in particular were alarmed at the news. Calm was restored, but things were not off to a good start.[34] When negotiations began, dissention disrupted the governor's calibrations. Those Miamis not under the sway of Little Turtle attacked the veteran of the Glaize as a Harrison stooge. The Weas—a Miami-speaking tribal group—sent word of their decision "on no account ever to part from another foot of their lands."[35] Indeed, the recalcitrant Miamis made known their understanding that "the Governor had no instructions from the President to make the purchase but that he was making it upon his own authority to please the white people whom he governed."[36]

That accusation was only partially true. Harrison had some legal authority for what he did. Nonetheless, those Indians who objected knew the political stakes, and they knew Harrison's concern was his own political future. If there was a cultural misunderstanding, it was perhaps the notion that Harrison could be shamed out of his intentions—that concepts of honor and justice would trump his gamble for power. Despite the passion of Native American pleas, it is unlikely Harrison ever understood the concept of land among the peoples of the Ohio and Mississippi Rivers. Even as he explained his plans for new cessions to Eustis, Harrison related a story he had heard from "an Indian chief." That nameless man asked Harrison why the Americans took their lands, whereas the French had lived "in common with us—they plant'd where they pleas'd & they cut wood when they pleas'd & so did we—but now, if a poor Indian attempts to take a little bark from a Tree, to cover him from the Rain, up comes a white man & threatens to shoot him, claiming the Tree as his own."[37] The story went to show, Harrison wrote, that the Indians preferred the French and would likely ally with France should America end up at war with Napoleon. If he gleaned anything else from the chief's story about Indian understanding of resources, land, or community, he did not feel it important enough to record.

Other Native Americans understood the white approach to land perfectly well. Those Indians wanted to sell land at Fort Wayne, but only for the going rate, as the Miami chief Owl made clear: "We are willing to sell you some for the price that it sells for amongst yourselves."[38] It was the only way, Owl explained to the recalcitrant Miamis, "to put a stop to the encroachments of the whites who were eternally purchasing their lands for less than the real value."[39] Harrison declared that policy "entirely out of the question."[40]

Harrison offered up impassioned speeches—mostly containing the same promises of the benefits of Western-style agriculture that the U.S. government had so often spoken of and rarely delivered. He chided the tribes as "too apt to impute their poverty and the scarcity of Game to the encroachments of White Settlers." In truth, the fault lay in "their own improvidence" and reliance on the British fur trade.[41]

Though the Potawatomi and Delaware delegations agreed to a sale, and although Little Turtle promised Harrison he would "exert himself to the utmost of his power" to get the treaty through, Owl and other Miami leaders literally held their ground. Some wanted two dollars an acre; others committed themselves "never to sell another foot." Some of the Miami "young men" surprised the entire proceedings by arriving laden with goods from the British at Malden and displaying them to the Indians. The young men, it seems, wanted to demonstrate that the British also offered gifts, without the threat of land sales.[42]

Harrison complained that he had never felt such "mortification and disappointment," especially since the treaty "would be beneficial to all." The governor once again had the temerity to ask the Miamis, "Have you not always received justice from the hands of your father?"[43] Owl had an answer. He pointed to Greenville, where the Americans had told them to sell lands and promised them a border. Indeed, the American negotiators in 1795 had warned the Miamis to "consider well before we sell them"—meaning, of course, not to sell to the Spanish or British. "This was good advice," Owl told Harrison, for "when things are scarce they are dear." Owl aimed to follow American instructions exactly: they could have certain lands for two dollars an acre, and only if the Miamis were present when the land was surveyed. Owl presumably knew of Harrison's penchant for "discovering" that the lands he purchased were larger after surveys than they were in treaties.[44]

Harrison attempted to pressure the Miamis by gathering all the Indians together for a round of oratory. The Potawatomies did not disappoint, and their speaker, Winamac, threatened war with the Miamis unless the latter signed, before slavishly promising Harrison, "You have asked for land, we will give it to you." Owl held fast for two dollars an acre. In desperation, Harrison broke out the alcohol for the chiefs, his earlier pledges and proclamations against it notwithstanding. It did not alter the negotiations.[45]

On the night of September 30, two weeks into the negotiations, Harrison visited the Miami chiefs accompanied only by his interpreter, explaining that he came "not as the Representative of the President but as an old friend," trying to discover if two dollars an acre was truly an inflexible point. An Eel River chief suggested that perhaps it was not. The Miamis had the strongest claim to the land, a claim acknowledged by the Treaty of Grouseland. By dealing with the Potawatomies and Delawares on equal terms with the Miami, Harrison had inadvertently broken his own word and slighted the tribe. Harrison saw his opening. Perhaps if the Miamis received more than the Potawatomies and Delawares but less than two dollars an acre, the treaty might go forward? The collected Miami chiefs—not all of whom opposed the treaty to begin with—finally agreed. The treaty was revised to give the Miamis twice what the other tribes received, with more if the Kickapoos would concur with the treaty later that month. Harrison listened to a litany of complaints about the misconduct of white settlers and the Indian agents of the U.S. government. Harrison promised to look into it. Then he again opened the whiskey casks for his guests.[46] The assembled Indians consumed a phenomenal amount of alcohol, with more than 218 gallons issued, all under the watchful eye of a governor who so often had pledged with heartfelt words his intention to fight the presumed Indian addiction to demon rum.[47]

Harrison completed the work over the next few weeks. In accordance with his strategy, he brought the treaty to the less pliable tribes of the Indiana Territory. Once again he used the law as a weapon: the treaties recognized the land as belonging to the tribes who had already signed, which meant that the U.S. government would begin surveying and settling the lands. Those tribes left out of the negotiations could also sign on and receive some annuities, or else find themselves surrounded by white settlement and receive nothing. Those tribes—in this case, the Kickapoos and a division of the Weas—opted to sign. Harrison seemed particularly pleased at getting Kickapoo consent. The area ceded contained "a very rich copper mine" that Americans had not been able to explore. What Americans could not buy outright, Harrison obtained through legal legerdemain.

One of Harrison's most remarkable traits was an unshakable self-confidence. He counted all his plans as successes even before they were implemented, and believed failure came only when someone else cheated—hence his perpetual worries about cabals, intriguers, spies, and religious impostors. In the case of the 1809 treaty, Harrison believed it would "excite no disagreeable apprehension." In his summation, the treaty—with its withheld annuities, piecemeal signing, and gallons of whiskey—was "just to all."[48]

Other white American officials shared in the enthusiasm. Illinois governor Ninian Edwards eagerly anticipated that "it will add much to increase emigration from the old states."[49] The treaty handed over the rights to two and a half million acres on both sides of the Wabash—"some of the finest land in all the United States," as Johnston wrote to Cincinnati's *Liberty Hall*. The newspaper published the good news on October 11. Other papers reprinted the information over the course of the fall, sometimes adding the kind of commentary Harrison loved to hear: "The acquisition of a country so much desired and promising such advantages, must be highly gratifying to every well-wisher to his country." Through the newspapers, whites everywhere could learn how the United States was once again expanding into Native territory.[50]

So could the Indians. Had Harrison or Johnston paid closer attention, they might have spoken with a little more caution or a little less publicity. Tenskwatawa faced his own challenges in 1809, but even Indians recently disaffected with the Prophet continued to remind American officials of the impossibility of future land sales. Even as the Indians gathered at Fort Wayne, Ottawa and Ojibwe chiefs at Michilimackinac declared that the land "belonging to the Nations" was "common and undivided."[51] Unfortunately, even as these chiefs acknowledged that their nations had "suffered severely" by listening to the Prophet, they also insisted that Indian lands were not for sale. The American officials who were their audience seem to have ignored the latter caveat.[52]

Fort Wayne brought all of the Indian fears and suspicions back to the surface. After two years of relatively good relations required by the embargo, the treaty did exactly what Tenskwatawa had warned Indians the whites would do. Harrison had played one tribe against another and pocketed the profits. The accommodationist chiefs had caved to Harrison before, of course, and the nativists had complained, and nothing had come of it. That is probably why Harrison thought "no disagreeable apprehension" would result. But this time was different because of the pointed political reaction from Prophetstown.

Tenskwatawa refused to recognize the treaty, and together with Tecumseh declared that he would not permit the surveying of the newly purchased tracts. Tecumseh spoke ominously of maintaining "arms, ammunition and provisions" at the nation of Prophetstown.[53]

It was a savvy political move, similar to Harrison's own gamble to retain political relevance by crafting the treaty in the first place. Harrison assumed the weakened Prophet would not offer any significant resistance, just as the nativists had not in his previous decade in office. What was different was the existence of Prophetstown, a city of Indians near the territory Harrison purchased. Tenskwatawa, "much exasperated at the cessions," decided not to talk his way out of this Harrisonian maneuver. Instead, he chose this moment to defy the governor, and thereby push what one historian called the generational and ideological divide that had always animated his movement into the forefront.[54]

As news of the treaty spread across the frontier, the tribes of the Northwest began to split. Those who had signed the Treaty of Fort Wayne saw their influence collapse. Little Turtle found his warriors unwilling to listen and watched as they committed themselves to instead "British Indians." Winamac toured his villages after signing the treaty, and everywhere he found warriors abandoning him for the Prophet.[55] Even William Wells eventually concluded that after this "purch[ase] made by the united states . . . they threw themselves into the arms of the Shawnese proph[e]t."[56]

In a way, the Treaty of Fort Wayne helped both men keep their jobs. Tenskwatawa received renewed support and the loyalty of dispossessed Indians and an infuriated warrior class. Harrison's work repaired his damaged reputation—or in the words of the *Scioto Gazette,* it "put a seal on the slanderous tongue of faction." (For good measure, the *Gazette* accused anyone who opposed the treaty of British sympathies.)[57] In November 1809, the Indiana legislature passed a resolution recommending Harrison for a fourth term, due in part to his "virtue, talent, and republicanism" and his "influence over the Indians." Only one member voted against it.[58] President James Madison duly renominated the onetime ensign from Berkeley. Harrison had what he wanted, but the thaw in relations with the Prophet was over.

13

The Gathering

PROPHETS STALKED THE United States in those days. Some people thought then—as before and since—that the events passing before their eyes were signs of the end times. A great comet appeared in the sky in early 1811, "thought to be designed for bringing about great and fatal changes to the earth itself." Samuel Ingalls dreamed on September 2, 1809, that three angels descended upon Vermont and destroyed the houses across the river in New Hampshire. In her house flanked by whale bones, Moll Pitcher, the Massachusetts seer, wove her dark predictions about sailors' voyages. Luman C. Davis believed Napoleon was "the Lord of the Locusts" promised in Revelation. An author calling himself the "Wildman of the Woods" disagreed: Napoleon was clearly "the great beast with two horns like a lamb" from elsewhere in Revelation. Another pseudonymous prophet, "King John," sided with the Wildman and warned that a French invasion of England would trigger Armageddon.[1]

The years 1809–11 saw an abundance of apocalyptic prophecies, perhaps not without reason. In Europe, the Napoleonic Wars plunged the continent into chaos, and in North America, rumors of war whispered that the Western Hemisphere was next. Prophecy need not come from professionals, either: *The Complete Fortune Teller or An Infallible Guide to the Hidden Decrees of Fate*, a grimoire explaining how to read the future by cards, dreams, stars, and lines on the face and hands, went through five printings in the early republic.[2] "Strange things indeed sometimes take place," mused Michigan's Governor Hull. After all, "a man of the small Island of Corsica has become Emperor of France." From Detroit, Hull wondered whether "the old [Indian] Nations will consent, that a man on the Wabash and of the young Shawanese Nation, shall become *their* Emperor."[3]

After denouncing the Treaty of Fort Wayne and vowing not to allow its surveyors into the territory, the Prophet became once again an object of pilgrimage. Old allies renewed their pledges, disaffected tribes returned, and the formerly uncommitted began taking him seriously. In January, groups of Miamis "had been so intimidated as to agree to attend his council," while the Wyandots needed no such prompting; according to the *Vincennes Sun*, they now considered the Treaty of Greenville "void and good for nothing" and were "determined to stop the progress of the white settlements."[4] Charles Jouett, an Indian agent, reported that Sac Indian tribes had pledged themselves to the Prophet, and sought others "to join them in hostility agt. the U.S."[5] Word reached the Iowas, across the Mississippi, where Chief Mansegoa had to argue against "the young men" of his tribes, who had already sent (with the Winnebagoes) a company of more than a thousand on a pilgrimage to Tenskwatawa.[6] A Potawatomi who spent several days in Prophetstown described its composition as consisting of "nearly all the Kickapoo; a number of Winnebagoes, some Hurons [Wyandot] from Detroit, who have lately joined him," as well as Potawatomies, Shawnees, Ojibwes, and Ottawas.[7] If Hull thought the "old Nations" would not make Tenskwatawa their emperor, he knew well enough that "the young Warriors" of the Northwest might do exactly that.[8]

As always, Tenskwatawa drew his support from a younger generation supporting rejection of the tribal political structures that had allowed accommodationist chiefs to retain power. Winamac—who received an icy reception when he visited Prophetstown in the spring of 1810—reported that the Prophet had declared that the existing chiefs sought to prevent Indian opposition to "the encroachments of the white people." According to Winamac, the Prophet promised to murder them all. Little wonder Winamac made a hurried exit from Prophetstown.[9]

Tenskwatawa still explained his presence at Prophetstown as a dictate from the Master of Life, but his proclamations became more frequent and pointed. In addition to reminding his followers that "the express order of the Great Sprit" had placed them in Prophetstown, he also emphasized to all Indian peoples that he was the leader who opposed American expansion—and that with the Treaty of Fort Wayne such opposition was no longer simply a religious imperative but a matter of survival.[10]

This new direction was also apparent in the specificity of demands and declarations coming from Prophetstown. All of the leaders assembled at Prophetstown met in a council in May 1810 and "agreed, that the Tract on the N. West side of the Wabash should not be surveyed."[11] Tenskwatawa then called for a broader council to be held at Parc aux Vaches, Michigan, in late June to discuss how the tribes might work in concert to enact this platform.[12]

What had once been religious aphorisms to avoid land sales and contact with whites had now become defiance of a particular land treaty. It was Tecumseh who explained this to American officials when he "acknowledged that they could never be good friends with the United States until [the Americans] abandoned the idea of acquiring lands by purchase from the Indians, without the consent of all tribes."[13] Harrison himself understood the implications of such a position when he worried that Tenskwatawa wanted to "follow in the footsteps of the great Pontiac"—the leader of 1763 who also had insisted that all the tribes owned the land collectively.[14]

Tenskwatawa had an important if unpredictable ally in Main Poc, a holy man of the Potawatomies. His name meant "Crippled Hand," for his left hand had no thumb or fingers. The two prophets, Shawnee and Potawatomi, made political but not religious common cause. Main Poc embodied an older form of Native American religious practice. A tall figure of "brooding countenance," he engaged in the ecstatic dances of the *wabeno* tradition most common to the Menominee and Ojibwe tribes. Main Poc ignored the Prophet's ban on alcohol and rarely consented to place his warriors under Prophetstown's aegis. In 1808, Wells began funneling gifts to Main Poc in an effort to make the Potawatomi mystic a potential counterweight to Tenskwatawa. In truth, Wells thought Main Poc "a dangerous man" and "the pivot on which the mind of all the western Indians turned." Main Poc certainly pivoted—he pledged himself to the Prophet the same month Wells initiated his scheme. By the summer of 1810, rumors placed Main Poc's army as one of the central branches of a presumed Prophet-led Indian uprising.[15]

Harrison and other American officials had few means to keep tabs on these convoluted movements; they could only rely on visiting Indians, rumor, and spies. In the chaotic jumble of loyalties, nationalities, languages, and laws that constituted the early American state system, spies provided valuable intelligence—or, more commonly, rumor and paranoia. In 1807, with war looming, Harrison approved the arrest of a suspected British spy, in part because he believed that any "supposed prisoner for two years among the Indians would not have such clean underwear beneath his buckskin suit."[16] Harrison in turn received intelligence that Tenskwatawa had "some Person or Persons in or about Vincennes" informing Prophetstown of "every thing almost that transpires."[17] A British spy designated "Nancy" took stock of all American port defenses in 1808 and wrote to the spymaster in Halifax that aside from gunboats in New York, the Americans had made no preparations for war, which probably contributed to Britain's failure to take the embargo very seriously.[18]

Harrison's own spy was a Frenchman named Michel Brouillette, instructed by Harrison to journey to Prophetstown to watch Tenskwatawa's movements and to discover the loyalties of various Potawatomi groups. The job entailed considerable risk, including "private assassination," and somehow Harrison thought Brouillette's cover story would work well even though the other French traders had abandoned the Indian settlement.[19]

Brouillette had little good news to impart. The Francophone spy told stories of secret meetings among the Indians and Tenskwatawa's personal animosity toward Harrison, whom he apparently threatened to fight "in single combat." Brouillette's mission ended abruptly in June when the Prophet exposed him as an American infiltrator. The Prophet's followers forced Brouillette to recant his American sympathies, called him "an American dog," and ransacked his house.[20]

Harrison received conflicting reports throughout the spring and summer of 1810 as to whether the Prophet intended war. One informed him that it was an absolute certainty.[21] Another claimed that the Prophet intended to come to Vincennes "in the guise of friendship," then murder Harrison and massacre everyone in the town.[22] Others maintained that this tale of impending war was "an old story." Harrison himself wrote, "I am still of the opinion however that the Indians will not dare commence hostilities, unless the U. States should go to war with England."[23]

Before he was exposed, Brouillette gave Harrison an important piece of information that contradicted rumors of war: the council at Parc aux Vaches had not gone the Prophet's way. "The affairs of the Prophet received a great shock," wrote Brouillette, when "the tribes that were assembled unanimously agreed not to go to war with the United States." Apparently the Ottawas and Ojibwes acknowledged the importance of resisting the surveys but could not commit themselves to armed resistance. If such a declaration indeed had been Tenskwatawa's intention, he failed. He may, however, have only been seeking to sound out the tribes of Michigan, alerting them to his policy and asking for support.[24]

The Prophet might not have not sought war at Parc aux Vaches, though his movement was certainly not averse to violence or conflict. The Vincennes *Sun* reported that when a salt annuity arrived in Prophetstown, Tecumseh chided the Frenchmen delivering the U.S. salt, "shaking [one] violently by the hair" and demanding to know whether they were Americans.[25] The Francophone crew denied that they were, and hurried off.

The salt incident provoked Harrison to call out the militia. News of the event reached Harrison before news of Parc aux Vaches, and the governor issued a flurry of demands. He sent Toussaint Dubois, another French trader who had aided Brouillette on his secret mission, to ask the Prophet directly whether he intended any violence. The Prophet denied it; the *Sun*, however, printed the Prophet's reputed warning that Americans "should not come any nearer to him, that they should not settle on the Vermillion river—he smelt them too strong already."[26]

It was not what Harrison likely wanted to hear, but it was at least clear; his previous emissaries to Prophetstown—John Conner and Brouillette—had not made much headway. More important, the Prophet wanted to make his objectives even clearer to the governor, and so he sent his own emissary, the man Harrison called "the Moses of the family": Tecumseh.[27]

The rise of Tecumseh came as a direct result of the Treaty of Fort Wayne and the politicization of Prophetstown. Chroniclers of the Indian wars (beginning with Benjamin Drake in 1840 and continuing to the present) have assumed Tecumseh provided the backbone of Indian resistance and Tenskwatawa merely a front. Such an arrangement makes sense only if the entire religious structure of the early movement was mere window dressing for its true political nature, and Tenskwatawa's ministry a "career of cunning and pretended sorcery, which enabled him to sway the Indian mind in a wonderful degree."[28] The documents of Tenskwatawa's own time show precisely the opposite arrangement: Tenskwatawa was the primary leader in the early years, and Tecumseh his follower. Before 1810, white writers rarely called Tecumseh by name; he was simply "the Prophet's Brother." Notaries sent to Greenville always met with the Prophet and often failed to mention any relatives. The emergence of Tecumseh—Prophetstown's war chief—suggests that by 1810, the movement had sharpened its political edge and extended its military preparations.[29]

Tecumseh ("shooting star" in the Shawnee language) came into the world in 1768, the fifth child of his parents. Unlike his little brother, Tecumseh knew their father, albeit briefly, before the man's death in 1774. Later recollections place him with his brother at the Battle of Fallen Timbers two decades later. Unlike Lalawauthika, Tecumseh escaped the battle with his reputation intact and led a small group of Ohio Shawnees for several years afterward.[30]

Contemporary sources have little to say on Tecumseh's reign in Ohio and his early days as a disciple of his brother; later stories told about Tecumseh—and there are many—sometimes suggested that he followed Tenskwatawa only to advance his own political purposes. Such accusations usually come from those who assumed Tenskwatawa was a mere charlatan anyway. Yet Tecumseh seems to have been an ideal convert: abstemious, moral, and disdainful of American practices, but more careful than aggressive. His reputation as a war chief and his extensive oratorical skills also fit well with the leadership structures of Prophetstown.

Tenskwatawa began employing Tecumseh as a senior diplomat by at least 1808, when the latter represented the movement to British officials at Amherstburg, Canada.[31] Tecumseh's traveling diplomacy intensified after the

Treaty of Fort Wayne, although as biographer John Sugden has pointed out, some of these travels are undoubtedly apocryphal.[32] In 1809, Tecumseh had a very productive summit with the Sac tribe, who had lost their lands in an unscrupulous deal with Louisiana governor Meriwether Lewis, the explorer. The Sac tribes became some of the Prophet's most reliable adherents.[33] Other travels went less well. Tecumseh traveled to the Glaize in the spring of 1810 and received a stony reception. When the preacher Stephen Ruddell handed him a response, "the brother of the Prophet took it from his hands and threw it in the fire, declaring, that if Governor Harrison was there, he *would* serve him so."[34]

That attitude would have made Tecumseh an unusual choice to treat with the governor in the summer of 1810. On the other hand, such defiance might have been precisely the tack Tenskwatawa wanted to take; he may have felt more comfortable in his power then than in 1808, or he may have realized that his 1809 détente had permitted the Treaty of Fort Wayne to happen. It was also true that with Blue Jacket gone—he died at home in 1808—Tecumseh was now the foremost diplomat and military leader at Prophetstown, and the entire point of Prophetstown was that the Master of Life wanted the war chiefs in charge of affairs.[35] Finally, if Tenskwatawa was as well informed about events at Vincennes as the governor feared he was, he may well have sent Tecumseh precisely to antagonize Harrison, in an effort to further undermine the governor, for whom 1810 was turning out to be a political catastrophe.

For Harrison, the successes occasioned by the Treaty of Fort Wayne began to seem more like a reprieve than progress. He had taken his praises from the legislature in 1809, but there had been complaints as well. John Badollet informed Albert Gallatin in Washington that the legislatures were mere creatures of Harrison, for Harrison was the "moral chameleon" whose "despotic self-conceit" would ruin Indiana.[36]

Harrison's disastrous electoral fortunes continued, despite the governor's supposed powers of silencing dissent. Having lost the last round of balloting in 1809 when the anti-slavery Jonathan Jennings was elected as a delegate to the U.S. Congress, Harrison then watched as Jennings arranged for a congressional ban on gubernatorial nominations to territorial legislatures. Harrison's response did not win many sympathies. In his address to the Indiana legislature in October, he attacked those who criticized him as British sympathizers who wished "to excite our Indian neighbors to hostilities against us." He defended his heavy-handed leadership, mentioning in particular "unfounded jealousies of the accumulation of power in the hands of the Executive." Harrison went so far as to point out that as territorial governor, he was "independent of the people," and he told the legislature to be more like the militia in that they should be more loyal to him personally.[37]

Harrison had to call for new legislative elections in April 1810, and the majority fell to his opponents. Even when Harrison's men won their elections, it was often "close work," which the partisans blamed on the "business of electioneering" and "many illegal votes."[38] The loss unmade the central legislation of Harrison's reign: in late 1810, the legislature revoked the laws permitting slavery and indentured servitude in Indiana. This time the upper house of the legislature was not stuffed with Harrison appointees who could prevent its passage. (The legislature went on in the next four years to limit suffrage to free white men and to levy a tax on free black men. The legislature still wanted a white republic, just one without slavery.)[39]

After so many years of watching Harrison dominate them, his opponents could hardly stop at mere legislative victory. Even as relations with the Indians deteriorated, the opposition tried to have him removed from office. Harrison's former ally William McIntosh brought charges that the governor had arranged the Treaty of Fort Wayne to line his own pockets, that he had deliberately misled the Indians, and that he had committed fraud against the people of Indiana. Harrison had faced such accusations before; indeed, as governor, he extensively speculated in lands (and ultimately lost money doing so).[40] This time, however, McIntosh alleged that the heightened tension with the Indians came about because Harrison had cheated them: the governor "defrauded the Indians in the purchase of their lands & . . . made them . . . enemies to the government of the United States." Harrison eventually won the legal battle. The presiding judge was a Harrison appointee.[41]

McIntosh's object was solely political theater. Indeed, there are few Americans in history more infamous for their callousness regarding Indian rights to land, for in 1823, McIntosh was the defendant in *Johnson v. McIntosh*, in which Chief Justice John Marshall agreed with McIntosh's attorneys that all Indians were "an inferior race" and therefore had no rights to the lands they lived on. The case reflected a political reality possible only after Indian political alternatives to land ownership had already been defeated. McIntosh in 1810, on the other hand, represented the possibilities of a political system in which Indian entities represented a real political threat, and he was still willing to support Native rights to their lands—as long as it benefitted him. Taking down Harrison might necessitate greater independence for the Indians of the Old Northwest.[42]

Thus, when Tecumseh and Harrison finally met in August 1810, each man had an agenda to defend. Both stood to gain by sticking to a hard line in the negotiations. Given that situation, the summit was mostly for show.

And it was quite a show. Tecumseh arrived with an honor guard of seventy-five warriors, a diplomatic flourish that did not go over well with a Vincennes population accustomed to hearing rumors about the Prophet's plans to sack the town.[43] The decision to bring a military escort was already an act of defiance, as previously Harrison had sent word to Prophetstown that the presence of Indian warriors in large numbers would be "improper." Tecumseh and Tenskwatawa, however, likely had their own concepts of what was proper—especially given how unarmed and unescorted Indian diplomats had sometimes fared in American custody.[44] Harrison was not to be outdone and ordered two companies of militia in from the hinterlands and set them to twice-daily parades.[45]

Harrison and Tecumseh met in the arbor just outside Grouseland. Perhaps the only leader at the conference without guards was Winamac, whom Harrison had invited in yet another effort to employ accommodationist chiefs to assuage nativist sentiment. Having already chased Winamac out of Prophetstown, Tecumseh was in no mood to brook his presence at a council. He denounced Winamac loudly and at length. Winamac—surrounded by Americans—ominously began loading his pistol. Harrison attempted to intervene, protesting the fairness and justice of American treaties. Tecumseh—in Shawnee—called Harrison a liar.[46] Unfortunately, one of the army officers with Harrison spoke Shawnee, and on hearing the insult, he ordered his soldiers forward. Tecumseh's forces rose to meet them. The American soldiers closed ranks. The peace council was about to become a bloodbath.

After a long moment, Harrison chose the better part of valor. He condemned Tecumseh's action and asked the Shawnee leader to leave, saying he would send word of the U.S. response in writing. Harrison's actions gave everyone a chance to separate and cool off for the evening. On the following morning, Tecumseh offered his apology for the outburst. The council went forward, although Harrison called two more militia companies into Vincennes.[47]

What followed the next day did not produce any changes in relations, but it did produce some of the most eloquent explanations and defenses of the Prophetstown position on land ownership. Tecumseh explained the divine nature of their opposition. "He asserted," according to the *Sun*, "that the Great Spirit has given them as common property to all the Indians, and that they could not, nor should not be sold without the consent of all. That all the tribes of Indians on the continent formed but one nation." To achieve these goals, as always, required a political revolution they had already undertaken: "They were determined to have no more chiefs, but in future to have everything done under the direction of the warriors."[48] It was time "to level all distinctions to destroy the village chiefs by whom all mischief is done."[49]

Harrison had his own eloquent replies, and insisted that everything he and other American agents had done was perfectly consistent with trustworthiness and propriety. Harrison's correspondence with Washington confirms that the governor believed "the United States have upon all occasions manifested the strictest justice in their transactions with the Indians," but given Harrison's penchant for negotiating with tribes with weak land claims, his desire to keep Indians ignorant of the true price of land, and his opening of the casks at Fort Wayne, his claims to justice are difficult to substantiate.[50] But he needed those claims: surrounded by the citizens of Vincennes who had come to watch the proceedings, Harrison took the opportunity to grandstand, saying the American treaties had been a "fair purchase" and that "the right of the U. States would be supported by the sword."[51]

Tecumseh was wise to Harrison's gambit and to the political possibilities that internal white rivalries offered Prophetstown. He told Harrison that he knew "the people here were equally divided," with only "half adhering to the Governor." Moreover, Tecumseh also knew that Harrison knew that the treaties had not been fairly obtained—and that other whites intended to make those irregularities the undoing of the governor. Americans had visited Prophetstown, Tecumseh claimed, and explained that "the Governor had only two years more to remain in office, and if he (the Shawanoe) could prevail upon the Indians who sold the lands, not to receive their annuities for that time, then the Governor would be displaced, and a good man appointed in his room, who would restore to the Indians all the lands which had been purchased of them."[52]

Tecumseh, Tenskwatawa, and the Prophetstown partisans apparently understood the American political situation far better than they were generally given credit for. Harrison wondered why Tenskwatawa's allies would ever "be willing to measure their strength" against the United States, but based on Tecumseh's words, a war does not appear to have been the object of the military forces at Prophetstown.[53] Tenskwatawa and Tecumseh had adopted the strategy that many small states have chosen when facing a more populous, better-armed opponent: prepare for a defensive war and hold out until the greater power deemed the price of victory too high. That strategy had worked for the Americans against the British in 1783, and it would work for North

Vietnam against the Americans in 1975. It is the same strategy cited almost endlessly by historians (and counterfactual histories) as the best possible path to Confederate victory in the American Civil War.[54] Harrison knew that his contentions with the Indians were part of a domestic agenda, and Tecumseh knew that Harrison knew.

Tecumseh was not above a little grandstanding of his own. "You said," he reminded Harrison, "if we could shew that the land was sold by persons who had no right to sell—you would restore it." The tribes who had sold the Fort Wayne lands were not the rightful owners—the rightful owner, Tecumseh declared, "was *me*" and "the tribes with me." Not that those tribes owned all the land, but that *all* the tribes had to agree to sell the land, and Tecumseh and his followers had not agreed. "If the land is not restored to us," Tecumseh warned, "it will be very hard & produce great troubles among us." Then Tecumseh took a final swipe at the presumed logic of the Christian civilization the Americans had so long promoted and so rarely funded: "How can we have confidence in the white people—when Jesus Christ came upon the earth you kill'd him and nail'd him to a cross, you thought he was dead but you were mistaken."[55]

After he finished speaking, spokesmen from the Wyandot, Kickapoo, Potawatomi, Ottawa, and Winnebago nations declared that "their tribes had entered into the Shawanoe confederacy, and would support the principles laid down by Tecumseh, who they had appointed their leader." Harrison had planned for the Wea chief Laproussier to stand up and defy Tecumseh, but after Tecumseh's bravado, Laproussier decided to remain in his seat.[56]

When Harrison specifically asked if the Prophetstown brothers would allow the surveyors to measure the treaty land, Tecumseh said, "I look at the land, and pity the Women & Children," neatly inverting Harrison's own rhetoric about the need of Indians to care for their families by selling land. Tecumseh repeated that taking the land would make the whites "the Cause of trouble between us & the Tribes who sold it."[57] Harrison agreed to send on Tecumseh's speeches to President Madison. He also wrote to Secretary Eustis that they needed to be "ready to support our rights with the Sword."[58]

The revival of the Prophet's influence was also apparent at a second council a few weeks later at Brownstown, a Wyandot center. This time, the accommodationist chiefs gathered in an attempt to coordinate efforts to reverse the accumulation of power in the hands of Tenskwatawa, who was, according to the Iroquois chief Red Jacket, "endeavouring to destroy the authority of the old chiefs, assume the power himself, and depend upon the inconsiderate young warriors for support."[59] The assembled chiefs—those of the

Cayuga and Mohawk excepted—signed a letter to the Shawnee nation generally, reminding them that "you are the youngest of our nations" and asking, "Why have you discarded your good old chiefs, and committed the management of your affairs to inexperienced young men?"[60] Hull served as the American ambassador to the council, and read to them an account of Tecumseh's meeting with Harrison. According to Hull, the council chiefs rose in an uproar: "The Idea of distroying the authority of the old Chiefs, and committing the authority to the young warriors, with the Prophet at the head, excited the most pointed contempt and indignations."[61]

The council, however, could only agree to send a series of warnings and assurances to American officials, including a letter to President Madison. Although the council featured representatives from numerous tribes who had lost members to the Prophet's growing movement, the council's pronouncements seem less directed at the Prophet than at American officials who wanted reassurance that the "true" chiefs were dedicated to the accommodationist program, despite its manifold failures. To Madison, for example, they declared, "We have a confidence in your goodness." They then added a short note requesting the rights to a small piece of land that was claimed by the United States but which they felt belonged to some of the Wyandots.[62]

Even more stunning was their letter to their own nations, which once again offered a fawning paean to the accommodationist ideology. "Every day we become more connected to our white brethren," declared the assembly; "we see them offering us their assistance," particularly in agriculture, which theoretically obviated "the uncertainty of hunting and fishing." The letter even praised "the influence of the same protecting providence."[63] Such language sounds so much like American accommodationist ideology as to suggest that the entire meeting was merely an effort to tell American officials what they wanted to hear in exchange for goods and a slice of land. Hull thought that if he had not offered to host the council, the chiefs would have held the meeting near "the British Post," where "they would have been supplied by them, and it is difficult to say what would have been the result." He hoped the council would "check the insolence of the Prophet." Yet even Hull knew that these professions of loyalty amounted at most to a promise to stay out of any fighting between America and Prophetstown.[64]

Tecumseh and Tenskwatawa, meanwhile, continued to watch and gather allies. Tenskwatawa knew what happened at Brownstown, since he had two emissaries at the conference.[65] Tecumseh met with the Potawatomies and Ottawas in Michigan; messages went from Prophetstown to the Iowa tribes.[66] In November, Tecumseh traveled to Canada to make his case to the British.

He offered them a wampum belt with a design of the hands of Indians and the British united. "This Belt, Father," Tecumseh said, "our great Chiefs have been sitting upon . . . keeping it concealed, and ruining our Country. Now the warriors have taken all the chiefs and turned their faces towards you never again [to] look towards the Americans, and we the warriors now manage the affairs of our Nation."[67] Tecumseh then urged the British to keep the Indians supplied with arms and ammunition as a precaution. Rather than the British encouraging the Indians, as Harrison assumed, the Indians were encouraging the British and attempting to entice them into an alliance.

Preserving relationships with the disaffected Indians of the *pays d'en haut* was a crucial security concern for the British. That concern did not necessarily mean Canada would rush to aid the Indians. Lord Castlereigh, the future foreign minister of Britain, wrote to Lower Canada on "the subject of the Indian Tribes as viewed in a political light." Contrary to the fears of Harrison and others, Castlereigh did not intend to employ Indian tribes as an aggressive strike force against U.S. settlements. He voiced more concern "that if in a contest they are not employed to act with us, they will be engaged to act against us." He wanted to keep Indians as allies because he feared "their Destructiveness as Enemies."[68]

More intriguing was Castlereigh's suggestion that, should peace break out, the Americans and British might create "some Joint system as to the treatment of Indian nations." His suggestion required an unlikely "amicable adjustment" between Britain and its ex-colonies, but the idea echoed the perennial British notion of an Indian border state between Canada and America. In the days to come, that possibility was suggested with greater frequency as British military prospects brightened.[69]

Once again, war looked likely on the frontier. Governor Edwards in Illinois wrote to Washington that "the celebrated Indian Prophet is but too successful in exciting hostility toward the United States, in various tribes of Indians." West of the Mississippi, Edwards continued, Main Poc's bands were "certainly gaining confidence from impunity, and their conduct is getting entirely insufferable."[70] William Clark's spies told him the Prophet intended to "commence hostilities, as Soon as he thinks himself Sufficiently Strong."[71]

Harrison contributed a religious cast to the growing panic. The yearly warnings he gave to the territorial legislature, reprinted in the *Sun*, grew ever more specific regarding the danger that the Prophet posed *as a prophet*. In 1808—before Fort Wayne and before he lost control of his legislature—Harrison's gubernatorial address assured listeners that "there is every prospect of a continuance of that harmony and a good understanding with our

Indian neighbors, which is so mutually beneficial."[72] In 1809, he advocated that the legislature find ways to "humanize their fierce souls by the mild precepts of christianity," warning that neighboring Indians were balanced between "a scene of savage fury, of misery and superstition, or the delightful spectacle of man in a state of progressive improvement in morals, the arts of civilized life, and, above all, worshipping his Creator in the manner which he has himself prescribed."[73]

By 1810—with the opposition in control of the legislature and Fort Wayne undermining his authority at Vincennes—Harrison dispensed with any hope that Christian light could cure the heathen: "We have indeed been threatened with hostilities by a combination formed under the auspices of a bold adventurer, who pretends to act under the immediate inspiration of the Deity."[74] Under British stewardship, this religious takeover had disrupted the legitimate and traditional modes of power in Indian nations: "The personage of the Prophet is not a chief of the tribe to which he belongs, but is an outcast from it, rejected and hated by the real chiefs, the principal of whom was at the treaty [of Fort Wayne]."[75] Harrison's summation for the legislators explained the true Christian character of the impending crisis: "Is one of the fairest portions of the globe to remain in a state of nature, the haunt of a few wretched savages, when it seems destined by the Creator to give support to a large population, and to be the seat of civilization, of science, and of true religion?"[76]

So much for a "mild religion" that advanced only by argumentation. Harrison's rhetorical question arrayed many of the tenets of Christian deism—providentialism, a nonspecific deity, and perennial human advancement. More ominous, however, was the shift in tactic. Harrison was no longer discussing defensive measures to resist Indian encroachments; he was now arguing that the armies of civilization needed to absorb and adapt the world to fit God's plan. And though he did not say so to the legislature, all of these efforts were also critical to Harrison's goal of advancing his own career by adding Indiana's star to the American flag.

But Harrison's enthusiasm for fighting was not matched by President Madison, whose efforts with the Non-Intercourse Act and Macon's Bill Number Two were no more successful than Jefferson's had been with the embargo. In fact, they might have been worse: these congressional acts continued commercial restrictions when it had become clear they were unpopular, and thus inflicted further political as well as economic damage. And as a bonus headache, there was a possible war impending with Spain regarding the West Florida territory. Madison could not afford an Indian war on the frontier.[77]

Thus, though Harrison requested federal troops for Vincennes and permission to build a fortification on the Wabash, the government in Washington turned him down.[78] Harrison was neither to deploy troops nor to enact the surveys; it was "not expedient," and "peace with all the Indian tribes should be preserved."[79] Worse, Harrison's surveyors had decided not to attempt to work just yet.[80] Harrison had little choice but to inform the secretary glumly that "the President's injunctions with regard to the preservation of peace with the Indians, shall be faithfully attended to."[81]

Harrison was perhaps regretting the equivocations he had previously made regarding the Prophet's strength. Throughout 1810, he had written several letters to Eustis based on the fluctuating intelligence reports received at Vincennes. Those letters expressed the opinion that the Prophet represented little to no danger. Even after Tecumseh's threats at Vincennes, Harrison told the secretary, "I am far from believing that an Indian war is inevitable."[82] Indeed, Harrison even sent Brouillette back to Prophetstown to meet with Tenskwatawa, and this time the emissary was treated with "unusual friendship," though the Prophet still "expressed his determination not to permit the lands lately purchased to be Surveyed." Nevertheless, Harrison concluded that "there is not the least probability that he will make any hostile attempt."[83]

Harrison's reports changed dramatically, however, after Eustis rejected his call for military support. Even as he promised to abide by the presidential injunction for peace, he wrote that "the Prophet's principle, that their lands should be considered common property is either openly avowed or secretly favored by all the tribes, west of the Wabash." Without land sales, "tide of emigration from Pennsylvania & the State of Ohio" would cease, and that would poison "public opinion." "Our back-woods-Men," Harrison wrote, "are not of a disposition to content themselves with lands of an inferior quality, when they see in their immediate neighbourhood the finest Country as to soil in the world, occupied by a few wretched savages."[84] It was not the last time Harrison would imply that public opinion—and perhaps Republican electoral hopes—depended on shutting down Prophetstown. He urged Eustis to let him pursue yet another treaty. Eustis said no.[85]

Harrison kept at it, informing the Madison administration that his plans for more land treaties were inspired by instructions "from the late president [Jefferson], in his own hand writing."[86] Nothing changed in Washington. Harrison then warned that while he would try to keep the peace, "encroachment upon the rights and property of those, who will not resist it, is a characteristic of every savage," and again called for the authority to build a fort.[87] No authority came. When the Prophet was accused of possessing stolen horses and subsequently returned them to the Americans, Harrison wrote that such action "was merely intended to lull our vigilance."[88]

Of course, Eustis and Madison were unlikely to give Harrison the authority to conduct new treaties while the governor fought a lawsuit over the old ones. In the spring of 1811, McIntosh's suit against Harrison was still in court and undoubtedly harming Harrison's reputation with both Washington and Prophetstown. When Harrison read the charges, he tore up the paper that contained them and threw it into the fire. He felt "humiliated by the Contest" and worried that such charges would attach "the greatest Stigma" to his name.[89]

Thus Harrison's increasing propensity for war was not a simple reflection of a deteriorating security situation. Indeed, the Prophet and Tecumseh seem to have gone out of their way to pursue fair policies with the Americans—with the exception of allowing surveyors into the Fort Wayne lands. And while western governors (particularly in Illinois and Louisiana) faced sporadic violence in 1810–11, they had been dealing with such outbreaks consistently since 1808. Harrison, in short, was proposing a military solution to a political issue.

There was one way to ensure that Tenskwatawa and Tecumseh would break their careful diplomacy: by sending out teams of surveyors.[90] That is precisely what Harrison did. In the spring of 1811, he finally cajoled the survey team into heading out into Indian lands—after firing one of the surveyors for being "deeply engaged with an infamous faction at this place" (i.e., support of the anti-Harrison politicians).[91] The results provided political grist for Harrison, though they were less pleasant for the surveyors. Members of the Wea tribe—formerly reliable Harrison allies—surprised the team and took two members hostage. They released them the next day. One surveyor decided to postpone his work until the fall. The other fled to Cincinnati. The Weas, Harrison thought, "would not have dared to interrupt him if they had not been encouraged to do so, and assured of support from above." It was, Harrison told Eustis, "intended to feel our pulse"—though that statement more properly applied to Harrison, since it was the governor who sent out the surveyors.[92]

The Prophet added fuel to the fire. Harrison had sent a quantity of salt up the Wabash, intended for several tribes north of Prophetstown. Previously Tecumseh had chased salt merchants out of Prophetstown; this time the Prophet seized all the salt, explaining simply that he had thousands of people to feed and he needed it.[93]

It was a terrible blunder, and Harrison took advantage. Using the salt seizure as a pretext, he wrote Eustis his most alarmist letter yet, explaining that the Prophet planned to "come to this place with as many men as he can raise and if the land which was lately purchased is not immediately given up to commence the war." Once again, the reality did not match the rhetoric; Harrison had heard the same rumor in October and dismissed it out of hand as ridiculous.[94] Now, however, he felt certain that the Prophet "will come and equally so of his bad intentions. The whole force I could collect for many miles would not equal his number." For the next five months, Harrison sent a steady drumbeat for war in his missives to Washington: "From all I can collect I have not the least doubt but a crisis with this fellow is approaching."[95]

Tenskwatawa tried to backtrack, sending word to Harrison that Tecumseh would come to Vincennes to sort things out. Summits at Vincennes had prevented violence before. This time, however, Harrison established violent overtones before the brothers even arrived, accusing them of plotting his murder. Harrison also wrote to the brothers explaining how he knew: "If I had no other evidence of your hostility to us, your seizing the salt which I lately sent up the Wabash is sufficient."[96]

Harrison's letter once again warned the brothers of the vast numbers of American troops that could be brought to bear, although again he did not mention that few of those troops were currently available. Tecumseh sent a message back, assuring the governor that he was going to Vincennes only "to wash away all the bad stories."[97] Harrison demanded the brothers make "satisfaction," since they had "insulted the government of the United States." Harrison, it seemed, was preparing for a duel.[98]

The governor had, in fact, made the decision for war even before Tecumseh arrived. The same day Tecumseh wrote to Harrison, the governor gave a series of toasts for the Fourth of July. He praised "the militia of Indiana—they have a bayonet for the British, the French or the Indians." He also offered a toast to his political future, that is, to "Indiana—Territory erased and State surmounted."[99] Also on that same day, Harrison wrote to Governor Edwards in Illinois suggesting they coordinate their efforts against the Prophet. He complained that the Madison administration failed to understand the situation; Eustis and others would have them "receive the Stroke before we are authorized to resist."[100] Then Harrison laid out a complete military strategy for Edwards: march troops to the Wabash, build a fortification, and draw strength from loyal chiefs. Even that plan was not what Harrison really thought would be necessary. To make their point to the Prophet, "we must strike them at their Towns Capture their Women & Children & by distroying their Corn & eternally harassing them oblige them to sue for peace." By July 1811, Harrison had decided on a preemptive strike. "In Indian warfare," Harrison wrote, "there is no security but in offensive Measures."[101]

Harrison's continual tocsins were at last wearing down officials in Washington. In July he wrote, "If some decisive measures are not speedily adopted we shall have a general combination of all Tribes against us." He again warned of a soured public opinion, arguing that "the minds of the people have become so irritated in consequence of the depredations which they continually suffer from the Prophets party."[102] He warned of vigilante actions against loyal tribes unless he was allowed to march troops to the Wabash and demand the dispersion of the Prophet's "Banditti."[103] Harrison helpfully sent along a petition to President Madison in July 1811 protesting that "the safety of the persons and property of this frontier can never be effectually secured" except by smashing Prophetstown.[104] The resolution adopted by the citizens of Vincennes mentioned both plotter and plot by name: "We are fully convinced that the formation of this combination headed by the Shawnese prophet, is a British scheme."[105]

Secretary Eustis finally gave his man in Indiana the military authorization he needed to enforce the treaty. His letter of July 17, 1811, still urged that every effort be made to preserve peace, but "if the prophet should commence, or seriously threaten, hostilities he ought to be attacked."[106] Harrison would use a very broad definition of what constituted a threat. A month before Tippecanoe, Harrison intimated that he had more on his mind than a mere show of strength. "I sincerely wish," he wrote, "that my instructions were such as to authorize me to march immediately to the Prophets Town. . . . I have no reason to doubt the issue of a contest with the savages." This eagerness for battle would later provide his critics with reasons for doubting the wisdom of Harrison's war plans.[107]

The July 1811 summit with Tecumseh, therefore, was largely a waste of time. Tecumseh likely hoped to smooth out misunderstandings; Harrison, committed to a preemptive strike, had no such limitations on his deportment. He immediately took offense that Tecumseh came with so many warriors despite being asked not to do so. It proved the "insolence which is manifested by the Shawnoe." However, given that he was "under the obligations" of presidential order, Harrison nevertheless agreed to "bear with him as much as is possible."[108] Harrison spent most of the council barking demands at Tecumseh. Why had they seized the salt? Why had they permitted western tribes to terrorize families in Illinois? Why would they not remove from the lands the Americans had bought?

Tecumseh answered Harrison with another round of eloquent and memorable speeches. He compared Prophetstown and the Confederacy to the

United States: "They really meant nothing but peace," as Harrison himself later paraphrased it. The "U. States had set him the Example of forming a strict union amongst all the *fires* that compose their confederacy—That the Indians did not complain of it—Nor should his white brothers complain of him for doing the same thing."[109] Tecumseh apologized for the salt seizure and depredations. As for the lands, he once again inverted the American rhetoric. The Indians were the ones who needed the land for settlement, he said. He expected thousands of Indians to arrive at Prophetstown by winter, and they would need the Fort Wayne treaty lands for hunting grounds. Now it was Tecumseh who advised Harrison to move his people elsewhere, lest Indian braves accidentally kill their livestock. At the very least, the question of settling the tract ought to wait until Tecumseh returned from another diplomatic journey—this time to the Creeks and Choctaws in the South.[110]

The council lasted late into the night. Harrison continued to vent his spleen. He pointed at the moon shining down on the men and their armies. It would sooner fall to earth, Harrison told Tecumseh, "than the President would suffer his people to be murdered with impunity—and that he would put his warriors in petticoats sooner than he would give up a country he had fairly acquired."[111]

All in all, it was not a very successful summit. But then, Harrison had never intended it to be; he had already decided on a military solution to the Prophetstown problem, developed a strategy for it, and received the long-sought authority to carry out his plans.[112]

Harrison pursued this strategy even though he worried about the readiness of his armed forces. And lest the citizens of Vincennes doubt the wisdom of such a course, Harrison's inveterate ally, the publisher of the *Sun*, offered this summary of Tecumseh's visit just after the war chief left town:

> Stript of the thin disguise with which he attempted to cover his intentions, the plain English of what he said appeared to be this.— "In obedience to the orders of my master, the British, I have now succeeded in uniting the northern tribes of Indians in a confederacy for attacking the United States, and I am now on my way to stir up the southern Indians. I wish you, however, to remain perfectly quiet until I return—do not attempt to obtain any satisfaction for the injuries you may sustain, or for such as you have already received; I am not yet quite ready to resist you." . . . We hope, however, that the government will take immediate and effectual measures for breaking up this confederacy.

Harrison had decided on a preemptive strike. As Tecumseh went south to continue his mission, Harrison continued his efforts to round up volunteers to make the frontier safe for science, civilization, and his own "mild religion." One of the soldiers wrote home that Harrison's plan would likely frighten away the Prophetstown Indians without much danger: "Make your self as Contented as pos[s]ible," wrote John Drummens to his spouse, "the Governor says that he will insure every man safe home to his wife." John Drummens was killed at the Battle of Tippecanoe on November 7, 1811.[113]

14

Fiasco

HARRISON FAMOUSLY PRAISED Tecumseh as a man who, under different circumstances, "would perhaps be the founder of an Empire that would rival in glory that of Mexico or Peru." Historians have pointed to this letter as evidence of the governor's sense of kinship with Tecumseh, though it also emphasizes a view of Tecumseh as the noble savage and his brother as the barbarian.[1]

Harrison's praise had a purpose, part of a buildup to a personal war. He wrote those words to Secretary of War Eustis, intending to startle Eustis into a confirmation of Harrison's stratagem. If the United States did not keep Prophetstown in check, Tecumseh could create an empire like that of the Aztecs or Incas: "You see him today on the Wabash and in a short time you hear of him on the shores of Lakes Erie or Michigan, or on the banks of the Mississippi and wherever he goes he makes an impression favorable to his purposes." Tecumseh, Harrison wrote, was "one of those uncommon geniuses, which spring up occasionally to produce revolutions and overturn the established order of things." Given that the Americans believed they were the established order, these words were a dire warning. Harrison's praise of Tecumseh ended with a call to arms: "To ensure success some military force must be brought into view." Eustis forwarded the message to James Madison and informed the president that he had approved the march up the Wabash. He reassured Madison that there was "a strong presumption that hostilities will not be commenced by the Indians." Madison breezily agreed that hostilities were unlikely and approved Harrison's war on August 24, 1811.[2]

Despite his bluster to Tenskwatawa, Harrison had meager confidence in his military forces. Years of pleading had changed little. The Jeffersonian legislatures, both state and national, feared government spending and a standing army: "They have supposed that nothing was necessary to effect their wishes, than to cause the men to be enrolled and formed into companies," Harrison grumbled. The result was Harrison's perpetual military headache. "The militia of this section of the Union are vastly inferior," he admitted to Eustis in 1810. "In an encounter with the Indians they would inevitably be beaten unless *greatly* superior in numbers." Watching the local militia practice maneuvers, Harrison concluded that muster days were worse than useless, "devoted to riot and intemperance," and "of those who command . . . few are better than the men whom they attempt to teach."[3]

Nor was Harrison complacent about the Prophet's forces. While subsequent historians deemed Indian success a delusion and an impossibility, Harrison did not. He particularly worried that if the Prophet scored an early military victory, those Indians who had theretofore denied his religion and his state would quickly join ranks with him. Already, Harrison told Edwards, the Prophet had succeeded in strengthening his forces compared to 1810—a year when Harrison wrote that even a small Prophetstown force was still "capable, from the nature of our frontier settlements, of spreading slaughter & devastation to an immense extent."[4]

Then there was the problem of geography. Asked to assess the security situation in the Old Northwest in 1809, Harrison concluded, "I am persuad'd one hundred thousand men would not be able to form a Cordon along the frontiers of this Territory, Michigan, and the state of Ohio, sufficiently compact to preserve our settlements . . . in case of a general combination of the North Western Tribes against us." Forts could not protect the population, he wrote, nor were there any natural choke points to prevent ingress or egress of enemy forces, not even a hill "that can be dignified with the name of mountain" to permit observation of enemy movements.[5] To defeat the Indians of the Northwest, Americans would have to command the waterways, thereby preventing the Native Americans from obtaining reinforcement and resupply from Canada. Of course, the Jeffersonians had not spent much on the navy, either. Harrison often ended such assessments with breezy assurances that Indians likely would not "measure their strength" against the Americans. He felt certain "the Indians will not dare commence hostilities"—as indeed they did not. Harrison started this war.[6]

Thus, the plans Harrison constructed before ever receiving permission to strike Prophetstown called for the movement of American forces up the Wabash and the construction of a military fort on the river to regulate commerce and supply forward forces. He also hoped that this kind of forward operating base would encourage and strengthen the anti-Prophet factions among the Northwest Indians, who would then aid the Americans (openly or tacitly) in the expulsion of the Prophet—thereby limiting Harrison's need to rely on militia forces.

Harrison honored the letter of his promise to Eustis to seek peace by offering Tenskwatawa an ultimatum. He sent a message on August 7, 1811, that all non-Shawnees should leave Prophetstown. Then, in coordination with the governors of Ohio and Michigan, he followed this demand with an

ultimatum to all tribes in the Northwest to cease the flow of warriors and goods into Prophetstown. Meanwhile, he instructed John Johnston to determine how many of the "old chiefs" could provide support or assistance. "Ascertain how far the disaffection may have extended amongst the tribes of your agency," he wrote, and reminded the Indian agent to "assure the fidelity of those who s[t]ill continue faithful or who may be fluctuating."[7] Confident of victory, Harrison assured Eustis that "it is only by placing the danger before his eyes, that a savage is to be control'd."[8]

Tenskwatawa understood the nature of Harrison's demand; the call for non-Shawnees to leave the city was a call for the end of pan-Indianism. Yet Prophetstown was a city for all Indians. That had been the Great Spirit's command. The Prophet could never comply with Harrison's demand for non-Shawnees to abandon the town and still remain true to his faith.

In the past, Tenskwatawa had defused Harrison's recalcitrance by avoiding the governor's demands. On receiving the orders from Harrison, Tenskwatawa tried the same tactic and chose not to answer them directly. Instead, he sent a delegation from Prophetstown to Vincennes to explain the Prophet's peaceful intentions. He also petitioned the Kickapoos, Potawatomies, and Miamis for more soldiers. On September 25, Harrison rebuffed the delegation from Prophetstown, claiming that he had evidence from informers of "designs against us." Evidence of these designs never materialized. Indeed, Harrison had perpetually heard rumors of Indian designs against Americans; only now, with his political situation threatened, did he decide to credit them. Tenskwatawa's policies remained the same; it was Harrison who shifted.[9] The next day he marched from Vincennes with his hodgepodge army.

Harrison was not the only one enthusiastic at the prospect of war. Black Hoof did not mind at all when Harrison proposed to remove the man who had overshadowed him for years. From Ohio, Black Hoof assured the Americans that he had nothing to do with the Prophet, and also that "in the purchase of land you made of the Indians at Fort Wayne two years ago we know you used no deception in it." In Illinois, Governor Edwards was elated. "If we are to have a british war," he wrote to Missouri's Benjamin Howard, "then the more severely we now punish the Indians when we can fight them single handed the more they will be deterred—and the more difficult of course will it be to rally them against us."[10]

Punishing "the Indians" would require a much broader war, and Harrison made some aggressive moves in that direction before he marched from Vincennes. He informed the Potawatomies and various Miami tribes that the Americans were determined to end the Prophet's career. Harrison's

message to the Wea and Eel River tribes described a "dark cloud hanging over" the Wabash.[11] Perhaps Harrison believed his words would strengthen the pro-American factions of the tribes. A group of Miami chiefs sent back a terse message, disavowing any connection with the Prophet but also warning Harrison that he should keep his forces out of Miami land: "If our lands are invaded, we will defend them to the utmost, and die with the land."[12] In Illinois, the pro-American Potawatomi Little Chief expressed exasperation: "The Shawanoe Prophet the man who talks with the father of life—blames us for not listening to him—you do the same. We are like a bird in a bush beset and not knowing which way to fly for safety." Nevertheless, Little Chief warned Harrison against allowing any whites to make war on his people: "Perhaps you take us for little children, we whip little children but men will defend themselves."[13]

Little Chief had good reason to fear that the march on Tenskwatawa's town would devolve into a general war against the Indians. Harrison himself worried about unleashing a racial war, where "the innocent will frequently suffer for the guilty"—that had been his ostensible reason for the clumsy warnings to the Miamis and Potawatomies.[14] For Harrison, the Indian "problem" was still not a question of race—it was an issue of culture. Those who wished to join the United States and surrender their lands and lifeways to the superior civilization should receive protection. Those who chose not to do so were enemies and threats to republicanism.

The men who signed up for the expedition, however, did not always share Harrison's views. Robert McAfee joined up from Kentucky out of "an abhorrence of those principles and practices of the savages, and their British allies."[15] The citizens of Knox County who had petitioned Madison reminded the president that their intent was that "the savages be made sensible that every aggression from them will meet with a correspondent punishment."[16] Lydia Bacon, a camp follower traveling with her quartermaster husband, knew only that "the Indians are committing depredations on the White inhabitants," but she could also imagine, as she traveled to the frontier, "the Indians with their Tomahawks, & scalping knives, peeping at us, from behind the bushes."[17] Bacon's fears in part originated in the stories whites told about the Indians: "How often have I read, & heard of Indian fights, till my blood chilled, in my veins."[18]

As tensions on the Jeffersonian frontier intensified, the stories whites told themselves about Indians changed. In 1808, Archibald Loudon published *A Selection of Some of the Most Interesting Narratives, of Outrages, Committed by the Indians, in Their Wars with the White People*, in two volumes. It told tales

dating back fifty years and more; the teachings of Neolin, the Delaware prophet of the 1760s, were first published in English by Loudon, as part of the captivity account of John McCullough.[19]

Most of Loudon's tales, however, did not linger on the nuances of Indian religion. They followed a simpler format: short, staccato accounts of Indian depredations on innocent whites, with particular emphasis on the barbarity and gruesomeness of the Indian way of war. The captivity narrative of Hugh Gibson featured the story of a white woman stripped naked and branded with irons in front of a crowd of her countrymen, while the "ruthless barbarians were deaf to her agonizing shrieks and prayers; and continued their cruelty till death released her from the torture of these hellish fiends."[20] Another explained the Indian "manner of torture . . . on multitudes of the unhappy settlers, who expected to obtain an easy affluence through honest industry."[21] In one case, the Indians allowed captive blacks to rule over captive whites, "to domineer and tyrannize over the prisoners, frequently whipping them," in a story of racial role reversal probably intended to maximize the fears of a slaveholding society.[22]

Such stories circulated orally as well. In the first decade of the nineteenth century a former Revolutionary soldier, preacher, and businessman from Connecticut named Solomon Spaulding collected local legends about the pre-Columbian Indians into a story about ancient Romans blown off course into "a country inhabited by savages" in "this butt end of the world."[23] Some such local tales managed to get committed to paper, as when John Greenleaf Whittier collected folklore about Indian demon worship, their "knowledge of the doings of Satan in witchcraft and astrology."[24] Thaddeus M. Harris, a clergyman from Massachusetts, imagined that the Indian mounds across the Northwest had once been "PLACES OF SACRIFICE."[25] Bacon herself had stopped to see some of those mounds on her way to Vincennes, which may have contributed to her belief that "the Indians . . . are deceitful in the extreme," even though at the same time she admitted they "have not manifested any hostility towards our Troops."[26] She thanked God, though, for the providence in preserving her husband from an accident with gunpowder, and admired his determination to continue on to Prophetstown. On October 1, she praised this "kind providence," then walked outside to observe the great comet of 1811 as it made its way across the sky.[27]

THE STORY OF the Battle of Tippecanoe is usually told as a rousing frontier battle wherein fire-hardened U.S. troops whipped an unprepared Indian force. That concept, however, owes more to Harrison's presidential campaign materials from 1840 than to the actual events in the fall of 1811. In fact,

Tippecanoe was a disaster for both sides. While Harrison eventually managed to spin the defeat into a political asset, in reality the strike was ill-planned, costly, and militarily insignificant. Within weeks the town had been rebuilt. Harrison almost instantly retreated, and though feted in Vincennes, he was condemned and nearly court-martialed in Washington.[28]

Harrison led a force of around thirteen hundred members of the regular army under Colonel John Boyd, plus seven hundred volunteers, about half of whom were members of the underwhelming Indiana militia. Other volunteers included Kentucky mounted troops and riflemen, including troops led by Joseph Daviess, a U.S. district attorney from Kentucky. The bulk of Harrison's forces were the men he once had denounced as members of the "lazy and intemperate" class.[29]

Harrison therefore proceeded in a slow march, and like his mentor Wayne, he drilled the militia along the way. Seventy miles from Prophetstown, he stopped and built a fort (named after himself) on the Wabash. By October, Fort Harrison was ready, but the delay allowed a fever to run riot among the troops, "a tedious painful disease," as Lydia Bacon called it, treated by "a medicine to vomit me" that she never actually tasted, for the smell alone "had the desired effect." Harrison also discovered that the army had not procured sufficient flour, and so he put his soldiers on half rations.[30]

When Harrison finally did move on Prophetstown, he managed to march his troops through the boggiest, most tiring route. He continually broadcast his position and his proximity to Tenskwatawa by sending emissaries with a series of demands to the Prophet throughout October. Harrison was so confident of victory that although he heard that the forces at Prophetstown were ready for him, he didn't believe it. He wrote to Secretary Eustis that Tenskwatawa "and his followers were confident of success," but "I know not from whence this confidence can be derived." Harrison also assumed that only religious credulity inspired the Indians, charmed by Tenskwatawa's "ridiculous and superstitious pranks."[31]

Harrison failed to understand the relationship between the Prophet's actions and his teachings. Harrison believed trickery had brought the Prophet to prominence. Like all charlatans, Harrison wrote to Eustis, Tenskwatawa sought not truth but tyrannical power. At one point Harrison even accused the British of creating the Prophet's religion itself in order to trick the United States: "The Prophet is inspired by the superintendent of Indian affairs for upper Canada, rather than the Great Spirit."[32]

For his part, Tenskwatawa seemed determined to keep the peace. Most reports agree that Tecumseh had advised (some say ordered) his brother not to engage in hostilities until the mission returned from the south. Drake, McAfee, and other later chroniclers assumed that the Prophet gleefully launched into war once Tecumseh left, in an effort to subvert his brother's growing influence. The evidence points to the contrary: Tenskwatawa appears to have worked assiduously to avoid conflict. In September he offered a compromise, representing his best effort at maintaining peace; he sent a former accommodationist chief to deliver the message, possibly hoping for some fellow feeling, and asked for talks to begin in the new year. Harrison spurned the delegation, saying that he would march the next day and enforce American demands. If the Indians resisted, there would be "retribution for the past."[33]

As Harrison advanced, Tenskwatawa focused on defensive preparations. "They had fortified their town with care & with astonishing labour for them, all indicating that they there meant to Sustain the Shock," Harrison later wrote.[34] Tenskwatawa also sent out spies and scouting parties that occasionally engaged in brief exchanges of fire with their American counterparts. Nevertheless, even when Harrison crossed the Wabash and arrived within striking distance of Prophetstown, the Prophet still urged peace. A delegation met with Harrison as he was encamped by the Wabash, and again offered to hold peace talks. This time, against the advice of his officers, Harrison agreed. On November 6, on a cold and wet evening, Harrison and his troops made camp about a mile from Prophetstown, on a slightly elevated piece of land above the marshy Wabash. Beyond the camp, a soldier named John Tipton heard Indian voices in the night that may have been prayers or war cries, or possibly both.[35]

Shabonee, an Ottawa at Prophetstown who afterward switched to the American side, suggested later in life that Tenskwatawa's offers of peace were a deception.[36] A ruse was certainly possible, and many historians have surmised that the Prophet did indeed plan a sneak attack that evening. (Such an explanation usually comes with the accusation that the Prophet guaranteed victory, promising the assembled Indian forces that they would be immune to bullets.) The Prophet's forces, in this view, eased themselves forward under cover of darkness and opened fire on the Americans.

The alternative, as explained by Alfred A. Cave in the most thorough examination of the Battle of Tippecanoe to date, is that the battle itself was a mistake. Indian units were making regular patrols that night; Tenskwatawa had the same doubts about Harrison's trustworthiness as Harrison had about the Prophet's. According to one of the Prophet's Kickapoo supporters, the American sentinels accidentally panicked and shot two Winnebago warriors on one such patrol. As this news spread through Prophetstown, the Indians "determined to be revenged" and made for the Americans in the early morning hours. Such an explanation—wherein the forces at Prophetstown held on to the peace until blood was shed—seems more consistent with Tenskwatawa's pacific overtures. After all, the Prophet had had ample opportunities to strike the Americans while they moved through muddy thickets in unfamiliar territory in the weeks before they arrived at the gates of Prophetstown. Such an explanation also avoids the assumption that religious people will believe anything they are told by a holy man—and it is consistent with what Tenskwatawa himself said in 1816: "The Winnebagoes with me at Tippecanoe struck your people. I was opposed but could not stop it."[37]

Harrison had already decided on war, whether or not Tenskwatawa planned a first strike. Several weeks after the battle, he reflected on the action to a confidant in Kentucky. He had already made up his mind when he met with the Prophetstown delegation on November 6, he wrote. He would make his demands, which he "did not believe they would accede to," and once negotiations had failed, he could "attack & burn the Town on the following night." Harrison wanted a military victory, knowing that military laurels would buttress his perilous political situation. That much was revealed in the same letter, when he recalled his conundrum of how to initiate action against Prophetstown while minimizing political risk; an open assault in the daytime would seem barbaric and cruel, he wrote, while a night attack would seem cowardly. A "nightly incursion" by the nativists "was precisely what I wished because from Such a one only could I hope for a close & decisive action." Whether or not Harrison initiated the action, the battle that ensued was precisely what he wanted.[38]

Ultimately no one will ever know who fired first—Harrison's green troops or a Winnebago patrol from Prophetstown. The firefight began just at dawn. Some reports said that the Americans had been sleeping on their rifles in anticipation of the attack and thus quickly joined the action, but others asserted that American soldiers were shot before they even got out of their tents.[39] For the first two hours there was "continewel firing," with Indians charging in and retreating from the camp, "so that we Could not tell the indians and our men apart," as participant John Tipton wrote.[40] Harrison's failure to erect breastworks undoubtedly aided the assault.[41]

Harrison was awake when the fighting began, at least according to McAfee, and found the camp under attack on three sides. He sent Daviess to lead a contingent of dragoons against the enemy forces. When Daviess charged, however, few men followed. McAfee blamed the incident on Daviess' insufficiently commanding voice; lack of discipline seems as likely an explanation. In any event, the charge failed, and Daviess himself was mortally wounded.[42]

The Prophetstown forces hoped to decapitate the Americans by killing Harrison, and to that end, they had arranged a bitter harvest, given the governor's energetic pursuit of the expansion of slavery. They had contacted one of Harrison's ex-slaves, a wagon driver named Ben, who led a contingent of Indian warriors in a strike against Harrison's tent. Ben's unit thought they had spotted the governor on his usual gray horse, and shot the rider. But Harrison rode a black horse that day; he had given his gray horse to Abraham Owen, his aide-de-camp, who died in Harrison's place. The assassination squad became confused and were caught. It was, Harrison later wrote, "*providential* interference."[43]

Harrison's forces took far heavier casualties, more than 180. "I have seen the wounded arrive, my God! what heart rending sight," wrote John Badollet later that month. The Prophetstown forces lost somewhere around fifty soldiers. Low on ammunition, the Indian forces retreated.[44]

Tenskwatawa evacuated Prophetstown. While perhaps a sound military decision, the flight from Prophetstown gave Harrison the chance to claim a triumph. The Americans "took" the city without further bloodshed. Yet they too were short on provisions and ammunition. Having sustained heavy casualties, and with rumors swirling that Tecumseh was on his way with reinforcements, the Americans beat a hasty retreat. But Harrison had long planned for this moment. He ordered the troops to set fire to the city— especially to the fields and the storehouses. It was another tactic from his days in Wayne's army. Elias Darnell, serving under Harrison, helped destroy a settlement that gave the lie to white claims that traditional Indians had no agriculture: "We cut up their corn and put it in piles, sixty or eighty acres, so that it might rot. A variety of beans were found growing with their corn; potatoes, pumpkins, water-melons, and cucumbers . . . all burnt by the orders of General Harrison."[45] Tenskwatawa's forces had not retreated far; they were perhaps three miles away and likely saw the smoke rising from their town.[46] There was no winner at Tippecanoe. There was just the smoldering city and the barren fields.

HARRISON SPENT MUCH of the next several weeks assuring his superiors that Tippecanoe had been a complete and total victory. He was also immensely pleased with his own performance, writing, "The Indians have never sustained so severe a defeat since their acquaintance with white people."[47] Nonetheless, conflicting reports of the battle began to creep into newspapers and official correspondence. Harrison soon discovered that "enemies of the Administration in Kentucky have endeavored to raise a clammor from some supposed defect in the planning or in the execution of the late expedition."[48] Harrison once again suspected a conspiracy. "My personal enemies have united with the British agents in representing that the expedition was entirely useless."[49]

Harrison's critics included John Johnston, who wrote to Secretary Eustis, "I am afraid the Governour has been outgeneralled by them." The Indians, Johnston informed Eustis, had suffered few casualties, even though Tecumseh had been absent. Worse, "the result of the late battle has however not conveyed to the natives any great idea of our prowess in War"; if Harrison's goal had been to frighten the Indians into submission, the effort had been worse than doing nothing. Indeed, the Prophetstown Indians had been so incensed at the burning of their village that after the Americans withdrew, they "returned to the Battle ground dug up our dead strip[p]ed them and left them lying above ground."[50]

Criticism came from closer to home as well: Harrison's own second in command, John Boyd. Frustrated by the newspaper reports praising the militia and condemning the regular army, Boyd wrote to Eustis a month after Tippecanoe, complaining that the regular army had delivered victory, while "the dastardly conduct of some whole militia companies led to exposure." Militia captains hid during battle, Boyd wrote, and that cowardice caused the high casualty rate.[51] Though Boyd exonerated Harrison for the militia's conduct, his letter appeared in the national newspapers and added to the criticism of what increasingly looked to many like a debacle. The Indiana legislature was also skeptical of the strike at Prophetstown. When Harrison's allies in the Indiana legislature submitted a resolution praising the governor's action, it failed to pass the upper house. The pro-Harrison men adopted the resolution without a quorum and sent it on to President Madison anyway, who duly issued a proclamation to Congress honoring Harrison.[52]

Newspaper reports, particularly in the anti-war Northeast, provided another venue for condemnation. "Governor Harrison's account of the battle with the Indians, in general, is not very satisfactory," reported the *Long Island Star*. "The administration . . . will certainly do well to terminate these hostilities as speedily as possible," was the comment from the *Commercial Advertiser*. "War in any form is not their element" and "The one in which they are now engaged will be found, we fear . . . to be a most 'un-*prophet*-able contest.'"[53]

If anything, the strike on Prophetstown made Tenskwatawa's movement stronger. William Clark's prediction that "the Defeat of the Prophet" would push Indians "into the Measures of their [old] chiefs" did not come true. In fact, the opposite happened; Tippecanoe alerted wavering Indian towns, tribes, and leaders that Tenskwatawa had told the truth. An unprovoked American attack, a people dispersed, and a village burned did not encourage accommodation. The Prophet himself undoubtedly lost face because of the defeat, and yet the resort to arms without clear provocation—and the continued nativist occupation of Prophetstown—brought more Indians and tribes into the Prophet's orbit.[54]

Indian agent Jacob Lalime reported from Chicago that despite his retreat from Prophetstown, the Prophet nevertheless had given the Indians of the Northwest the conviction that they could win. "It appears that they have an idea that they have gained a victory over our army, and that if it had not been for want of Ammunition they would have defeated the whole. . . . They hold a very unfavorable idea of the Americans being able to stand a battle with them." Over the next few months, new Indians and entire tribes joined the Prophet's movement. Gomo, a longtime accommodationist Miami leader, announced he could no longer influence his tribe. The Sioux sent representatives and warriors to Indiana. In Illinois, groups of Winnebago soldiers began raiding the frontiers freely in revenge for their brethren killed at Tippecanoe.[55] And most astonishingly, the Wyandots of Michigan did not even bother with the frontier bureaucrats and intermediaries. Under pressure to sell more lands, they wrote to the House of Representatives that several missionaries had "told us the religion of the whites consisted in a few words; that was, to do unto other as we wish that others would do unto us. . . . we wish you to put the above Christian rule into practice." Instead, they found that when American bought land, "all our nations are assembled; a large sum of money is offered; the land is occupied probably by one nation only; nine-tenths have no actual interest in the land wanted; if the particular nation interested refuses to sell, they are generally threatened by the others, who want the money or goods offered, to buy whiskey." Indian disaffection increased in the wake of Tippecanoe.[56]

Several stories emerged over the next few years about the loss, including the legend that Tecumseh nearly killed Tenskwatawa when he heard the news. Other stories about the battle focused on the magical protection the Prophet had supposedly promised and failed to provide his followers during the Battle of Tippecanoe. Such stories in turn were invariably used as evidence to prove that the battle had broken the political power of the Prophet—a claim that was manifestly untrue, though it has persevered in the historiography. One of Harrison's contacts reported to him that the Prophet had promised his followers on the night before the battle that he would devise an "enchantment" over the enemy that would render half of the enemy army "dead and the other half bewildered or in a state of distraction." After the battle, Harrison's correspondent explained, when the surviving warriors demanded to know why the magic had failed, Tenskwatawa "held his head down between his knees" and admitted that "his composition was lost in consequence of it being with his wife the time of her monthly visitation."[57] This story of defeat by menstruation has been repeated by both nineteenth- and twentieth-century historians.[58]

All these stories come from Harrison allies, and from white men. The particular story of Tenskwatawa's supposed excuse is both plausible (because of the cultural taboos on blood in Eastern Woodlands cultures) and implausible (because it is not verified by any Indian source). Nor was the source of the story, a captain under Harrison's command named Josiah Snelling, an eyewitness. A report from "a Kickapoo chief," recorded by British Indian agent Matthew Elliott and subsequently reprinted in the Alexandria *Gazette* in 1812, makes no mention of the Prophet's magic or his loss of leadership.[59] In fact, the Kickapoo reported, "The Prophet and his people do not appear as a vanquished enemy; they re-occupy their former ground." Two months after the battle, Harrison received notice that "many of them [the Kickapoos] retained their confidence in the Prophet" and "believed that they would all die as soon as the Prophet was put to death."[60]

And then there was the earthquake. In the early morning of December 11, a massive quake struck near New Madrid, in what is now Missouri. Modern seismological estimates suggest the initial shock had a magnitude of 8.1. The earth shook in Louisville, Detroit, Quebec, New England, and Louisiana; church bells rang in Charleston, South Carolina, and the pavement cracked in Washington, D.C.[61] In New Madrid itself, houses, streets, and a graveyard plunged into the river as what had been bayou thrust upward to become dry land. The river itself seemed torn to pieces; it shifted course, flooded the town, erupted with new rapids and waterfalls. According to witnesses, the Mississippi ran backward for a few minutes. Such a catastrophe spawned calls of divine punishment. "New Madrid had been designated as the metropolis of the New World," wrote the itinerating Lorenzo Dow, "but God sees not as man sees."[62] In Congress, Virginia's Thomas Randolph cried out that war was imminent: "We are on the brink of some dreadful scourge—some great desolation—some awful visitation from that Power whom, I am afraid, we have as yet, in our national capacity, taken no means to conciliate."[63]

The devastation among Indian villages along the Mississippi must have been as severe as at New Madrid. By the end of the month, however, the legend had arisen that "the *Shawanese Prophet* has caused the earthquake to destroy the whites."[64] Later legends made the earthquake the result of Tecumseh stamping his foot. Whites took the earthquake as a sign of chastisement; Indians took it as a call to action and a divine vindication of the Prophet's power.

Meanwhile, Harrison's own correspondence revealed the murky results of the battle. On December 11, he reported that the Prophet remained dangerous, and requested more federal troops. In Canada, Matthew Elliot reported that the raid had failed and that the Prophet and his people had already reoccupied Prophetstown. On the same day, Colonel Boyd issued that stinging reproof of the governor's handling of the ambush. Finally, on January 12, Secretary Eustis commanded Harrison to make peace with the Prophet, and Harrison was (humiliatingly) forced to send a delegation to the very place he thought he had burned to the ground.

Tippecanoe also failed to secure the frontiers for white settlement; with Indian attacks increasing, white settlers began to leave. Governor Edwards' informants saw wagon trains heading east. In Dark County, Ohio, a citizens group begged for either military protection or "peace with the Indians," or else "most if not all the inhabitants here will move."[65]

Tenskwatawa, for his part, regrouped. He and his brother rejected Secretary Eustis' peace feelers, but in May, Tecumseh convened a massive pan-Indian congress at Mississinewa; Tecumseh urged peace but warned the Americans that the Treaty of Fort Wayne should not be enforced. A few weeks later, Tenskwatawa sent out messengers to various far-flung tribes such as the Otos, Creeks, and Sioux with a religious and political plea for support. Tenskwatawa, it seemed, was still in charge of his movement.

Harrison, on the other hand, seemed about to lose his. Political discontent had provoked a congressional investigation into whether the British had fomented the Indian resistance, and of "the orders by which the campaign [against the Indians] was authorized and carried on." The report concluded that Harrison's campaign "to march against, and disperse, the armed combination under the Prophet" was justified. Its conclusion depended, however, on the logic that because an Indian rebellion would "hazard the large annuities" supplied by the United States, the Native Americans therefore must have been receiving British aid. No Indian could possibly value freedom or land more than annuities and supplies. In other words, Congress retroactively approved Harrison's decisions because it accepted his contention of a British plot, based solely on the argument that no Indian grievance could possibly justify war. To whites' minds, the Indian willingness to fight was a sign of British perfidy. The legality and wisdom of Harrison's treaties, the failures of the annuity system, and Harrison's own machinations were not considered in the brief report, which was issued on June 13, 1812—five days before Congress declared war on Great Britain.[66]

The war declaration stunned Americans and British alike. It also saved Harrison's career. Congressional debates over whether to declare war were held in secret, and they were among the most acrimonious in American history. In part, the advocates for war—whose nickname, "War Hawks," became an entrenched part of the American political vocabulary—accepted Harrison's Jeffersonian logic. Harrison's military gaffe was ultimately pardoned because his political party succeeded in extending the war across the nation. And with a war on, Harrison's political opportunities would be unparalleled.

The advocates of war shared some of Harrison's other characteristics, too. In the recommendation for war that John C. Calhoun presented to Madison, the U.S. Congress concluded that war was necessary and that God was on their side: "The Lord of Hosts will go with us to Battle."[67]

15

"A War of Extirpation"

WHAT FOLLOWED WAS a catastrophe. The United States has had its share of military debacles, conflicts entered into without sufficient resources or with a vast underestimate of the actual military objectives at hand. Even among such blunders, the War of 1812 stands out. America entered the war—its first as an independent government and its first without General Washington—in a poisonous atmosphere of political division that prompted talk of secession and actual military mutiny. Michigan, Maine, and the District of Columbia fell to invading armies; the White House burned. As historian Jon Latimer points out, it was not a war "both sides won," as popular opinion has it (when anyone even remembers the event). It was fundamentally "a failed war of conquest."[1]

The object of conquest was clear to almost everyone in 1812. Perpetual congressional curmudgeon John Randolph lambasted the case for war as "one monotonous tone—Canada! Canada! Canada!"[2] Jefferson, on the other hand, was positively gleeful in his reaction to the news, and wrote that the subjugation of Canada would be a "mere matter of marching." Henry Clay insisted that "the conquest of Canada is in your power." It would, he declared, "extinguish the torch that lights up savage warfare."[3]

Madison sent his request for a declaration of war to Congress on June 1, 1812. The president listed the "injuries and indignities which have been heaped on our Country." These indignities included the impressment of American sailors, the violation of neutral shipping rights, naval blockades—and Tippecanoe. "Our attention is necessarily drawn to the warfare just renewed by the Savages, on one of our extensive frontiers; a warfare which is known to spare neither age nor sex, and to be distinguished by features peculiarly shocking to humanity." The evidence for a presumed conspiracy between British Canada and the Indian rebellions, so often promoted by Harrison in defense of his conduct, and so rarely substantiated, had made it into Madison's justification for war. The president even used the same logic Harrison had: any Indian rebellion necessitated the existence of a British connection:

"It is difficult to account for the activity, and combinations . . . among tribes in constant intercourse with British traders and garrisons, without connecting their hostility with that influence." In a reversal of his long effort to keep peace on the frontier, Madison had finally adopted (at least rhetorically) the notion that Indian resistance flowed not from American malfeasance, injustice, or land hunger but from British malevolence.[4]

Yet the Father of the Constitution should probably be cleared of the charge of sloppy logic in favor of the charge of political survival. Like the Battle of Tippecanoe that preceded it, the War of 1812 was a political war, pushed hardest by one faction within one party to enhance its power and to secure electoral success. Madison had never been the universal choice of Republicans to succeed Jefferson. Jefferson's policies had often sidestepped his pre-election philosophies about state liberties. The Louisiana Purchase, the fanatical pursuit of Burr, and the embargo prompted some congressional Republicans to seek a candidate ideologically better than Madison, who had once been a Federalist himself. Fears of a Virginia-dominated union led a Republican faction to back George Clinton of New York in 1808. Madison survived the challenge to become the candidate in the general election, with Clinton as his running mate.[5]

These divisions intensified after Madison's election. He attempted to balance his own supporters and the "malcontents" when he made his presidential appointments; this move actually led more Republicans into opposition.[6] As historian Robert V. Remini has pointed out, the Republican Party of 1809 "instilled no discipline," and with Jefferson gone, constant efforts began to decapitate their own party.[7] Madison's ineffectual efforts to preserve peace while trying to intimidate Britain did not stem the tide of criticism. By July 4, 1811, while Governor Harrison was drinking to the destruction of Prophetstown, other Republican leaders were drinking to the dismantling of the president. In New York, Maryland, and Pennsylvania, Republicans celebrated Independence Day in usual raucous antebellum fashion—but did not drink to Madison or to his reelection. A Swedish visitor in New York State made what he thought was an appropriate toast praising the president. It received no cheers.[8]

The War Hawks found themselves in position by the spring of 1812 to force a change. When Madison sent a peace mission to Britain in April 1812, Henry Clay and a group of congressional Republicans paid a visit to the White House and in no uncertain terms told the president that if he did not seek an "open and direct war . . . they would forsake him and be opposed to him." If Madison lost the War Hawks and the "malcontents," he was finished.[9]

Madison's brother-in-law, James G. Jackson, urged the president to move toward war. The electorate would presumably follow, he explained, and "the war will become more & more popular every day.[10]

Republicans hoped to bring back the political fortunes of 1800, when Jeffersonians talked grandiloquently about being the one true American political cause. Felix Grundy, a War Hawk, declared that once hostilities began, "the distinction of Federalists and Republicans will cease." Similarly, Jefferson feared that if Madison could not get the Republicans to act together, then "our *nation* will be undone. For the Republicans are the nation."[11]

Madison therefore had strong motives to ask Congress for war preparations in October 1811. Congress puttered for a while but eventually authorized additional troops to supplement the tiny American army. In theory, the 20,000 new regulars, 50,000 volunteers, and 100,000 militiamen authorized presumably were a preparation with "a view to enable the Executive to step right into Canada," as Madison wrote to Jefferson.[12] The question of peace or war, wrote British envoy Augustus Foster, was the "question on which depended the election of the next Presidency."[13]

The vote for war in Congress followed political lines, and it was breathtakingly close. In the House, the debates were held in secret. Federalist James Milnor attempted and failed to open the proceedings to the public. The strategy to unite the Republicans succeeded. Every Federalist voted against it, but only sixteen of the "malcontents" broke with their party to join the opposition. In the end, the measure passed, 78–45.[14]

In the Senate, the Madisonians were outnumbered; at most, the president could rely on fifteen votes out of thirty-four. Worse, administration loyalist Thomas Worthington of Ohio refused to support the war declaration. He had seen the results of Harrison's kind of war and feared that broadening the conflict would instigate Indian attacks throughout Ohio. As in the House, all the Federalists planned to vote against it, as did Philip Reed of Maryland and Nicholas Gilman of Vermont, who were only nominal Jeffersonians. Antiwar sentiment in New England convinced Jeremiah Howell to save his career rather than Madison's, and another frontier senator (Pope of Kentucky) shared Worthington's concerns about the results of a war. That gave the opposition eleven votes; they needed eighteen to defeat the measure.

Conveniently, at least eight senators—anti-Madison Republicans all— were wavering. These included Alexander Gregg, who preferred letters of marque to formal war, and Michael Leib, who simply disliked Madison. Obadiah German, John Smith, and John Lambert came from mid-Atlantic and New England states impoverished by embargo and soured toward war.

William Giles of Virginia came out against it. Samuel Smith of Maryland talked on both sides of the issue, and Senator Richard Brent was often so drunk it was impossible to know what he thought.[15]

On June 10, the Senate voted to approve letters of marque rather than declare war—a move that would keep the conflict on the seas and thereby prevent an invasion of Canada and attacks on Indians. The motion passed 17–13, and it looked as though the push to war would wither. On June 12, however, the Senate reconsidered. This time the motion failed on a tie vote. "The suspense we are in," wrote one observer, "is worse than hell!!!!"[16]

On June 15, after a series of delaying tactics, Leib once again brought up his proposal to substitute letters of marque. The motion failed, 17–15. That defeat likely convinced other waverers that continued opposition was pointless or politically dangerous. The Senate passed the declaration of war, 19–13. The key vote was that of Giles, who had voted for letters of marque on June 10 but against them on June 12 and 15. German, Gilman, and Lambert voted with the Federalists, but everyone else threw in with Madison. Even Leib and Gregg, once they realized their alternative would not pass, voted for the declaration. Had they, Giles, and Samuel Smith voted no—as all of them, at one time or another, had said they would—the declaration would have failed. In this way, America limped into war.

Despite the impassioned assurances Harrison and other western governors gave about their citizens' enthusiasm and support for war, the congressional representatives of the western states knew better. Kentucky and Ohio—the two states that surely would see the most violence in a western war—had a Senate delegation that voted 3–1 against the war. Ohio's only congressman also voted no. Transmontane Virginia—the closest thing the Old Dominion had to a western country—exhibited so little enthusiasm for war that it elected a Federalist to Congress in 1810 for the first time in twenty years. He also voted against the war.[17] The West was apparently not brimming with war fever and a hunger for Indian lands; some of their leaders might have been, but plenty of constituents, it seems, would rather have left well enough alone.[18]

Oddly enough, the British government had revoked the Orders-in-Council that hampered American shipping—one day before the Senate voted for war. Britain itself faced a political and military crisis that dwarfed Madison's; in May, with the country at war with Napoleonic France, an assassin had shot Prime Minister Spencer Perceval at point-blank range. The fact that Parliament managed to pull together a new government and address the American complaints in a matter of weeks was astonishing in itself. News did not reach

the United States for more than a fortnight, however, and by then war had been declared, and plans for the conquest of Canada had begun.

Political wars are often executed with a political ideology. In the case of the War of 1812, this tendency hobbled the war effort. The Jeffersonians were the anti-war, anti-standing-army party; Harrison's perpetual concerns about the militia were not shared by most of his party members. Clay, for example, had suggested that "the militia of Kentucky are alone competent to place Montreal and Upper Canada at your feet."[19] Jefferson and Madison had assiduously cut military budgets, and the Twelfth Congress had done the same. In 1810, the Republicans in Congress had actually reduced the size of the army and navy, despite the possibility of war with Britain and France simultaneously. Their successors in 1812 voted *for* war but *against* the construction of further naval vessels. Some Republicans, such as Nathaniel Macon of North Carolina, voted against all military expansion before and after he voted to send the country to war.[20]

The basis for this paradox derived from perennial fears of a standing army in the British Whig tradition, adopted by anti-Federalists in America. The notion that a standing army in peacetime, forming a distinct class, would eventually oppress liberty acted as "a kind of axiom" in this Anglo-American ideology.[21] More recently, the Republican political success of the 1800s had been forged, in part, in opposition to the military ambitions of Federalist leaders; the plans of John Adams and Alexander Hamilton to increase the military in order to intimidate the British and tamp down dissent had sparked the turn to Jefferson. Jefferson himself opposed military spending, given that he believed military acumen derived solely from the "love of liberty, and republican government, which carried us triumphantly through the [Revolutionary] war." Military planning, skill, and funding were unnecessary to a nation or a people with moral purpose. Yeoman farmers, formed into militia ranks, could defeat all foes. Money was not needed for the war effort. What was required was that yeoman militia fight valiantly. War could be fought on guts and perseverance. When Senators Giles and Gregg, in the run-up to the war, tried to dissuade their countrymen from war given that the army would have far more volunteers than regulars, they earned a mocking rebuke from General Bradley, who declared that Vermont alone could produce 10,000 volunteers, "who could beat a similar force of the best appointed legions of Napoleon." They could "whip the 25,000 regulars of Mr. Giles," drive the British from Canada, and "would not ask whether the constitution authorized the president to march them into Canada." The "country was all fire and fight," Bradley assured the Senate, and Congress "pusillanimous."[22]

Bradley was exactly wrong. The country was not on fire for war, the militia did not measure up to trained British regulars, Canada did not fall to the United States, and—astonishingly—militia squadrons from Pennsylvania and New York actually *did* stop at the border of Canada because they did not believe the president had the authority to order them to invade foreign territory. (They were "unfortunately seized with constitutional scruples," as Robert McAfee put it.)[23] Militiamen showed up, collected their pay, and went back home. The volunteer forces—a designation separate from the militia—almost never met their recruitment quotas.[24] Senator Worthington learned that the 160 acres offered as a bounty did not encourage volunteerism when one of his constituents informed him that "many wished every member of Congress had 160 acres of land stuffed up his xxxx." Britain's General Isaac Brock, in charge of facing these sorts of American units, had a simple assessment of their worth: "They die very fast."[25]

Madison had warnings of this lack of military preparedness. A report on the military in April 1811 warned that there were garrisons staffed by men who had never fired a cannon. Coastal defenses at Norfolk were rusting and "unworthy of the name of a fort." Army muskets and rifles were of poor quality and inaccurate; the officer class was "generally ignored & conceited."[26] War Hawks were not worried about the absence of preparation; they had decided "to get married & buy the furniture afterwards," joked Congressman Robert Wright.[27] The joke might have been lost on the soldiers of the Northwest. Even when Congress managed to provide matériel, American leadership bungled the job: Hull famously sent U.S. war supplies to Canada by mistake.[28]

Providentialists swung into action nonetheless, declaring that nature and nature's God wanted the war to go forward. "Such a war," declared John Stevens in his pulpit, "God considers as his own cause, and to help in such a cause is to come to the help of the Lord."[29] The Baptist churches in particular gave religious support to the conflict; they had long been supporters of Republicans generally and Madison in particular for his consistent support of religious freedom and disestablishment. Baptist churches came to Madison in his hour of need, asserting in their numerous yearly meetings the necessity of fighting. Georgia Baptists compared volunteering for the war to the sufferings of the early Christians, couching both as seekers of liberty.[30] Kentucky's Samuel McDowell wrote, "It is remarkable that the capture of the British fleet on Erie happened on the fast day appointed by the President." The American victory actually came several days after the fast, but nevertheless, McDowell said hopefully, "Providence is on our side."[31]

The war proved least popular in mercantile New England, where the deist strain of Christianity had foundered against long-standing Congregationalist piety. The tacit alliance with the French state (traditionally Catholic, recently atheist) against Britain spawned the usual biblical imagery: "Wormwood, it is the gall, which the wrath of heavens have mingled for the nations," declared Federalist congressman George Sullivan. American losses through the first year of the war were a sure sign "that the LORD is not on our side."[32] Massachusetts governor Caleb Strong issued a fast day recommendation, asking Massachusetts residents (who still had a state church) to ask forgiveness of God for setting them to war against "the nation from which we are descended" and which was "the *Bulwark* of our religion" against France. Strong's proclamation also included the fear that the war in the Northwest could mean the end of civilizing programs for Native Americans; it asked Massachusetts citizens to pray "that He would dispose the people of these States to do justice to the Indian tribes, to enlighten and not to exterminate them."[33]

At least one minister used Strong's fast day as a platform to lambaste the Harrisonian logic that Indians had only made war on Americans under British prompting. "There is no evidence of the fact laid before the people," sermonized Kiah Bayley. The Battle of Tippecanoe had been not an Indian attack on Americans but an American attack on Indians: "Without any express act of Congress, an expedition was last year set on foot, and prosecuted into Indian territory" not ceded to the United States. Had "we made war upon Indians, or they upon us?"[34] Congregationalist divine Benjamin Bell had no great love for the Indians, but he told his parishioners that Tippecanoe had been little more than the marching of an army into Indian territory simply because Indians were "dissatisfied," having been cheated by Indian agents licensed by the U.S. government.[35] An anonymous author believed that Indian victories were the result of a just providence: "This War was first urged by *Kentucky, Ohio* and the inland States . . . and a righteous Providence is now inflicting on them its direst horrors."[36] The aging John Lathrop—once the interpreter of the Dark Day—quoted Strong's call for justice to Indians and wondered whether American privateering did not amount to the same kind of warfare practiced by "savage" nations.[37]

Not to be outdone, Madison recommended a fast day to the nation for September 1813 and 1814. These and other fast days did not result only in antiwar religious crusades; one sermon praised "the leading patriots of the Nation, fired with fervent zeal for the prosperity of Columbia's cause," and urged them "humbly to implore the aid, assistance, and protection of our father's God, and the Author of our National Independence."[38] In 1814, Timothy Merritt called the conflict a *"righteous* war," warned that "we provoke heaven by lightly esteeming real national character," and compared those who opposed it to "those Jews who clamored against the life of the Saviour, and said, 'His blood be on us, and on our children.'"[39]

Divine sanction for the war had advocates among Native American populations as well, and not just among the followers of Tenskwatawa. Tecumseh's recruiting journey to the Gulf Coast had not unified the northern and southern tribes, but it had sparked a stiffer resistance to the assimilationist policy of the Creek National Council. Among the Muskogee-speaking Creeks in what eventually became Alabama, Little Warrior and a number of religious leaders led a revolt against American authority when the War of 1812 got under way. Unlike Tenskwatawa's movement, which condemned traditional authority, the Red Stick Rebellion was largely led by the established shamans among Muskogee-speaking peoples and did not have a primary prophet or central political headquarters. Nevertheless, the Red Sticks declared that their high god—the Maker of Breath—would preserve their homeland and terrify their enemies. Most of the fighting in the American South during the war—up to and including the Battle of Horseshoe Bend—would involve Americans fighting the vast Red Stick rebellion, which numbered perhaps four thousand.[40]

Estimates of the Prophet's forces in the Northwest are unclear, but Thomas Forsythe—who politely declined the post of Indian agent of a United States on the brink of war—set the number at around five thousand. Henry Rowe Schoolcraft, writing after the war, put the number at over eight thousand. In June 1812, while Congress debated a war that would pit Americans against nativist Indians, Harrison reassured them that the problems at Prophetstown had been solved. Forsythe wrote, however, "I am afraid that Govr Harrison has not the proper information from the Prophet's town, as his party must be great at present."[41]

Harrison's confusion was part of Tenskwatawa's plan. The Prophet made efforts to feign submission to American officials. In councils held in March and May 1812, his followers blamed the Prophet for their troubles, and Isadore Chaine—a Métis in the service of Britain—presented white wampum belts of peace to the Americans. When U.S. officials had left, Chaine gave black wampum belts, signifying alliance, to the other tribes.[42] Similarly, the Prophet himself met with American officials at Fort Wayne in July, ostensibly for the funeral of Little Turtle, who had finally succumbed to gout and dropsy.[43] Tenskwatawa offered the Americans "a large white belt of wampum, with a small spot of purple." The purple spot represented Prophetstown, he explained, and one end of the belt extended to Vincennes and the other to Fort Wayne. Tenskwatawa even declared to the Americans that he was ready "to relinquish all claim to the land conveyed to the US by the Treaty of Fort Wayne of 1810."[44]

The Prophet's promises were a ruse; he had already conferred with Chaine about the importance of quietly stockpiling weapons at Prophetstown. Nevertheless, Tenskwatawa also sent messengers around the Northwest to consolidate the discontent that had simmered since Tippecanoe. His messengers called for Indians—especially soldiers—to join him at Prophetstown. One Kickapoo visitor to a Sac council spoke "in behalf of the Prophet" in a much more martial tone than before:

> Your Friend, the great Narrator on the Wabash River has sent to each of you this Wampum & Pipe for you to reverence and join him at his village when the corn is made, so we all can agree there when & where to strike on the Americans. They are a bad People and never will tell you the truth, they will also cheat you out of your lands and keep you and your families in poverty.[45]

The Kickapoo speaker boasted about his own clothing—a sign of the goods derived from the British alliance Tecumseh was formalizing that very season. Tecumseh would be in Upper Canada when William Hull, in command of U.S. forces, attempted to invade. Tenskwatawa remained at Prophetstown, making the Wabash "more conspicuous as a point of danger," in Edwards' terms. Far from being finished after Tippecanoe, the Prophet and his movement were stronger than before, and about to achieve their greatest victory.[46]

THE WAR OF 1812 was the first war fought from Washington rather than Philadelphia and Valley Forge. In this initial conflict, born of political meanderings, fought with swagger but not foresight, the Americans were coming up badly short. In the West, however, a war against Canada allowed Harrison and his allies to pursue their "war of extirpation" against recalcitrant Indian tribes. A week after war was declared, Napoleon invaded Russia, tying up British land forces and leaving the Great White North undersupplied. The American generals thanked providence for what was obviously a divine design for them to take Canada.

Harrison longed to join the fray, but his miscalculations at Tippecanoe had made both Madison and Eustis wary of accepting the governor's offers of help. Madison named Michigan's governor, William Hull—a veteran of the Revolution—the major-general in the West, and then put James Win-chester in charge of the second army. Harrison received no orders, forcing him to write to the governor of Kentucky to see if, perhaps, "the volun-teers from your state would serve under me." Eustis, however, ordered Harrison to fortify and defend his territory. He would not be receiving a military commission.[47]

Hull took command, but his confidence outweighed his wisdom. He began by letting the soldiers have a parade thrown for them by grateful Ohio citizens. He then marched his troops through Ohio, cutting a new road to Detroit.[48] Hull outlined the purpose of the march to his soldiers: "In march-ing through a wilderness memorable for savage barbarity, you will remember the causes by which the barbarity had been heretofore excited. In viewing the ground stained with the blood of your fellow citizens, it will be impossible to repress the feelings of indignation."[49] Before the war even began, white gen-erals were preparing their troops to think of Indians as subhuman brutes. Hull also repeated the axiom that Britain had prompted all Indian malfea-sance against the encroaching Americans.

Across the border, the "savage" Tecumseh had an army numbering in the thousands, and had allied with the British and Canadian forces, which would prove surprisingly eager to defend their country. American war plans had assumed Canadians would rise up and join the invaders to throw off Britain, forgetting that many Canadians had immigrated there because of loyalist predilections during the American Revolution. They had built their own royalist state in Upper Canada and had little interest in rejoining rebel-lious countrymen.[50]

Indeed, almost as soon as the war began, the Indian and Canadian forces struck a crushing blow. U.S. strategy involved a three-pronged attack on Can-ada: against the capital of Upper Canada (York, now Toronto), the British naval centers on Lake Ontario, and the Niagara.[51] The campaign for the Niag-ara was repulsed at the Battle of Queenstown Heights in October; the Yanks captured York in 1813 but decided to burn it rather than hold it. Washington, D.C., would pay for this act of hubris when the British captured it about a year later.

But of all the failures, the assault on Kingston, the primary British naval port on Lake Ontario, was the most spectacular. Hull entered Canada with an army split by factions and personal animosities. He then trained his troops in British territory for two weeks without advancing. On hearing that a com-bined Indian, Canadian, and British force had taken the American fort at Michilimackinac, Hull withdrew to Detroit. The northern allies pursued, and in August they placed the city under siege. British commanders informed Hull that he ought to surrender to prevent a "war of extermination." Hull apparently believed his own rhetoric about the depravity of Indian warfare, and rather than face it, he surrendered Detroit on August 16, 1812. The war was only two months old, and already Tecumseh and his allies had retaken part of their homeland from the Americans.[52]

The day before the victory at Detroit, the Americans had evacuated Fort Dearborn and let the Indian and British forces take control there. Many were killed as they fled—including William Wells.[53] These victories put Michigan firmly under Indian-British control; while British strategy remained focused on the defeat of Napoleon (North America was a sideshow until then), the victory seemed to be in keeping with the Indian war strategy. Lack of Native sources for Tenskwatawa's movement during the war makes identifying their war aims difficult. Several white Americans, however, thought they had surmised the situation. Ninian Edwards believed that the Indians' object was to frighten white settlers off the land in northern Indiana and Illinois while opening larger military offenses on key American positions.[54]

Tenskwatawa's actions seemed to bear out Edwards' analysis. By September, the Prophet's forces had assaulted Fort Wayne and Fort Harrison. The Americans holed up at Fort Wayne heard that Tecumseh had promised the Miamis "that he was coming on to the Wabash with 7000 Indians and a great number of English, that he should put his foot on Fort Wayne as he came along, and crush it."[55] The Prophet, it seemed, wanted to secure and hold the territory he had claimed for this people prior to the Battle of Tippecanoe.[56]

Many white observers also felt sure that Tecumseh and the Prophet wanted to open a second front in the South—which occurred when the Red Sticks rebelled. General Andrew Jackson took command in the South, and while he heard Cherokees and Creeks claim they were not listening to the Prophet, he suspected that the tribes were "secretly influenced in a greater or lesser degree by these malcontents."[57]

For Harrison, however, Hull's failure at Detroit was a windfall. The governor journeyed from Vincennes to Kentucky to meet with Scott, Shelby, and other Kentucky Republicans. This party meeting—not the officials at Washington—determined that Harrison should take up command of the army in the West. Rather than recommend Harrison to Madison, however, Governor Scott instead appointed Harrison the general of the Kentucky militia. According to the Kentucky state constitution, militia commanders had to live or have been born in Kentucky; Harrison had done neither. But command of a state militia without real legal justification was precisely the kind of murky situation that would allow Harrison to write his own rules.[58]

Harrison then made his own power play. James Monroe planned to march an army to assist in the recapture of Detroit, but when Henry Clay told him that Harrison had the support of Kentucky's Republicans, Monroe decided to delay his mission. That left only James Winchester's regular army in the western theater. When Winchester and Harrison met in Cincinnati in late August, Harrison demanded control of Winchester's forces. Winchester caved, and Madison had little choice but to make Harrison the supreme commander in the West, which he did on September 27, 1812. Passed over on the basis of his qualifications and questionable results in the field, Harrison had reclaimed command based on the support of an ideological faction within the ruling party and his ability to intimidate officials. Harrison was not a general who became a politician; he was a politician who became a general.[59]

A politician who had never served in the military—James Madison—was meanwhile sweating out his reelection campaign. Voters in 1812 did not see candidates themselves trolling for votes or attending rallies; indeed, in many states, the presidential electors were not chosen by direct popular vote. Much of the electioneering involved swaying political leaders and prominent officials, as Madison did with his decision for war.

But a war that goes badly is rarely popular, and Madison had not kept all of his Republicans loyal. DeWitt Clinton, a New York Jeffersonian, had chosen to seek the presidency himself, and he feted supporters by attacking Madison's mishandling of the war, the loss of Michigan, and the dangers of a "Virginia dynasty" ruling the nation (three of four presidents thus far had come from the Old Dominion). The Federalists in turn lined up behind Clinton, hoping that this time the alliance that had nearly scuttled the war vote in the Senate might end the war by taking the White House.[60]

Clinton's candidacy came breathtakingly close. Not until December, when vote tallies were confirmed in Ohio and Pennsylvania, did Madison know he had won. The president certainly won the popular vote—such as it was in 1812—but Clinton could have won the electoral college (and thus the presidency) by winning Pennsylvania, which would have given him a razor-thin 104–103 majority. Pennsylvania was also the state that had elected Madison antagonist Senator Leib, and where newspaperman William Duane had predicted in 1810 that "Mr Madison will be thrown out at the next election." But Duane returned to the president's fold with the war declaration, and so did Pennsylvania. Madison therefore took both the popular vote and the Electoral College, 128–89. The war, and perhaps Madison's mishandling of it, would continue.[61]

TENSKWATAWA HAD ALSO assumed military leadership. Prophetstown was reoccupied, the Prophet's forces were larger than before, and he wielded command among the Indian forces (although he remained subordinate to his brother). Nevertheless, while Tecumseh fought in Michigan, Tenskwatawa oversaw the war in Indiana from Prophetstown.

He sent his forces in an attack on Fort Harrison in September. The American commanding officer was Zachary Taylor (yet another president who rose to fame by fighting the Prophet). A saboteur from Tenskwatawa's army set fire to the wooden stockade, hoping to burn a hole in the perimeter to allow Indian access. Taylor managed to rally his men, who contained the fire and threw up temporary blockades behind the burning palisades. Without a clear point of entry, Tenskwatawa's troops withdrew.

The siege on Fort Wayne had better prospects of success; in August, five hundred of Tenskwatawa's forces surrounded a fort held by seventy Americans. "For God sake Call on Gov. Meigs for to Assist us in sending More Men," wrote the often-intoxicated commanding officer, Captain James Rhea, just before the siege settled in. The Americans managed to hold, however, until Harrison arrived to relieve them on September 12. With these strikes stymied, Tenskwatawa withdrew, and the American forces initiated guerilla attacks on Indian settlements, burning crops and killing animals. In a canny counterstrike, the Prophet sent a group of Potawatomies, who claimed to be heading to a peace summit at Piqua, to Fort Harrison after the siege. They stayed at the fort at American expense until their hosts demanded that they leave. Then they rioted, destroying staples and animals. Guerilla warfare continued throughout the war, although both whites and Indians had largely abandoned their villages once the war began. For two years Indiana was a war zone.[62]

Harrison's first targets were the Miamis. The Miamis had often sided with Harrison in the battles with the Prophet, but no matter; they were in the way. As Johnston justified it to Eustis, "The Indian War is becoming more and more general on the frontiers and along the Roads, there is scarcely a day but announces some murder which generally falls on the defenceless and unprotected."[63] Harrison ordered an attack on the Indians closest to him, and proceeded to lead his forces on a sack of all the Indian villages and fields within two days' march of Fort Wayne. Little Turtle's old village, and the site where the longtime accommodationist's bones were buried, went up in flames.[64]

Having turned on the Miamis, Harrison attempted to strike at Tenskwatawa. That meant mounting another expedition against Prophetstown. Harrison sent Samuel Hopkins and the Kentucky militia to sack the town. Once
again, the militia—praised by their contemporaries as fearless and characterized by historians as hell-bent for Indian blood—suffered heavy desertions in
the wilderness, where they also got lost. Harrison had to take action, and
moved against the town a second time. Tenskwatawa and his followers had
fled before they arrived. Harrison again burned the city—and again abandoned the scene of battle.[65]

Harrison did not hold Prophetstown, but he did build a new fort on the
Maumee, which he named Fort Meigs after the governor of Ohio. Tecumseh
and British commander Henry Procter twice descended from the occupied
territory of Michigan to assault the fort. In keeping with British promises of a
buffer state, Procter promised Michigan as a new homeland for Indians. Neither siege held, however; the first, in May 1813, saw Indian forces deal a devastating blow to Harrison's troops. Assuming they had won the battle, many of
Tecumseh's warriors left for the planting season—as did many Canadian militiamen. But Harrison had not been dislodged, and the siege failed.[66]

In September 1813, a close American victory changed the tenor of the
northwestern front. On September 10, America's Admiral Perry wrested a victory over the British navy, despite an 80-percent casualty rate on his own flag-
ship. The victory prompted the famous battlefield report, "We have met the
enemy and they are ours." It also effectively closed the western Great Lakes
(and hence the Northwest Territory) to further resupply. Harrison, now with
more than five thousand men, made plans to take back Michigan. Procter
decided to retreat back to British North America. He informed Tecumseh
and his Indian allies of this decision on September 18, 1813.[67]

Tecumseh burned with indignation that Procter would retreat when the
British had promised to garrison the confederated Indians; he compared
Procter to a "fat animal." The speech he gave contained the pathos, passion,
and determination that fed the legend of Tecumseh in the centuries that followed. They could not retreat, Tecumseh said, while the "Americans have not
yet defeated us on land." If Procter wanted to retreat, Tecumseh asked him to
leave the guns and ammunition for the Indians. They would fight—and die, if
necessary—for their land and their god: "As for us, our lives are in the hands
of the great Spirit. We are determined to defend our lands, and if it be his wish
to leave our bones upon them."[68]

Tecumseh believed that heaven had set aside this land for his people, and
those who died would ultimately fulfill an ancient purpose. His words were

almost exactly the same as those Harrison wrote concerning his dead soldiers after Tippecanoe: "If they were selected by divine providence as the price of an important Victory there is nothing left us but to honor their memory & to bow submissively to a decree which we cannot alter."[69]

Observers saw the Indians electrified by Tecumseh's words, some breaking into war cries on the spot. Procter, along with Matthew Elliott, asked for three days to prepare a response. The two sides finally made a compromise: they would retreat only as far as it took to reach a defensible position—on the Thames River, near Moraviantown in Lower Canada. Tecumseh agreed, but it must have galled him terribly to leave the land he had reconquered from the Americans in the name of the Master of Life.

The rank and file must have felt more gall than wisdom, for Indian forces left Tecumseh in droves after the decision to retreat. With the abandonment of Michigan, there was no longer anything to fight for. The lands for which Tenskwatawa negotiated, on which he built his cities, and which he claimed the Master of Life had promised to the Indians were located between British and American territories. Tecumseh had perhaps two thousand warriors at Detroit when they retreated. He had only hundreds weeks later when they met Harrison at Moraviantown. The rest had given up—or, more precisely, did not believe that a military retreat into Canada would fulfill their political and religious objectives in fighting. The defeat of Tenskwatawa's forces did not come from poor management, nor was it an inevitable question of numbers; it came because the British lost a naval battle on the Great Lakes and deprived the allied forces in Michigan of supplies and ammunition.[70]

Harrison now stood on the verge of real military glory, succeeding where so many others had failed: an invasion of Canada. He pursued Procter's retreating army into Upper Canada, taking his men across the site of the river Raisin, where thirty Americans had been massacred by rebellious Indians months before. The American forces saw the still-unburied bodies of Americans. McAfee recalled the crossing three years afterward: "The bleaching bones still appealed to heaven, and called on Kentucky to avenge this outrage." Surely this battle would live in infamy, thought McAfee, for "not while there is a recording angel in heaven, or a historian upon earth, will the tragedy of the river Raisin ever be suffered to sink into oblivion." Most Americans of the twenty-first century could not find the Raisin River on a map, much less describe what happened there two centuries ago.[71]

They met in October, in the forests outside Moraviantown. Harrison's forces broke through Procter's poorly constructed lines and engaged in close combat with the remaining Indian forces. The battle ended when an American soldier fired ball and buckshot into Tecumseh's heart, and the Prophet's brother died. Although it is not clear who ultimately fired the gun that killed Tecumseh, Richard Mentor Johnson would forever be feted as the man that did the deed; indeed, when the play *Tecumseh, or The Battle of the Thames*—a fawning account of Johnson's life—was performed in Baltimore a quarter century later, advertisements for the show boasted that the play featured the authentic pistol used to shoot the Shawnee warrior. The American soldiers at the actual Battle of the Thames took more visceral souvenirs: Tecumseh's clothing, hair, and skin. One soldier, in his own words, proudly took "two pieces of his yellow hide home with me to my Mother & Sweet Harts."[72]

Tenskwatawa fled the battle on horseback, just ahead of pursuing American forces. He rode away from the defeat, but not toward anything; he regrouped in Upper Canada only to meet the Canadian winter. Short on supplies, he could not provide for the thousand or so Indians encamped at Dundas who remained loyal to him. Indeed, his major accomplishment after the Thames was probably merely keeping his people alive. In April 1814, Tenskwatawa would be recognized by the British as "the principal Chief of all the Western Nations" and was "presented with the Sword & Pistols, from His Royal Highness." But by then, the British showed little enthusiasm for pursuing the war in the West; their attentions had shifted to the eastern seaboard, where Native American fighters were a non-factor. After Tecumseh's death, Tenskwatawa only ever marched to one battle—for which he arrived late.[73]

The British were largely hemmed in and could not resupply their Indian allies easily. Their success in the East merely compounded their apathy for the West. With Napoleon defeated and exiled to Elba in the summer of 1814, the crown sent the full brunt of its forces to America, and on August 25, 1814, British forces sacked Washington. The British would have done far more damage had they burned a major commercial center—New York, Philadelphia, or Baltimore. In fact, they tried. In September they bombarded Baltimore's harbor, and a disheveled lawyer named Francis Scott Key got to watch the firestorm at Fort McHenry. He wrote a poem about it—"The Defense of Fort McHenry." Americans know it today as "The Star-Spangled Banner."

Most know Key's work as a song and not a poem—and even then, only the first stanza. The full text, however, revels in providentialist rhetoric about America's divine war for conquest: "Conquer we must, for our cause it is just, / And this be our motto: in God is our trust." Americans were "free men," the British "hirelings and slaves" whose "foul footsteps" had been washed away by blood. War—even a catastrophically mismanaged war—had made America: "Praised be the power that preserved us a nation." Key implicitly assumed the cause *was* just, even as Baltimore harbor burned around him. Little had changed from the prewar religious justifications for the invasion of Canada.

Canada also developed an anthem from the war. "The Bold Canadian," written in the wake of the capture of Michigan, called "the Yankee boys" the "unnatural foe" who "did invade us, / To kill and to destroy." This rousing war anthem celebrated law rather than untrammeled liberty: "Come all ye bold Canadians, / Enlisted in the cause, / To defend your country, / And to maintain all your laws." It ended with the traditional "God save the King!" Americans did not have a monopoly on creating national self-definition by defaming their enemies.

Only the Native American forces, in the Northwest and in the South, seemed to lack a wartime song of self-definition. They undoubtedly had songs, but they did not have the massive newsprint operations that allowed Canadian and American anthems to be shared over vast distances. Though not a song, Tecumseh's 1811 speech to the Choctaws and Chickasaws had much the same tone as "The Bold Canadian" or "The Star-Spangled Banner": the Americans "are a people fond of innovations, and quick to put their schemes into execution, no matter how great the wrong and injury to us; while we are content to preserve what we already have." Let Indians, then, "form one body, one heart, and defend to the last warrior our country, our homes, our liberty, and the graves of our fathers."[74]

The defense of Fort McHenry (the battle, not the poem) probably preserved the United States as well as its flag. Washington, D.C., possessed little actual importance as a center of trade or urban life. ("Wilderness City," some called it, for almost no one lived there.) The British burned the capital for psychological effect—their own, in retaliation for the torching of York. One observer recalled that no one in Washington could sleep: "They spent the night gazing on the fires and lamenting the disgrace of the city."[75] Margaret Bayard Smith famously wrote of looking at the ruins of the White House and Congress, "now nothing but ashes, and it was in these ashes, now trodden under foot by the rabble, which once possess'd the power to inflate pride, to gratify vanity."[76] Yet British commanders, having ensured that every public building was ruined, left the city for the more substantial target of Baltimore.

Had that city fallen, the Americans would have lost a significant production and naval center. Coupled with coastal raids and an easy control of northern Virginia and Maryland (given the British routing of American forces en route to Washington), the fall of Baltimore might have forced the United States into a much more humiliating peace—especially if the impending invasion down the Hudson River had successfully severed anti-war New

England from the rest of the states, allowing a separate peace. The Hartford Convention of 1814, rife with anti-war leaders and bitter Federalists, considered just such a proposition. The notion of a separate peace was rejected, although most Republican newspapers passed over this technicality.

But the invasion from Canada also sputtered. While the British could exult in their humiliation of the haughty ex-colonials, the failure to take Baltimore meant they could not gain their territorial ambitions (control of Great Lakes). For their part, the Americans realized they could never achieve theirs (Canada). In treaty negotiations at Ghent, in Belgium, the Americans and the British settled for *status quo ante bellum*. As usual, the Indians were not invited to the negotiating table.

In the West, it would be different. Tenskwatawa's forces had been either defeated or confined to Canada. Other Indian warriors had simply returned home. Indian villages of the Old Northwest had suffered American invasions and military destruction. In the South, Andrew Jackson defeated the Creek rebels and forced them into a peace that removed them from their land and gave it to the United States. He rewarded his Creek allies who had not rebelled by taking their land as well. It was a sign of things to come. Military destruction (and not white population pressures) shifted the balance of power on the frontier. Removal of the Northwest Indians was now a political possibility— and an easy political decision—since at this point it would subject few white people (voters) to security threats. Tenskwatawa's war for a homeland—a war Harrison started—resulted in the end of a dream for an Indian state.

Could the Indians have won? If the dissolution and defeat of the main Northwestern Indian–British army was indeed due to the British failure to defeat American naval forces at Lake Erie, the Indian and Canadian forces came quite close to winning. Procter held out the promise of an Indian buffer state should the Indians take Fort Meigs, and General Isaac Brock was adamant after the occupation of Michigan that some kind of an Indian homeland be established in any peace settlement.[77] Had those battles gone another way, the war's end might have been quite different for Tecumseh and Tenskwatawa. Despite the myth that Tecumseh fought for a lost cause, the brothers in fact came close to achieving what they believed to be their political and religious destiny.

Few historians, however, have spent much time exploring the repercussions of an Indian-Canadian victory in North America. Instead, most scholars have assumed that Indian defeat in the Northwest—indeed, across the continent—was inevitable. It is an assumption very nearly hardwired into the historiography of America. From the moment of English settlement in

1607, Indians were doomed, and the longer colonization continued, the worse things became. Numbers, technology, immunities, and racial hatreds made white expansion unstoppable and effective Indian resistance essentially futile. Historians of the last few decades have done a phenomenal job recovering the stories of the Indian experience in post-Revolutionary America, but the power of the lost-cause argument endures.[78]

Some historical writing—and very good historical writing at that—maintains such a view even when considering evidence that suggests the contrary. Consider the account of John Keating (written in 1823), who included an anecdote heard from a correspondent that when preaching to the Sacs, Tenskwatawa encountered Indian skeptics who demanded he perform a resurrection to prove his divine mission. Tenskwatawa refused. A recent historical work cites the incident as evidence that the Prophet "made few Sac converts," buttressing the larger argument that existing political animosities doomed Tenskwatawa's movement. In fact, however, Keating's correspondent made exactly the opposite point: "Many were satisfied and did as he bid them." Tenskwatawa's answers satisfied Indian critics and made his movement stronger, even in the face of traditional divisions. Failure was not foreordained.[79]

Acknowledging that white American expansionists had considerable advantages over their Indian neighbors does not constitute evidence of inevitability. Accepting any outcome as inevitable involves the tricky logic of assuming that the way things are is the way they must have been. Tecumseh's eloquent paean to martyrdom at the evacuation of Detroit makes it easy to assume that his entire movement had possessed similar pathos, but in fact, had Perry lost on Lake Erie, the speech never would have existed. In wars, and particularly in a war as badly managed and poorly fought as the War of 1812, contingency must trump inevitability as a mode of analysis. The Indian forces could well have won their war. It would have been unlikely—but the history of the Napoleonic era is full of unlikely victories: the slave uprising in Haiti in 1791, the ultraconservative revolution of Mexico in 1821, and the surprising national awakening of Canada in 1815.

Moreover, the idea of Indian nations in inevitable decline has its own troubling history. Jefferson and Harrison had considered the idea; it was part of the supposed logic of the accommodationist program. Henry Rowe Schoolcraft took this assumption and made it a historical determinant when he published his account in 1857. Speaking of the Treaty of Greenville, he wrote, "This result could not, under any possible circumstances, have been averted." Even if the Indians had possessed better leadership, it would not have mattered. "As the war was, in fact, a direct issue between civilization and barbarism, the ultimate result would have been precisely similar. The reasoning powers of the Indians did not, probably, enable them to arrive at this conclusion."[80] American victory, Schoolcraft wrote, was a result of the fitness of Americans and the folly of the Indians; "the fury of savages" could not overcome "a people inured to hardships, and educated for centuries in the principles of political self-reliance, and faith in God."[81] The historical contention that Indians were destined to fail in their wars of resistance did not originally emerge from a close comparison of military or economic forces. It derived from a nationalist (and racist) cultural comparison wherein American civilization was ipso facto superior to the cultural innovations of Native Americans. In other words, the assumption of inevitable American victory is itself the kind of nationalist cultural hubris that was a *result* of the victories of Americans in the War of 1812. "Inevitability" was a result of the contingencies of war, not an explanation of them.

Some documents from the war do speak in this language of inevitability, promising that limitless American soldiers would easily crush Indian resistance. Those documents were usually intended for consumption by voters in the West. Actual security assessments from the frontier, however, emphasize the contingent nature of the conflict. The reports made by Americans and Canadians during the war contained the understanding that the outcome was no sure thing. General Hull, for example, wrote as early as 1810, "It is difficult however to determine what the consequences on this frontier would be, if hostilities should take place on the Wabash."[82] When Hull actually went to fight the war, his assessments got worse; originally the Indians seemed "neutralized," but "the surrender of Michilimackinac opened the northern hive of Indians, and they were swarming down in every direction." Then, of course, Hull surrendered.[83]

Governor Edwards in Illinois similarly foresaw destruction, as Indian forces larger than the Prophet's would have free rein to pillage his territory.[84] His prediction of war was far different from Schoolcraft's post hoc assurances: "If the Illinois Indians become hostile, they will overrun this Territory."[85] Then of course there were Harrison's private fears and complaints about the American militia, in marked contrast to his public pronouncements on the indomitable frontier spirit that animated such men. It was true that such words stirred hearts. It was also true that the United States never came close to meeting its recruitment quotas throughout the war.

Moreover, with the British alliance in place, the nativist forces had much better odds of victory than they had had at Greenville two decades previously. Such an alliance added manpower, ammunition, supplies, and diplomatic heft. British commanders in Canada even resurrected the idea of an Indian buffer state between Canada and the United States as a reward for Prophetstown and allied Indians should the coalition successfully defeat the Americans. In 1812, Lord Bathurst, the newly appointed minister for war, wrote an official paper backing "the necessity of securing the territories of the Indians from encroachment."[86] Isaac Brock recommended that the entire "tract of country fraudulently usurped from them"—a possible reference to the Fort Wayne Treaty—should be restored as a condition of peace.[87]

Such a peace never came about, but it could have. As late as August 1814, British diplomats continued to insist on a buffer state as the price of peace. American commissioners complained that such a boundary meant "establishing an independent Country" for Indians, which would "arrest the course of civilization and the extension of Christianity." Americans were not really in a position to bargain, however; Henry Clay, a War Hawk now seeking peace, wrote from Belgium, "I tremble, indeed, whenever I take up a News paper," fearing reports of a total collapse of the American movement. The favorable terms of Ghent came about only when potential rivalries at the peace treaty in Vienna threatened to undo British victory against its Continental foes, and the British government opted for a quick peace with the Americans.[88]

What if the war's outcome had tilted decidedly in favor of Britain and the Indians in 1813? Such counterfactual considerations are rarely undertaken on behalf of Indian wars, although shelves of such books (both wise and foolish) have imagined alternative outcomes to the Civil War and World War II. In the case of the War of 1812, a failure of U.S. naval forces on Lake Erie would have ensured continued British supply of Michigan and the nativists. Lack of ammunition and supplies is often cited as a reason for the inevitability of American victory, but this result was contingent on the closing of the Great Lakes. (Additionally, American forces were also often short on ammunition, foodstuffs, and pay.)[89] A victory at Fort Meigs would have extended British holdings into Ohio—which then could have been returned to the United States in exchange for Michigan as a permanent Indian territory.

A theoretical Indian territory probably would not have looked like a modern state, with a centralized capital, national bureaucracy, and extensive legal code; the decentralized political structures of Eastern Woodlands cultures would not have fit easily with the consolidating tendencies of the modern state. Such a state would, however, have had modern national characteristics—a sense of citizenship based on common origins (in this case, Tenskwatawa's revived notion that all Indians formed one tribe) and perhaps a common religion (Tenskwatawa's teachings about the Master of Life). Tecumseh certainly would have been a paramount leader in such a state, and his considerable charisma and reputation might well have served as a political glue to maintain a loose order on the Michigan peninsula. Ultimately, such an Indian state might have looked like the Comanche Empire of the eighteenth century—a nexus of trade and diplomacy ruled by cultural rather than political persuasion, and which employed force primarily to dictate borders and maintain autonomy.[90]

Such a counterfactual state might not have lasted long, as a significant faction of white America supported territorial expansion. Kentucky's Samuel McDowell, for example, wrote in 1814, "I would never buy a Peace at the expense of one foot of Terotary nor have the Indians Even Named in a treaty of Piece with England." The McDowells of America would be a significant threat to a permanent Indian state—but McDowell also identified the very reason why such sentiments were not the only factor: "I fear that the President Ruling Powers of our Country have not Energy Sufficient to Act with Promptness and Decision."[91] Given the fragile military situation and the precarious political positioning of the U.S. government in 1813, a peace such as McDowell would have hated was nevertheless possible. (Indeed, his fear of it suggests how real such a possibility seemed to him.) Another war might have arisen in which the United States attempted to take back Michigan—or perhaps the presence of such an autonomous buffer state, to which the United States had no claim, would have dampened the ardor and confidence of later land grabs. Would Georgia's hunger for Cherokee land in the 1830s have been stymied if an independent state led by Tenskwatawa and Tecumseh belied assumptions of white superiority and Indian decline? Having seen successful native resistance, would the American government have felt as easy about moving the Ohio accommodationist tribes across the Mississippi in the 1820s—or would they have continued to work to build alliances with them as a counterweight to Tenskwatawa's country?

The aggressive policy of removal that emerged in the 1820s was possible only because the security threats in the Northwest and Florida had been defeated and because of the myth of inevitability that had been created by 1815; military concerns were no longer paramount, and politicians could impose their will on Native groups without much fear of Indian reprisals upon white voters. Had Tenskwatawa and Tecumseh succeeded, the military situation in the Northwest would have continued, with a viable Indian military force maintaining a presence in the area. The road to American expansion would have taken a more difficult path, and concepts and assurances of American destiny would have been quite different.

The war changed the fate of the gods, too. The Master of Life—or at least his Prophet—had been defeated. Harrison (now a successful general) was essentially able to dictate terms to the defeated Indian tribes, with whom the Americans made a separate peace. Under the 1815 Treaty of Spring Wells, Tenskwatawa would be allowed to return to the United States, but only as a subject of Black Hoof in Ohio; he could have no religious role. Tenskwatawa refused to sign the treaty. Most of his followers returned to the United States without him. He attempted to shepherd a handful of followers through life in Canada.[92]

Yet Harrison's god also suffered in the war. The providentialist god who would see America through any calamity seemed noticeably absent in the War of 1812. McDowell railed against the "Majority of Atheists and Dayests" who ruled the country "for at least 14 years." God had brought defeat to the United States "to bring them to a proper sense of their wickedness." The string of defeats followed by the surprising victory of New Orleans (which came after the war officially ended) seemed less indicative of a clockmaker god whose design could be discerned and more like the work of a capricious but ultimately loving god who demanded worship rather than good works and reason. The postwar United States would undergo a vigorous series of revivals that would bring Methodist and Baptist rejections of deism to the fore; it would also see the construction of the religiously based reform movements intended to win America for Christ by making its government Christian—a movement that began in 1815 with a vast letter-writing campaign intended to convince the U.S. government that the capital had been burned because Americans allowed mail to be circulated on the Sabbath.[93]

The true religious postscript to the war came when a young man named William Miller grew melancholy after the fighting ended. He had withstood the British assault at Plattsburgh and seen men killed by British cannon a few feet from him. He lapsed into a depression, his homegrown deism no longer answering his concerns. On the anniversary of the battle, in the very building where he had first accepted deistic thought, he heard a Baptist sermon, and joined the church.[94] Miller's conversion led to his intensive study of the Bible, and he would eventually become convinced that Christ's return was imminent; he set the date for 1843, and revolutionized American religion. Though his date would pass without worldwide cataclysm, his movement eventually gave birth to the Seventh-Day Adventist movement and the Jehovah's Witnesses. More important, it brought the idea of an increasingly depraved world that could be saved only by an imminent Second Coming—premillennialism, in Christian theological parlance—to the fore. With Miller's success, American Christianity tilted away from the notion that things were improving, that humanity was reaching its goal, and that nature and reason made for good Christianity. Over the years, Miller's vision of a crumbling world, where humans could be saved only by knowledge of Christ, who would come very soon to judge the quick and the dead, would become the dominant theme of American Protestantism. The personal god of American Christianity created his apostle at the close of the War of 1812, when the British decided not to storm Miller's regiment. If the War of 1812 can be read as a struggle between the clockmaker god and the Master of Life, then both may have become too exhausted by the fighting to establish their empire. A new religion took their place.

Epilogue

The Funeral

THE GUNS FIRED at dawn. Clusters of people, on foot, on horseback, gathered on the streets for the funerary procession, while above the pell-mell residents of Washington peered from windows or balconies to watch. In the East Room of the White House, the furniture, chandeliers, and mirrors had been draped in black, as had the mansion's columns. The office seekers and power brokers filed past the corpse of their president, dead after just thirty days in office. A cavalry squadron waited outside with the funeral car, a single wheeled platform draped in velvet and drawn by six white horses. A team of pallbearers, one from each American state and territory, brought the coffin out of the White House, settled it on the bier, and moved in prescribed fashion to the Congressional Burying-Ground.

Harrison had not been sick long. The persistent claim that Harrison caught cold while giving a protracted inaugural address is almost certainly untrue. No reports of the March inaugural of 1841 mention rain or snow; indeed, plans had been made to move the inaugural inside should weather prove inclement, yet the festivities had remained outdoors. Nor was the president unprepared for cold weather; he wore a frock coat and a wool suit. Certainly the speech was overlong; observers clocked it anywhere between one and two hours, making it the longest inaugural address in American history. Nonetheless, Harrison could at least be said to have kept one of his pledges he made in that speech: "Under no circumstances will I consent to serve a second term." Yet none of the medical reports issued after his death mention the inaugural address in association with the president's illness. Harrison made a habit of venturing out into the cold during the winter of 1841 and had ample opportunities to contract the pneumonia that killed him. The attending physician called it "one of our ordinary fevers of low grade." Nor did the medical advice he received improve his chances for survival; the doctors treated him with the best of antebellum American medicine, including laxatives, opium, and bloodletting.[1]

The story that it was the speech that killed him did not emerge until Freeman Cleaves' 1939 biography, *Old Tippecanoe*. Here, almost one hundred years later, can be found the first reference to the story of Harrison appearing hatless and coatless.[2] Cleaves cited two observers' accounts, but neither of the cited reports mentioned either Harrison's outfit or inclement weather; indeed, one of them remarked, "The day was fine."[3] Perhaps the poetic justice of a politician done in by his own verbosity was too tempting for Cleaves to pass up. And so the story subsequently found its way into popular culture.

It is, of course, just a footnote to history. And yet if the story of Harrison catching cold at the inaugural is not true—and that story is the only thing most Americans know about him—what else about Harrison and his record might have escaped notice? What else that we think we know about American history is wrong?

His death was hardly unexpected; he had been the oldest man elected to the office to date. Harrison's age had been a factor in the 1840 campaign, but he and his Whig Party had successfully buried it under a tumult of hoopla, parades, and campaign songs—aided in part by the incompetence of the Van Buren administration. Some historians consider the 1840 campaign to be the first "modern" political campaign. Both parties introduced banners, songbooks, slogans, and electioneering into general use. The 1840 efforts should not be thought of as an exact parallel to contemporary campaign boosterism, wherein electoral fortunes are organized by an ever-expanding professional class of handlers whose job is not to formulate policy but to win elections. The Whigs of 1840 had an economic and political agenda; they did, however, see to it that a healthy dose of propaganda assured voters that a cider-drinking, honest, hardworking backwoodsman would be carrying out those policies. The parallel to modern times, perhaps, is that campaign literature and rhetoric transformed William Henry Harrison into something he was not.[4]

One of the things he was not was a devout Christian. Deism died before Harrison did, so campaign materials had to intensify Harrison's vague faith. They called him "a sincere Christian," a "church-going man," "one who highly respects religion." One campaign biographer claimed he often found Harrison "on his knees at his bedside, absorbed in his devotions to his Maker."[5] In Massachusetts, Senator William Sprague told Whigs to demand the surrender of the Democrats "in the name of the great god Jehovah."[6] Yet campaign literature should not be taken at face value; Harrison had still never joined a church. He had been married by a justice of the peace, not a minister of the gospel.[7] His only reference to God in his inaugural address—vague pabulum about "a profound reverence for the Christian religion"—had been inserted by Secretary of State Daniel Webster.[8]

But he was well cast in death as a Christian martyr. More than one hundred sermons memorializing Harrison were printed, and in nearly all of them both he and his country were sealed to a religious destiny, a slightly more intense providence than Harrison had had faith in during his lifetime. He was a man of "decided evangelical principle," "a believer in the inspiration and authority of the bible," "a good and faithful servant to the joy of his Lord." His sudden death was "a martyrdom" and "a death such as a Christian statesman might desire."[9] Virtually every sermon mentioned Harrison's (in reality, Webster's) allusion to the power of the Christian religion in his inaugural address. The sermons and memorials similarly mentioned a Bible Harrison had purchased on his first day in office—even though no reference to such a Bible occurred before he died. Harrison's greatness and fidelity were compared to those of King David, with the American people drafted to play the role of Israelites.[10] Harrison, "anointed of liberty," had been in the service of the Lord of Hosts—why else would God call him home?[11] John Quincy Adams called Harrison's passing a "providential revolution in its [America's] Government" and claimed that God had visited the calamity on America because the "moral condition of this country is degenerating."[12] Harrison's death was God's lesson to America because Harrison's life embodied God's plan for America.

Part of that plan involved the destruction of heathen Indians and the opening of the western frontier for white settlers. The eulogies were fairly consistent on this point. When Harrison fought the Northwest Indians from 1811 to 1813, he fought the "screams of the savage . . . with consummate skill and heroism," and "by divine blessing stayed the threatened devastation of our frontiers."[13] Harrison rode out against an infidel enemy as the representative of "the Christian Government."[14] His actions prevented the creation of "an Indian Empire . . . in an extensive and important part of the territory, solemnly acknowledged as ours."[15] Harrison's Christian destiny had been to defeat the Indians in the West and thereby allow Christian America to occupy that territory. Indeed, Harrison seemed so indestructible, alleged the Reverend Reuben Sears of Albany, that even the "Indian foes he chastised and quelled" began to see Harrison as preternatural, and "came at length to consider him as under the special favor and protection of the Great Spirit!"[16]

A man who actually thought himself favored by the Master of Life had a more ignominious postwar history. In 1816, Tenskwatawa attempted to convince Michigan's governor, Lewis Cass, to allow him to establish a new city for his followers on the Raisin River—where the Americans had been massacred three years before. Cass refused and kept the Prophet in Canada for the next several years. Across the Old Northwest, meanwhile, the accommodationist chiefs were back in charge, including the hated Black Hoof.

Harrison was selected (unsurprisingly) to oversee a separate peace treaty (i.e., land negotiation) with nine Indian tribes in 1815. At his own request, he asked Congress to investigate the continuing charges that he had benefitted from land speculation as governor and as general. While the investigation continued, he was elected to Congress from Ohio, which surely must have helped his case. In a stunning reversal, he declared himself opposed to slavery, likely because Ohio (his new political base) was largely anti-slavery. Though he was cleared of the charges, Harrison's career stalled in 1820—he lost a bid for the Senate, was passed over for several ambassadorships, and failed in his effort to regain his House seat. By 1824, both Harrison and Tenskwatawa were stuck.

But that year, their prospects brightened. Moses Dawson published *A Historical Narrative of the Civil and Military Services of Major-General William H. Harrison*, and C. C. Trowbridge interviewed Tenskwatawa in Upper Canada. Dawson's book was unapologetic propaganda, designed to refurbish Harrison's image, systematically going through and vindicating all of Harrison's efforts. Indeed, according to Dawson, Harrison's letter to the Prophet in 1806 had ended the witch trials by fiat, "arrested the fanatical fury which seemed to pervade the whole tribe, and no doubt saved the lives of many."[17] The eclipse the letter prompted—and the subsequent rise of Tenskwatawa— went unmentioned. This questionable text was the source for numerous myths and stories about Tenskwatawa as a cunning master of a kind of anti-Christianity, the lord of "dark and midnight councils held among the Indians, through the influence of the Shawanese prophet."[18]

Trowbridge's interview, meanwhile, recorded Tenskwatawa's religious system in its most complete form. This interview is our best source for the Prophet's own view of his conversion, conviction, and religious practices. He explained how the Shawnees had been the first people born in the world, and that when the Shawnees ceased to be, so would the world. By contrast, white people had been so poor and imbecilic at the beginning of things that the Master of Life took pity on them. In what appeared to be a new development in his religious thought since 1815, the Prophet claimed that there were two spirits that ran the world, one for the Indians and one for the whites. He explained the nature of eclipses; he elucidated the nature of the afterlife, where humans would inhabit another clay body, just as they did in this world. He mourned that human lifetimes had once lasted two hundred years, until the scheming and foolishness of the whites had ruined it. It is difficult to ascertain, given how little history has left us from Tenskwatawa, but these final musings seemed tinged with sadness, or perhaps resignation.[19]

In 1825, Tenskwatawa also saw both an opportunity to return to the United States and a chance to strike back at the accommodationists who had usurped his position. One of the last Indian groups still living in the Old Northwest were the Shawnees of Black Hoof's tribe. Michigan's Cass was trying hard to remove them to a reservation in what is now Kansas. Tenskwatawa took the bait, and with Cass' patronage, he returned to the United States as an advocate of Indian removal. Cass moved Tenskwatawa and his followers to Black Hoof's Wapakoneta, where Tenskwatawa preached removal. Black Hoof refused to sell.

But Tenskwatawa was back in America, and he tried one last time to found a city. In 1826, he led his followers and some dissatisfied members of Black Hoof's tribe to the Missouri Shawnees, who had been living in the Louisiana Territory since its days as a Spanish protectorate. His arrival was not popular. His efforts to accrue leadership in Missouri failed, and he finally arrived in Kansas in 1828. He died there in 1836.

It was also in 1836 that Harrison completed one of the most remarkable political comebacks in history. After a fairly unsuccessful decade of politicking, he tried for the vice presidential spot on John Quincy Adams' ticket in 1828. He failed in that, but, showing his political acumen, he nevertheless managed to wrangle a diplomatic appointment from Adams' successful opponent, Andrew Jackson—perhaps because of their shared history in Indian fighting. Jackson made Harrison minister to Colombia. Roughly a year later, he was kicked out of Bogotá on suspicion of involvement in a plot to overthrow the government. Harrison offered a careful defense of his actions, but given his penchant for autocracy and scheming, it is hard not to believe the rumors were true.[20]

Jobless, Harrison sold most of his land to pay his debts, and once again the scion of Virginia looked finished. But then Richard Mentor Johnson dredged up the old charges against Harrison in order to promote his own candidacies; popular culture lauded Johnson, as in the 1836 play *Tecumseh, or the Battle of the Thames*, by Richard Emmons. American theater-goers could see the Prophet, played by a Mr. Raffile, dance the war dance around a human sacrifice, and hear him explain, "The Great Spirit now commands the Prophet to appease his wrath by the lingering death of the victim ... glut thy wrath before Manitou bids his prophet to hunting grounds repair."[21] Emmons' Tecumseh asks in pidgin English if Richard M. Johnson is a warrior, and in good republican style he is told, "Yes, he must a warrior be—but in the Senate."[22]

Johnson became vice president in 1836, but he was not the only legendary Indian-killer on the ballot. Harrison created the "Tippecanoe

Clubs" to counter Johnson's charges against his record. In 1836, the clubs nominated Harrison for president in various states. The Whig party nominated several men that year, and Harrison—shockingly—outperformed his better-connected rivals Daniel Webster and Hugh White.

The rise of the Tippecanoe Clubs produced a flood of campaign literature, turning Harrison into "Tippecanoe." These pamphlets and songbooks made the wellborn general out to be a folksy woodsman, a hero of the West, a man who had acquired "FIFTY-ONE MILLIONS of the finest land ever owned by the United States . . . the aboriginal title extinguished. They are now worth, at least, SIXTY-THREE MILLIONS, and are far better than that much in BARS OF GOLD. *Who has done more?* There is NOT ONE." In order to get at "the aboriginal title," Harrison needed a villain, an opposite number similarly dedicated, who had forfeited the right to land and whose defeat at Harrison's hands had prevented the kind of disastrous future the nation had avoided in 1811 but might face if they failed to put Harrison in the White House. The Shawnee brothers fit the bill admirably. Sometimes the religious tomfoolery was Tecumseh's: "Tecumseh found it necessary to subsidize the superstition of the tribes to his purpose. With this view he affected to treat his brother as a being of superior order; and by artifice succeeded completely in imposing on them." This kind of leadership meant that "the savages fought with all the fury of religious fanaticism," and only "the moral influence of Harrison's positions subdued this son of the woods." This portrayal, from the 1836 *Sketch of the Life of Major General William Henry Harrison*, concluded its discussion of Tippecanoe with veiled threats of the descent into violence bred by medieval superstition: "Far different would have been the scene had the Prophet triumphed—towns would have been sacked, hamlets burned, and the peaceful tenement of the settler offered up as a sacrifice to savage fury."[23]

Campaign biographies in 1840 had an additional advantage: perceived incompetence and financial mismanagement by the Van Buren administration. Subtle hints in this second campaign drew parallels between the deceptive Tenskwatawa and the skullduggery of the Democrats. The Van Burenites might "hope to escape detection and its just punishment by falsehood, chicanery, and low cunning," but Harrison was on the scene to end "a long night of misrule."[24] The author used the same language to describe the Shawnee brothers: crafty impostors "who preferred tactics and secret management to open violence." As for the Prophet, "cunning, artful, and treacherous, he was no warrior, but an accomplished and persuasive orator," which perhaps sketched a parallel between the Shawnee "*medicine man* or magician" and the notorious Little Magician in the White House. "This administration," the anonymous author reminded his readers, "has so long been weighing" on the country, "like an oppressive incubus."[25]

Harrison won the election, receiving 234 electoral votes to Van Buren's 60. When the president-elect visited his defeated rival at the White House for a surprisingly amiable dinner, Van Buren declared Harrison was "as tickled with the Presidency as is a young woman with a bonnet." John Quincy Adams found Harrison and his supporters "showy-shabby." His criticisms aside, Adams was crushed when Harrison died just a few days later.[26]

Not everyone felt that way. Andrew Jackson chuckled that Harrison's death was divine retribution to the American people for voting the Democrats out of office. The flinty William Cullen Bryant regretted Harrison's death only insofar as it had not given the president time enough to prove his incompetence for the office.[27] But the preachers who published sermons captured the more widespread notion that Harrison had been a Christian president of a Christian nation, and though it might be that "God has a controversy with this nation," the glory of God would nevertheless be the glory of America.[28]

These speeches were not quite Manifest Destiny; that term would not enter American parlance for a few more years.[29] The idea that providence had made the continent for white settlement was an old one, though, and as the sermons said, Harrison made it possible. Indeed, Harrison insisted on it, and because he insisted on it, it came to be. Certainly the Indians were less numerous than white Americans, and certainly both groups harbored suspicion, resentment, and hatred toward the other. But those facts alone did not cause the war or allow for the transformation of white-Indian relations from accommodation to removal. That political reality was ultimately created by the political and military decisions on the frontier—decisions cast by Harrison and the Prophet. Had Harrison not pursued the Prophet with such fanatical vigor, or had his initial missteps continued into 1813, the geopolitics of the Northwest would have looked very different. Harrison's victory and the Prophet's defeat—which balanced precariously for a year—were what made the mythology of American providence seem true. They "proved" the supposition that America was indeed made for whites, even as they changed the direction of that destiny from north into Canada to west into Mexico.

Harrison's death also changed the fate of nations. John Tyler became president and quickly succeeded in alienating both political parties. He then tried to forge a third movement (with himself at its head) by pushing for the annexation of Texas. He finally got his way on his last day in office, but he had whipped much of the country into a war frenzy for Texas, then engaged in a bitter sovereignty debate with Mexico. Tyler's successor, James K. Polk, won

election (barely) on a Tyleresque pro-Texas platform and then plunged the
country into war, eventually adding Texas, California, and the American
Southwest to the United States. For the next forty years, American military
and militia forces would be engaged in an effort to "pacify" the independent
Native American nations of the Plains, the Rockies, and the Pacific Northwest—but the continental American map was complete.

Yet if Harrison had not survived his perilous political life as well as he did;
if he had obeyed his superiors' orders not to enforce the Treaty of Fort Wayne;
if he had not defeated John Badollet's challenge; if he had not escaped
court-martial in 1812; and if he had not touted Tippecanoe as the perfect victory he imagined instead of the meaningless draw it was—then the now familiar map of the United States would never have come to be. Without Harrison,
Eustis might have negotiated a peace, and perhaps even a border, with Tenskwatawa. Perhaps there would have been no Tippecanoe and no guerilla war
for Indiana. And without Tippecanoe, there would have been no Harrison
presidency—and thus no Tyler presidency, no push for Texas, no war with
Mexico, no annexation of the Southwest. The map that seems so inevitable is
revealed to be the result of highly contingent events—a historical accident,
based on the unlikely outcome of an unlikelier holy war.

Though his enemies derided him, Tenskwatawa was at least right in one
thing: in his decisions rested the fate of nations. When he related his stories
to Trowbridge in Michigan, near the end of his life, he included the story of
the Cannibal Monsters—a trio of hideous creatures who consumed an entire
human village but ultimately were outwitted by Wren and the young man
named Pthe'kawa. Tenskwatawa had now seen the Americans victorious, and
it is hard not to see in the Cannibal Monsters the Americans themselves. But
as he often did in his ministry, Tenskwatawa ended with a song of hope: the
monsters defeated, Pthe'kawa built a great sweat lodge on the shores of a vast
lake. The survivors of the monsters gathered the bones of the victims and
placed them in the lake, and "a great many bounded out as whole living men,
women, and children who had been borne in as gnawed bones. Every one of
the murdered-ones had been restored to life, cleansed and purified in the
sweat-house." The resurrected village, "freshened and vigorous," thanked the
heroic Pthe'kawa, but "some had been dead so long they had no memory
whatever of former times." These few Pthe'kawa gathered unto himself, "our
clan together," and they returned to his grandmother's lodge, "where they
lived together with great happiness for many years." And there, with an old
man dreaming of resurrection, the tale ends.[30]

Notes

PROLOGUE: THE ECLIPSE

1. For the Prophet's powers, see the Draper Manuscripts 12YY8, 6YY123; Benjamin Youngs, "A Journey to the Indians March 1807," Winterthur Library, Andrews Collection 860, 23; Richard McNemar, *The Kentucky Revival* (New York, 1848 [Cincinnati, 1808]), 123–49.

2. Draper Manuscripts 12YY20; Washington *National Intelligencer*, September 10, 1806, "Extract of a Letter from S. Griswold . . . Giving an Account of the Total Eclipse, June 16, 1806, As It Appeared at Detroit, and Its Effect on the Indians."

3. *Intelligencer*, September 10, 1806.

4. Draper Manuscripts 12YY29. Native American reactions are taken from Joseph Badger, *A Memoir of Rev. Joseph Badger*, ed. Henry Noble Day (Hudson, OH, 1851), 147, and the *Intelligencer*, September 10, 1806.

5. Draper Manuscripts 3YY59.

6. Youngs, "A Journey," 120.

7. Aaron Burr to James Wilkinson, September 26, 1805, in *The Political Correspondence and Public Papers of Aaron Burr*, ed. Mary-Jo Kline (Princeton, 1983), 2:940.

8. William Henry Harrison (henceforth WHH) to William Eustis, December 24, 1810, in *Messages and Papers of William Henry Harrison*, ed. Logan Esarey (Indianapolis, 1922), 1:498.

9. Washington's religious views and behavior have been detailed for two centuries. See Frank E. Grizzard Jr., *The Ways of Providence: Religion and George Washington* (Buena Vista, VA, 2005), ch. 1, and David L. Holmes, *Faiths of the Founding Fathers* (New York, 2006), ch. 6. Quote from George Washington to Burwell Bassett, April 20, 1773, *The Papers of George Washington, Digital Edition*, ed. Theodore J. Crackel (Charlottesville, VA, 2008); also cited in Grizzard, *Ways*, 5.

10. George Washington to Maryland Legislature, January 20, 1790, in *The Papers of George Washington*. See also Washington to Lucretia Wilhemina van Winter, March 30, 1785, Washington to Jonathan Trumbull, July 20, 1788, and Washington to Annis Boudinot Stockton, August 31, 1788.

11. WHH to General Assembly, July 29, 1805, *Messages and Papers* 1:153–55.

12. Quotes from WHH to the Delawares, undated, 1806, *Messages and Papers* 1:183–84.

13. Ibid., 1:183.

14. The best "firsthand" accounts are in fact, old memoirs—Anthony Shane's interview with Benjamin Drake in 1821 (12YY in the Draper Manuscripts) and Joseph Badger's autobiography, an 1851 publication of an 1806 journal.

15. Benjamin Drake, *The Life of Tecumseh and of His Brother the Prophet* (Charleston, SC, 2006 [Cincinnati, 1841]), 87.

16. Draper Manuscripts 3YY58–59; *New York Mirror*, September 12, 1829.

17. R. David Edmunds, *The Shawnee Prophet* (Lincoln, NE, 1983), 48; Glenn Tucker, *Tecumseh: Vision of Glory* (New York, 1973), 99; Robert M. Owens, *Mr. Jefferson's Hammer: William Henry Harrison and the Origins of American Indian Policy* (Norman, OK, 2007), 126; Colin G. Calloway, *The Shawnees and the War for America* (New York, 2007), 134; Anthony F. C. Wallace, *Jefferson and the Indians: The Tragic Fate of the First Americans* (Cambridge, MA, 1999), 309.

18. Edmunds, *Shawnee Prophet*, 142; Andrew R. L. Cayton, *Frontier Indiana* (Bloomington, IN, 1996), 207.

19. R. M. Devens, *Our First Century* (Springfield, MA, 1977), 199–200.

20. *Oram's New-Jersey and New-York Almanac* (Trenton, 1805).

21. Several times in 1807, the Prophet required a translator to communicate with Americans. See Draper Manuscripts 7BB49 and McNemar, *Kentucky Revival*, 125.

22. *Intelligencer*, September 10, 1806. This report comes from a white author describing nameless Indians reacting to the eclipse he had informed them was coming, and should be used cautiously. It does, however, attest to the possibility that Native Americans could have known about the eclipse.

23. See, for example, Black Hawk, *The Life of Black Hawk, or Ma-ka-tai-me-she-kia-kiak: Dictated by Himself*, ed. J. Gerald Kennedy (New York, 2008), 12, 37; or the narrative of Neolin's vision in Henry Rowe Schoolcraft, *Algic Researches: North American Indian Folktales and Legends* (Mineola, NY, 1999 [1839]), 118.

24. It is tempting but inaccurate to think of Native American religion as an unchanging constant that arose with the Beringian migrations and has continued unbroken ever since. That is almost certainly not the case—nor is it true that there is a single "Native American" religion. While the difficulties of reconstructing history based on archaeological evidence are manifold, some broad contours can be sketched of the development of Native American religious traditions of eastern North America, with increasing (but never absolute) definitiveness after French contact. And in the latter half of the twentieth century, it began to influence many modern-day Americans outside of Native American culture. Philip Jenkins, *Dream Catchers: How Mainstream America Discovered Native Spirituality* (New York, 2004).

25. Stuart Clark, *Thinking with Demons: The Idea of Witchcraft in Early Modern Europe* (New York, 2005), 8. I also borrow from Ramsey MacMullen, *Christianizing*

the Roman Empire (New Haven, CT, 1984), esp. 1–27. Vincent Brown makes a similar comment regarding the study of death: it is possible to record a people's beliefs and practices regarding the afterlife—and explain how those beliefs shaped their actions and power structures—without any speculation on the metaphysical accuracy of those beliefs; indeed, such an evaluation can get in the way of explaining how beliefs inspire action. Vincent Brown, *The Reaper's Garden: Death and Power in the World of Atlantic Slavery* (Cambridge, MA, 2008), 5.

26. Daniel K. Richter, *Facing East from Indian Country: A Native History of Early America* (Cambridge, MA, 2001), 230.

27. J. C. A. Stagg, *Mr. Madison's War: Politics, Diplomacy, and Warfare in the Early Republic, 1783–1830* (Princeton, NJ, 1983), 178. (Stagg's citation refers back to Wallace's original revitalization article.)

28. Wallace's theory first appeared in "Revitalization Movements," *American Anthropologist* 58, no. 2 (April 1956): 264–81, and received fuller treatment in *The Death and Rebirth of the Seneca* (New York, 1969). Wallace's theories are associated with Tenskwatawa in Stagg, *Mr. Madison's War*, 178; Edmunds, *Shawnee Prophet*, 25–27 and 34–41; Gregory Evans Dowd, *A Spirited Resistance: The North American Indian Struggle for Unity, 1745–1815* (Baltimore, 1992), 121–31; and Alfred A. Cave, *Prophets of the Great Spirit: Native American Revitalization Movements in Eastern North America* (Lincoln, NE, 2006), 6–10.

29. Anthony F. C. Wallace, *Religion: An Anthropological View* (New York, 1966), 264–65. I was led to this citation in Rodney Stark, *What Americans Really Believe* (Waco, TX, 2008), 115–16.

30. Pekka Hämäläinen, *The Comanche Empire* (New Haven, CT, 2008), 7, 367n8.

31. McNemar, *Kentucky Revival*, 125.

32. Patrick Spero gives an excellent summary of these shifts in "Matters of Perspective: Interpreting the Revolutionary Frontier," *Pennsylvania Magazine of History and Biography* 132, no. 3 (July 2008): 261–70.

CHAPTER 1: THROWN AWAY

1. Tenskwatawa's tales are collected in James Clifton, *Star Woman and Other Shawnee Tales* (Lanham, MD, 1984). Quotes from Thrown Away are on 37, and dating on 64–65.

2. See Robert F. Berkhofer Jr., *The White Man's Indian: Images of the American Indian from Columbus to the Present* (New York, 1978) and Alice B. Kehoe, "Eliade and Hultkrantz: The European Primitivism Tradition," *American Indian Quarterly* 20, nos. 3–4 (Summer/Fall 1996): 377–92; for the particular shifts in the Jacksonian age and after, see S. Elizabeth Bird, "Introduction: Constructing the Indian, 1830s–1990s," in *Dressing in Feathers: The Construction of the Indian in American Popular Culture*, ed. S. Elizabeth Bird (Boulder, CO, 1996), 1–12.

3. Some historians have taken the stories recorded in 1824 as the traditional Shawnee myth from which Tenskwatawa then defected. It seems problematic, however, to take the oratory of a transformative religious figure as evidence of the nature of the religion prior to the transformation. See R. David Edmunds, *The Shawnee Prophet* (Lincoln, NE, 1983), 48, 201n13; Gregory Evans Dowd, *A Spirited Resistance: The North American Indian Struggle for Unity, 1745–1815* (Baltimore, 1992), 10–11.

4. Edmund Atkin, quoted in Colin G. Calloway, *The Shawnees and the War for America* (New York, 2007), 3.

5. John Sugden, *Tecumseh: A Life* (New York, 1998), 7.

6. Dowd, *Spirited Resistance*, 24.

7. Tenskwatawa's pan-tribal genesis is well treated in Gregory Evans Dowd, "Thinking and Believing: Nativism and Unity in the Ages of Pontiac and Tecumseh," in *American Encounters: Natives and Newcomers from European Contact to Indian Removal, 1500–1850*, ed. Peter C. Mancall and James H. Merrell (New York, 2000), 379–403. A broader discussion of the difficulties of using modern political terms such as "tribes" and "chiefs" when discussing the Native American past is found in Timothy R. Pauketat, *Chiefdoms and Other Archaeological Delusions* (Lanham, MD, 2007).

8. Gary B. Nash, *The Urban Crucible: Social Change, Political Consciousness, and the Origins of the American Revolution* (Cambridge, MA, 1979), 55.

9. See Theda Perdue and Michael D. Green, *The Cherokee Nation and the Trail of Tears* (New York, 2007), 11–35; Linda S. Cordell and Bruce D. Smith, "Indigenous Farmers," 234–45, in *The Cambridge History of the Native Peoples of the Americas*, vol. 1: *North America*, ed. Bruce G. Trigger and Wilcomb E. Washburn (New York, 1996), 201–66; Daniel K. Richter, *Facing East from Indian Country: A Native History of Early America* (Cambridge, MA, 2001), 55–61.

10. D. W. Menig, *The Shaping of America: A Geographical Perspective on 500 Years of History* (New Haven, CT, 1986), 1:210.

11. For New England Puritan "praying towns," see Harold W. Van Lonkhuysen, "A Reappraisal of the Praying Indians: Acculturation, Conversion, and Identity at Natick, Massachusetts, 1634–1730," in *New England Encounters: Indians and Euroamericans ca. 1600–1850*, ed. Allen T. Vaughn (Boston, 1999), 205–32. I adopt Van Lonkhuysen's interpretation of the New England praying towns as a cultural innovation, rather than a response to cultural destruction.

12. John Sugden, *Blue Jacket: Warrior of the Shawnees* (Lincoln, NE, 2000), 28; Timothy J. Shannon, *Iroquois Diplomacy on the Early American Frontier* (New York, 2008), 116; Richard White, *The Middle Ground: Indians, Empires, and Republics in the Great Lakes Region, 1650–1815* (New York, 2006 [1991]), 267; Dowd, *Spirited Resistance*, 23–24.

13. Christian Frederick Post, "Post's Second Journal, 1758," in *Early History of Western Pennsylvania* (Pittsburgh, 1848), 99–129, 109.

14. Dowd, *Spirited Resistance*, 23.

15. Calloway, *Shawnees and the War*, 4–5.

16. Shannon, *Iroquois Diplomacy*, 34–35; Daniel K. Richter, *The Ordeal of the Long-house: The Peoples of the Iroquois League in the Era of European Colonization* (Chapel Hill, NC, 1992), 65–66.

17. Patrick Griffin, *The People with No Name: Ireland's Ulster Scots, America's Scots Irish, and the Creation of a British Atlantic World, 1689–1764* (Princeton, NJ, 2001), 1–8; Menig, *Shaping of America*, 80; Carla Gardina Pestana, "Religion," in *The British Atlantic World, 1500–1800*, ed. David Armitage and Michael J. Braddick (New York, 2002), 69–89.

18. Albert J. Raboteau, *Slave Religion: The "Invisible Institution" in the Antebellum South* (New York, 2006 [1978]), ch. 1.

19. Quoted in William M. Clements, *Oratory in Native North America* (Tucson, AZ, 2002), 37, 58. Four Guns quoted in Colin G. Calloway, "Times Are Altered with Us Indians," in *The World Turned Upside Down: Indian Voices from Early America*, ed. Colin G. Calloway (New York, 1994), 17.

20. Richter, *Ordeal of the Longhouse*, 4–7; Calloway, *Shawnees and the War*, 17–18; James Axtell, "Ethnohistory: A Historian's Viewpoint," *Ethnohistory* 26 (1979): 1–13.

21. Clifton, *Star Woman*, 47. Clifton's afterword (63–68) and White, *Middle Ground*, 520–21, suggest a related reading of Tenskwatawa's stories.

22. Richter, *Facing East*, 41, 61.

23. Francis Jennings, *Ambiguous Empire: The Covenant Chain Confederation of Indian Tribes with English Colonies from Its Beginnings to the Lancaster Treaty of 1744* (New York, 1984), 49–50; Dowd, *Spirited Resistance*, 23.

24. White, *Middle Ground*, 1–4, 29.

25. The concept of an "Iroquois Empire" is a controversial one in American historiography; many scholars feel the term is outdated. The Iroquois did not possess a Roman-style military machine and bureaucracy, but rather a system of what Jennings terms "voluntary associations, military conquest, and combinations of the two in confederation with tributary allies" (Jennings, *Ambiguous Empire*, 93–94). While some scholars prefer the term "modern Indian politics" to describe the Iroquois situation (as Richter does in *Ordeal of the Longhouse*), the Five Nations did show remarkable ability to project political power over distance—which is, in essence, what an empire is. I therefore use the term here, albeit cautiously. On the terminology and its applicability to the history of the Iroquois, see Richard Aquila, *The Iroquois Restoration: Iroquois Diplomacy on the Colonial Frontier, 1701–1754* (Detroit, 1997 [1983]).

26. Pekka Hämäläinen, *The Comanche Empire* (New Haven, CT, 2008).

27. Ibid., 7, 367–68n8; Jennings, *Ambiguous Empire*; Alan Taylor, *American Colonies* (New York, 2001), ch. 5; Aquila, *Iroquois Restoration*; Colin G. Calloway, *Crown and Calumet: British-Indian Relations, 1783–1815* (Norman, OK, 1987), 17; White, *Middle Ground*, 1–5.

28. White, *Middle Ground*, ix–xvi.
29. Quoted in Shannon, *Iroquois Diplomacy*, 41.
30. Quoted in Jennings, *Ambiguous Empire*, 309.
31. Quoted in Shannon, *Iroquois Diplomacy*, 110.
32. Jennings, *Ambiguous Empire*, 361.
33. The description of Canasetego is quoted from Richard Peters in Bruce E. Johansen, "'By Your Observing the Methods Our Wise Forefathers Have Taken, You Will Acquire Fresh Strength and Power': Closing Speech of Canassatego, July 4, 1744," in *Native American Speakers of the Eastern Woodlands: Selected Speeches and Critical Analyses*, ed. Barbara Allen Mann (Westport, CT, 2001), 83–106, quote at 91.
34. Jennings, *Ambiguous Empire*, 361; *A Treaty, Held at the Town of Lancaster . . .* (Philadelphia, 1744), 11. Jennings, 297, points out that treaties in 1722 laid out the legal foundation for the Treaty of Lancaster in 1744.
35. Calloway, *Shawnees and the War*, 23; Jennings, *Ambiguous Empire*, 357.
36. White, *Middle Ground*, 237–38.
37. Jennings, *Ambiguous Empire*, 307, 335–41.
38. Shannon, *Iroquois Diplomacy*, 138.
39. While the Iroquois ceded parts of the Shenandoah Valley, the treaty language potentially included much more. It claimed the Iroquois ceded "all the lands within the said colony [Virginia] as it is now or hereafter may be"—that is, the Treaty at least nominally included all of the Ohio Valley beyond the Shenandoah, and potentially, all the land to the Pacific. See Jennings, *Ambiguous Empire*, 361.
40. Ibid., 362.
41. Sugden, *Blue Jacket*, 28.
42. Calloway, *Shawnees and the War*, 24–26.
43. Colin G. Calloway, *The Scratch of a Pen: 1763 and the Transformation of North America* (New York, 2006), xi.
44. Calloway, *Shawnees and the War*, 30–33.
45. Missiweakiwa quoted in ibid., 30–31.
46. Dowd, *Spirited Resistance*, 24–25.
47. Clifton, *Star Woman*, 48.

CHAPTER 2: MASTER OF LIFE

1. Barbara Alice Mann, "Are You Delusional? Kandiaronk on Christianity," in *Native American Speakers of the Eastern Woodlands: Selected Speeches and Critical Analyses*, ed. Barbara Alice Mann (Westport, CT, 2001), 35–81, quotes at 63–64. Mann details the historiographical arguments over Kandiaronk as recorded in Lahontan's 1703 dialogue; I accept her contention that Lahontan's Kandiaronk/Adario is trustworthy as a Wyandot voice.
2. Colin G. Calloway, ed., *The World Turned Upside Down: Indian Voices from Early America* (New York, 1994), 47. Calloway notes that this conversion was para-

phrased and likely edited together by John Eliot as a training manual for Native American ministers; it is therefore not an exact conversation, but a summation of the arguments Native Americans of eastern North America produced against Christianity. Its surprisingly frank objections to the Christian message, however, suggest that Eliot accurately transcribed the theological objections of Native peoples of the time.

3. Quoted in William G. McLoughlin, *Cherokees and Missionaries, 1789–1839* (New Haven, CT, 1984), 21.

4. John Filson, *The Discovery, Settlement, and Present State of Kentucky* (Wilmington, 1784), 365–66.

5. John Heckewelder, *Notes, Amendments, and Additions to Heckewelder's History of the Indians*, Wallace Papers, Series II, American Philosophical Society, 8.

6. Gregory Evans Dowd, *A Spirited Resistance: The North American Indian Struggle for Unity, 1745–1815* (Baltimore, 1992), 17.

7. Black Hawk, *Life of Black Hawk*, ed. J. Gerald Kennedy (New York, 2008), 45.

8. Thomas Ridout, "Narrative of the Captivity Among the Shawanese Indians, in 1788, of Thomas Ridout," in *Ten Years of Upper Canada in Peace and War, 1805–1815*, ed. Matilda Edgar (Toronto, 1890), 371. A note dates the narrative to 1799.

9. See James Axtell, ed., *The Indian Peoples of Eastern America: A Documentary History of the Sexes* (New York, 1981), xv–xxi, 171–73; Dowd, *Spirited Resistance*, 1–22; Anthony F. C. Wallace, *The Death and Rebirth of the Seneca* (New York, 1969), 59–107; R. Murray Thomas, *Manitou and God: North-American Indian Religions and Christian Culture* (Westport, CT, 2007).

10. Society for the Propagation of the Gospel Among Indians and Others Papers, Kirkland diaries, Box 1, Folder 6, 9–10; David Brainerd, *Memoirs of the Rev. David Brainerd*, ed. Jonathan Edwards and Serebo Dwight (New Haven, CT, 1822), 345.

11. Dowd argues that this transition was very close to traditional Eastern Indian practice; Cave sees it as a fundamentally novel departure. See Alfred A. Cave, *Prophets of the Great Spirit: Native American Revitalization Movements in Eastern North America* (Lincoln, NE, 2006), 1–5; Dowd, *Spirited Resistance*, 27–46.

12. This version of Neolin's message is drawn from Henry Rowe Schoolcraft, *Algic Researches: North American Indian Folktales and Legends* (Mineola, NY, 1999 [1839]), 116–21.

13. Dowd, *Spirited Resistance*, 29–31.

14. J. G. E. Heckewelder, *History, Manners, and Customs of the Indian Nations* (New York, 1971 [1819]), 293–96; Dowd, *Spirited Resistance*, 32–33.

15. Richard White, *The Middle Ground: Indians, Empires, and Republics in the Great Lakes Region, 1650–1815* (New York, 2006), 281.

16. Ibid., 271, 281.

17. Ibid., 289.

18. Ibid., 271.

19. Ibid., 308.

20. Patrick Griffin, *American Leviathan: Empire, Nation, and Revolutionary Frontier* (New York, 2007), 46–47.
21. Benjamin Franklin, *Narrative of the Late Massacres* (Philadelphia, 1764), 27, 10. The Paxton Boys play a crucial role in Griffin's *American Leviathan* and Peter Silver, *Our Savage Neighbors: How Indian War Transformed Early America* (New York, 2007).
22. Franklin, *Narrative*, 13.
23. Thomas Barton, *Conduct of the Paxton-Men* (Philadelphia, 1764), 6; Heckewelder quoted in Paul A. W. Wallace, *Travels of John Heckewelder in Frontier America* (Pittsburgh, 1985 [1958]), 72. On the secular nature of the Paxton revolt, see Daniel K. Richter, *Facing East from Indian Country: A Native History of Early America* (Cambridge, MA, 2001), 201ff.
24. Thomas, *Manitou and God*, 10–11; White, *Middle Ground*, 503; Alan Taylor, *American Colonies* (New York, 2001), 435. The general (and fallacious) logic of revitalization is at work here: religion is a site for taxonomy and the search for the cultural sources of a new religious message, rather than the examination of the effects the message has on historical outcomes.
25. Journal of James Kenny, *Pennsylvania Magazine of History and Biography* 37 (1913): 152–53.
26. Thomas, *Manitou and God*, 11.
27. Dunmore's War is sometimes cited as a key event in the rising and increasingly racialized tensions on the American frontier (Richter, *Facing East*, 210–15). To an extent, Silver's *Our Savage Neighbors* makes the same argument about racial definitions and the creation of an "anti-Indian sublime," though his watershed occurs earlier. Yet as Patrick Griffin (*American Leviathan*, 113–22) has pointed out, such tensions did not make war an inevitability; Dunmore's War and its conclusion depended heavily on decision making by Dunmore and colonial officials. Cultural forces shaped developments, but the final arrangement of the first American frontier owed more to political, economic, and military considerations that played out for the next forty years.
28. A summary of these conditions can be found in D. W. Menig, *The Shaping of America: A Geographical Perspective on 500 Years of History* (New Haven, CT, 1986), 1:205–13.
29. Timothy J. Shannon, *Iroquois Diplomacy on the Early American Frontier* (New York, 2008), 136–41, 162.
30. White, *Middle Ground*, 353–56.

CHAPTER 3: PRIMOGENITURE

1. Freeman Cleaves, *Old Tippecanoe: William Henry Harrison and His Times* (New York, 1939), ix.
2. Ibid., 4.

3. John Adams on Benjamin Harrison V, quoted in Edmund S. Morgan, "The Puritan Ethic and the American Revolution," *William and Mary Quarterly* (3rd ser.) 24, 1 (January 1967): 4–43; quote at 31.

4. Michael J. Braddick, "Civility and Authority," in *The British Atlantic World, 1500–1800*, ed. David Armitage and Michael J. Braddick (New York, 2002), 93. See also John Ragosta, *The Wellspring of Liberty: How Virginia's Religious Dissenters Helped Win the Revolution and Secured Religious Liberty* (New York, 2010), ch. 1; Devereux Jarratt, *The Life of the Reverend Devereux Jarratt* (Baltimore, 1806), 14.

5. Howard W. Smith, *Benjamin Harrison and the American Revolution* (Williamsburg, VA, 1978), 26.

6. Inoculation of slaves and free whites was a patchwork affair in the early republic. See Elizabeth A. Fenn, *Pox Americana: The Great Smallpox Epidemic of 1775–82* (New York, 2001), 57–58.

7. *Virginia Gazette*, September 24, 1772, December 23, 1767, October 18, 1770, May 6, 1773, January 14, 1775.

8. *Virginia Gazette*, July 19, 1776.

9. Adams quoted in Smith, *Benjamin Harrison*, 26.

10. Thomas Jefferson to Benjamin Rush, April 21, 1803, in *The Portable Thomas Jefferson*, ed. Merrill D. Peterson (New York, 1985), 490–94.

11. See, for example, David Barton, *Benjamin Rush, Signer of the Declaration of Independence* (Aledo, TX, 1999), and the sections on Rush in Tim LaHaye, *Faith of Our Founding Fathers* (Green Forest, AR, 1996).

12. Benjamin Rush, *Selected Writings of Benjamin Rush*, ed. Dagobert Runes (New York, 1947), 126.

13. The best primer on deist varietals is David L. Holmes, *The Faiths of the Founding Fathers* (New York, 2006), 39–52. Joseph Priestly, deist discoverer of oxygen, held to the eternal nature of matter.

14. Thomas Jefferson to John Adams, April 11, 1823, in *The Writings of Thomas Jefferson*, ed. Andrew A. Lipscomb and Albert Ellery Bergh (Washington, DC, 1905), 15:426.

15. *Oxford English Dictionary*.

16. Jonathan Edwards quoted in Elihu Palmer, *The Principles of Nature*, ed. Kerry Walters (Wolfeboro, NH, 1990 [1806]), 22. See also Gerald R. McDermott, *Jonathan Edwards Confronts the Gods: Christian Theology, Enlightenment Religion, and Non-Christian Faiths* (New York, 2000), ch. 2.

17. Ibid., 79.

18. Thomas Jefferson to Peter Carr, August 10, 1787, *The Papers of Thomas Jefferson, Digital Edition*, ed. Barbara B. Oberg and J. Jefferson Looney (Charlottesville, VA, 2008).

19. Palmer, *Principles*, 79.

20. Paine quoted in Kerry S. Walters, *Rational Infidels: The American Deists* (Durango, CO, 1992), 131–32.

21. Ethan Allen, *Reason the Only Oracle of Man* (Bennington, VT, 1784), 225, 233.

22. Holmes, *Faiths*, ch. 12. Stephen Waldman, *Founding Faith: Providence, Politics, and the Birth of Religious Freedom in America* (New York, 2008), 58–59, discusses how Washington's few references to Christ have been widely (over) quoted, and sometimes concocted outright.

23. See William G. McLoughlin, *Revivals, Awakenings, and Reform: An Essay on Religious and Social Change in America* (Chicago, 1978); Rhys Isaac, *The Transformation of Virginia, 1740–1790* (Williamsburg, VA, 1982); George Marsden, *A Short Life of Jonathan Edwards* (Grand Rapids, MI, 2008), 134.

24. Jon Butler, *Awash in a Sea of Faith: Christianizing the American People* (New Haven, CT, 1990), 195.

25. Jewel L. Spengler, *Virginians Reborn: Anglican Monopoly, Evangelical Dissent, and the Rise of the Baptists in the Late Eighteenth Century* (Charlottesville, VA, 2008), 204–8; Ragosta, *Wellspring of Liberty*.

26. Janice Potter, *The Liberty We Seek: Loyalist Ideology in Colonial New York and Massachusetts* (Cambridge, UK, 1983), 12–13.

27. Morgan, "Puritan Ethic," 31; Holmes, *Faiths*, 139.

28. Allen, *Reason*, 258.

29. Thomas Prince, *Earthquakes the Works of God and Tokens of His Just Displeasure* (Boston, 1755), 12. Other 1755 variations on providence and earthquakes are found in James Cogswell, *The Danger of Disregarding the Works of God* (New Haven, CT, 1755); John Burt, *Earthquakes the Effects of God's Wrath* (Newport, RI, 1755); Eliphalet Williams, *The Duty of a People, Under Dark Providences* (New London, CT, 1756). European reaction to the Lisbon quake of 1755 produced markedly different results. For analysis, see Robert Ingram, "'The Trembling Earth Is God's Herald': Earthquakes, Religion, and Public Life in Britain During the 1750s," in *The Lisbon Earthquake of 1755: Representations and Reactions*, ed. Theodore E. D. Braun and John B. Radner (Oxford, 2005), 97–115.

30. Thomas Jefferson to John Adams, April 11, 1823, in *Writings*, 15:426. Also cited in Waldman, *Founding Faith*, 83.

31. Jacob Cushing, *Divine Judgments upon Tyrants, and Compassion to the Oppressed: A Sermon Preached in Lexington, April 20th, 1778* (Boston, 1778), 5.

32. Anonymous [William Wolcott], *Grateful Reflections on the Divine Goodness* (Hartford, CT, 1779), 58.

33. Ann Hulton, *Letters of a Loyalist Lady* (New York, 1971), 65.

34. Here I apply the arguments of Alexandra Walsham, who identified this same construction of providence regarding the English Civil War. See her *Providence in Early Modern England* [New York, 2001]. I am indebted to but disagree with the unilateral attribution of American providentialism with American nationalism, as argued in John F. Berens, *Providence and Patriotism in Early America, 1640–1815* (Charlottesville, VA, 1978). Examples are found in Samuel Cooke, *The Violent Destroyed and the Oppressed Delivered, a Sermon Preached at Lexington,*

April 19, 1777 (Boston, 1777), 21; *Cow-Chase, in Three Cantos, Published on the Occasion of the Rebel General Wayne's Attack of the Refugees Block-House* (New York, 1780), 45.

35. John Gates Diaries, entry for May 19, 1780, reel 4.6, Pre-Revolutionary War Diaries, Massachusetts Historical Society, Boston, MA. Punctuation added.

36. For descriptions of the Dark Day, see Samuel P. Savage, Memoranda Book, entry for May 19, 1780, Massachusetts Historical Society; Massachusetts *Spy*, June 1, 1780; Boston *Independent Chronicle and Universal Advertiser*, May 25, June 8, and June 15, 1780; Providence *American Journal*, June 7, 1780; Samuel Williams, "An Account of a Very Uncommon Darkness," *Memoirs of the Academy of Arts and Sciences*, January 1, 1785, A234–46; William McLoughlin, ed., "Olney Winsor's 'Memorandum' of the Phenomenal 'Dark Day' of May 19, 1780," *Rhode Island History*, Winter 1967, 88–90; Boston *Continental Journal*, November 23, 1780.

37. Williams, "An Account," 234; Boston *Independent Chronicle and Universal Advertiser*, June 15, 1780; Norwich *Packet*, May 22, 1780.

38. Farmer, in the State of Massachusetts-Bay, *Some Remarks on That Great and Unusual Darkness, That Appeared on Friday, May 19* . . . (Danvers, MA, 1780), 3, 4 (emphasis added).

39. Samuel Gatchel, *The Signs of the Times* (Danvers, MA, 1781) (emphasis added). Gatchel was a deacon of the Second Congregational Church in Marblehead. See Ira V. Brown, "Watchers for the Second Coming: The Millenarian Tradition in America," *Mississippi Valley History Review* 39, no. 3 (December 1952): 441–58.

40. Walsham, *Providence*, 5, 218; Farmer, *Remarks*, 5 (emphasis added), 7, 10, 13.

41. Gatchel, *Signs*, 13, 15–16. A third interpretation also circulated around the colonies in 1780: the Shaker sect of New England apparently took the Dark Day as a sign to declare to the world that their leader, Ann Lee, was the Second Coming of Jesus Christ. See Stephen J. Stein, *The Shaker Experience in America: A History of the United Society of Believers* (New Haven, CT, 1992), 11–12.

42. Hugh Henry Brackenridge, *The Death of General Montgomery, at the Siege of Quebec* (Philadelphia, 1777), 22.

43. Patrick Griffin, *American Leviathan: Empire, Nation, and Revolutionary Frontier* (New York, 2007), 29.

44. See James E. Force, "Hume and Johnson on Prophecy and Miracle: Historical Context," *Journal of the History of Ideas* 43, no. 3 (July–September 1982): 473; Christopher J. Berry, "Hume on Rationality in History and Social Life," *History and Theory* 21, 2 (May 1982): 246.

45. Griffin, *American Leviathan*, 19–22, 29–31; Nicholas Phillipson, "Providence and Progress: An Introduction to the Historical Thought of William Robertson," in *William Robertson and the Expansion of Empire*, ed. Stewart J. Brown (Cambridge, UK, 1997), 55–73.

46. Anthony Pagden, *The Fall of Natural Man: The American Indian and the Origins of Comparative Ethnology* (New York, 1982), esp. 192–97.

47. Sir Walter Scott, *The Pirate* (New York, 1910), 208–9. I was alerted to Scott's work by Ronald Hutton, *Triumph of the Moon: A History of Modern Pagan Witchcraft* (New York, 1999), 7.

48. Philip Freneau, "Indian Burying Ground," in *The Poems of Philip Freneau: Poet of the American Revolution*, ed. Fred Lewis Pattee (Princeton, NJ, 1903), 2:369–70.

49. John Adams to Thomas Jefferson, May 12, 1812, in *The Papers of Thomas Jefferson, Retirement Series*, ed. J. Jefferson Looney (Princeton, NJ, 2008), 5:70.

50. Robert J. Miller, *Native America, Discovered and Conquered: Thomas Jefferson, Lewis and Clark, and Manifest Destiny* (Lincoln, NE, 2008).

51. Colin G. Calloway, *The Shawnees and the War for America* (New York, 2007), 65–77.

52. Speech of United Indian Nations, November 28 and December 12, 1786, *American State Papers: Indian Affairs* (Washington, DC, 1832–34), 1:8–9.

53. Gregory Evans Dowd, *A Spirited Resistance: The North American Indian Struggle for Unity, 1745–1815* (Baltimore, 1992), 93.

54. Griffin, *American Leviathan*, 191–93; Richard White, *The Middle Ground: Indians, Empires, and Republics in the Great Lakes Region, 1650–1815* (New York, 2006), 444; Calloway, *Shawnees and the War*, 88.

55. Cleaves, *Old Tippecanoe*, 4.

56. Thomas Jefferson to William Short, December 14, 1789, in *The Papers of Thomas Jefferson, Digital Edition*, ed. Barbara B. Oberg and J. Jefferson Looney (Charlottesville, VA, 2008).

57. David Rice, *A Sermon, on the Present Revival of Religion in this Country, Preached at the Opening of the Kentucky Synod* (Washington, KY, 1804), 9–11. Paul Conkin connects Hampden-Sydney to later revivals in *Cane Ridge: America's Pentecost* (Madison, WI, 1990), 50–53.

58. Miller, *Native America*, 42–43; Peter Onuf, "The Importance of the Northwest Ordinance," in *Liberty's Legacy: Our Celebration of the Northwest Ordinance and the United States Constitution* (Columbus, OH, 1987), 7–15.

CHAPTER 4: DEFEAT

1. Arthur St. Clair, *Narrative of the Manner in Which the Campaign Against the Indians . . . Was Conducted* (Philadelphia, 1812), v–vi.

2. Colin G. Calloway, *Crown and Calumet: British-Indian Relations, 1783–1815* (Norman, OK, 1987), 195; Gordon Wood, *Empire of Liberty: A History of the Early Republic, 1789–1815* (New York, 2009), 129–30.

3. Alan Taylor, *The Divided Ground: Indians, Settlers, and the Northern Borderland of the American Revolution* (New York, 2006), 259.

4. Ibid., 166.

5. Taylor tells the tale of the treaty in ibid., 154–62; I disagree with his conclusions of its effectiveness.

6. Henry Lee Jr. to George Washington, February 16, 1786, in *The Papers of George Washington, Digital Edition*, ed. Theodore J. Crackel (Charlottesville, 2008).

7. Taylor, *Divided Ground*, 155–61.

8. Colin G. Calloway, *The Shawnees and the War for America* (New York, 2007), 78–79.

9. C. C. Trowbridge, *Shawnese Traditions: C. C. Trowbridge's Account*, ed. Vernon Kinietz and Erminie Wheeler-Voegelin (New York, 1980), 11.

10. Ibid., 11.

11. Jedidiah Morse, *A Report to the Secretary of War of the United States on Indian Affairs* (New York, 1970 [1822]), Appendix 98.

12. Trowbridge, *Shawnese Traditions*, 12.

13. Ibid., 12.

14. Ibid., 12–13.

15. Taylor, *Divided Ground*, 122.

16. James Madison, *Federalist* 48, in *The Federalist with the Letters of "Brutus,"* ed. Terence Ball (New York, 2003), 240–44.

17. Taylor, *Divided Ground*, 20; John Sugden, *Blue Jacket: Warrior of the Shawnees* (Lincoln, NE, 2000), 65–68.

18. Daniel K. Richter, *Facing East from Indian Country: A Native History of Early America* (Cambridge, MA, 2001), 222–23.

19. Sugden, *Blue Jacket*, 68.

20. Stewart Rafert, *The Miami Indians of Indiana: A Persistent People, 1654–1994* (Indianapolis, 1996), 47–48.

21. Hendrick Aupamat, "A Narrative of an Embassy to the Western Indians," *Memoirs of the Historical Society of Pennsylvania* 2 (1827): 110. Aupamat himself was a Mohican, but lived in Iroquois territory and spoke both Iroquoian and Algonquian languages. Alan Taylor, "Captain Hendrick Aupamat: The Dilemmas of an Intercultural Broker." *Ethnohistory* 43, no. 3 (Summer 1996): 431–57.

22. John Heckewelder, "Narrative of the Cuyahoga Indian Settlement, 1785," in *Visions of the Western Reserve: Public and Private Documents of Northeastern Ohio, 1750–1860*, ed. Robert Wheeler (Columbus, OH, 2000), 41.

23. Quoted in Peter Silver, *Our Savage Neighbors: How Indian War Transformed Early America* (New York, 2007), 275. Accounts of the dynamics of anti-Indian racism and its effect on Revolutionary America and the United States include, among many, James H. Merrell, *Into the American Woods: Negotiators on the Pennsylvania Frontier* (New York, 1999); Richter, *Facing East*, chs. 5–6; and Richard Drinnon, *Facing West: The Metaphysics of Indian-Hating and Empire Building* (Minneapolis, 1980).

24. Silver, *Our Savage Neighbors*, 288.

25. Patrick Griffin, *American Leviathan: Empire, Nation, and Revolutionary Frontier* (New York, 2007), 202–3.

26. Congress approved the survey of the lands in 1785, and further codified the process in the 1787 Northwest Ordinance. Frazer Dorrian McGlinchey, "'A Superior Civ-

ilization': Appropriation, Negotiation, and Interaction in the Northwest Territory, 1787–1795," in *The Boundaries Between Us: Natives and Newcomers Along the Frontiers of the Old Northwest Territory, 1750–1850*, ed. Daniel P. Barr (Kent, OH, 2006), 118–42.

27. Draper Manuscripts 23U22.

28. Oliver M. Spencer, *Indian Captivity: A True Narrative of the Capture of Rev. O. M. Spencer* (New York, 1852), 92.

29. Helen Hornbeck Tanner, "The Glaize in 1792: A Composite Indian Community." *Ethnohistory* 25, no. 1 (Winter 1978): 15–39.

30. John Sugden, *Tecumseh: A Life* [New York, 1998], 55–66.

31. Ibid., 131.

32. Gerard T. Hopkins, *A Mission to the Indians from the Indian Committee of the Baltimore Yearly Meeting to Fort Wayne in 1804* (Philadelphia, 1862), 54.

33. Tanner, "The Glaize in 1792," 28.

34. Sugden, *Blue Jacket*, 131; John Heckewelder, *Narrative of the Mission of the United Brethren . . . to the Close of the Year 1808*, ed. William Elsey Connelley (Cleveland, 1907 [1819]), 410; Consul Willshire Butterfield, *An Historical Account of the Expedition Against Sandusky Under Col. William Crawford in 1782* (Cincinnati, 1873), 211.

35. Quoted in Sugden, *Blue Jacket*, 72.

36. Aupamat, "Narrative," 118–19.

37. Ibid., 119–20, 123.

38. Spencer, *Indian Captivity*, 75.

39. Ibid., 97–98.

40. Leroy V. Eid, "American Indian Military Leadership: St. Clair's Defeat," *Journal of Military History* 57, no. 1 (January 1993): 71–88.

41. Sugden, *Blue Jacket*, 74–75; Ebenezer Denny, *The Military Journal of Ebenezer Denny* (Philadelphia, 1859), 94.

42. Quoted in Griffin, *American Leviathan*, 206.

43. Michael S. Warner, "General Josiah Harmar's Campaign Reconsidered: How the Americans Lost the Battle of Kekionga," *Indiana Magazine of History* 83, no. 1 (March 1987): 43–64; Griffin, *American Leviathan*, 205–6.

44. The continual failure of the militia complicates Silver's argument about the importance of Indian-hating as a historical force, since those who supposedly hated the Indians the most (the frontier militia types) often performed the worst against Indian armies. On the early republic's tendency to value militia over trained professionals, see Daniel Walker Howe, *What Hath God Wrought* (New York, 2007), 13, 17–18.

45. My summary of St. Clair's command is from Eid, "American Indian Military Leadership," 71–76.

46. Ibid., 83–85.

47. Ibid., 71.

48. St. Clair to George Washington, March 26, 1792, in *Papers of George Washington*.

49. Spencer, *Indian Captivity*, 98.

50. Historians who move rapidly from St. Clair's defeat to Anthony Wayne's victory include Alfred A. Cave, *Prophets of the Great Spirit: Native American Revitalization Movements in Eastern North America* (Lincoln, NE, 2006), 59–60; Edmunds, *Shawnee Prophet*, 16; and Wood, *Empire of Liberty*, 129–31. John Sugden, *Blue Jacket*, and Gregory Evans Dowd, *A Spirited Resistance: The North American Indian Struggle for Unity, 1745–1815* (Baltimore, 1992), take a more careful look at the years following St. Clair's defeat.

51. I. R. Jackson, *Life of William Henry Harrison of Ohio* (Philadelphia, 1840), 19.

52. William Maclay, *Sketches of Debate in the First Senate of the United States*, ed. George Harris (Harrisburg, PA, 1880), entry for February 1, 1791, 288.

53. Quoted in Stanley M. Elkins and Eric L. McKitrick, *The Age of Federalism* (New York, 1993), 271.

54. Dorothy Burne Goebel, *William Henry Harrison: A Political Biography* (Philadelphia, 1974 [1926]), 19.

55. WHH to Carter Harrison, November 27, 1794, quoted in Robert M. Owens, *Mr. Jefferson's Hammer: William Henry Harrison and the Origins of American Indian Policy* (Norman, OK, 2007), 37; WHH to Nathaniel Massie, January 17, 1800, in *The Papers of William Henry Harrison, 1800–1815*, ed. Douglas E. Clanin (microfilm) (Indianapolis, 1999), 1:9.

56. Owens, *Mr. Jefferson's Hammer*, 39.

57. Ibid., 15, 253n35; Harrison to Brooks, July 20, 1839, Harrison MSS, quoted in Freeman Cleaves, *Old Tippecanoe: William Henry Harrison and His Times* (New York, 1939), 7. Washington duly sent along the nomination to the Senate on October 31, 1791. See *Papers of George Washington*.

58. St. Clair to Knox, November 9, 1791, in Henry Trumbull, *History of the Discovery of America . . . to Which Is Annexed the Defeat of Generals Braddock, Harmar, and St. Clair* (Norwich, CT, 1812), 151.

59. Speech to the Delawares and Other Tribes, October 6, 1792, in Rufus Putnam, *Memoirs of Rufus Putnam*, ed. Rowena Buell (Marietta, OH, 1903), 368.

60. Instructions to Benjamin Lincoln et al., December 4, 1793, *American State Papers, Indian Affairs* (Washington, DC, 1832), 1:340–41. See also Lisa Brooks, "Two Paths to Peace: Competing Visions of Native Space in the Old Northwest," in *The Boundaries Between Us: Natives and Newcomers Along the Frontiers of the Old Northwest Territory, 1750–1850*, ed. Daniel P. Barr (Kent, OH, 2006), 87–117.

61. Robert Gray Gunderson, *The Log Cabin Campaign* (Lexington, KY, 1957), 7.

62. WHH to the General Assembly, November 4, 1806, in *Papers*, 2:660.

63. Theodore J. Crackel, *Mr. Jefferson's Army: Political and Social Reform of the Military Establishment, 1801–1809* (New York, 1987), 90–91.

64. Andrew R. L. Cayton, *Frontier Indiana* (Bloomington, IN, 1996), 119, 149.

65. Richard B. Stott, "Commentary," in William Otter, *History of My Own Times, or the Life and Adventures of William Otter, Sen.*, ed. Richard B. Stott (Ithaca, NY, 1995), 202.

66. W. J. Rohrabaugh, *Alcoholic Republic: An American Tradition* (New York, 1979), 139.

67. Deposition of Christopher Wyant, May 9, 1795, Indianapolis Historical Society, William English Collection, Box 30, Folder 2.

68. Rohrabaugh, *Alcoholic Republic*, 79–80, 151.

69. Owens, *Mr. Jefferson's Hammer*, 21.

70. Anthony Wayne's Orderly Book, July 21, 1792, *Historical Collections: Collections and Researches Made by the Michigan Pioneer and Historical Society* (Lansing, 1905), 34:351.

71. Ibid.

72. Ibid., May 26, 1792, 347.

73. Ibid.

74. Owens, *Mr. Jefferson's Hammer*, 18.

75. Wayne to Henry Knox, August 3, 1792, in *Anthony Wayne: A Name in Arms*, ed. Richard C. Knopf (Westport, CT, 1960), 55–58; Gunderson, *Log Cabin Campaign*, 10.

76. Andrew R. L. Cayton, "Power and Civility in the Treaty of Greenville," in *Contact Points: American Frontiers from the Mohawk Valley to the Mississippi, 1750–1830*, ed. Andrew R. L. Cayton and Fredrika J. Teute (Chapel Hill, NC, 1998), 243.

77. Anthony Wayne's Orderly Book, November 11, 1792, 401–3.

78. Ibid., October 18, 1792, 396–97. Harrison was assigned to Smith's company on September 10, 1792 (ibid., 381).

79. Ibid., July 19, 1792, 355–56.

80. Ibid., August 9, 1792, 358.

81. Ibid., September 1, 1792, 370–71.

82. Sugden, *Blue Jacket*, 143–44.

83. Aupamat, "Narrative," 118.

84. Ibid., 89.

85. "Indians to General Washington," February 1793, in *Historical Collections: Collections and Researches Made by the Michigan Pioneer and Historical Society* (Lansing, 1892), 20:315.

86. Alexander McKee to Joseph Chew, Miami Rapids, February 1, 1794, *Historical Collections*, 20:325–26. See also William Johnson Chew to Joseph Chew, October 24, 1794, in ibid., 380.

87. William Clark, "William Clark's Journal of General Wayne's Campaign," ed. R. C. McGrane, *Mississippi Valley Historical Review* 1, no. 3 (December 1914): 421.

88. Ibid., 424.

89. Ibid., 425.

90. Ibid., 428–29; David Paul Nelson, *Anthony Wayne: Soldier of the Early Republic* (Bloomington, IN, 1985), 262–67.

91. Clark, "William Clark's Journal," 430.

92. Edmunds, *Shawnee Prophet*, 16; Cave, *Prophets of the Great Spirit*, 60; Calloway, *Crown and Calumet*, 225–26.

93. McKee to Joseph Chew, August 27, 1794, in *Historical Collections*, 20:372.

94. Alan D. Gaff, *Bayonets in the Wilderness: Anthony Wayne's Legion in the Old Northwest* (Norman, OK, 2004), 317–18.

95. Nelson, *Anthony Wayne*, 270.

96. Ibid., 269, 271.

97. Joseph Brant to Joseph Chew, October 22, 1794, in *Historical Collections*, 20:376. Wayne's diplomacy and conduct are at the center of Cayton's analysis of the treaty in "Power and Civility."

98. William Johnson Chew to Joseph Chew, October 24, 1794, in *Historical Collections*, 20:380.

99. George Ironside to McKee, December 13, 1794, in *Historical Collections*, 20:386; Gaff, *Bayonets in the Wilderness*, 304.

100. My understanding of Jay's Treaty derives from conversations with Lawrence B. A. Hatter at the University of Virginia, as well as his article "The Jay Charter: Rethinking the American National State in the West, 1796–1819," in *Diplomatic History* (forthcoming). See also Jerald A. Combs, *The Jay Treaty: Political Battleground of the Founding Fathers* (Berkeley, CA, 1970); Todd Estes, *The Jay Treaty Debate, Public Opinion, and the Evolution of Early American Political Culture* (Boston, 2006).

101. E. B. Littlehales to Francis Le Maistre, September 21, 1794, in *Historical Collections*, 20:375.

102. Gaff, *Bayonets in the Wilderness*, 331; Peter C. Mancall, *Deadly Medicine: Indians and Alcohol in Early America* (Ithaca, NY, 1995); *Territorial Papers of the United States*, ed. Clarence Edwin Carter (Washington, DC, 1934), 3:421–27. On Native Americans and alcoholism, see Richard W. Thatcher, *Fighting Firewater Fictions: Moving Beyond the Disease Model of Alcoholism in First Nations* (Toronto, 2004), esp. ch. 7, and Mancall, 256–59.

103. Mancall, *Deadly Medicine*, 75–77.

104. Quoted in Owens, *Mr. Jefferson's Hammer*, 25.

CHAPTER 5: THE CAREERIST

1. Andrew R. L. Cayton, *Frontier Indiana* (Bloomington, IN, 1996), 167; Thomas Jefferson to John Cleves Symmes, June 22, 1792, in *The Papers of Thomas Jefferson, Digital Edition*, ed. Barbara B. Oberg and J. Jefferson Looney (Charlottesville, 2008); John Cleves Symmes to Robert Morris, June 22, 1795, in *The Intimate Letters of John Cleves Symmes and His Family*, ed. Beverly W. Bond Jr. (Cincinnati, 1956), 97–99; John Cleves Symmes to Silas Condict, February 28, 1796, in *Intimate Letters*, 102–3.

2. John Cleves Symmes to Silas Condict, February 28, 1796, in *Intimate Letters*, 102–3.

3. John Cleves Symmes to WHH, September 9, 1796, in *Intimate Letters*, 140; John Cleves Symmes to Jonathan Dayton, August 10, 1796, in *The Correspondence of John Cleves Symmes*, ed. Beverly W. Bond Jr. (New York, 1926), 182–83; Robert M. Owens, *Mr. Jefferson's Hammer: William Henry Harrison and the Origins of American Indian Policy* (Norman, OK, 2007), 43–45.

4. John Cleves Symmes to Anna Tuthill Symmes Harrison, September 11, 1809, in *Correspondence*, 300; John Cleves Symmes to Jonathan Dayton, June 17, 1795, in *Correspondence*, 166.

5. Owens, *Mr. Jefferson's Hammer*, 46.

6. Rufus Putnam to Fisher Ames, n.d. [1790], in *Memoirs of Rufus Putnam*, ed. Rowena Buell (Cambridge, MA, 1903), 237; McHenry to James Wilkinson, August 20, 1797, War of 1812 MSS, Lilly Library, University of Indiana. See also Wilkinson-Miro correspondence, Filson Historical Society.

7. McHenry to James Wilkinson, November 3, 1797, War of 1812 MSS, Lilly Library, University of Indiana.

8. Gordon Wood, *Empire of Liberty: A History of the Early Republic, 1789–1815* (New York, 2009), 183.

9. Ibid., 186–87.

10. Doron Ben-Atar and Barbara Oberg, "The Paradoxical Legacy of the Federalists," in *Federalists Reconsidered*, ed. Doron Ben-Atar and Barbara Oberg (Charlottesville, VA, 1998), 2.

11. Peter Onuf, *Jefferson's Empire: The Language of American Nationhood* (Charlottesville, VA, 2000), 93–94. See also Jean M. Yarborough, *American Virtues: Thomas Jefferson on the Character of a Free People* (Lawrence, KS, 1998), 102–52; Douglass G. Adair, *The Intellectual Origins of Jeffersonian Democracy: Republicanism, the Class Struggle, and the Virtuous Farmer* (New York, 2000 [1964]), 153–64.

12. Tappan, quoted in Vernon Stauffer, *The Bavarian Illuminati in America: The New England Conspiracy Scare, 1798* (Mineola, NY, 2006 [1918]), 92.

13. Joanne B. Freeman, *Affairs of Honor: National Politics in the New Republic* (New Haven, CT, 2001), 174.

14. Stanley M. Elkins and Eric L. McKitrick, *The Age of Federalism* (New York, 1993), 525.

15. Saul Cornell, *The Other Founders: Anti-Federalism and the Dissenting Tradition in America, 1788–1828* (Chapel Hill, NC, 1999), 233.

16. Circular Letter of Robert Goodloe Harper, February 10, 1799, in *Circular Letters of Congressmen to Their Constituents, 1789–1829*, ed. Noble E. Cunningham Jr. (Williamsburg, VA, 1978), 1:146.

17. Cornell, *The Other Founders*, 231.

18. The malleability of the switch from local to national—as well as the intensity of elections based around a developing definition of American nationalism—is

neatly treated in David Waldstreicher, *In the Midst of Perpetual Fetes* (Chapel Hill, NC, 1997); the election of 1800 is dealt with specifically on 184–216.

19. Quoted in Freeman, *Affairs of Honor*, 233.
20. *Gazette of the United States*, September 10, 1800, quoted in Robert S. McDonald, "Was There a Religious Revolution of 1800?" in *The Revolution of 1800: Democracy, Race, and the New Republic*, ed. James Horn, Jan Ellen Lewis, and Peter S. Onuf (Charlottesville, VA, 2002), 182.
21. "A Republican" [Jonathan Russell], quoted in McDonald, "Was There a Religious Revolution," 185.
22. Owens, *Mr. Jefferson's Hammer*, 48.

CHAPTER 6: GROUSELAND

1. Anonymous, *Journal of a Trip from Champaign County, Ohio . . . 1805–06* (SC2148), Abraham Lincoln Presidential Library and Museum.
2. Robert M. Owens, *Mr. Jefferson's Hammer: William Henry Harrison and the Origins of American Indian Policy* (Norman, OK, 2007), 56–58.
3. Peter S. Onuf, "The Northwest Ordinance," in *Roots of the Republic: American Founding Documents Interpreted*, ed. Stephen L. Schechter (Lanham, MD, 1990), 251.
4. Onuf, "Ordinance," 254; David Brion Davis, "Significance of Excluding Slavery from the Old Northwest 1787," *Indiana Magazine of History* 84, no. 1 (March 1988): 75–89.
5. Quoted in Daniel Owen, "Circumvention of Article VI of the Ordinance of 1787," in *Indiana Magazine of History* 36, no. 2 (June 1940): 111–12.
6. Ibid., 112.
7. Ibid.; Owens, *Mr. Jefferson's Hammer*, 193.
8. Owens, *Mr. Jefferson's Hammer*, 68.
9. Earl E. McDonald, "Disposal of Negro Slaves by Will in Knox County," *Indiana Magazine of History* 26, no. 2 (June 1930): 145.
10. Owens, *Mr. Jefferson's Hammer*, 68.
11. Indiana *Gazette and Western Sun*, September 11 and 18, 1804. See also McDonald, "Disposal of Negro Slaves," 295n19.
12. Owens, *Mr. Jefferson's Hammer*, 71.
13. Owen, "Circumvention," 115–16; Owens, *Mr. Jefferson's Hammer*, 109–11.
14. Owens, *Mr. Jefferson's Hammer*, 69–70.
15. Benjamin Drew, *The Refugee, or the Narrative of Fugitive Slaves in Canada* (Boston, 1856), 273, 373.
16. Owens, *Mr. Jefferson's Hammer*, 72–73.
17. Robert Morrison to Joseph Morrison, December 31, 1805, Robert Morrison Letters (SC 1079), Abraham Lincoln Presidential Library and Museum (henceforth ALPLM).

18. Owens, *Mr. Jefferson's Hammer*, 193–94; *Census for 1820* (Washington, DC, 1821), 18. Note that I here disagree with Owens about the significance of the increased slave population.

19. Journal of William Foster, in *Indiana as Seen by Early Travelers*, ed. Harlow Lindley (Indianapolis, 1916), 257.

20. Owens, *Mr. Jefferson's Hammer*, 54, 75.

21. Andrew R. L. Cayton, *Frontier Indiana* (Bloomington, IN, 1996), 233.

22. Entry for January 28, 1802, *Executive Journal of Indiana Territory, 1800–1816*, ed. William Wesley Woollen, Daniel Wait Howe, and Jacob Piatt Dunn (Indianapolis, 1985), 16.

23. Minutes and Proceeding of the Vincennes University as Transacted by the Board of Trustees, Indiana Territory; Lilly Library, Indiana University.

24. Samuel Finch et al. to WHH, undated (before November 20, 1804), in *The Papers of William Henry Harrison, 1800–1815*, ed. Douglas E. Clanin (microfilm) (Indianapolis, 1999), 2:41.

25. Minutes and Proceeding of the Vincennes University as Transacted by the Board of Trustees, Indiana Territory.

26. WHH, Message to the General Assembly, November 4, 1806, in *Papers of William Henry Harrison*, 2:655.

27. WHH, Proclamation, December 5, 1804, in *Papers of William Henry Harrison*, 2:56.

28. Samuel Finch et al. to WHH, undated (before November 20, 1804), in *Papers of William Henry Harrison*, 2:41.

29. Indiana *Gazette*, July 21, 1804.

30. *Executive Journal of Indiana Territory*, 34.

31. Ibid., 36–37.

32. Ibid., 35.

33. Thomas Jefferson to WHH, April 28, 1805, in *Papers of William Henry Harrison*, 2:159; Owens, *Mr. Jefferson's Hammer*, 92–93.

34. See Cayton, *Frontier Indiana*, ch. 9.

35. WHH to Thomas Worthington, December 25, 1804, in *Papers of William Henry Harrison*, 2:64.

36. *Executive Journal of Indiana Territory*, 38.

37. Solomon Sibley to WHH, December 2, 1799, in *Papers of William Henry Harrison*, 1:1.

38. Thomas Jefferson to WHH, February 27, 1803, in *Thomas Jefferson: Writings*, ed. Merrill D. Peterson (New York, 1984), 1117–20.

39. Jefferson to Livingston, April 18, 1802, in *The Portable Thomas Jefferson*, ed. Merrill D. Peterson (New York, 1985), 485.

40. Henry Dearborn to WHH, July 29, 1802, in *Papers of William Henry Harrison*, 1:342.

41. Thomas Jefferson to WHH, February 27, 1803, in *Thomas Jefferson: Writings*, ed. Merrill D. Peterson (New York, 1984), 1117–20.

42. Ibid.

43. Ibid. My interpretation of the Jeffersonian project derives from the work of Peter S. Onuf, *Jefferson's Empire: The Language of American Nationhood* (Charlottesville, VA, 2000).

44. Gerard T. Hopkins, *A Mission to the Indians from the Indian Committee of the Baltimore Yearly Meeting to Fort Wayne in 1804* (Philadelphia, 1862), 77.

45. John Francis McDermott, "Audubon's 'Journey Up the Mississippi,'" *Journal of the Illinois State Historical Society* 35:1 (1942): 154. On gender roles in Shawnee and related Indian communities, see Richter, *Facing East from Indian Country*, 55–58; Gregory Evans Dowd, "Thinking and Believing: Nativism and Unity in the Ages of Pontiac and Tecumseh," in *American Encounters: Natives and Newcomers from European Contact to Indian Removal, 1500–1850*, ed. Peter C. Mancall and James H. Merrell (New York, 2000), 387–88.

46. Hopkins, *Mission*, 77.

47. Ibid., 85.

48. Thomas Jefferson's Reply to the Delaware and Shawnee Delegation, February 2, 1802, in *The Papers of Thomas Jefferson*, ed. Barbara Oberg (Princeton, NJ, 2009), 36:522–23.

49. Dowd, "Thinking and Believing," 386–88.

50. WHH speech at Indian Council, September 12, 1802, in *Papers of William Henry Harrison*, 1:374, 377.

51. Owens, *Mr. Jefferson's Hammer*, 61–64.

52. Heckewelder, *The History, Manners, and Customs of the Indian Nations* (Philadelphia, 1876), 256; Constantin F. Volney, *A View of the Soil and Climate of the United States* (New York, 1968 [1804]), 404, 420–21.

53. Paul A. Hutton, "William Wells: Frontier Scout and Indian Agent," *Indiana Magazine of History* 74, no. 3 (September 1978): 203–4.

54. Ibid.

55. Stewart Rafert, *The Miami Indians of Indiana: A Persistent People, 1654–1994* (Indianapolis, 1996), 66–68; Conference with Little Turtle and Miami, Wea, and Potawatomi Chiefs, January 1802, reprinted in the Shawnee File of Glenn A. Black Laboratory of Archaeology, Ohio Valley–Great Lakes Ethnohistory Archive, Indiana University.

56. Dorothy Burne Goebel, *William Henry Harrison: A Political Biography* (Philadelphia, 1974 [1926]), 101; Owens, *Mr. Jefferson's Hammer*, 77–80.

57. Conference with Delaware and Shawnee, February 1802, Shawnee File, Great Lakes Ethnohistory Archive.

58. Owens, *Mr. Jefferson's Hammer*, 80; Wallace, *Jefferson*, 227. The Fort Wayne Treaty came in June, and the treaty with Piankeshaws in August.

59. WHH to Indian Council, August 12, 1802, in *Messages and Papers of William Henry Harrison*, ed. Logan Esarey (Indianapolis, 1922), 1:53.

60. WHH to Henry Dearborn, February 25, 1806, in *Papers of William Henry Harrison*, 2:502.

61. Treaty with the Sauk and Foxes, November 3, 1804, in *Papers of William Henry Harrison*, 2:3–7.
62. WHH to Henry Dearborn, August 10, 1805, in *Papers of William Henry Harrison*, 2:282; Treaty with the Piankeshaw, December 30, 1805, in *Papers of William Henry Harrison*, 2:446–48.
63. WHH to Henry Dearborn, January 1, 1806, in *Papers of William Henry Harrison*, 2:472.
64. My analysis here follows that of N. Bruce Duthu, *American Indians and the Law* (New York, 2008), 69–72. The ramifications of *Johnson v. McIntosh* are cogently analyzed in Lindsay G. Robertson, *Conquest by Law: How the Discovery of America Dispossessed Indigenous Peoples of Their Lands* (New York, 2005), and Robert J. Miller, *Native America, Discovered and Conquered: Thomas Jefferson, Lewis and Clark, and Manifest Destiny* (Lincoln, NE, 2008).
65. WHH to Thomas Jefferson, May 12, 1804, in *Papers of William Henry Harrison*, 1:797–99.
66. WHH to Thomas Jefferson, August 29, 1805, in *Papers of William Henry Harrison*, 2:328, emphasis added.
67. Dearborn to Jouett, April 2, 1805, *American State Papers, Indian Affairs* (Washington, DC, 1832), 1:703.
68. WHH to Henry Dearborn, August 26, 1805, in *Papers of William Henry Harrison*, 2:325.
69. Hull to Henry Dearborn, September 22, 1805, Shawnee File, Great Lakes Ethnohistory Archive.
70. WHH to Henry Dearborn, March 3, 1805, in *Papers of William Henry Harrison*, 2:104.
71. Conference with Delaware and Shawnee, February 1802, Shawnee File, Great Lakes Ethnohistory Archive.
72. Speech of Sandusky Indians to Hull, May 19, 1805, *Michigan Historical Collections* (Lansing, 1929), 40:61.
73. James Wikinson to Henry Deaborn, December 3, 1805, Shawnee File, Great Lakes Ethnohistory Archive.
74. Hull to Wyandots, May 6, 1807, *Michigan Historical Collections* (Lansing, 1929), 40:61, 115.
75. Hull to Henry Dearborn, October 28, 1805, *Michigan Historical Collections* (Lansing, 1929), 40:77; James Bruff to James Wilkinson, March 12, 1805, *Territorial Papers of the United States*, 13:101.
76. *Journal of a Trip from Champaign County, Ohio . . .*, ALPLM.
77. Barton Warren Stone, *The Biography of Elder Barton Warren Stone, Written by Himself*, ed. John Rogers (New York, 1972 [1847]), 68.
78. John Lyle diary, June 14, 1801, Kentucky Historical Society.
79. Paul Conkin, *Cane Ridge: America's Pentecost* (Madison, WI, 1990), 52–53.

80. James MacGready, "A Short Narrative of the Revival of Religion in Logan County," *Western Missionary Magazine*, March 1803, 46; Conkin, *Cane Ridge*, 43, 55–56.

81. George Baxter to Archibald Alexander, January 1, 1802, reprinted in *Western Missionary Magazine*, August 1803, 263.

82. Stone, *A Short History of the Life of Barton Warren Stone, Written by Himself*, in *Voices from Cane Ridge*, ed. Rhodes Thompson (St. Louis, 1954), 70.

83. Lorenzo Dow, *History of Cosmopolite* (Cincinnati, 1854), 184.

84. *Increase of Piety, or Revivals of Religion in the United States of America* (Newburyport, MA, 1802), 90.

85. MacGready, "A Short Narrative," 54.

86. Journal of Robert Breckinridge McAfee, 1803–7, Filson Historical Society, Louisville, Kentucky. Entries for 1804: April 21, February 9, February 12, April 29, July 22, July 31.

87. Symmes to WHH, March 30, 1801, in *Papers of William Henry Harrison*, 1:134.

88. Richard McNemar, *The Kentucky Revival* (New York, 1848 [1808]), 132.

CHAPTER 7: PROPHECY

1. George Bluejacket, *History of the Shawanoes*, Lilly Library, US History MSS, entry for October 29, 1829.

2. Richard McNemar, *The Kentucky Revival* (New York, 1848 [1808]), 114.

3. *National Intelligencer*, October 9, 1807.

4. Wells to Henry Dearborn, March 31, 1807, Shawnee File, Great Lakes Ethnohistory Archive.

5. Speech of the Trout, May 4, 1807, enclosure in Dunham to Hull, May 20, 1807, *Michigan Historical Collections* (Lansing, 1929), 40:123.

6. John Tanner, *The Falcon: A Narrative of the Captivity and Adventures of John Tanner* (New York, 2000 [1830]), 145.

7. Prophet to WHH, August 1, 1808, in *Messages and Papers of William Henry Harrison*, ed. Logan Esarey (Indianapolis, 1922), 1:299–300; Thomas Forsythe to William Clark, December 23, 1812, quoted in *The Indian Tribes of the Upper Mississippi Valley*, ed. Emma Helen Blair (Cleveland, 1912), 2:277.

8. *The Moravian Indian Mission on White River: Diaries and Letters*, ed. Lawrence Henry Gipson, trans. Harry E. Stocker, Herman T. Frueauff, and Samuel C. Zeller (Indianapolis, 1938), 407.

9. Prophet to WHH, August 1, 1808, in *Messages and Papers of William Henry Harrison*, ed. Logan Esarey (Indianapolis, 1922), 1:299–300.

10. McNemar, *Kentucky Revival*, 114.

11. Deposition of Charles McLivane, February 1806, Draper Manuscripts 7BB25 and 2YY5; see also McNemar, *Kentucky Revival*.

12. McNemar, *Kentucky Revival*, 124.

13. Benjamin Youngs, "A Journey to the Indians March 1807," Winterthur, Andrews Collection 860, 2.

14. Ibid., 11–12.

15. John Sugden, *Blue Jacket: Warrior of the Shawnees* (Lincoln, NE, 2000), 239.

16. McNemar, *Kentucky Revival*, 127–28.

17. Youngs, "Journey," 17–18.

18. Ibid., 20.

19. McNemar, *Kentucky Revival*, 129.

20. See for example Sugden, *Blue Jacket,* 241.

21. Hull to Henry Dearborn, September 9, 1807, *Michigan Historical Collections* (Lansing, 1929), 40:197.

22. Eli Langford to Thomas Kirker, September 5, 1807, Draper Manuscripts 7BB45.

23. Wells to Henry Dearborn, March 31, 1807, Shawnee File, Great Lakes Ethnohistory Archive; Jouett to Henry Dearborn, December 1, 1807, *Territorial Papers of the United States* (Washington, DC, 1939), 7:496–97.

24. Sugden, *Blue Jacket*, 238; Draper Manuscripts 2YY108; Sandy Antal, *A Wampum Denied: Procter's War of 1812* (Ottawa, 1997), 58–59n.

25. Wells to Secretary of War, May 19, 1807, Shawnee File, Great Lakes Ethnohistory Archive.

26. Speech of the Trout, May 4, 1807, 128.

27. William Wells, Speech to the Shawnees residing at Greenville, April 22, 1807, Shawnee File, Great Lakes Ethnohistory Archive.

28. Draper Manuscripts 7BB45.

29. Kirk to Drake, September 16, 1809, Draper Manuscripts 3YY74.

30. Intelligence Report of Simon Kenton et al., Draper Manuscripts 7BB46.

31. Shawnee Chiefs in Public Council to the Governor, March 20, 1806, Draper Manuscripts 7BB31.

32. Report of Worthington and McArthur to Kirker, September 22, 1807, Draper Manuscripts 7BB49.

33. *Moravian Indian Mission*, 403.

34. Draper Manuscripts 12YY53.

35. *Moravian Indian Mission*, 413; Dunham to Hull, May 20, 1807, *Michigan Historical Collections* (Lansing, 1929), 40:123; Charles Reame to Dunham, June 4, 1807, Shawnee File, Great Lakes Ethnohistory Archive.

36. Paul Radin, *The Winnebago Tribe* (Washington, DC, 1970 [1923]), 23.

37. William Keating, *Narrative of an Expedition to the Source of St. Peter's River* (London, 1825), 1:235–36.

38. Thomas Morris quoted in Cave, *Prophets of the Great Spirit*, 77. On medicine bundles, see *Native North American Spirituality of the Eastern Woodlands*, ed. Elisabeth Tooker (New York, 1979), ch. 5; Lee Irwin, *Coming Down from Above: Prophecy, Resistance, and Renewal in Native American Religions* (Norman, OK,

2008), 180–82. On the place of medicine bundles in the contemporary religious life of some Native Americans, see John A. Grim, "Traditional Ways and Contemporary Vitality: Absaroke/Crow," in *Native Religions and Cultures of North America*, ed. Lawrence E. Sullivan (New York, 2000), 53–84.

39. Forsythe in Blair, *Indian Tribes of the Upper Mississippi,* 2:277.
40. Cave 79, Trowbridge 43–46, quote at 45.

CHAPTER 8: WITCHCRAFT

1. Wolfgang Behringer, *Witches and Witch Hunts: A Global History* (Malden, MA, 2004), xvii.
2. John Demos, *The Enemy Within: 2000 Years of Witch-hunting in the Western World* (New York, 2008), 274–81.
3. Jay Miller, "The 1806 Purge Among the Indiana Delaware: Sorcery, Gender, Boundaries, and Legitimacy," *Ethnohistory* 41, no. 2 (Spring 1994): 245–66. Miller and Robert M. Owens (*Mr. Jefferson's Hammer: William Henry Harrison and the Origins of American Indian Policy* [Norman, OK, 2007], 269n67) describe Beata as an independent prophetess; her appearance just after the Prophet's vision (in the winter of 1804–5) and her deference to the Prophet suggest otherwise.
4. *The Moravian Indian Mission on White River: Diaries and Letters*, ed. Lawrence Henry Gipson, trans. Harry E. Stocker, Herman T. Frueauff, and Samuel C. Zeller (Indianapolis, 1938), entry for January 25, 1806, 401.
5. Ibid., entry for February 13, 1805, 333.
6. Ibid., entry for February 13–16, 1805, 333–35.
7. Ibid., entries for January 31 and February 17, 1805, January 25 and September 29–30, 1806, 331, 335, 401–2, 451.
8. Ibid., entry for January 25, 1806, 401–2.
9. Ibid., entry for January 28, 1806, 403.
10. Ibid., entry for January 25, 1806, 402.
11. Ibid., entry for February 19, 1806, 407–8.
12. Ibid., entry for January 25, 1806, 401–2.
13. See Ibid., entries for July 1 and 3, 1805, 365 and 368–69.
14. Ibid., entry for January 25, 1806, 401–2.
15. Ibid., entry for February 17, 1806, 407.
16. Ibid., entry for December 3, 1805, 392.
17. Ibid., entry for March 14, 1805, 339–40.
18. Ibid., entry for March 15, 1806, 414.
19. The Shawnee Prophet's witch hunts are often used as an argument for Wallace's theory of revitalization. As I demonstrate here, the witch hunts do not seem to fit the model of witchcraft as revitalization, but they do fit Stuart Clark's model of witchcraft beliefs as beliefs. See Clark, *Thinking with Demons: The Idea of Witchcraft in Early Modern Europe* (New York, 2005), 1–10, 550.

20. Benjamin Youngs, "A Journey to the Indians March 1807," Winterthur, Andrews Collection 860, 32–33.

21. Ibid., 30.

22. Henry Rowe Schoolcraft, *History and Statistical Information Respecting the History, Conditions, and Prospects of the Indian Tribes of the United States* (Philadelphia, 1851), 4:495.

23. *Journal of Pontiac's Conspiracy*, ed. Mary Agnes Burton (Detroit, 1912), online version at americanjourneys.com, Document AJ-135, p. 22.

24. Massachusetts Historical Society, SPG Papers, Kirkland diaries, Box 1, Folder 6, p. 5.

25. Michael E. Bell, *Food for the Dead: On the Trail of New England's Vampires* (New York, 2001), 301, 253–55.

26. Ibid., 202–3.

27. Edward Augustus Kendall, *Travels Through the Northern Parts of the United States in the Years 1807 and 1808* (New York, 1809), 3:84.

28. Alan Taylor, "The Early Republic's Supernatural Economy: Treasure Seeking in the American Northeast, 1780–1830," *American Quarterly* 38, no. 1 (Spring 1986): 12, 16.

29. Rochester *Gem*, May 15, 1830, reprinted in Francis W. Kirkham, *A New Witness for Christ in America: The Book of Mormon* (Salt Lake City, 1959), 2:48; also cited in Taylor, "Early Republic's Supernatural Economy," 12.

30. Quoted in Fawn M. Brodie, *No Man Knows My History: The Life of Joseph Smith* (New York, 1995 [1945]), 18.

31. Charleston, SC, *Southern Patriot*, May 22, 1835.

32. John Greenleaf Whittier, *Legends of New England* (Hartford, CT, 1831), 57–58.

33. Whittier to Sarah Josepha Hale, January 24, 1832, *Letters of John Greenleaf Whittier*, ed. John B. Pickard (Cambridge, MA, 1975), 1:71; Amasa Delano, *A Narrative of Voyages and Travels in the Northern and Southern Hemispheres* (Boston, 1817), 30; Alonzo Lewis, *History of Lynn* (Boston, 1829), 207.

34. Paul Coffin, *A Tour to Hanover, N.H., with a Design to Enter Charles Coffin as a Freshman in Dartmouth College, 1795*, excerpted in *Memoir and Journals of Rev. Paul Coffin*, ed. Cyrus Woodman (Portland, ME, 1855), 70.

35. I have outlined the newspaper evidence for witchcraft and anti-witchcraft mobs in "Were There Really Witches? Magic and Spellcasting in the United States, 1787–1860," paper presented at Queen's College, Belfast, May 2010. See also Portland *Eastern Herald and Gazette of Maine*, November 17, 1796; Alexandria *Herald*, September 18, 1822; Yvonne P. Chireau, *Black Magic: Religion and the African American Conjuring Tradition* (Berkeley, CA, 2003), 69–71.

36. *The Trial Record of Denmark Vesey*, ed. John Oliver Killens (Boston, 1970), 13–14, 76, 137.

37. Jortner, "Were There Really Witches?"

38. Philadelphia *Independent Gazetteer*, May 9, 1787. See also Edmund Morgan, "The Witch and We, the People," *American Heritage*, August–September 1983, 6–11.

39. Philadelphia *Independent Gazetteer*, May 17, 1787.

40. Ibid., July 23, 1787.

41. *Moravian Indian Mission*, entry for July 3, 1806, 365.

42. Ibid., entry for July 23, 1806, 369–70.

43. Ibid., entries for February 21 and 22, 1806, 408–9.

44. Ibid., entries for March 3 and 10, 1806, 410–12.

45. Ibid., entry for March 13, 1806, 412.

46. John Heckewelder, *Narrative of the Mission of the United Brethren* (Philadelphia, 1820), 410.

47. *Moravian Indian Mission*, entries for December 3, 1805, and February 17, 1806, 392, 407.

48. Ibid., entry for March 10, 1806, 412.

49. Ibid., 420. The entry for April 9, 1806, records that seven were to be killed that day; to that are added Tetapatchsit, Charity, and the "peaceable Indian" executed on April 1.

50. Draper Manuscripts 12YY14; Miller, "The 1806 Purge," 254–55. Miller suggests that Charity was an outspoken critic of Beata, although his only evidence for this assertion is the fact that they were both women. See also Heckewelder, *Narrative*, 415–16. I have relied in this account of the trial primarily on the Moravian documents, using Anthony Shane's interview with Benjamin Drake in 1821 (Draper Manuscripts 12YY) where necessary. Some of the more spectacular stories about the trials, however, derive from nineteenth-century secondary sources.

51. *Moravian Indian Mission*, entry for March 10, 1806, 412.

52. Draper Manuscripts 12YY14–15.

53. *Moravian Indian Mission*, entry for March 15, 1806, 412–14.

54. Ibid., entry for March 18, 1806, 418.

55. Draper Manuscripts 12YY8.

56. *Moravian Indian Mission*, entry for March 17, 1806, 415–16.

57. Ibid., entry for March 17, 1806, 416.

58. Ibid., entry for April 1, 1806, 420.

59. Ibid., entry for March 9–10, 1806, 420–21.

60. Joseph A. Badger, *A Memoir of Rev. Joseph Badger*, ed. Henry Noble Day (Hudson, OH, 1851), entry for May 13, 1806, 145.

61. Ibid., entry for May 13, 1806, 145.

62. *Moravian Indian Mission*, entry for August 9, 1806, 445.

63. Forsythe in Blair, *Tribes of the Upper Mississippi*, 2:278; Wyandots of Sandusky to Hull, June 27, 1810, Shawnee File, Great Lakes Ethnohistory Archive. See also Alfred A. Cave, *Prophets of the Great Spirit: Native American Revitalization Movements in Eastern North America* (Lincoln, NE, 2006), 87, and John Sugden, *Tecumseh: A Life* (New York, 1998), 209, 436–37n13. Sugden's analysis concludes that these trials were internal to the Wyandot settlement and not prompted by the Prophet.

64. Draper Manuscripts 12YY13–14.
65. Miller, "The 1806 Purge," 248, 251.
66. Cave, *Prophets*, 88.
67. Sugden, Cave, Gregory Evans Dowd, *A Spirited Resistance: The North American Indian Struggle for Unity, 1745–1815* (Baltimore, 1992), and R. David Edmunds, *The Shawnee Prophet* (Lincoln, NE, 1983), all agree that the Prophet had political aims in mind in his identification of witches, and I certainly do not mean to cast aspersion on their work by correlating them with the leaky scholarship of a previous generation. My point here, however, is that Tenskwatawa's witchcraft accusations were not simply an effort to remove political enemies, but a way of introducing a new political thesis of leadership.
68. Cave, *Prophets*, 83.
69. Ibid., 85. See also *Moravian Indian Mission*, entries for September 7 and 10, 1806, 453.
70. *Moravian Indian Mission*, entry for May 17, 1806, 431.
71. Dunham to Hull, May 20, 1807, *Michigan Historical Collections* (Lansing, 1929), 40:123.
72. The Delawares, of course, had been among the first to be forced west by British colonial and American law and weapons, and the first to support a nativist prophet. Thus these trials should not be seen as only the efforts of Tenskwatawa, but as a combined effort of Tenskwatawa and the young warrior caste of the Delaware to reorient the communitas and leadership structure of the Delawares, 1806–7.
73. Clark, *Thinking with Demons*, 550.
74. *Moravian Indian Mission*, entry for August 9, 1806, 444–45.
75. Ibid., entry for August 2, 1806, 443.
76. Ibid., entries for September 29–30 and October 7, 1806, 451, 453.
77. Ibid., entry for April 18, 1806, 421–22.

CHAPTER 9: CONSPIRACIES

1. Robert Morrison to Thomas, December 6, 1808, Jesse B. Thomas Letters, Folder 2, ALPLM.
2. Vincennes *Western Sun*, August 27, 1808, quoted in James D. Rees, "The Bond-Jones Duel and the Shooting of Rice Jones by Dr. James Dunlap: What Really Happened in Kaskaskia, Indiana Territory, on 8 August and 7 December 1808?" *Journal of the Illinois State Historical Society* 97, no. 4 (Winter 2004–5), 272–85. Rees' claim that the shooting occurred in self-defense is based almost exclusively on an anonymous account of the murder written over a year after the event (276). He does not consult the Morrison letters at the ALPLM.
3. Rees, "Bond-Jones Duel," 274.
4. Ibid., 275, 281; Robert Morrison to Thomas, December 1808, ALPLM.

5. Badollet to Gallatin, November 13, 1809, in *The Correspondence of John Badollet and Albert Gallatin, 1804–1836,* ed. Gayle Thornbrough (Indianapolis, 1963), 119.

6. See Richard Buel Jr., *America on the Brink: How the Political Struggle over the War of 1812 Almost Destroyed the Young Republic* (New York, 2005), 4; Joanne Freeman, *Affairs of Honor: National Politics in the New Republic* (New Haven, CT, 2001).

7. Elijah Backus to Robert Morrison, August 7, 1808 (SC 58), ALPLM.

8. Robert M. Owens, *Mr. Jefferson's Hammer: William Henry Harrison and the Origins of American Indian Policy* (Norman, OK, 2007), 183.

9. Freeman, *Affairs of Honor,* ch. 4.

10. Ibid., 172.

11. Ben C. Truman, *The Field of Honor: Being a Complete and Comprehensive History of Dueling in All Countries* (New York, 1884), 383.

12. Andrew Burstein, *The Passions of Andrew Jackson* (New York, 2004), 55–61.

13. The best recent effort to explain the fantastic history of Aaron Burr is Nancy Isenberg, *Fallen Founder: The Life of Aaron Burr* (New York, 2007), but see also (out of many) Milton Lomask, *Aaron Burr: The Conspiracy and Years of Exile, 1806–1836* (New York, 1982).

14. Hull to Henry Dearborn, May 15, 1807, *Michigan Historical Collections* (Lansing, 1929), 40:119–20.

15. Hill to the Sandusky, September 11, 1805, Shawnee File, Great Lakes Ethnohistory Archive.

16. WHH to Henry Dearborn, July 11, 1807, *Michigan Historical Collections* 40:839–40.

17. Henry Dearborn to Hull, March 24, 1807, Shawnee File, Great Lakes Ethnohistory Archive.

18. Thomas Jefferson to the Shawnee Nation, February 19, 1807, *Territorial Papers of the United States* (Washington, DC, 1949), 14:112; Louis Lorimier to Joseph Brown, February 19, 1807, Shawnee File, Great Lakes Ethnohistory Archive.

19. Journal of the Treaty Negotiations with the Osage, October 14, 1805, in *The Papers of William Henry Harrison, 1800–1815,* ed. Douglas E. Clanin (microfilm) (Indianapolis, 1999), 2:362.

20. Wells to Henry Dearborn, April 25, 1807, Shawnee File, Great Lakes Ethnohistory Archive.

21. Wells to Henry Dearborn, July 14, 1807, Shawnee File, Great Lakes Ethnohistory Archive.

22. Hull to Henry Dearborn, July 25, 1807, *Michigan Historical Collections* 40:159–60.

23. WHH to Jared Mansfield, August 8, 1806, in *Papers,* Clanin 2:615. Richard White has suggested the Native American alliance against the Osage formed "the core of anti-American resistance" and that Tenskwatawa "tapped" this resource. White, *The Middle Ground: Indians, Empires, and Republics in the Great Lakes Region, 1650–1815* (New York, 2006), 512–13.

24. WHH, Address to the General Assembly, November 4, 1806, in *Papers,* 2:654–62.

25. Jon Latimer, *1812: War with America* (Cambridge, MA, 2007), 21; Alan Taylor, *The Civil War of 1812: American Citizens, British Subjects, Irish Rebels, and Indian Allies* (New York, 2010), 100–101.

26. Latimer, *1812*, 22–25; Peter P. Hill, *Napoleon's Troublesome Americans: Franco-American Relations, 1804–1815* (Washington, DC, 2005), 18–19.

27. Latimer, *1812*, 21; Adams quoted in Gordon Wood, *Empire of Liberty: A History of the Early Republic, 1789–1815* (New York, 2009), 641.

28. John Askin to his father, September 8, 1807, *John Askin Papers*, ed. Milo M. Quaife (Detroit, 1928), 2:572.

29. Wood, *Empire of Liberty,* 642; Latimer, *1812*, 21.

30. *Pittsburgh Gazette*, July 14, 1807.

31. *National Intelligencer*, August 7, 1807.

32. *Scioto Gazette*, June 30, 1807.

33. Resolutions of Citizens of Green and Champaign County, Ohio, August 4, 1807, Draper Manuscripts 7BB41.

34. Hull to Henry Dearborn, July 25, 1807, *Michigan Historical Collections* 40:159–60.

35. WHH address to General Assembly, August 18, 1807, in *Papers*, 2:877ff. and 887n1.

36. WHH to Henry Dearborn, July 11, 1807, in *Papers*, 2:840.

37. WHH to Henry Dearborn, August 29, 1807, in *Papers*, 2:912.

38. A. J. Langguth, *Union 1812: The Americans Who Fought the Second War of Independence* (New York, 2006), 134–35; Latimer, *1812*, 22.

39. See Buel, *America on the Brink*, 37–38, 65.

40. Robert Troup to John Trumbull, February 9, 1809, Lilly Library MSS.

41. Masters quoted in Buel, *America on the Brink*, 67; *Palladium* quoted in ibid., 73.

42. Robert Morrison to John Messinger, December 31, 1805, ALPLM.

43. Andrew R. L. Cayton, *Frontier Indiana* (Bloomington, IN, 1996), 246.

44. Jones to Thomas, November 7, 1808, Jesse B. Thomas letters, Folder 2, ALPLM.

45. Rob Morrison to Thomas, December 18, 1808, and Robert Morrison to Thomas, December 1808, ALPLM.

CHAPTER 10: GREENVILLE

1. Benjamin Youngs, "A Journey to the Indians March 1807"; Winterthur, Andrews Collection 860.

2. Richard McNemar, *The Kentucky Revival* (New York, 1848 [1808]), 124, 128–29.

3. A. B. Woodward, Report of Indian Alarms, August 14, 1807, *Michigan Historical Collections* 40:174ff.

4. Frederick Bates to Henry Dearborn, October 22, 1807, *Life and Papers of Frederick Bates*, ed. Thomas Maitlan Marshall (St. Louis, 1926), 1:221–23.

5. Alfred A. Cave, *Prophets of the Great Spirit: Native American Revitalization Movements in Eastern North America* (Lincoln, NE, 2006), 67–68; Draper Manuscripts 11YY19.

6. John Law, *Colonial History of Vincennes,* quoted in Draper Manuscripts 3YY110–114.

7. Draper Manuscripts 1YY95; Sugden, *Tecumseh: A Life* (New York, 1998), 426n2.

8. Dunham to Henry Dearborn, June 12, 1807, Shawnee File, Great Lakes Ethnohistory Archive.

9. Hull to Henry Dearborn, July 23, 1807, *Michigan Historical Collections* (Lansing, 1929), 40:158.

10. John Tanner, *The Falcon: A Narrative of the Captivity and Adventures of John Tanner* (New York, 2000 [1830]), 145; Edmunds, *Shawnee Prophet,* 52–53.

11. Wells to Henry Dearborn, April 25, 1807, Shawnee File, Great Lakes Ethnohistory Archive.

12. Dowd lists Trout as yet another independent prophet, but both the text of the Trout's speech and Dunham's response leave little doubt that the Trout followed the Shawnee Prophet.

13. Dunham to Hull, May 20, 1807, *Michigan Historical Collections* 40:123.

14. Dunham, Enclosure, Speech of Indian Chief to Various Tribes, *Michigan Historical Collections,* 40:127–32.

15. Dunham to Henry Dearborn, June 12, 1807, Shawnee File, Great Lakes Ethnohistory Archive.

16. Peter Cartwright, *The Autobiography of Peter Cartwright*, ed. Charles L. Wallis (Nashville, TN, 1984), 214.

17. Entry for October 20, 1796, in Lorenzo Dow, *History of Cosmopolite* (Cincinnati, 1859), 34.

18. Dunham, "Address to the Ottawas and Chippewas of Arbre Croche and Michilimackinack," May 25, 1807, Shawnee File, Great Lakes Ethnohistory Archive.

19. WHH to General Assembly, August 18, 1807, in *The Papers of William Henry Harrison, 1800–1815,* ed. Douglas E. Clanin (microfilm) (Indianapolis, 1999), 2:877ff.

20. WHH to Henry Dearborn, August 29, 1807, in *Papers,* 2:911.

21. Speech reprinted in Benjamin Drake, *Life of Tecumseh and of His Brother, the Prophet* (Cincinnati, 2006 [1841]), 96–97; see also Harrison, *Papers,* 1:919. The dating of this message is approximate; it was reprinted in the *Western Sun* in 1808, but Harrison's letter of September 5, 1807, puts its composition and delivery near the end of August 1807. See Harrison, *Papers,* 2:918n1, 925.

22. WHH to Henry Dearborn, September 5, 1807, in *Messages and Papers of William Henry Harrison*, ed. Logan Esarey (Indianapolis, 1922), 1:247–48.

23. Drake, *Life of Tecumseh,* 97.

24. Thomas Jefferson to Henry Dearborn, August 12, 1807, in *The Writings of Thomas Jefferson,* ed. H. A. Washington (Washington, DC, 1853), 5:162–63; Henry Dearborn to WHH, September 17, 1807, in *Papers,* 2:965.

25. Thomas Jefferson to Henry Dearborn, August 12, 1807, in *The Writings of Thomas Jefferson,* 5:163. Jefferson later gave orders for the governors to hold interviews and promote the policy of acculturation and quiescence. See John Smith (for Henry Dearborn) to WHH and Hull, September 27, 1807, in *Papers,* 2:974.
26. WHH to Henry Dearborn, September 5, 1807, in *Papers,* 2:925–27.
27. Hull to Henry Dearborn, November 4, 1807, Chippewa File, Great Lakes Ethnohistory Archive.
28. McKee to Prideaux Selby, Amherstburg, February 3, 1808, Chippewa File, Great Lakes Ethnohistory Archive.
29. Hull to Henry Dearborn, December 28, 1807, in *Michigan Historical Collections* 40:240. For further examples of perfidy involving the Treaty of Detroit, see William Claus to Francis Gore and Gore to Sir James Craig, in *Michigan Historical Collections* 23:45ff.
30. WHH to Hargrove, November 4, 1807, in *Messages and Papers,* 1:272.
31. Ibid., 1:273.
32. Hendrick Aupamat to Wells, February 26, 1808, Shawnee File, Great Lakes Ethnohistory Archive.
33. Wells to Henry Dearborn, March 6, 1808, *Territorial Papers of the United States* (Washington, DC, 1939), 7:531–32.
34. Harrison to Dearborn, February 18, 1808, in *Messages and Papers,* 1:284.
35. WHH to General Assembly, September 8, 1807, in *Papers,* 2:935.
36. Indiana Territorial Act Concerning the Introduction of Negroes and Mulattoes, September 17, 1807, in *Papers,* 2:960.
37. Resolutions of Loyalty by the French, September 20, 1807, in *Messages and Papers,* 1:258.

CHAPTER 11: THE NATION OF PROPHETSTOWN

1. William Wells to Henry Dearborn, April 20, 1808 (addendum, April 22), Shawnee File, Great Lakes Ethnohistory Archive.
2. Ibid.
3. These possibilities are discussed in Edmunds, *Shawnee Prophet,* 67–70, and Alfred A. Cave, *Prophets of the Great Spirit: Native American Revitalization Movements in Eastern North America* (Lincoln, NE, 2006), 97.
4. Tenskwatawa quoted in Vincennes *Western Sun,* July 7, 1810.
5. Recollections of Anthony Shane, Draper Manuscripts 12YY52.
6. Report of Worthington and McArthur to Kirker, reprinted in the *National Intelligencer,* October 9, 1807.
7. William Wells to Henry Dearborn, April 20, 1808 (addendum, April 22), Shawnee File, Great Lakes Ethnohistory Archive.
8. John Conner's statement before William Wells, Fort Wayne, June 18, 1808, Shawnee File, Great Lakes Ethnohistory Archive.

9. Harrison to Eustis, July 10, 1811, in *Messages and Papers of William Henry Harrison*, ed. Logan Esarey (Indianapolis, 1922), 1:533; David Turpie, *Sketches of My Own Times* (Indianapolis, 1903), 170–71.

10. Michael Strezewski, James R. Jones III, and Dorothea McCullough, *Archaeological Investigations at Site 12-T-59 and Two Other Locations at Prophetstown State Park, Tippecanoe County, Indiana*, Report of Investigations 513, Indiana University–Purdue University Fort Wayne (Fort Wayne, 2006), 20–21.

11. *American State Papers, Indian Affairs* (Washington, DC, 1832), 1:131–32, 135.

12. Turpie, *Sketches*, 171; Strezewski, Jones, and McCullough, *Archaeological Investigations*, 32.

13. John Tipton, "John Tipton's Tippecanoe Journal," *Indiana Magazine of History* 2, no. 4 (December 1906): 180.

14. Description is from Turpie, *Sketches*, 170–71.

15. WHH to Eustis, June 14, 1810, in *Messages and Papers*, 1:425.

16. Census materials from http://www.census.gov/population/www/documentation/twps0027.html.

17. William Wells to Henry Dearborn, April 20, 1808 (addendum, April 23), Shawnee File, Great Lakes Ethnohistory Archive.

18. John Johnston, *Recollections of Sixty Years* (1846), reprinted in Leonard U. Hill, *John Johnston and the Indians in the Land of the Three Miamis* (Piqua, OH, 1957), 155.

19. Canada's entire population was around 300,000 at the start of the war. Upper Canada, the colony that saw the most fighting, had only 75,000. The Native American population in the early republic is difficult to estimate, but in 1822, Jedidiah Morse reported to the secretary of war that the Indian population of the Old Northwest and western territories to the Rocky Mountains was 230,000; he put the Native population of Indiana, Illinois, and Michigan in 1822 at 45,000. The numbers were likely higher prior to the devastation of the War of 1812, and therefore the population comparison seems apt, although definitive numbers can never be known. See Alan Taylor, *The Civil War of 1812: American Citizens, British Subjects, Irish Rebels, and Indian Allies* (New York, 2010), 140; Jon Latimer, *1812: War with America* (Cambridge, MA, 2007), 42; and Jedidiah Morse, *A Report to the Secretary of War of the United States on Indian Affairs* (New York, 1970 [1822]), Appendixes 362–75. Morse's total is derived from adding together his numbers for Michigan and the Northwest Territory, Indiana and Illinois, tribes west of the Mississippi and north of the Missouri, tribes between the Missouri and Red rivers, and tribes between the Mississippi and the Rocky Mountains. Alternative population totals can be found in Robert M. Owens, *Mr. Jefferson's Hammer: William Henry Harrison and the Origins of American Indian Policy* (Norman, OK, 2007), 274n1.

20. "Indian Speech of Techkumthai Brother to the Shawenese Prophet," Amherstburg, November 15, 1810, *Historical Collections: Collections and Researches Made by the Michigan Pioneer and Historical Society* (Lansing, 1896), 25:275–77.

21. Vincennes *Western Sun*, August 25, 1810.

22. Turpie, *Sketches*, 170; "Reply of the Bearer of the Prophet's Speech," in *Messages and Papers*, 1:295. Tipton described a mile of corn in 1811; George Imlay's report from the 1791 village at the same site reported 200 acres (one-third of a mile square). That suggests an increase, but the shift from one to two dimensions prevents a final determination.

23. Winter Papers, cited in Strezewski, Jones, and McCullough, *Archaeological Investigations*, 33; ash and slag noted in Ibid., 39.

24. For mining operations by Indians across the Mississippi, see William Clark to Eustis, July 3, 1811, Shawnee File, Great Lakes Ethnohistory Archive.

25. Strezewski, Jones, and McCullough, *Archaeological Investigations,* 38–39, 115.

26. Ibid., 130.

27. William Wells to Henry Dearborn, April 20, 1808 (addendum, April 22), Shawnee File, Great Lakes Ethnohistory Archive.

28. WHH to Henry Dearborn, May 19, 1808, in *Messages and Papers*, 1:290–91.

29. Henry Dearborn to WHH, March 22, 1808, in *The Papers of William Henry Harrison, 1800–1815*, ed. Douglas E. Clanin (microfilm) (Indianapolis, 1999), 3:131.

30. Connor quoted in Cave, *Prophets*, 102. A typical denunciation of the Prophet's leadership regarding food security is Wells to Henry Dearborn, April 2, 1808, *Territorial Papers of the United States* (Washington, DC, 1939), 7:540–41. Benjamin Drake, *Life of Tecumseh and of His Brother, the Prophet* (Cincinnati, 2006 [1841]), 99, Edmunds, *Shawnee Prophet*, 75–76, and Cave, *Prophets*, 101–2, all suggest the Prophet mismanaged his followers into the 1808 famine.

31. *The Moravian Indian Mission on White River: Diaries and Letters*, ed. Lawrence Henry Gipson, trans. Harry E. Stocker, Herman T. Frueauff, and Samuel C. Zeller (Indianapolis, 1938), 460.

32. Dunham to Henry Dearborn, May 24, 1807, Shawnee File, Great Lakes Ethnohistory Archive.

33. Frederick Bates to Henry Dearborn, October 22, 1807, in *Life and Papers of Frederick Bates*, ed. Thomas Maitlan Marshall (St. Louis, 1926), 1:221–23.

34. Prophet to WHH, June 24, 1808, in *Messages and Papers*, 1:291.

35. John Conner's statement before William Wells, Fort Wayne, June 18, 1808, Shawnee File, Great Lakes Ethnohistory Archive.

36. Proceedings of a Private Meeting with the Shawnees, Amherstburg, March 25, 1808, in *Historical Collections: Collections and Researches Made by the Michigan Pioneer and Historical Society* (Lansing, 1896), 25:242–43.

37. Prophet to WHH, June 24, 1808, in *Messages and Papers*, 1:291.

38. Ibid., 1:291–92.

39. WHH to Prophet, June 24, 1808, in *Messages and Papers*, 1:292.

40. Diary of Col. William Claus, 1808, in *Historical Collections*, 23: 23, 47–60, quote at 53.

41. Edmunds, *Shawnee Prophet*, 74–75; Sugden, *Tecumseh: A Life* (New York, 1998), 170–71.
42. WHH to Prophet, in *Messages and Papers*, 1:292.
43. WHH to Dearborn, September 1, 1808, in *Papers*, 3:228–29; WHH to Dearborn, November 9, 1808, in *Papers*, 3:302.
44. Cave, *Prophets*, 104.
45. Vincennes *Western Sun*, April 15, 1809.

CHAPTER 12: THE BARGAIN

1. David J. Costa, "Illinois," in "Three American Placenames," in *The Society for the Study of the Indigenous Languages of the Americas Newsletter* 25, no. 4 (January 2007): 9–12.
2. Indiana Historical Society, William English Collection, Box 30, Folder 12; Wallace Taylor to Thomas Randolph, June 3, 1809, in Varney-Porter Papers, Box 1, Folder 1; G. Hunt to Randolph, October 31, 1810, Varney-Porter Papers, Box 1, Folder 2; Minutes and Proceeding of the Vincennes University as Transacted by the Board of Trustees, Indiana Territory, Lilly Library, Indiana University, entry for September 5, 1807.
3. WHH to Thomas Jefferson, July 16, 1808, in *The Papers of William Henry Harrison, 1800–1815*, ed. Douglas E. Clanin (microfilm) (Indianapolis, 1999), 3:193.
4. Thomas Jefferson to Delawares, December 1808, in *Messages and Papers of William Henry Harrison*, ed. Logan Esarey (Indianapolis, 1922), 1:330–32; Minutes and Proceeding of the Vincennes University, entries for December 6, 1806, and September 5, 1807.
5. WHH to Eustis, December 24, 1810, in *Messages and Papers*, 1:498.
6. Johnston to Henry Dearborn, April 15, 1809, *Territorial Papers of the United States* (Washington, DC, 1939), 7:647.
7. Johnston to P. E. Thomas, April 15, 1809, in *Letter Book of the Indian Agency at Fort Wayne, 1809–1815*, ed. Gayle Thornbrough (Indianapolis, 1961), 41.
8. Shawnee Chiefs to the President and Secretary of War, April 10, 1809, in *Letter Book*, 47.
9. Henry Dearborn to Johnston, May 23, 1809, Shawnee File, Great Lakes Ethnohistory Archive.
10. Vincennes *Western Sun*, May 13, 1809.
11. Wells to Eustis, March 31, 1809, Shawnee File, Great Lakes Ethnohistory Archive.
12. W. S. Messinger to John Messinger, April 3, 1810, John Messinger Papers, ALPLM.
13. William Claus, "Diary of William Claus," *Historical Collections: Collections and Researches Made by the Michigan Pioneer and Historical Society* (Lansing, 1895), 23:53, 54, 60.
14. Wells to Eustis, March 31, 1809, Shawnee File, Great Lakes Ethnohistory Archive.

15. Wells to Henry Dearborn, June 5, 1808, Shawnee File, Great Lakes Ethnohistory Archive.

16. Clark to Eustis, April 5, 1809, in *Messages and Papers*, 1:336.

17. WHH to Eustis, April 18, 1809, in *Messages and Papers*, 1:340.

18. WHH to Eustis, April 26, 1809, in *Papers*, 3:399–401.

19. WHH to Eustis, May 3, 1809, in *Papers*, 3:409–10.

20. WHH to Eustis, May 16, 1809, in *Papers*, 4:424.

21. Hull to Eustis, June 16, 1809, Shawnee File, Great Lakes Ethnohistory Archive.

22. WHH to Eustis, April 18, 1809, in *Messages and Papers*, 1:340.

23. WHH to Eustis, May 16, 1809, in *Messages and Papers*, 1:346.

24. Johnston to the Prophet, May 3, 1809, *Letter Book*, 49; John Johnston to Eustis, July 1, 1809, Shawnee File, Great Lakes Ethnohistory Archive. Given the relative strength of the Prophet through the rest of 1809–11, I incline toward Johnston's explanation that the conflict between the Prophet and the Ojibwes or Ottawas was mostly feigned, which accounts for the continued adherence of Ojibwe and Ottawa groups to the Prophet. Cave and Edmunds follow Wells' warning that the Ottawas and Ojibwes meant the Prophet harm because his supernatural powers had failed to provide food. Wells' explanation corresponds with modern conceptions about "testing" supernatural claims (and is thus suspect, to my mind). However, given the lack of sources from Prophetstown itself, this point remains debatable.

25. WHH to Eustis, July 5, 1809, in *Papers*, 3:446ff.

26. WHH to Eustis, July 14, 1809, in *Messages and Papers*, 1:356.

27. WHH to Eustis, May 16, 1809, in *Papers*, 3:424.

28. Eustis to WHH, June 5, 1809, in *Papers*, 3:429; and Eustis to WHH, July 15, 1809, in *Papers*, 3:458; WHH to Eustis, July 14, 1809, in *Messages and Papers*, 1:356.

29. Henry Dearborn to Johnston, June 3, 1809, Shawnee File, Great Lakes Ethnohistory Archive.

30. Wells to Eustis, December 20, 1811, Shawnee File, Great Lakes Ethnohistory Archive.

31. Thomas Jefferson to Little Turtle, Shawnee File, Great Lakes Ethnohistory Archive.

32. WHH to Eustis, August 29, 1809, in *Papers*, 1:470–71.

33. Robert M. Owens, *Mr. Jefferson's Hammer: William Henry Harrison and the Origins of American Indian Policy* (Norman, OK, 2007), 205–6.

34. Henry Jones, *Journal of the Proceedings, Indian Treaty, Fort Wayne, September 30th, 1809* (Connersville, IN, 1910), 10.

35. Ibid., 11.

36. Ibid., 13–14.

37. WHH to Eustis, July 25, 1810, in *Papers*, 1:453.

38. Jones, *Journal*, 18.

39. Ibid., 13.

40. Ibid., 19.

41. Ibid., 12.

42. Ibid., 13, 16, 17.

43. Ibid., 14, 15.

44. Ibid., 17–18.

45. Ibid., 20. For alcohol, see ibid., 13, 17, and WHH Proclamation, August 23, 1809, in *Papers*, 3:468.

46. Jones, *Journal*, 20–22. For annuities paid to the assembled tribes, see "Delawares and Others," *American State Papers, Indian Affairs* (Washington, DC, 1832), 1:760–62, and Stewart Rafert, *The Miami Indians of Indiana: A Persistent People, 1654–1994* (Indianapolis, 1996), 71–72.

47. Owens, *Mr. Jefferson's Hammer*, 201. By comparison, Owens notes, six gallons of alcohol were issued at Fort Wayne in July.

48. Quoted in Owens, *Mr. Jefferson's Hammer*, 206.

49. Edwards to Henry Brown, September 26, 1809, Indiana Historical Society, Indiana Territory Collection, Folder 1.

50. Johnston to the editors of *Liberty Hall*, October 3, 1809, in *Letter Book*, 65–66, 66n49; *Scioto Gazette*, November 6, 1809. The message from Johnston also appears in the *Chillicothe Supporter* on October 27 and the Washington *National Intelligencer* on October 30.

51. Ottawas and Chippewas of Michilimackinac, Speech to the Brethren Residing in the Southward, August 30, 1809, Chippewa File, Great Lakes Ethnohistory Archive.

52. Speech of the Ottawa and Chippewa Nation to Hull, Michilimackinac, August 30, 1809, Shawnee File, Great Lakes Ethnohistory Archive.

53. Statement of Broulliet, in *Papers*, 4:81–83.

54. Virtually all scholars of the Old Northwest cite Fort Wayne as a turning point. See Gregory Evans Dowd, *A Spirited Resistance: The North American Indian Struggle for Unity, 1745–1815* (Baltimore, 1992), 139; Edmunds, *Shawnee Prophet*, 81; Andrew R. L. Cayton, *Frontier Indiana* (Bloomington, IN, 1996), 215–16; Richard White, *The Middle Ground: Indians, Empires, and Republics in the Great Lakes Region, 1650–1815* (New York, 2006), 515. The comment on fragmentation comes from Stagg, 180–81.

55. R. David Edmunds, *Tecumseh and the Quest for Indian Leadership* (Boston, 1984), 124.

56. Wells to Eustis, December 20, 1811, Shawnee File, Great Lakes Ethnohistory Archive.

57. *Scioto Gazette*, November 6, 1809.

58. *National Intelligencer*, December 8, 1809.

CHAPTER 13: THE GATHERING

1. Samuel Ingalls, *A Dream, or Vision by Samuel Ingalls of Dunham* (Windsor, VT, 1810), broadside; William C. Davis, *The Millennium, or a Short Sketch on the Rise*

and Fall of the Antichrist (Salisbury, NC, 1811), 44; "Wildman of the Woods," *A Short Address to the People of America* (Cazenovia, NY, 1809); *The Comet, Explained and Improved* (Boston, 1812); "King John," *Observations on the Prophecies Which Relate to the Rise and Fall of Antichrist* (Chambersburg, MD, 1809).

2. D. Michael Quinn, *Early Mormonism and the Magic World View* (Salt Lake City, 1998), 18.

3. Hull to Eustis, July 20, 1810, Shawnee File, Great Lakes Ethnohistory Archive. Emphasis added.

4. Vincennes *Sun*, June 23, 1810.

5. Hull to Eustis, July 12, 1810, Shawnee File, Great Lakes Ethnohistory Archive.

6. Speech of Man Se Go A (Iowa), May 1811, Winnebago File, Great Lakes Ethnohistory Archive.

7. WHH to Eustis, May 16, 1810, in *The Papers of William Henry Harrison, 1800–1815*, ed. Douglas E. Clanin (microfilm) (Indianapolis, 1999), 4:15.

8. Hull to Eustis, July 12, 1810, Shawnee File, Great Lakes Ethnohistory Archive.

9. WHH to Eustis, June 26, 1810, in *Papers*, 4:67.

10. WHH to Eustis, July 4, 1810, in *Messages and Papers of William Henry Harrison*, ed. Logan Esarey (Indianapolis, 1922), 1:438–40.

11. Statement of Brouillette, in *Papers*, 4:82.

12. WHH to Eustis, May 16, 1810, in *Papers*, 4:15, 18n4.

13. Vincennes *Western Sun*, August 4, 1810.

14. WHH to Eustis, June 14–19, 1810, in *Papers*, 4:38–47.

15. Wells to Henry Dearborn, April 2, 1808, *Territorial Papers of the United States* (Washington, DC, 1939), 7:540–41; William Wells to Henry Dearborn, April 20, 1808, Shawnee File, Great Lakes Ethnohistory Archive; Alfred A. Cave, *Prophets of the Great Spirit: Native American Revitalization Movements in Eastern North America* (Lincoln, NE, 2006), 97–99; Gregory Evans Dowd, *A Spirited Resistance: The North American Indian Struggle for Unity, 1745–1815* (Baltimore, 1992), 144; extract from letter, John Johnston to WHH, June 24, 1810, printed in Vincennes *Western Sun*, July 14, 1810.

16. WHH to Hargrove, October 12, 1807, in *Messages and Papers*, 1:266.

17. Statement of Broulliet, in *Papers*, 4:83.

18. "Nancy" to Vice-Admiral G. C. Berkeley, January 18, 1808, War of 1812 Manuscripts, Lilly Library, Indiana University. For other examples of spies on the frontier, see Clark to Eustis, July 3, 1811, Shawnee File, Great Lakes Ethnohistory Archive, and Milo M. Quaife, ed., "A Diary of the War of 1812," *Mississippi Valley Historical Review* 1, no. 2 (September 1914): 272–78.

19. WHH to Eustis, May 2, 1810, in *Papers*, 4:1.

20. Statement of Broulliet, in *Papers*, 4:81–83; WHH to Eustis, June 14–19, 1810, in *Papers*, 4:38–47; Edmunds, *Shawnee Prophet*, 86–87.

21. WHH to Eustis, May 15, 1810, in *Papers*, 4:15.

22. WHH to Eustis, June 14–19, 1810, in *Papers*, 4:38–47.

23. John Johnston to Eustis, July 25, 1810, Shawnee File, Great Lakes Ethnohistory Archive; WHH to Eustis, May 16, 1810, in *Papers*, 4:16.

24. Statement of Broulliet, in *Papers*, 4:81–83; WHH to Eustis, July 4, 1810, in *Papers*, 4:78.

25. Vincennes *Western Sun*, June 23, 1810.

26. Vincennes *Western Sun*, June 23 and July 7, 1810.

27. WHH to Eustis, August 6, 1810, in *Messages and Papers*, 1:456.

28. Benjamin Drake, *The Life of Tecumseh and of His Brother the Prophet* (Charleston, SC, 2006 [1841]), 82.

29. See, for example, documents as late as 1810, including Vincennes *Western Sun*, June 23, 1810, and the *Raleigh Register*, September 20, 1810. Cave and Edmunds argue against the prominence of Tecumseh in this early period, against older interpretations such as Tucker's and modern books such as Langguth's. Sugden reminds readers that Tecumseh was "no minor chief" in the early years of the movement, but it is also true that in the first few years, Tecumseh rarely left Ohio. See John Sugden, "Tecumseh's Travels Revisited," *Indiana Magazine of History* 96, no. 2 (June 2000): 150–68.

30. See R. David Edmunds, *Tecumseh and the Quest for Indian Leadership* (Boston, 1984), ch. 2.

31. William Claus, "Diary of William Claus," June 11–13, 1808, *Historical Collections: Collections and Researches Made by the Michigan Pioneer and Historical Society*, vol. 23 (Lansing, 1895).

32. Sugden, "Tecumseh's Travels," 152.

33. Ibid., 159.

34. Extract from John Johnston to WHH, June 24, in Vincennes *Sun*, July 14, 1810.

35. Blue Jacket's death has no contemporary sources. See John Sugden, *Blue Jacket: Warrior of the Shawnees* (Lincoln, NE, 2000), 254.

36. Badollet to Gallatin, November 13, 1809, in *The Correspondence of John Badollet and Albert Gallatin, 1804–1836*, ed. Gayle Thornbrough (Indianapolis, 1963), 117.

37. WHH Message to the General Assembly, October 17, 1809, in *Messages and Papers*, 1:383.

38. Andrew R. L. Cayton, *Frontier Indiana* (Bloomington, IN, 1996), 251; Robert M. Owens, *Mr. Jefferson's Hammer: William Henry Harrison and the Origins of American Indian Policy* (Norman, OK, 2007), 191; John D. Barnhart, "The Democratization of Indiana Territory," *Indiana Magazine of History* 43, no. 1 (March 1947): 20; Thomas Randolph to Samuel Vance, April 17, 1810, and James Dill to Randolph, April 12, 1810, Indiana Historical Society, Varney-Porter Papers, Box 1, Folder 2.

39. Owens, *Mr. Jefferson's Hammer*, 191–92.

40. Ibid., 74–75.

41. Ibid., 207–8.

42. See Robert J. Miller, *Native America, Discovered and Conquered: Thomas Jefferson, Lewis and Clark, and Manifest Destiny* (Lincoln, NE, 2008), 50–53; Lindsay G.

Robertson, *Conquest by Law: How the Discovery of America Dispossessed Indigenous Peoples of Their Lands* (New York, 2005).

43. Vincennes *Sun*, June 23, 1810.
44. Vincennes *Sun*, August 4, 1810.
45. Vincennes *Sun*, August 25, 1810.
46. Edmunds, *Tecumseh*, 132–33.
47. Negotiations at an Indian Council, Vincennes, August 12–20, 1810, in *Papers*, 4:144–50; WHH to Eustis, August 22, 1810, in *Papers*, 4:168–75.
48. Vincennes *Sun*, August 25, 1810.
49. Quoted in Dowd, *Spirited Resistance*, 140.
50. WHH to Eustis, June 14–19, 1810, in *Papers*, 4: 38–47.
51. Vincennes *Sun*, August 25, 1810.
52. Ibid.
53. WHH to Eustis, June 26, 1810, in *Papers*, 4:67.
54. Academics rightly view with skepticism extensive counterfactual suppositions. Well-grounded counterfactual history presents an opportunity to evaluate contingent moments, and therefore to assess the historical stakes of a given moment and the relative importance and staying power of cultural, political, and economic forces. Ideal efforts on this approach are Gary Kornblith, "Rethinking the Coming of the Civil War: A Counterfactual Exercise," *Journal of American History* 90, no. 1 (2003): 76–105; Edward L. Ayers, *In the Presence of Mine Enemies: Civil War in the Heart of America* (New York, 2004); and Gary W. Gallagher, *The Confederate War* (Cambridge, MA, 1999).
55. Speeches of Tecumseh, August 20–21, 1810, in Harrison, *Papers*, 4:156ff.
56. WHH to Eustis, August 28, 1810, in *Papers*, 4:178.
57. Speeches of Tecumseh, August 20–21, 1810, in Harrison, *Papers*, 4:164.
58. WHH to Eustis, August 22, 1810, in *Papers*, 4:167n23, 168.
59. Speech of Red Jacket at Brownstown, Shawnee File, Great Lakes Ethnohistory Archive; Hull to Johnston, September 27, 1810, in Gayle Thornbrough, ed., *Letter Book of the Indian Agency at Fort Wayne, 1809–1815* (Indianapolis, 1961), 83–86, 83n65.
60. Assembled Chiefs to Our Younger Brethren the Shawnee, September 26, 1810, in Thornbrough, ed., *Letter Book*, 86–87.
61. Hull's report to Secretary of War on Brownstown, October 4, 1810, Shawnee File, Great Lakes Ethnohistory Archive.
62. Chiefs at Brownstown to the President of the US, September 26, 1810, Shawnee File, Great Lakes Ethnohistory Archive.
63. To the Brethren of the Several Nations, September 26, 1810, in Thornbrough, ed., *Letter Book*, 87–90.
64. Hull's report to Secretary of War on Brownstown, October 4, 1810, Shawnee File, Great Lakes Ethnohistory Archive.

65. Johnston to Eustis, October 20, 1810, Shawnee File, Great Lakes Ethnohistory Archive.

66. Edmunds, *Tecumseh*, 140.

67. Indian Speech of "Techkumthai Brother to the Shawenese Prophet," Amherstburg, November 15, 1810, in *Historical Collections: Collections and Researches Made by the Michigan Pioneer and Historical Society* (Lansing, 1896), 25:275–77.

68. Castlereigh to Sir James Craig, April 8, 1809, in Claus, "Diary of William Claus," *Historical Collections,* 23:69.

69. The counterfactual possibility of a buffer state should be approached with caution. As Colin G. Calloway writes (*Crown and Calumet: British-Indian Relations, 1783–1815* [Norman, OK, 1987], 17), the British had developed a bad habit of making promises to the Indians only to sell them out later. In all the cases Calloway cites, however, the necessary military victory to back such diplomatic dreams was lacking. A buffer state was therefore possible, if not probable.

70. Ninian Edwards to Eustis, June 20, 1811, Shawnee File, Great Lakes Ethnohistory Archive.

71. Clark to Eustis, July 3, 1811, Shawnee File, Great Lakes Ethnohistory Archive.

72. WHH to Dearborn, April 12, 1807, in *Messages and Papers*, 1:207.

73. WHH, Annual Message to the General Assembly, October 17, 1809, in *Messages and Papers*, 1:383.

74. WHH Annual Message, November 12, 1810, in *Messages and Papers*, 1:487–88.

75. Ibid., 1:489.

76. Ibid., 1:492–93.

77. For Madison's fate regarding Macon's Bill and Non-Intercourse, see Richard Buel Jr., *America on the Brink: How the Political Struggle over the War of 1812 Almost Destroyed the Young Republic* (New York, 2005), 84–85, 98–111.

78. WHH to Eustis, August 22, 1810, in *Papers*, 4:172; WHH to Eustis, October 5, 1810, in *Papers*, 4:217–18.

79. Eustis to WHH, October 26, 1810, in *Papers*, 4:251–52.

80. WHH to Jared Mansfield, October 3, 1810, in *Papers*, 4:216.

81. WHH to Eustis, December 24, 1810, in *Papers*, 4:291.

82. WHH to Eustis, August 22, 1810, in *Papers*, 4:172. For letters denying the strength of the Prophet's faction, see WHH to Eustis, August 28, October 5, and October 10, 1810, in *Papers*, 4:178ff., 218, 227.

83. WHH to Eustis, October 17, 1810, in *Papers*, 4:241.

84. WHH to Eustis, December 24, 1810, in *Papers*, 4:291–99.

85. Eustis to WHH, March 7, 1811, in *Papers*, 4:413.

86. WHH to Eustis, February 6, 1811, in *Papers*, 4:384.

87. WHH to Eustis, April 23, 1811, in *Papers*, 4:486.

88. WHH to Eustis, June 6, 1811, in *Papers*, 4:538–48.

89. WHH to John Eppes, January 22, 1811, in *Papers*, 4:329.

90. Most works on Tippecanoe intimate that Harrison's predilection to see Indian threats helped propel him to Tippecanoe, but they do not connect Harrison's political fortunes to the decision to attack in 1811 rather than earlier. See R. David Edmunds, *The Shawnee Prophet* (Lincoln, NE, 1983), 102–6; Owens, *Mr. Jefferson's Hammer*, 214; Cayton, *Frontier Indiana*, 224; Jon Latimer, *1812: War with America* (Cambridge, MA, 2007), 29.

91. WHH to Jared Mansfield, March 6, 1811, in *Papers*, 4:408.

92. WHH to Eustis, June 6, 1811, in *Papers*, 4:540.

93. Edmunds, *Tecumseh*, 141.

94. WHH to Eustis, October 5, 1810, in *Papers*, 4:281.

95. WHH to Eustis, June 19, 1811, in *Papers*, 4:574–75.

96. Message to the Shawnee Prophet and Tecumseh, June 24, 1811, in *Papers*, 4:581–84.

97. Tecumseh to WHH, July 4, 1811, in *Papers*, 4:623.

98. Message to the Shawnee Prophet and Tecumseh, June 24, 1811, in *Papers*, 4:581–84.

99. Vincennes *Sun*, July 6, 1811, in *Papers*, 4:625–26.

100. WHH to Edwards, July 4, 1811, in *Papers*, 4:613.

101. Harrison's missive makes it hard to credit Owens' argument that Harrison did not "single-handedly" cause the war at Tippecanoe. Owens points out that the expedition was popular—and it was. Nevertheless, the war undoubtedly came from Harrison's planning and prompting, largely undertaken to defend his own political career and in defiance of the broader Indian policies of the Madison administration.

102. WHH to Eustis, July 2, 1811, in *Papers*, 4:604–5.

103. WHH to Eustis, July 11, 1811, in *Papers*, 4:635.

104. Resolution Concerning Indians, July 31, 1811, in *Messages and Papers*, 1:540–42.

105. Reprinted in the Bennington (VT) *Green-Mountain Farmer*, August 12, 1811.

106. Eustis to WHH, July 17, 1811, in *Messages and Papers*, 1:537–38.

107. WHH to Eustis, October 6, 1811, in *Messages and Papers*, 1:595.

108. WHH to Eustis, July 24, 1811, in *Papers*, 4:657.

109. WHH to Eustis, August 6, 1811, in *Papers*, 4:671.

110. Council between WHH and Tecumseh, in *Papers*, 4:663–64.

111. WHH to Eustis, August 6, 1811, in *Papers*, 4:675.

112. Harrison had outlined his plans and asked permission prior to the meeting; Eustis had authorized the mission prior to the meeting as well, but the message was likely in transit at the time of the summit.

113. John Drummens to Rebecca Drummens, October 14, 1811, John Drummens Letters, Filson Historical Society.

CHAPTER 14: FIASCO

1. WHH to Eustis, August 7, 1811, in *The Papers of William Henry Harrison, 1800–1815*, ed. Douglas E. Clanin (microfilm) (Indianapolis, 1999), 4:684–88. The

historical and cultural predilection for seeing the Shawnee brothers as two halves of one stereotype is expertly explained in Alfred A. Cave, "The Shawnee Prophet, Tecumseh, and Tippecanoe: A Case of Historical Myth-Making," *Journal of the Early Republic* 22, no. 4 (Winter 2002): 636–73. I closely follow Cave's analysis here, which in turn was influenced by the commentary of Gregory E. Dowd, "Thinking and Believing: Nativism and Unity in the Ages of Pontiac and Tecumseh," *American Indian Quarterly* 26 (Summer 1992): 322–27.

2. WHH to Eustis, August 7, 1811, in *Papers*, 4:684–88; Eustis to James Madison, August 21, 1811, *Papers of James Madison*, Presidential Series, ed. J. C. A. Stagg (Charlottesville, VA, 1999), 3:426–27; James Madison to Eustis, August 24, 1811, *Papers of James Madison*, 3:429.

3. WHH to Eustis, June 14–19, 1810, in *Papers*, 4:47; WHH to Charles Scott, March 10, 1810, 3:761.

4. WHH to Edwards, July 4, 1811, in *Papers*, 4:613–22; WHH to Eustis, May 16, 1810, in *Papers*, 4:15.

5. WHH to Eustis, July 5, 1809, in *Messages and Papers of William Henry Harrison*, ed. Logan Esarey (Indianapolis, 1922), 1:448.

6. WHH to Eustis, June 26, 1810, in *Papers*, 4:67; WHH to Eustis, May 16, 1810, in *Papers*, 4:15.

7. Extract from WHH to John Johnston, August 6, 1811, Draper Manuscripts 1X25.

8. WHH to Eustis, August 7 and 13, 1811, in *Papers*, 4:713–17.

9. Andrew R. L. Cayton, *Frontier Indiana* (Bloomington, IN, 1996), 221; Alfred A. Cave, *Prophets of the Great Spirit: Native American Revitalization Movements in Eastern North America* (Lincoln, NE, 2006), 116–18.

10. Speeches of Capt. Lewis and Black Hawk, sent by John Johnston to Liberty Hall in Cincinnati, Shawnee File, Great Lakes Ethnohistory Archive; Edwards to Gov. Benjamin Howard, August 1, 1811, Draper Manuscripts 1X21–23.

11. WHH to the Miami et al., August 1811, in *Papers*, 4:731.

12. Miami Chiefs to WHH, September 4, 1811, Shawnee File, Great Lakes Ethnohistory Archive.

13. Speech of Little Chief, August 17, 1811, Shawnee File, Great Lakes Ethnohistory Archive.

14. Extract from WHH to John Johnston, August 6, 1811, Draper Manuscripts 1X25.

15. Robert McAfee, *History of the Late War in the Western Country* (Bowling Green, KY, 1919 [1816]), 5.

16. Inhabitants of Knox County to James Madison, July 31, 1811, *Papers of James Madison*, 3:397.

17. Lydia Bacon, "Mrs. Lydia B. Bacon's Journal, 1811–1812," ed. Mary M. Crawford, *Indiana Magazine of History* 40, no. 4 (1944): 374.

18. Ibid., 383.

19. Archibald Loudon, *A Selection of Some of the Most Interesting Narratives, of Outrages, Committed by the Indians, in Their Wars with the White People* (Carlisle, PA,

1808), 2:187, 208–9. Loudon's stories are often taken as primary-source evidence for the events of 1763—as, for example, in Peter Silver, *Our Savage Neighbors: How Indian War Transformed Early America* (New York, 2007), 165–67; Richter, *Facing East from Indian Country: A Native History of Early America* (Cambridge, MA, 2001), 196–98, and this very book—because other sources are so scarce. The book's origin in the Jeffersonian era, however, raises questions about its ability to speak for people from fifty years earlier. Certainly, in terms of the rhetoric of the stories and their impact on white Americans who heard them, it should be considered as an 1808 document.

20. Loudon, *Selection*, 2:182.

21. Ibid., 2:187.

22. Ibid., 2:76.

23. Solomon Spaulding, *The Manuscript Found* (Salt Lake City, 1886), 7. Spaulding's manuscript has survived only because it was accused of being an apocryphal source for the later Book of Mormon.

24. Robert Greenleaf Whittier, *Legends of New England* (Hartford, CT, 1831), 81.

25. Thaddeus M. Harris, *Journal of a Tour into the Territory Northwest of the Allegheny* (Boston, 1805), 158.

26. Bacon, "Mrs. Lydia B. Bacon's Journal," 374, 381.

27. Ibid., 379–80.

28. It is dangerous—but perhaps inevitable—to re-create any particular battle through the memoirs of its participants. Historian Mark Sheftall summarizes a vast body of work on historical memory in military history when he writes that not only would no two participants remember the battle in the same way, but also the re-creation of war through memory is often filtered through "opposing political and social agendas" seeking to "appropriate the meaning of the war in ways that served their claims to authority and legitimacy." Mark David Sheftall, *Altered Memories of the Great War* (New York, 2010).

29. Robert M. Owens, *Mr. Jefferson's Hammer: William Henry Harrison and the Origins of American Indian Policy* (Norman, OK, 2007), 214–15; Florence G. Watts, "Lieutenant Charles Larrabee's Account of the Battle of Tippecanoe, 1811," *Indiana Magazine of History* 57, no. 3 (September 1961): 225–47.

30. Bacon, "Mrs. Lydia B. Bacon's Journal," 380; McAfee, *History of the Late War*, 28–29.

31. WHH to Eustis, October 13, 1811, in *Messages and Papers*, 1:601.

32. WHH to Eustis, June 26, 1810, in *Messages and Papers*, 1:435.

33. WHH to Eustis, September 25, 1811, in *Papers*, 4:816–21.

34. WHH to Charles Scott, December 31, 1811, in *Papers*, 5:146.

35. McAfee, *History of the Late War*, 37.

36. Shabonee's account was also recorded decades later, after Harrison's ascension to the presidency and Shabonee had been put on the federal payroll for his services to the United States; he quit the Prophet's movement in 1813 and went on to become a prominent accommodationist chief. His account is riddled with

inaccuracies—Tecumseh is said to be Tenskwatawa's younger brother, and "hundreds" of women were killed by Americans after the battle. See Shabonee, "Shabonee's Account of Tippecanoe," ed. J. Wesley Wickar, *Indiana Magazine of History* 17, no. 4 (December 1921): 353n1, 355, 360.

37. See Cave, *Prophets*, 114–29, and Cave, "Shawnee Prophet," 652–56.

38. WHH to Charles Scott, December 13, 1811, in *Papers*, 5:146–54.

39. WHH to Charles Scott, December 13, 1811, in *Papers*, 5:146.

40. John Tipton, "John Tipton's Tippecanoe Journal," *Indiana Magazine of History* 2, no. 4 (December 1906): 181.

41. WHH to Charles Scott, December 13, 1811, in *Papers*, 5:154.

42. McAfee, *History of the Late War*, 39.

43. Owens, *Mr. Jefferson's Hammer*, 217–19.

44. John Badollet to Albert Gallatin, November 19, 1811, in *The Correspondence of John Badollet and Albert Gallatin, 1804–1836*, ed. Gayle Thornbrough (Indianapolis, 1963), 207–9; Owens, *Mr. Jefferson's Hammer*, 218.

45. Elias Darnell Journal, Shawnee File, Great Lakes Ethnohistory Archive.

46. Forsyth to Howard, February 18, 1812, in *Territorial Papers of the United States* (Washington, DC, 1939), 14:535–36.

47. WHH to Eustis, December 4, 1811, in *Papers*, 5:104–7.

48. WHH to Eustis, December 24, 1811, in *Messages and Papers*, 1:683.

49. WHH to Charles Scott, December 31, 1811, in *Papers*, 5:146.

50. Johnston to Eustis, November 28, 1811, Shawnee File, Great Lakes Ethnohistory Archive. The grave desecration is mentioned in numerous secondary sources as being done by the Americans, but Johnston's remark is the only citation that suggests it took place, and was performed by the Prophet's forces. Americans had disturbed Indian graves before, at Fallen Timbers in 1794 and elsewhere.

51. Boyd to Eustis, December 11, 1811, reprinted in the *National Intelligencer*, January 12, 1812.

52. John Badollet to Albert Gallatin, December 17, 1811, in *The Correspondence of John Badollet and Albert Gallatin*, 211–13.

53. Long Island *Star*, December 4, 1811; New York *Commercial Advertiser*, December 4, 1811.

54. Clark to Eustis, November 23, 1812, Shawnee File, Great Lakes Ethnohistory Archive.

55. Edwards to Eustis, January 25, 1812, Shawnee File, Great Lakes Ethnohistory Archive.

56. Jacob Lalime to Howard, February 4, 1812, in *Territorial Papers of the United States* (Washington, DC, 1939), 14:536–37; Edwards to Eustis, February 10, 1812, Shawnee File, Great Lakes Ethnohistory Archive; Wyandots to House of Representatives, February 28, 1812, *American State Papers, Indian Affairs* (Washington, DC, 1832), 1:795. For disaffection increasing, see also John Johnston to Eustis, May 21, 1812, Shawnee File, Great Lakes Ethnohistory Archive.

57. Josiah Snelling to WHH, November 20, 1811, in *Messages and Papers*, 1:643–44. His report on the status of Prophetstown came secondhand from a Miami chief.
58. Harrison used the story to claim he had protected America from "mysterious rites." WHH to Eustis, November 26, 1811, in *Messages and Papers*, 1:651. The Shawnee taboo against menstruation, Dowd suggests, should be read as a generalized taboo against blood, but the insinuation was probably intended in Snelling's recounting as humiliation of both military valor and masculinity. See Gregory Evans Dowd, *A Spirited Resistance: The North American Indian Struggle for Unity, 1745–1815* (Baltimore, 1992), 4–16.
59. Elliott to Brock, January 12, 1812, in *Messages and Papers*, 1:616, also printed in *Alexandria Gazette*, March 5, 1812.
60. WHH to Eustis, January 7, 1812, in *Messages and Papers*, 2:5. For interpretations of Tecumseh's reaction to Tenskwatawa after the battle, see Cave, "Shawnee Prophet," and Dowd, "Thinking and Believing," 391–97.
61. James L. Penick, *The New Madrid Earthquakes of 1811–1812* (Columbia, MO, 1976), 6–9; Jelle Zeilinga de Boer and Donald Theodore Sears, *Earthquakes in Human History* (Princeton, NJ, 2005), 117.
62. Penick, *New Madrid Earthquakes*, 39, 53; Lorenzo Dow, *History of Cosmopolite* (Cincinnati, 1854), 243, 245.
63. *Annals of Congress*, 12th Congress, 1st session, 1386.
64. Draper Manuscripts 1YY38.
65. Edwards to Eustis, February 10, 1812, and Thomas Fish and Enos Terry to Meigs, January 14, 1812, Shawnee File, Great Lakes Ethnohistory Archive.
66. *American State Papers, Indian Affairs*, 1:795.
67. John C. Calhoun, "Report on the Causes and Reasons for War," June 3, 1812, in *The Papers of John C. Calhoun*, ed. Robert L. Meriwether (Columbia, SC, 1959), 1:109–25, quote at 122.

CHAPTER 15: "A WAR OF EXTIRPATION"

1. Jon Latimer, *1812: War with America* (Cambridge, MA, 2007), 3–4.
2. Quoted in ibid., 31.
3. Clay quoted in Robert V. Remini, *Henry Clay: Statesman for the Union* (New York, 1991), 60.
4. James Madison to Congress, June 1, 1812, in *Papers of James Madison*, Presidential Series, ed. J. C. A. Stagg (Charlottesville, VA, 1999), 4:432–42.
5. J. C. A. Stagg, *Mr. Madison's War: Politics, Diplomacy, and Warfare in the Early American Republic* (Princeton, NJ, 1983), 48–49.
6. Ibid., 49–50.
7. Remini, *Henry Clay*, 60. See also Kate Caffrey, *The Twilight's Last Gleaming: Britain vs. America, 1812–1815* (New York, 1977), ch 5.
8. Stagg, *Mr. Madison's War*, 74–75.

9. The story of Clay's warning comes from Senator Thomas Worthington, quoted in Latimer, *1812*, 33.

10. Jackson to James Madison, April 13, 1812, in *Papers of James Madison*, 4:317.

11. Quoted in Gordon Wood, *Empire of Liberty: A History of the Early Republic, 1789–1815* (New York, 2009), 667, 670.

12. James Madison to Thomas Jefferson, February 7, 1812, in *Papers of James Madison*, 4:168. See also Stagg, *Mr. Madison's War*, 79.

13. Quoted in Stagg, *Mr. Madison's War*, 110.

14. *Annals of Congress*, 12th Cong., 1st session, 1633–34.

15. Stagg, *Mr. Madison's War*, 114–15; Bradford Perkins, *Prologue to War: England and the United States, 1805–1812* (Berkeley, CA, 1961), 410–14; Roger H. Brown, *The Republic in Peril: 1812* (New York, 1971), 110–20.

16. Jonathan Roberts to Matthew Roberts, June 17, 1812, quoted in Perkins, *Prologue*, 414.

17. Norman K. Risjord, "1812: Conservatives, War Hawks, and the Nation's Honor," *William and Mary Quarterly*, 3rd Ser., 18, no. 2 (April 1961): 197, 201.

18. An ancient historiographical debate concerns whether the voting patterns in Congress show party or regional loyalty. The contention that maritime rights (the ostensible cause) were in fact the driving force behind the war has had few defenders since Margaret K. Latimer presented the regional argument that the West and South sought a war for territorial aggrandizement in "South Carolina—A Protagonist of the War of 1812," *American Historical Review* 61 (1955–56): 921–29. Risjord and others claimed that national honor played a larger role. Stagg, *Mr. Madison's War*, contends that the war was political in its nature, as did John S. Pancake, "The 'Invisibles': A Chapter in the Opposition to President Madison," *Journal of Southern History* 21, no. 1 (February 1955): 17–37. The fact that western representatives were not hell-bent on war seems to support Stagg's more recent conclusions.

19. Quoted in Desmond Morton, *A Short History of Canada* (Edmonton, 1983), 38.

20. Wood, *Empire of Liberty*, 672; Norman K. Risjord, *The Old Republicans: Southern Conservatism in the Age of Jefferson* (New York, 1965), 127.

21. "Brutus," quoted in Max M. Edling, *A Revolution in Favor of Government: Origins of the U.S. Constitution and the Making of the American State* (New York, 2003), 89.

22. *Raleigh Register*, February 21, 1812, reprinted from the *Baltimore American*. The identity of "Gen. Bradley" is unclear; it is possibly Hugh Bradley, who never achieved the rank of general.

23. Graeme Wynn, "On the Margins of Empire," in *The Illustrated History of Canada*, ed. Craig Brown (Toronto, 2002), 209; Latimer, *1812*, 186; Stagg, *Mr. Madison's War*, 249; Robert McAfee, *History of the Late War in the Western Country* (Bowling Green, KY, 1919 [1816]), 393.

24. Stagg, *Mr. Madison's War*, 138.

25. A. J. Langguth, *Union 1812: The Americans Who Fought the Second War of Independence* (New York, 2006), 337; Worthington's constituent quoted in Stagg, *Mr. Madison's War*, 163; Brock quoted in Langguth, *Union 1812*, 212.

26. Unidentified correspondent to James Madison, April 25, 1811, *Papers of James Madison*, 3:289.

27. Quoted in Donald R. Hickey, *The War of 1812: A Forgotten Conflict* (Chicago, 1989), 47.

28. Hull to Eustis, July 7, 1812, Shawnee File, Great Lakes Ethnohistory Archives.

29. William Gribbin, *The Churches Militant: The War of 1812 and American Religion* (New Haven, CT, 1973), 61.

30. Ibid., 63, 79–80.

31. McDowell to Reid, September 22, 1813, Filson Historical Society.

32. *Columbian Centinel*, July 31, 1813, quoted in John F. Berens, *Providence and Patriotism in Early America, 1640–1815* (Charlottesville, VA, 1978), 152.

33. Caleb Strong, *A Proclamation for a Day of Public Fasting . . . June 26, 1812* (Boston, 1812).

34. Kiah Bayley, *War a Calamity to Be Dreaded . . .* (Hallowell, MA [ME], 1812), 13–14.

35. Benjamin Bell, *The Difference Between Present and Former Days* (Utica, NY, 1812), 31.

36. *Columbian Centinel*, February 17, 1813; Berens, *Providence and Patriotism*, 152.

37. John Lathrop, *The Present War Unexpected, Unnecessary, and Ruinous* (Boston, 1812), 19, 31.

38. Samuel Bloss, *Obedience to Magistrates* (Hartford, CT, 1813), 3.

39. Timothy Merritt, *Discourse on the War with England* (Hallowell, MA [ME], 1814), 5, 14.

40. Alfred A. Cave, *Prophets of the Great Spirit: Native American Revitalization Movements in Eastern North America* (Lincoln, NE, 2006), ch 4.

41. Forsyth to Gibson, July 26, 1812, Shawnee File, Great Lakes Ethnohistory Archives; Henry Rowe Schoolcraft, *History and Statistical Information Respecting the History, Conditions, and Prospects of the Indian Tribes of the United States* (Philadelphia, 1851), 5:708; Forsyth to Howard, June 9, 1812, in *Territorial Papers of the United States* (Washington, DC, 1939), 14:570–71; Edwards to Eustis, May 26, 1812, Shawnee File, Great Lakes Ethnohistory Archives.

42. R. David Edmunds, *The Shawnee Prophet* (Lincoln, NE, 1983), 121–22.

43. Harvey Lewis Carter, *The Life and Times of Little Turtle* (Chicago, 1987), 228.

44. Stickney to Eustis, July 19, 1812, Shawnee File, Great Lakes Ethnohistory Archives.

45. John Johnston to Howard, July 9, 1812, in *Territorial Papers of the United States* (Washington, DC, 1939), 14:578.

46. Edward to Eustis, August 8, 1812, Shawnee File, Great Lakes Ethnohistory Archives.

47. Dorothy Burne Goebel, *William Henry Harrison: A Political Biography* (Philadelphia, 1974 [1926]), 133–35.

48. Stagg, *Mr. Madison's War*, 196–97.

49. McAfee, *History of the Late War*, 63–64.

50. Alan Taylor, "A Northern Revolution of 1800? Upper Canada and Thomas Jefferson," in *The Revolution of 1800: Democracy, Race, and the New Republic*, ed. James Horn, Jan Ellen Lewis, and Peter S. Onuf (Charlottesville, VA, 2002), 383–409.

51. Wood, *Empire of Liberty*, 684.

52. Stagg, *Mr. Madison's War*, 201–5.

53. Stewart Rafert, *The Miami Indians of Indiana: A Persistent People, 1654–1994* (Indianapolis, 1996), 74.

54. Ninian Edwards to Scott, August 2, 1812, Ninian Edwards Letters, Folder 1, ALPLM.

55. Stickney to WHH, September 29, 1812, in Gayle Thornbrough, ed., *Letter Book of the Indian Agency at Fort Wayne, 1809–1815* (Indianapolis, 1961), 174.

56. Alfred A. Cave, "The Shawnee Prophet, Tecumseh, and Tippecanoe: A Case of Historical Myth-Making," *Journal of the Early Republic* 22, no. 4 (Winter 2002): 667–68.

57. Andrew Jackson to Blount, June 5, 1812, and Blount to Jackson, June 12, 1812, *The Papers of Andrew Jackson*, ed. Harold D. Moser and Sharon Macpherson (Knoxville, TN, 1984), 2:301, 303.

58. Stagg, *Mr. Madison's War*, 213.

59. Ibid., 214–15.

60. Ibid., 272–73; Langguth, *Union 1812*, 222–23.

61. Pennsylvania politics and Madison's fortunes are discussed in J. C. A. Stagg, "James Madison and the 'Malcontents': The Political Origins of the War of 1812," *WMQ*, 3rd ser., vol. 33, no. 4 (Oct 1976), 557–85, quote from Duane at 566.

62. Edmunds, *Shawnee Prophet*, 128–31; Latimer, *1812*, 69; Thornbrough, ed., *Letter Book*, 173 n176.

63. John Johnston to Eustis, October 14, 1812, Shawnee File, Great Lakes Ethnohistory Archives.

64. Rafert, *Miami Indians*, 74–75.

65. Edmunds, *Shawnee Prophet*, 131.

66. Sandy Antal, *A Wampum Denied: Procter's War of 1812* (Ottawa, 1997), 224–36; Edmunds, *Shawnee Prophet*, 134–36.

67. Latimer, *1812*, 184–85; R. David Edmunds, *Tecumseh and the Quest for Indian Leadership* (Boston, 1984), 203.

68. Edmunds, *Tecumseh*, 204–5; McAfee, *History of the Late War*, 402–4.

69. WHH to Charles Scott, December 13, 1811, in *The Papers of William Henry Harrison, 1800–1815*, ed. Douglas E. Clanin (microfilm) (Indianapolis, 1999), 5:154–55.

70. For accounts of disillusionment after the retreat, see Edmunds, *Shawnee Prophet*, 140, and Latimer, *1812*, 186.

71. McAfee, *History of the Late War*, 408.

72. Robert M. Owens, *Mr. Jefferson's Hammer: William Henry Harrison and the Origins of American Indian Policy* (Norman, OK, 2007), 229; Latimer, *1812*, 188–89.

73. Drummond to Prevost, April 19, 1814, in *Select British Documents of the Canadian War of 1812*, vol. 3, part 2 (New York, 1968), 720–21; Edmunds, *Shawnee Prophet*, 146–47.

74. Tecumseh, "Sleep No Longer," quoted in Horatio Bardwell Cushman, *A History of the Choctaw, Chickasaw, and Natchez Indians* (Greenville, TX, 1899), 313. As with many of Tecumseh's speeches, "Sleep No Longer" was transcribed. Its transmission to the modern day has been torturous; Horatio Cushman heard it from John Pitchlynn, who may not himself be reliable. Although this evidence should be used cautiously, the excerpts quoted appear to be consistent with Tecumseh's vision of a pan-Indian future in 1811.

75. Latimer, *1812*, 318–21.

76. Quoted in Caffrey, *The Twilight's Last Gleaming*, 247.

77. Brock to Prevost, September 28, 1812, in *Life and Correspondence of Major-General Sir Isaac Brock*, ed. Ferdinand Brock Tupper (London, 1845), 319–20.

78. See for example, Colin G. Calloway, *The Shawnees and the War for America* (New York, 2007), 86; Gregory Evans Dowd, *A Spirited Resistance: The North American Indian Struggle for Unity, 1745–1815* (Baltimore, 1992), 184.

79. Cave, *Prophets*, 114; William Keating, *Narrative of an Expedition to the Source of St. Peter's River* (London, 1825), 1:230.

80. Henry Rowe Schoolcraft, *General History of the North American Indians* (Philadelphia, 1857), 342.

81. Schoolcraft, *History of the Indian Tribes*, 6:357.

82. Hull to Eustis, July 20, 1810, Shawnee File, Great Lakes Ethnohistory Archive.

83. Hull to Eustis, August 26, 1812, *Michigan Historical Collections* (Lansing, 1929), 40:460ff., quote at 462.

84. Edwards to Eustis, May 12, 1812, Shawnee File, Great Lakes Ethnohistory Archive.

85. Edwards to Eustis, June 2, 1812, Shawnee File, Great Lakes Ethnohistory Archive.

86. Quoted in Antal, *A Wampum Denied*, 156.

87. *Life and Correspondence of Isaac Brock*, 320.

88. The American to the British Commissioners, August 24, 1814, in *The Papers of James A. Bayard, 1796–1815*, ed. Elizabeth Donnan (Washington, DC, 1971 [1915]), 2:322; Alan Taylor, *The Civil War of 1812: American Citizens, British Subjects, Irish Rebels, and Indian Allies* (New York, 2010), 417. Taylor summarizes the historical argument that American intransigence prevented the creation of a buffer state at Ghent. The commissioners did vehemently oppose such a condition, but it is a mistake to assume that American rhetoric dictated conditions to the British. With Washington burning, what the American commissioners wanted mattered little, and would have mattered even less had the British still controlled the Great Lakes.

As Taylor himself writes, America "needed a miracle" to survive at Ghent, and had the British still held Michigan, I contend that such an American miracle would have included an Indian buffer state.

89. For lack of supplies and the fate of Indian resistance, see Dowd, *Spirited Resistance*, 171, 181, and John Sugden, *Tecumseh: A Life* (New York, 1998), 264. For lack of American supplies, see Edwards to Eustis, March 2, 1813, Shawnee File, Great Lakes Ethnohistory Archive; John Johnston to Howard, July 21, 1812, Shawnee File, Great Lakes Ethnohistory Archive; and Jennings to Madison, May 4, 1812, in *The Unedited Letters of Jonathan Jennings*, ed. Dorothy Lois Riker (Indianapolis, 1932), 184–85.

90. See Pekka Hämäläinen, *The Comanche Empire* (New Haven, CT, 2008), esp. chs. 4 and 5.

91. McDowell to Reid, November 22, 1814, Filson Historical Society. For the Samuel McDowell–Andrew Hand correspondence, see *Filson Club Historical Quarterly* 16, no. 3 (July 1942): 172ff.

92. Edmunds, *Shawnee Prophet*, 156–61.

93. McDowell to Reid, November 22, 1814, Filson Historical Society; Gribbin, *Churches Militant*, 140–41.

94. David L. Rowe, *God's Strange Work: William Miller and the End of the World* (Grand Rapids, MI, 2008), ch. 2. On the changes in the American cultural conception of the godhead after 1800, see Nathan O. Hatch, *The Democratization of American Christianity* (New Haven, CT, 1989); Catherine A. Brekus, *Strangers and Pilgrims: Female Preaching in America, 1740–1845* (Chapel Hill, NC, 1998); and John B. Boles, *The Great Revival: Beginnings of the Bible Belt* (Lexington, KY, 1972).

EPILOGUE: THE FUNERAL

1. Boston *Medical and Surgical Journal*, June 2, 1841. Harrison's dress was described in the *Cleveland Daily Herald*, February 13, 1841; *Boston Courier*, March 4, 1841; and John Quincy Adams, *Memoirs of John Quincy Adams*, ed. Charles Francis Adams, entry for March 4, 1841 (New York, 1971 [1874–77]), 10:439. See also Daniel Walker Howe, *What Hath God Wrought* (New York, 2007), 589.

2. Freeman Cleaves, *Old Tippecanoe: William Henry Harrison and His Times* (New York, 1939), 336–37.

3. Philip Hone, *Diary of Philip Hone*, ed. Bayard Tuckerman, entry for March 4, 1841 (New York, 1889), 2:67.

4. The best work on the 1840 contest is Richard J. Carwardine's *Evangelicals and Politics in Antebellum America* (Knoxville, TN, 1997), ch. 2, but on the nature of and history of the Second Party System, see Harry L. Watson, *Liberty and Power* (New York, 1990); Michael F. Holt, *The Political Crisis of the 1850s* (New York, 1978); and Lynn H. Parsons, *The Birth of Modern Politics* (New York, 2009).

5. Carwardine, *Evangelicals and Politics*, 59.

6. Ibid., 65.

7. Andrew R. L. Cayton, *Frontier Indiana* (Bloomington, IN, 1996), 167.

8. Cleaves, *Old Tippecanoe*, 336.

9. Charles B. Haddock, *A Discourse Delivered at Hanover, on the Occasion of the Death of William Henry Harrison* (Windsor, VT, 1841), 13–14; Joseph Angier, *A Eulogy, on the Occasion of the Death of William Henry Harrison* (Boston, 1841), 3; Hewitt quoted in Carwardine, *Evangelicals and Politics*, 69; Theodore Frelinghuysen, "Oration," in *Report of the Committee of Arrangements for. . .Funeral Obsequies in Memory of William H. Harrison* (New York, 1841), 100.

10. Norwood Damon, *A Holy Voice: A Discourse* (West Cambridge, MA, 1841), 8; Palmer Dyer, *A Discourse on the Death of William Henry Harrison* (Whitehall, NY, 1841); George Bethune, *A Discourse on the Death of William Henry Harrison* (Philadelphia, 1841), 8.

11. Charles Jones Jenkins, *Eulogy on the Life and Character of William Henry Harrison* (Augusta, GA, 1841), 5; Howard H. Peckham, *Tears for Old Tippecanoe: Religious Interpretations of President Harrison's Death* (Worcester, MA, 1959), 17.

12. Adams, *Memoirs*, entry for April 6, 1841, 10:458.

13. Frelinghuysen, "Oration," 97.

14. James Birch, *An Address in Commemoration of the Life and Character of William Henry Harrison* (Missouri, 1841), 8.

15. Angier, *A Eulogy*, 17.

16. Reuben Sears, *A Discourse Delivered . . . on Account of the Death of William Henry Harrison* (Albany, 1841), 10.

17. Moses Dawson, *A Historical Narrative of the Civil and Military Services of Major-General William H. Harrison* (Cincinnati, 1824), 82–83.

18. Ibid., 100.

19. C. C. Trowbridge, *Shawnese Traditions: C. C. Trowbridge's Account*, ed. Vernon Kinietz and Erminie Wheeler-Voegelin (New York, 1980), 3, 10, 17, 21, 40.

20. Harrison, *Remarks of General Harrison, Late Envoy Extraordinary and Minister Plenipotentiary of the United States to the Republic of Colombia, on Certain Charges Made Against Him . . .* (Washington, DC, 1830).

21. Richard Emmons, *Tecumseh, or the Battle of the Thames* (New York, 1972 [1836]), 34.

22. Ibid., 8.

23. I. R. Jackson, *Sketch of the Life and Services of William Henry Harrison* (New York, 1836), 13, 14, 17, 18.

24. *The Life of William Henry Harrison, the People's Candidate for the Presidency* (Philadelphia, 1840), 4.

25. Ibid., 4.

26. Cleaves, *Old Tippecanoe*, 334; Adams, *Memoirs*, entry for March 4, 1841, 10:439.

27. Hone, *Diary of Philip Hone*, entry for April 4, 1841, 2:73.

28. Quote from William Ramsey in Peckham, *Tears for Old Tippecanoe*, 31.

29. Howe, *What Hath God Wrought*, 702.

30. James Clifton, ed., *Star Woman and Other Shawnee Tales* (Lanham, MD, 1984), 35.

Bibliography

MANUSCRIPT AND ARCHIVAL MATERIALS

Glenn A. Black Laboratory of Archaeology, Ohio Valley–Great Lakes Ethnohistory
    Archive, Indiana University, Bloomington, Indiana
        Chippewa [Ojibwe] File
        Potawatomi File
        Shawnee File
        Winnebago File
Lilly Library, Indiana University, Bloomington, Indiana
        War of 1812 Manuscripts
        Minutes and Proceedings of the Vincennes University as Transacted by the Board
        of Trustees
        George Bluejacket, *History of the Shawanoes*
Indiana Historical Society, Indianapolis
        Indiana Territory Collection
        William English Collection
        Varney-Porter Papers
Massachusetts Historical Society, Boston
        Society for Propagating the Gospel Among the Indians and Others in North
        America Papers
        Samuel P. Savage Memoranda Book
        Pre-Revolutionary War Diaries
Filson Historical Society, Louisville
        Journal of Robert Breckinridge McAfee
        John Drummens Letters
Abraham Lincoln Presidential Library and Museum, Springfield, Illinois
        Robert Morrison Papers
        Jesse B. Thomas Papers
        John Messinger Papers
        Ninian Edwards Letters
Kentucky Historical Society, Frankfort, Kentucky
        John Lyle Diary

American Philosophical Society, Philadelphia
    Wallace Papers, Series II
Winterthur Library, Winterthur, Delaware
    Andrews Collection
State Historical Society of Wisconsin, Madison
    Lyman Draper Manuscripts

PUBLISHED PRIMARY SOURCES

Adams, John Quincy. *Memoirs of John Quincy Adams.* Ed. Charles Francis Adams. New York, 1971 [1874–77].

Allen, Ethan. *Reason the Only Oracle of Man.* Bennington, VT, 1784.

American State Papers. Class II. Indian Affairs. 2 vols. Washington, DC, 1832.

Angier, Joseph. *A Eulogy, on the Occasion of the Death of William Henry Harrison.* Boston, 1841.

Askin, John. *John Askin Papers.* Ed. Milo M. Quaife. Detroit, 1928.

Aupamat, Hendrick. "A Narrative of an Embassy to the Western Indians." *Memoirs of the Historical Society of Pennsylvania* 2 (1827):76–131.

Bacon, Lydia. "Mrs. Lydia B. Bacon's Journal, 1811–1812." Ed. Mary M. Crawford. *Indiana Magazine of History* 40, no. 4 (1944):367–86.

Badger, Joseph. *A Memoir of Rev. Joseph Badger.* Ed. Henry Noble Day. Hudson, OH, 1851.

Badollet, John, and Albert Gallatin. *The Correspondence of John Badollet and Albert Gallatin, 1804–1836.* Ed. Gayle Thornbrough. Indianapolis, 1963.

Barton, Thomas. *Conduct of the Paxton-Men.* Philadelphia, 1764.

Bates, Frederick. *Life and Papers of Frederick Bates.* Ed. Thomas Maitlan Marshall. St. Louis, 1926.

Bayard, James A. *The Papers of James A. Bayard, 1796–1815.* Ed. Elizabeth Donnan Washington, DC, 1971 [1915].

Bayley, Kiah. *War a Calamity to Be Dreaded.* Hallowell, MA [ME], 1812.

Bell, Benjamin. *The Difference Between Present and Former Days.* Utica, NY, 1812.

Bethune, George. *A Discourse on the Death of William Henry Harrison.* Philadelphia, 1841.

Birch, James. *An Address in Commemoration of the Life and Character of William Henry Harrison.* Missouri, 1841.

Black Hawk. *The Life of Black Hawk, or Ma-ka-tai-me-she-kia-kiak: Dictated by Himself.* Ed. J. Gerald Kennedy. New York, 2008.

Bloss, Samuel. *Obedience to Magistrates.* Hartford, CT, 1813.

Bond, Beverly W., Jr., ed. *The Intimate Letters of John Cleves Symmes and His Family.* Cincinnati, 1956.

Brackenridge, Hugh Henry. *The Death of General Montgomery, at the Siege of Quebec.* Philadelphia, 1777.

Brainerd, David. *Memoirs of the Rev. David Brainerd*. Ed. Jonathan Edwards and Serebo Dwight. New Haven, CT, 1822.

Burr, Aaron. *The Political Correspondence and Public Papers of Aaron Burr*. Ed. Mary-Jo Kline. Princeton, NJ, 1983.

Burt, John. *Earthquakes the Effects of God's Wrath*. Newport, RI, 1755.

Butterfield, Consul Willshire. *An Historical Account of the Expedition Against Sandusky Under Col. William Crawford in 1782*. Cincinnati, 1873.

Calhoun, John C. *The Papers of John C. Calhoun*. Ed. Robert L. Meriwether. Columbia, SC, 1959.

Cartwright, Peter. *The Autobiography of Peter Cartwright*. Ed. Charles L. Wallis. Nashville, TN, 1984 [1956].

Clark, William. "William Clark's Journal Of General Wayne's Campaign." Ed. R. C. McGrane. *Mississippi Valley Historical Review* 1, no. 3 (December 1914): 418–44.

Claus, William. "Diary of William Claus." *Historical Collections: Collections and Researches Made by the Michigan Pioneer and Historical Society*, vol. 23. Lansing, 1895.

Clifton, James, ed. *Star Woman and Other Shawnee Tales*. Lanham, MD, 1984.

Coffin, Paul. *Memoir and Journals of Rev. Paul Coffin*. Ed. Cyrus Woodman. Portland, ME, 1855.

Cogswell, James. *The Danger of Disregarding the Works of God*. New Haven, CT, 1755.

The Comet, Explained and Improved. Boston, 1812.

Cooke, Samuel. *The Violent Destroyed and the Oppressed Delivered, a Sermon Preached at Lexington, April 19, 1777*. Boston, 1777.

Cow-Chase, in Three Cantos, Published on the Occasion of the Rebel General Wayne's Attack of the Refugees Block-House. New York, 1780.

Cunningham, Noble E., Jr., ed. *Circular Letters of Congressmen to Their Constituents, 1789–1829*. Williamsburg, VA, 1978.

Damon, Norwood. *A Holy Voice: A Discourse*. West Cambridge, MA, 1841.

Davis, William C. *The Millennium, or a Short Sketch on the Rise and Fall of the Antichrist*. Salisbury, NC, 1811.

Dawson, Moses. *A Historical Narrative of the Civil and Military Services of Major-General William H. Harrison*. Cincinnati, 1824.

Delano, Amasa. *A Narrative of Voyages and Travels in the Northern and Southern Hemispheres*. Boston, 1817.

Denny, Ebenezer. *The Military Journal of Ebenezer Denny*. Philadelphia, 1859.

Devens, R. M. *Our First Century*. Springfield, MA, 1877.

Dow, Lorenzo. *History of Cosmopolite*. Cincinnati, 1854.

Drake, Benjamin. *The Life of Tecumseh and of His Brother the Prophet*. Charleston, SC, 2006 [1841].

Drew, Benjamin. *The Refugee, or the Narrative of Fugitive Slaves in Canada*. Boston, 1856.

Dyer, Palmer. *A Discourse on the Death of William Henry Harrison*. Whitehall, NY, 1841.

Emmons, Richard. *Tecumseh, or the Battle of the Thames*. New York, 1972 [1836].

Farmer, in the State of Massachusetts-Bay. *Some Remarks on That Great and Unusual Darkness, That Appeared on Friday, May 19 . . .* Danvers, MA, 1780.

Filson, John. *The Discovery, Settlement, and Present State of Kentucky*. Wilmington, 1784.

Franklin, Benjamin. *Narrative of the Late Massacres, in Lancaster County, of a Number of Indians*. Philadelphia, 1764.

Frelinghuysen, Theodore. "Oration." In *Report of the Committee of Arrangements for . . . Funeral Obsequies in Memory of William H. Harrison*. New York, 1841.

Freneau, Philip. *The Poems of Philip Freneau: Poet of the American Revolution*. Ed. Fred Lewis Pattee. Princeton, NJ, 1903.

Gatchel, Samuel. *The Signs of the Times*. Danvers, MA, 1781.

Gipson, Lawrence Henry, ed. *The Moravian Indian Mission on White River: Diaries and Letters*. Indianapolis, 1938.

Haddock, Charles B. *A Discourse Delivered at Hanover, on the Occasion of the Death of William Henry Harrison*. Windsor, VT, 1841.

Harris, Thaddeus M. *Journal of a Tour into the Territory Northwest of the Allegheny*. Boston, 1805.

Harrison, William Henry. *Messages and Papers of William Henry Harrison*. Ed. Logan Esarey. Indianapolis, 1922.

———. *Remarks of General Harrison, Late Envoy Extraordinary and Minister Plenipotentiary of the United States to the Republic of Colombia, On Certain Charges Made Against Him*. Washington, DC, 1830.

———. *The Papers of William Henry Harrison, 1800–1815*. (Microfilm.) Ed. Douglas Clanin. Indianapolis, 1999.

Heckewelder, J. G. E. "Narrative of the Cuyahoga Indian Settlement, 1785." In *Visions of the Western Reserve: Public and Private Documents of Northeastern Ohio, 1750–1860*, ed. Robert Wheeler, 37–48. Columbus, OH, 2000.

———. *History, Manners, and Customs of the Indian Nations*. New York, 1971 [1819].

———. *Narrative of the Mission of the United Brethren . . . to the Close of the Year 1808*. Ed. William Elsey Connelley. Cleveland, 1907 [1819].

Hone, Phillip. *Diary of Philip Hone*. Ed. Bayard Tuckerman. New York, 1889.

Hopkins, Gerard T. *A Mission to the Indians from the Indian Committee of the Baltimore Yearly Meeting to Fort Wayne in 1804*. Philadelphia, 1862.

Hulton, Ann. *Letters of a Loyalist Lady*. New York, 1971 [1927].

Increase of Piety, or Revivals of Religion in the United States of America. Newburyport, MA, 1802.

Ingalls, Samuel. *A Dream, or Vision by Samuel Ingalls of Dunham*. Windsor, VT, 1810.

Jackson, Andrew. *The Papers of Andrew Jackson*. Ed. Harold D. Moser and Sharon Macpherson. Knoxville, TN, 1984.

Jackson, I. R. *Life of William Henry Harrison of Ohio*. Philadelphia, 1840.

Jefferson, Thomas. *The Papers of Thomas Jefferson Digital Edition*. Ed. Barbara B. Oberg and J. Jefferson Looney. Charlottesville, VA, 2008.

Jenkins, Charles Jones. *Eulogy on the Life and Character of William Henry Harrison.* Augusta, GA, 1841.

Jennings, Jonathan. *The Unedited Letters of Jonathan Jennings.* Ed. Dorothy Lois Riker. Indianapolis, 1932.

Johnston, John. *Recollections of Sixty Years.* In Leonard U. Hill, ed., *John Johnston and the Indians in the Land of the Three Miamis.* Piqua, OH, 1957.

Jones, Henry. *Journal of the Proceedings, Indian Treaty, Fort Wayne, September 30th, 1809.* Connersville, IN, 1910.

Keating, William. *Narrative of an Expedition to the Source of St. Peter's River.* London, 1825.

Kendall, Edward Augustus. *Travels Through the Northern Parts of the United States in the Years 1807 and 1808.* New York, 1809.

Kenny, James. "Journal of James Kenny." *Pennsylvania Magazine of History and Biography* 37 (1913):1–47, 152–201.

Killens, John Oliver, ed. *The Trial Record of Denmark Vesey.* Boston, 1970.

King John. *Observations on the Prophecies Which Relate to the Rise and Fall of Antichrist.* Chambersburg, MD, 1809.

Larrabee, Charles. "Lieutenant Charles Larrabee's Account of the Battle of Tippecanoe, 1811." Ed. Florence G. Watts. *Indiana Magazine of History* 57, no. 3 (September 1961): 225–47.

Lathrop, John. *The Present War Unexpected, Unnecessary, and Ruinous.* Boston, 1812.

The Life of William Henry Harrison, the People's Candidate for the Presidency. Philadelphia, 1840.

Loudon, Archibald. *A Selection of Some of the Most Interesting Narratives, of Outrages, Committed by the Indians, in Their Wars with the White People.* Carlisle, PA, 1808.

Maclay, William. *Sketches of Debate in the First Senate of the Unites States.* Ed. George Harris. Harrisburg, PA, 1880.

Madison, James. *Papers of James Madison,* Presidential Series. Ed. J. C. A. Stagg. Charlottesville, VA, 1999.

McAfee, Robert. *History of the Late War in the Western Country.* Bowling Green, KY, 1919 [1816].

McNemar, Richard. *The Kentucky Revival.* New York, 1848 [1808].

Merritt, Timothy. *Discourse on the War with England.* Hallowell, MA [ME], 1814.

Michigan Historical Commission. *Michigan Historical Collections.* 2 vols. Lansing, 1915–29.

Michigan Pioneer and Historical Society. *Historical Collections: Collections and Researches Made by the Michigan Pioneer and Historical Society.* 19 vols. Lansing, 1886–1912.

Morse, Jedidiah. *A Report to the Secretary of War of the United States on Indian Affairs.* New York, 1970 [1822].

Oram's New-Jersey and New-York Almanac. Trenton, NJ, 1805.

Palmer, Elihu. *The Principles of Nature.* Ed. Kerry Walters. Boston, 1990 [1806].

Post, Christian Frederick. "Post's Second Journal, 1758." In *Early History of Western Pennsylvania*, 99–129. Pittsburgh, 1848.

Prince, Thomas. *Earthquakes the Works of GOD and Tokens of His Just Displeasure*. Boston, 1755.

Putnam, Rufus. *Memoirs of Rufus Putnam*. Ed. Rowena Buell. Marietta, OH, 1903.

Quaife, Milo M. "A Diary of the War of 1812." *Mississippi Valley Historical Review* 1, no. 2 (September 1914): 272–78.

Rice, David. *A Sermon, on the Present Revival of Religion in this Country, Preached at the Opening of the Kentucky Synod*. Washington, KY, 1804.

Ridout, Thomas. "Narrative of the Captivity Among the Shawanese Indians, in 1788, of Thomas Ridout." In *Ten Years of Upper Canada in Peace and War, 1805–1815*, ed. Matilda Edgar, 339–75. Toronto, 1890.

Rush, Benjamin. *Selected Writings of Benjamin Rush*. Ed. Dagobert Runes. New York, 1947.

Schoolcraft, Henry Rowe. *Algic Researches: North American Indian Folktales and Legends*. Mineola, NY, 1999 [1839].

———. *History and Statistical Information Respecting the History, Conditions, and Prospects of the Indian Tribes of the United States*. Philadelphia, 1851.

Sears, Reuben. *A Discourse Delivered . . . on Account of the Death of William Henry Harrison*. Albany, NY, 1841.

Shabonee. "Shabonee's Account of Tippecanoe." Ed. J. Wesley Wickar. *Indiana Magazine of History* 17, no. 4 (December 1921): 353–63.

Spaulding, Solomon. *The Manuscript Found*. Salt Lake City, 1886.

Spencer, Oliver M. *Indian Captivity: A True Narrative of the Capture of Rev. O. M. Spencer*. New York, 1852.

St. Clair, Arthur. *Narrative of the Manner in the Which the Campaign Against the Indians . . . Was Conducted*. Philadelphia, 1812.

Stone, Barton Warren. *The Biography of Elder Barton Warren Stone, Written by Himself*. Ed. John Rogers. New York, 1972 [1847].

Strong, Caleb. *A Proclamation for a Day of Public Fasting . . . June 26, 1812*. Boston, 1812.

Symmes, John Cleaves. *The Correspondence of John Cleaves Symmes*. Ed. Beverly W. Bond Jr. New York, 1926.

Tanner, John. *The Falcon: A Narrative of the Captivity and Adventures of John Tanner*. New York, 2000 [1830].

Territorial Papers of the United States. Ed. C. E. Carter and J. P. Bloom. Washington, DC, 1934–75.

Thornbrough, Gayle, ed. *Letter Book of the Indian Agency at Fort Wayne, 1809–1815*. Indianapolis, 1961.

Tipton, John. "John Tipton's Tippecanoe Journal." *Indiana Magazine of History* 2, no. 4 (December 1906): 170–84.

A Treaty, Held at the Town of Lancaster, in Pennsylvania, by the Honorable Lieutenant-Governor of the Province . . . with the Indians of the Six Nations in June, 1744. Philadelphia, 1744.

Trowbridge, C. C. *Shawnese Traditions: C. C. Trowbridge's Account.* Ed. Vernon Kinietz and Erminie Wheeler-Voegelin. New York, 1980.

Trumbull, Henry. *History of the Discovery of America . . . to Which Is Annexed the Defeat of Generals Braddock, Harmar, and St Clair.* Norwich, CT, 1812.

Turpie, David. *Sketches of My Own Times.* Indianapolis, 1903.

Volney, Constantin F. *A View of the Soil and Climate of the United States.* New York, 1968 [1804].

Washington, George. *The Papers of George Washington Digital Edition.* Ed. Theodore J. Crackel. Charlottesville, VA, 2008.

Wayne, Anthony. Orderly Book. *Historical Collections: Collections and Researches Made by the Michigan Pioneer and Historical Society,* vol. 34. Lansing, 1905.

Whittier, John Greenleaf. *Legends of New England.* Hartford, CT, 1831.

———. *Letters of John Greenleaf Whittier.* Ed. John B. Pickard. Cambridge, MA, 1975.

Wildman of the Woods. *A Short Address to the People of America.* Cazenovia, NY, 1809.

Williams, Eliphalet. *The Duty of a People, Under Dark Providences.* New London, CT, 1756.

Williams, Samuel. "An Account of a Very Uncommon Darkness." *Memoirs of the Academy of Arts and Sciences,* January 1, 1785, A234–46.

Winsor, Olney. "Olney Winsor's 'Memorandum' of the Phenomenal 'Dark Day' of May 19, 1780." Ed. William McLoughlin. *Rhode Island History,* Winter 1967, 88–90.

Wolcott, William. *Grateful Reflections on the Divine Goodness.* Hartford, CT, 1779.

Woollen, William Wesley, Daniel Wait Howe, and Jacob Piatt Dunn, eds. *Executive Journal of Indiana Territory, 1800–1816.* Indianapolis, 1985.

SELECTED NEWSPAPERS

Philadelphia *Gazette of the United States*
Scioto (OH) *Gazette*
Richmond *Virginia Gazette*
Vincennes (IN) *Gazette* (1804–1806)
Vincennes (IN) *Western Sun* (1807–1820; also titled *Sun*)
Washington *National Intelligencer*

SECONDARY SOURCES

Antal, Sandy. *A Wampum Denied: Procter's War of 1812.* Ottawa, 1997.

Aquila, Richard. *The Iroquois Restoration: Iroquois Diplomacy on the Colonial Frontier, 1701–1754.* Detroit, 1997.

Axtell, James. "Ethnohistory: A Historian's Viewpoint." *Ethnohistory* 26 (1979):1–13.

Barnhart, John D. "The Democratization of Indiana Territory." *Indiana Magazine of History* 43, no. 1 (March 1947): 1–22.

Behringer, Wolfgang. *Witches and Witch Hunts: A Global History.* Malden, MA, 2004.

Bell, Karl. "Breaking Modernity's Spell—Magic and Modern History." *Cultural and Social History* 4, no. 1 (March 2007): 115–22.

Bell, Michael E. *Food for the Dead: On the Trail of New England's Vampires.* New York, 2001.

Ben-Atar, Doron, and Barbara Oberg, eds. *The Federalists Reconsidered.* Charlottesville, VA, 1998.

Berens, John F. *Providence and Patriotism in Early America, 1640–1815.* Charlottesville, VA, 1978.

Berkhofer, Robert F., Jr., *The White Man's Indian: Images of the American Indian from Columbus to the Present.* New York, 1978.

Berry, Christopher J. "Hume on Rationality in History and Social Life." *History and Theory* 21, no. 2 (May 1982): 234–47.

Bird, S. Elizabeth ed. *Dressing in Feathers: The Construction of the Indian in American Popular Culture.* Boulder, CO, 1996.

Boles, John B. *The Great Revival: Beginnings of the Bible Belt.* Lexington, KY, 1972.

Braddick, Michael J. "Civility and Authority." In *The British Atlantic World, 1500–1800,* ed. David Armitage and Michael J. Braddick, 93–112. New York, 2002.

Brekus, Catherine A. *Strangers and Pilgrims: Female Preaching in America, 1740–1845.* Chapel Hill, NC, 1998.

Briggs, Robin. "'Many Reasons Why': Witchcraft and the Problem of Multiple Explanation." In *Witchcraft in Early Modern Europe: Studies in Culture and Belief,* ed. Jonathan Barry, Marianne Hester, and Gareth Roberts, 49–63. New York, 1996.

Brodie, Fawn M. *No Man Knows My History: The Life of Joseph Smith.* New York, 1995 [1945].

Brooks, Lisa. "Two Paths to Peace: Competing Visions of Native Space in the Old Northwest." In *The Boundaries Between Us: Natives and Newcomers along the Frontiers of the Old Northwest Territory, 1750–1850,* ed. Daniel P. Barr, 87–117. Kent, OH, 2006.

Brown, Roger H. *The Republic in Peril: 1812.* New York, 1971 [1964].

Brown, Vincent. *The Reaper's Garden: Death and Power in the World of Atlantic Slavery.* Cambridge, MA, 2008.

Buel, Richard, Jr. *America on the Brink: How the Political Struggle over the War of 1812 Almost Destroyed the Young Republic.* New York, 2005.

Burstein, Andrew. *The Passions of Andrew Jackson.* New York, 2004.

Butler, Jon. *Awash in a Sea of Faith: Christianizing the American People.* New Haven, CT, 1990.

Caffrey, Kate. *The Twilight's Last Gleaming: Britain vs. America, 1812–1815.* New York, 1977.

Calloway, Colin G. *Crown and Calumet: British-Indian Relations, 1783–1815.* Norman, OK, 1987.

————. *The Scratch of a Pen: 1763 and the Transformation of North America*. New York, 2006.

————. *The Shawnees and the War for America*. New York, 2007.

————. "Times Are Altered with Us Indians." In *The World Turned Upside Down: Indian Voices from Early America,* ed. Colin Calloway, 1–19. New York, 1994.

Carter, Harvey Lewis. *The Life and Times of Little Turtle*. Chicago, 1987.

Carwardine, Richard J. *Evangelicals and Politics in Antebellum America*. Knoxville, TN, 1997.

Cave, Alfred A. *Prophets of the Great Spirit: Native American Revitalization Movements in Eastern North America*. Lincoln, NE, 2006.

————. "The Shawnee Prophet, Tecumseh, and Tippecanoe: A Case of Historical Myth-Making." *Journal of the Early Republic* 22, no. 4 (Winter 2002): 636–73.

Cayton, Andrew R. L. *Frontier Indiana*. Bloomington, IN, 1996.

————. "Power and Civility in the Treaty of Greenville." In *Contact Points: American Frontiers from the Mohawk Valley to the Mississippi, 1750–1830,* ed. Andrew R. L. Cayton and Fredrika J. Teute, 235–69. Chapel Hill, NC, 1998.

Clark, Stuart. *Thinking with Demons: The Idea of Witchcraft in Early Modern Europe*. New York, 2005.

Cleaves, Freeman. *Old Tippecanoe: William Henry Harrison and His Times*. New York, 1939.

Clements, William M. *Oratory in Native North America*. Tucson, AZ, 2002.

Combs, Jerald A. *The Jay Treaty: Political Battleground of the Founding Fathers*. Berkeley, CA, 1970.

Conkin, Paul. *Cane Ridge: America's Pentecost*. Madison, WI, 1990.

Cornell, Saul. *The Other Founders: Anti-Federalism and the Dissenting Tradition in America, 1788–1828*. Chapel Hill, NC, 1999.

Costa, David J. "Illinois." In "Three American Placenames." *The Society for the Study of the Indigenous Languages of the Americas Newsletter* 25, no. 4 (January 2007): 9–12.

Crackel, Theodore J. *Mr. Jefferson's Army: Political and Social Reform of the Military Establishment, 1801–1809*. New York, 1987.

Davies, Owen. *Witchcraft, Magic, and Culture, 1736–1951*. New York, 1999.

Davis, David Brion. "Significance of Excluding Slavery from the Old Northwest 1787." *Indiana Magazine of History* 84, no. 1 (March 1988): 75–89.

de Blécourt, Willem. "On the Continuation of Witchcraft." In *Witchcraft in Early Modern Europe: Studies in Culture and Belief,* ed. Jonathan Barry, Marianne Hester, and Gareth Roberts, 335–52. New York, 1996.

de Boer, Jelle Zeilinga, and Donald Theodore Sears. *Earthquakes in Human History*. Princeton, NJ, 2005.

Demos, John. *The Enemy Within: 2000 Years of Witch-hunting in the Western World*. New York, 2008.

Derounian-Stodola, Kathryn Zabelle, and James Arthus Levernier. *The Indian Captivity Narrative, 1550–1900*. New York, 1993.

Dowd, Gregory Evans. "Thinking and Believing: Nativism and Unity in the Ages of Pontiac and Tecumseh." In *American Encounters: Natives and Newcomers from European Contact to Indian Removal, 1500–1850*, ed. Peter C. Mancall and James H. Merrell, 379–403. New York, 2000.

———. *A Spirited Resistance: The North American Indian Struggle for Unity, 1745–1815.* Baltimore, 1992.

Drinnon, Richard. *Facing West: The Metaphysics of Indian-Hating and Empire Building.* Minneapolis, 1980.

Duthu, N. Bruce. *American Indians and the Law.* New York, 2008.

Edmunds, R. David. *The Potawatomis: Keepers of the Fire.* Norman, OK, 1978.

———. *The Shawnee Prophet.* Lincoln, NE, 1983.

———. *Tecumseh and the Quest for Indian Leadership.* Boston, 1984.

Eid, Leroy V. "American Indian Military Leadership: St. Clair's Defeat." *Journal of Military History* 57, no. 1 (Jan. 1993): 71–88.

Elkins, Stanley M., and Eric L. McKitrick, *The Age of Federalism.* New York, 1993.

Elmer, Peter. "Science, Medicine, and Witchcraft." In *Witchcraft Historiography*, ed. Jonathan Barry and Owen Davies, 33–51. New York, 2007.

Estes, Todd. *The Jay Treaty Debate, Public Opinion, and the Evolution of Early American Political Culture.* Boston, 2006.

Fenn, Elizabeth A. *Pox Americana: The Great Smallpox Epidemic of 1775–82.* New York, 2001.

Force, James E. "Hume and Johnson on Prophecy and Miracle: Historical Context." *Journal of the History of Ideas* 43, no. 3 (July–September 1982): 463–75.

Freeman, Joanne B. *Affairs of Honor: National Politics in the New Republic.* New Haven, CT, 2001.

Gaff, Alan D. *Bayonets in the Wilderness: Anthony Wayne's Legion in the Old Northwest.* Norman, OK, 2004.

Games, Alison. *Witchcraft in Early North America.* New York, 2010.

Goebel, Dorothy Burne. *William Henry Harrison: A Political Biography.* Philadelphia, 1974 [1926].

Gribbin, William. *The Churches Militant: The War of 1812 and American Religion.* New Haven, CT, 1973.

Griffin, Patrick. *American Leviathan: Empire, Nation, and Revolutionary Frontier.* New York, 2007.

———. *The People with No Name: Ireland's Ulster Scots, America's Scots Irish, and the Creation of a British Atlantic World, 1689–1764.* Princeton, NJ, 2001.

Grizzard, Frank E. Jr. *The Ways of Providence: Religion and George Washington.* Buena Vista, VA, 2005.

Gunderson, Robert Gray. *The Log Cabin Campaign.* Lexington, KY, 1957.

Hämäläinen, Pekka. *The Comanche Empire.* New Haven, CT, 2008.

Harkin, Michael E., ed. *Reassessing Revitalization Movements: Perspectives from North America and the Pacific Islands.* Lincoln, NE, 2004.

Hatch, Nathan O. *The Democratization of American Christianity*. New Haven, CT, 1989.

Hickey, Donald R. *The War of 1812: A Forgotten Conflict*. Chicago, 1989.

Hill, Peter P. *Napoleon's Troublesome Americans: Franco-American Relations, 1804–1815*. Washington, DC, 2005.

Holmes, David L. *Faiths of the Founding Fathers*. New York, 2006.

Holt, Michael F. *The Political Crisis of the 1850s*. New York, 1978.

Howard, James H. *Shawnee! The Ceremonialism of a Native Indian Tribe and Its Cultural Background*. Athens, OH, 1981.

Howe, Daniel Walker. *What Hath God Wrought*. New York, 2007.

Hutton, Paul A. "William Wells: Frontier Scout and Indian Agent." *Indiana Magazine of History* 74, no. 3 (September 1978): 183–222.

Hutton, Ronald. *Triumph of the Moon: A History of Modern Pagan Witchcraft*. New York, 1999.

Ingram, Robert. "'The Trembling Earth Is God's Herald': Earthquakes, Religion, and Public Life in Britain During the 1750s." In *The Lisbon Earthquake of 1755: Representations and Reactions*, ed. Theodore E. D. Braun and John B. Radner, 97–115. Oxford, UK, 2005.

Irwin, Lee. *Coming Down from Above: Prophecy, Resistance, and Renewal in Native American Religions*. Norman, OK, 2008.

Isaac, Rhys. *The Transformation of Virginia, 1740–1790*. Williamsburg, VA, 1982.

Isenberg, Nancy. *Fallen Founder: The Life of Aaron Burr*. New York, 2007.

Jenkins, Philip. *Dream Catchers: How Mainstream America Discovered Native Spirituality*. New York, 2004.

Jennings, Francis. *Ambiguous Empire: The Covenant Chain Confederation of Indian Tribes with English Colonies from Its Beginnings to the Lancaster Treaty of 1744*. New York, 1984.

Juster, Susan. *Doomsayers: Anglo-American Prophecy in the Age of Revolution*. Philadelphia, 2003.

Knopf, Richard C., ed. *Anthony Wayne: A Name in Arms*. Westport, CT, 1960.

Kornblith, Gary. "Rethinking the Coming of the Civil War: A Counterfactual Exercise." *Journal of American History* 90, no. 1 (2003): 76–105.

Langguth, A. J. *Union 1812: The Americans Who Fought the Second War of Independence*. New York, 2006.

Latimer, Jon. *1812: War with America*. Cambridge, MA, 2007.

Latimer, Margaret K. "South Carolina—A Protagonist of the War of 1812." *American Historical Review* 61 (1955–56): 921–29.

Mancall, Peter C. *Deadly Medicine: Indians and Alcohol in Early America*. Ithaca, NY, 1995.

Mann, Barbara Alice. "Are You Delusional?: Kandiaronk on Christianity." In *Native American Speakers of the Eastern Woodlands: Selected Speeches and Critical Analyses*, ed. Barbara Alice Mann, 35–81. Westport, CT, 2001.

Marsden, George. *A Short Life of Jonathan Edwards*. Grand Rapids, MI, 2008.

McDermott, Gerald R. *Jonathan Edwards Confronts the Gods: Christian Theology, Enlightenment Religion, and Non-Christian Faiths*. New York, 2000.

McDermott, John Francis. "Audubon's 'Journey Up the Mississippi,'" *Journal of the Illinois State Historical Society* 35, no. 1 (1942): 148–73.

McDonald, Earl E. "Disposal of Negro Slaves By Will in Knox County." *Indiana Magazine of History* 26, no. 2 (June 1930): 143–46.

McDonald, Robert S. "Was There a Religious Revolution of 1800?" In *The Revolution of 1800: Democracy, Race, and the New Republic*, ed. James Horn, Jan Ellen Lewis, and Peter S. Onuf, 173–98. Charlottesville, VA, 2002.

McGlinchey, Frazer Dorrian. "'A Superior Civilization': Appropriation, Negotiation, and Interaction in the Northwest Territory, 1787–1795." In *The Boundaries Between Us: Natives and Newcomers Along the Frontiers of the Old Northwest Territory, 1750–1850*, ed. Daniel P. Barr, 118–42. Kent, OH, 2006.

McLoughlin, William G. *Cherokees and Missionaries, 1789–1839*. New Haven, CT, 1984.

———. *Revivals, Awakenings, and Reform: An Essay on Religious and Social Change in America*. Chicago, 1978.

Menig, D. W. *The Shaping of America: A Geographical Perspective on 500 Years of History*. New Haven, CT, 1986.

Merrell, James H. *Into the American Woods: Negotiators on the Pennsylvania Frontier*. New York, 1999.

Miller, Jay. "The 1806 Purge Among the Indiana Delaware: Sorcery, Gender, Boundaries, and Legitimacy." *Ethnohistory* 41, no. 2 (Spring 1994): 245–66.

Miller, Robert J. *Native America, Discovered and Conquered: Thomas Jefferson, Lewis and Clark, and Manifest Destiny*. Lincoln, NE, 2008.

Morgan, Edmund S. "The Puritan Ethic and the American Revolution." *William and Mary Quarterly*, 3rd Ser., 24, no. 1 (January 1967): 4–43.

———. "The Witch and We, the People." *American Heritage*, August–September 1983.

Morton, Desmond. *A Short History of Canada*. Edmonton, 1983.

Nash, Gary B. *The Urban Crucible: Social Change, Political Consciousness, and the Origins of the American Revolution*. Cambridge, MA, 1979.

Nelson, David Paul. *Anthony Wayne: Soldier of the Early Republic*. Bloomington, IN, 1985.

Noll, Mark A. *America's God: From Jonathan Edwards to Abraham Lincoln*. New York, 2002.

Onuf, Peter. "The Northwest Ordinance." In *Roots of the Republic: American Founding Documents Interpreted*, ed. Stephen L. Schechter, 249–65. Lanham, MD, 1990.

———. *Jefferson's Empire: The Language of American Nationhood*. Charlottesville, VA, 2000.

Owen, Daniel. "Circumvention of Article VI of the Ordinance of 1787." *Indiana Magazine of History* 36, no. 2 (June 1940): 110–16.

Owens, Robert M. *Mr. Jefferson's Hammer: William Henry Harrison and the Origins of American Indian Policy*. Norman, OK, 2007.

Pagden, Anthony. *The Fall of Natural Man: The American Indian and the Origins of Comparative Ethnology*. New York, 1982.

Pancake, John S. "The 'Invisibles': A Chapter in the Opposition to President Madison." *Journal of Southern History* 21, no. 1 (February 1955): 17–37.

Parsons, Lynn H. *The Birth of Modern Politics: Andrew Jackson, John Quincy Adams, and the Election of 1828*. New York, 2009.

Pauketat, Timothy R. *Chiefdoms and Other Archaeological Delusions*. Lanham, MD, 2007.

Peckham, Howard H. *Tears for Old Tippecanoe: Religious Interpretations of President Harrison's Death*. Worcester, MA, 1959.

Penick, James L., Jr. *The New Madrid Earthquakes of 1811–1812*. Columbia, MO, 1976.

Perdue, Theda, and Michael D. Green. *The Cherokee Nation and the Trail of Tears*. New York, 2007.

Perkins, Bradford. *Prologue to War: England and the United States, 1805–1812*. Berkeley, CA, 1961.

Pestana, Carla Gardina. "Religion." In *The British Atlantic World, 1500–1800,* ed. David Armitage and Michael J. Braddick, 69–89. New York, 2002.

Porter, Roy. "Witchcraft and Magic in Enlightenment, Romantic, and Liberal Thought." In *Witchcraft and Magic in Europe: the Eighteenth and Nineteenth Centuries*, ed. Bengt Ankarloo and Stuart Clark, 191–274. Philadelphia, 1999.

Potter, Janice. *The Liberty We Seek: Loyalist Ideology in Colonial New York and Massachusetts*. Cambridge, UK, 1983.

Quinn, D. Michael. *Early Mormonism and the Magic World View*. Salt Lake City, 1998.

Raboteau, Albert J. *Slave Religion: The "Invisible Institution" in the Antebellum South*. New York, 2006 [1978].

Radin, Paul. *The Winnebago Tribe*. Washington, DC, 1970 [1923].

Rafert, Stewart. *The Miami Indians of Indiana: A Persistent People, 1654–1994*. Indianapolis, 1996.

Ragosta, John. *The Wellspring of Liberty: How Virginia's Religious Dissenters Helped Win the Revolution and Secured Religious Liberty*. New York, 2010.

Rees, James D. "The Bond-Jones Duel and the Shooting of Rice Jones by Dr. James Dunlap: What Really Happened in Kaskaskia, Indiana Territory on 8 August and 7 December 1808?" *Journal of the Illinois State Historical Society* 97, no. 4 (Winter 2004–5): 272–85.

Remini, Robert V. *Henry Clay: Statesman for the Union*. New York, 1991.

Richter, Daniel K. *Facing East from Indian Country: A Native History of Early America*. Cambridge, MA, 2001.

———. *The Ordeal of the Longhouse: The Peoples of the Iroquois League in the Era of European Colonization*. Chapel Hill, NC, 1992.

Risjord, Norman K. "1812: Conservatives, War Hawks, and the Nation's Honor." *William and Mary Quarterly,* 3rd Ser., 18, no. 2 (April 1961): 196–210.

———. *The Old Republicans: Southern Conservatism in the Age of Jefferson*. New York, 1965.

Rohrabaugh, W. J. *Alcoholic Republic: An American Tradition*. New York, 1979.

Rowe, David L. *God's Strange Work: William Miller and the End of the World*. Grand Rapids, MI, 2008.

Salisbury, Neal. *Manitou and Providence: Indians, Europeans, and the Making of New England, 1500–1643*. New York, 1984.

Shannon, Timothy J. *Iroquois Diplomacy on the Early American Frontier*. New York, 2008.

Sheftall, Mark David. *Altered Memories of the Great War*. New York, 2010.

Silver, Peter. *Our Savage Neighbors: How Indian War Transformed Early America*. New York, 2007.

Silverberg, Robert. *The Mound Builders*. Athens, OH, 1970.

Smith, Howard W. *Benjamin Harrison and the American Revolution*. Williamsburg, VA, 1978.

Snyder, Christina. *Slavery in Indian Country: The Changing Face of Captivity in Early America*. Cambridge, MA, 2010.

Spengler, Jewel L. *Virginians Reborn: Anglican Monopoly, Evangelical Dissent, and the Rise of the Baptists in the Late Eighteenth Century*. Charlottesville, VA, 2008.

Spero, Patrick. "Matters of Perspective: Interpreting the Revolutionary Frontier." *Pennsylvania Magazine of History and Biography* 132, no. 3 (July 2008): 261–70.

Stagg, J. C. A. "James Madison and the 'Malcontents': The Political Origins of the War of 1812." *William and Mary Quarterly*, 3rd Ser., 33, no. 4 (October 1976): 557–85.

———. *Mr. Madison's War: Politics, Diplomacy, and Warfare in the Early Republic, 1783–1830*. Princeton, NJ, 1983.

Stark, Rodney. *What Americans Really Believe*. Waco, TX, 2008.

Stauffer, Vernon. *The Bavarian Illuminati in America: The New England Conspiracy Scare, 1798*. Mineola, MN, 2006 [1918].

Stein, Stephen J. *The Shaker Experience in America: A History of the United Society of Believers*. New Haven, CT, 1992.

Stott, Richard B. "Commentary." In *History of My Own Times, or the Life and Adventures of William Otter, Sen*. Ed. Richard B. Stott. Ithaca, NY, 1995.

Strezewski, Michael, James R. Jones III, and Dorothea McCullough. *Archaeological Investigations at Site 12–T-59 and Two Other Locations at Prophetstown State Park, Tippecanoe County, Indiana*. Report of Investigations 513. Indiana University-Purdue University Fort Wayne. Fort Wayne, 2006.

Sugden, John. *Blue Jacket: Warrior of the Shawnees*. Lincoln, NE, 2000.

———. *Tecumseh: A Life*. New York, 1998.

———. "Tecumseh's Travels Revisited." *Indiana Magazine of History* 96, no. 2 (June 2000): 150–68.

Tanner, Helen Hornbeck. "The Glaize in 1792: A Composite Indian Community." *Ethnohistory* 25, no. 1 (Winter 1978): 15–39.

Taylor, Alan. *American Colonies*. New York, 2001.

———. "A Northern Revolution of 1800? Upper Canada and Thomas Jefferson." In *The Revolution of 1800: Democracy, Race, and the New Republic*, ed. James Horn, Jan Ellen Lewis, and Peter S. Onuf, 383–409. Charlottesville, VA, 2002.

———. *The Civil War of 1812: American Citizens, British Subjects, Irish Rebels, and Indian Allies*. New York, 2010.

———. *The Divided Ground: Indians, Settlers, and the Northern Borderland of the American Revolution.* New York, 2006.

———. "The Early Republic's Supernatural Economy: Treasure Seeking in the American Northeast, 1780–1830." *American Quarterly* 38, no. 1 (Spring 1986): 6–34.

Thomas, R. Murray. *Manitou and God: North-American Indian Religions and Christian Culture.* Westport, CT, 2007.

Truman, Ben C. *The Field of Honor: Being a Complete and Comprehensive History of Dueling in All Countries.* New York, 1884.

Tucker, Glenn. *Tecumseh: Vision of Glory.* New York, 1973.

Tuczay, Christa. "The Nineteenth Century: Medievalism and Witchcraft." In *Witchcraft Historiography*, ed. Jonathan Barry and Owen Davies, 52–68. New York, 2007.

Van Lonkhuysen, Harold W. "A Reappraisal of the Praying Indians: Acculturation, Conversion, and Identity at Natick, Massachusetts, 1634–1730." In *New England Encounters: Indians and Euroamericans ca. 1600–1850*, ed. Allen T. Vaughn, 205–32. Boston, 1999.

Waldman, Stephen. *Founding Faith: Providence, Politics, and the Birth of Religious Freedom in America.* New York, 2008.

Waldstreicher, David. *In the Midst of Perpetual Fetes.* Chapel Hill, NC, 1997.

Wallace, Anthony F. C. *The Death and Rebirth of the Seneca.* New York, 1969.

———. *Jefferson and the Indians: The Tragic Fate of the First Americans.* Cambridge, MA, 1999.

———. *Religion: An Anthropological View.* New York, 1966.

———. "Revitalization Movements." *American Anthropologist* 58, no. 2 (April 1956): 264–81.

Wallace, Paul A. W. *Travels of John Heckewelder in Frontier America.* Pittsburgh, 1985 [1958].

Walsham, Alexandra. *Providence in Early Modern England.* New York, 2001.

Walters, Kerry S. *Rational Infidels: The American Deists.* Durango, CO, 1992.

Warner, Michael S. "General Josiah Harmar's Campaign Reconsidered: How the Americans Lost the Battle of Kekionga." *Indiana Magazine of History* 83, no. 1 (March 1987): 43–64.

Warren, Stephen. *The Shawnees and Their Neighbors, 1795–1870.* Chicago, 2005.

Watson, Harry L. *Liberty and Power.* New York, 1990.

White, Richard. *The Middle Ground: Indians, Empires, and Republics in the Great Lakes Region, 1650–1815.* New York, 2006 [1991].

Wood, Gordon. *Empire of Liberty: A History of the Early Republic, 1789–1815.* New York, 2009.

Yarborough, Jean M. *American Virtues: Thomas Jefferson on the Character of a Free People.* Lawrence, KS, 1998.

Index

Note: Page numbers in *italics* refer to maps.